Early Medieval Spain

Unity in Diversity, 400–1000

NEW STUDIES IN MEDIEVAL HISTORY
General Editor: Maurice Keen

Published

Roger Collins, *Early Medieval Spain:*
Unity in Diversity, 400–1000

J. K. Hyde, *Society and Politics in Medieval Italy:*
The Evolution of the Civil Life, 1000–1350

Angus MacKay, *Spain in the Middle Ages:*
From Frontier to Empire, 1000–1500

Eric Christiansen, *The Northern Crusades:*
The Baltic and the Catholic Frontier, 1100–1525

Edward James, *The Origins of France:*
From Clovis to the Capetians, 500–1000

Chris Wickham, *Early Medieval Italy:*
Central Power and Local Society, 400–1000

Other volumes are in preparation

Early Medieval Spain

Unity in Diversity, 400–1000

ROGER COLLINS

New Studies in Medieval History
MAURICE KEEN

First published 1983 by
THE MACMILLAN PRESS LTD
London and Basingstoke
Companies and representatives
throughout the world

Filmsetting by Vantage Photosetting Co. Ltd,
Eastleigh and London

Printed in Hong Kong

ISBN 0 333 26282 4 (hc)
ISBN 0 333 26283 2 (pbk)

Contents

List of Maps

Preface

SPANISH history is not easy, and so it has perhaps been less popular outside of the Iberian peninsula than it deserves to be. For the medieval centuries the complications of a period unfamiliar, and inevitably alien in many aspects of its people's life and thought, are multiplied in Spain by the simultaneous existence of three, or occasionally more, Christian states, each with its own distinct history, culture and institutions, not to mention the one or more Muslim powers that dominated the south. In addition, the inescapable importance of the contributions of the Jewish and Basque communities only adds to the bewildering richness and complexity of the racial and cultural mix. However, neither the historian nor the inquiring general reader should be daunted by such a challenge, and indeed, it may be hoped that if they venture but a little way, they may be swept into sharing some of the enthusiasm of the small but devoted band of committed 'Hispanists'.

It has too long been assumed, and this again has been an excuse for neglect, that Spain, its history and culture, have been isolated from the mainstream of European development; that the peninsula has remained an exotic backwater, giving little, and little influenced by events beyond the Pyrenees. Yet in a world in which both Spain and Portugal may soon become members of the institutionalised European community, and in which their own creations, the states of Latin America, will come to play an increasingly prominent role, such an attitude is not only unjustified but also unwise. Nor, as will be seen, is it any more true of the Early Middle Ages, in which the study of the history of the peninsula leads us from the banks of the Danube to the deserts of Arabia. It may also be hoped that some consideration of the earlier history of Spain, of the continuities forced upon its peoples and their rulers by their past and by the geography of the land in which they live, will help in understanding the problems and aspirations of their modern successors.

A book on so limited a scale as this cannot hope to give a full and detailed treatment of all the subjects that need to be covered in the Early Medieval centuries of Spanish history. Selection is inescapable, and has to be essentially personal. My choice of topics and themes for extended treatment is in large measure a reflection of my own interests, though I have also been influenced by the prior existence of reasonable accounts in English of uncontroversial subjects, few as these have been, and to which reference is made in the first section of the Bibliography. However, despite the necessary limitations of this book in terms of size and in the providing of references, I hope to have avoided mere repetition of the conventional and received wisdom on the topics discussed. Even when space prevents the full elaboration of the alternative interpretations that I would seek to advance, I have preferred to give them, if only in outline, rather than to repeat more established views in which I have no confidence. Those already familiar with the subject may find the results unconventional, but possibly also challenging, either to approval or to disagreement. My own first interest in early Spanish history was aroused when, in another context, I read an article on one aspect of it, which so intrigued and also enraged me that I set to work to find out more, and have never stopped since. To its author, from whose many other writings I have gained much, both in provocation and in enlightenment, I remain forever grateful.

It was Denis Bethell who first suggested to me that I might write this book, and I greatly benefited from his advice and encouragement in the slow course of its composition. As editor and friend his untimely death was a sudden and terrible loss for all who knew him. I am most grateful to Maurice Keen, his successor in this series, for invaluable help in the final stages of preparation, and I should like to thank Sarah Mahaffy of Macmillans, not least for her patience in waiting for the more than a little overdue completion of this work. However little this book may be a tribute to their skills, I should like to record my great debt to my teachers and mentors, Michael Wallace-Hadrill, Peter Brown and John Prestwich. From the correction of the numerous errors of spelling and punctuation to the discussion and clarifying of my ideas, this book has been aided and improved by my wife. The same could be said of its author.

Chronological Table

	Damascus by the Abbāsids – one of the former dynasty, ʿAbd al-Raḥmān, takes refuge in Africa
756	ʿAbd al-Raḥmān crosses to Spain and, with the aid of the opponents of Yūsuf, defeats him and establishes an independent state, the Umayyad Amirate
759	Frankish conquest of Narbonne – use of their own law guaranteed to its Gothic inhabitants
763 and 777	Failure of Abbasid inspired revolts against ʿAbd al-Raḥmān I
776, 784, 786	Beatus of Liebana produced the three editions of his *Commentary on the Apocalypse*
778	Charlemagne's expedition into the Ebro valley – forced to withdraw from Zaragoza, his rearguard is destroyed by the Basques in the pass of Roncesvalles
791–842	Reign of Alfonso II in the Asturias: establishment of Oviedo as its capital, revival of Visigothic traditions in art and government, building of first church at Santiago de Compostela, contacts with the Frankish court
790s	Adoptionist controversy
801	Frankish conquest of Barcelona – beginning of the 'Spanish march'
803	Revolt of the Banu Kasim in Tudela – suppressed
806	Frankish conquest of Pamplona
c. 808/10	Frankish failure to take Tortosa and hold Tarragona limits the extension of the new march
816	Revolt against Frankish rule suppressed in Pamplona
824	Renewed revolt leads to the destruction of a Frankish army at the second Battle of Roncesvalles and the establishment of an independent kingdom in Pamplona
827	Barcelona held by Bernard 'of Septimania' against Gothic rebels with Umayyad assistance
839	Council of Cordoba
844	First Viking raid on Spain – defeated by Ramiro I, but went on to sack Seville
c. 847–862	Ascendancy of Mūsa ibn Mūsa of the Banu Kasim in the upper Ebro; 'the third king of Spain'

848–849	Seizure of Barcelona by William, son of Bernard 'of Septimania' (executed in 844) – suppressed by the forces of Charles 'the Bald'
851–859	The martyr movement in Cordoba
859	Execution of Eulogius, titular Metropolitan of Toledo, its chief apologist – second Viking raid on coasts of Andalucia – they captured and ransomed King Garcia of Pamplona
862	Defeat of Mūsa ibn Mūsa at Albelda by Ordoño I of the Asturias
866–910	Reign of Alfonso III in the Asturias: beginning of Christian repopulation of the Duero valley and of Castille
878	Establishment of Wifred I 'the Hairy' as Count of Barcelona, which office becomes hereditary in his family
880–917	Ascendancy of *muwallad* rebel Omar ibn Hafsun, centred upon Bobastro
886–912	Reigns of Al-Mundhir and 'Abd-Allah in Cordoba: growing violence in the south between Arabs and indigenous converts to Islam (*muwallads*), many revolts and effectively independent states created in Mérida and other regions
912–961	Reign of 'Abd al-Raḥmān III: restoration of the authority of Cordoba, suppression of revolts and the greater imposition of authority over the Christian realms in the north of the peninsula
917–927	Elimination of the sons of Ibn Hafsun
929–931	Suppression of revolt of the *muwallad* 'Abd al-Raḥmān al-Jilliki at Badajoz
929	'Abd al-Raḥmān III took the title of caliph
931–970	Fernan Gonzalez Count of Castille
939	Battle of Simancas
Mid tenth century	Umayyad Spain at its apogee: a centre of learning, especially under the caliph Al-Ḥakem II, with its rulers extending their power to North Africa, frequent diplomatic exchanges with Byzantium and Ottonian Germany
960	Sancho I 'the Fat' of Leon restored to his kingdom by the caliph
966, 971	Minor Viking raids

Maps

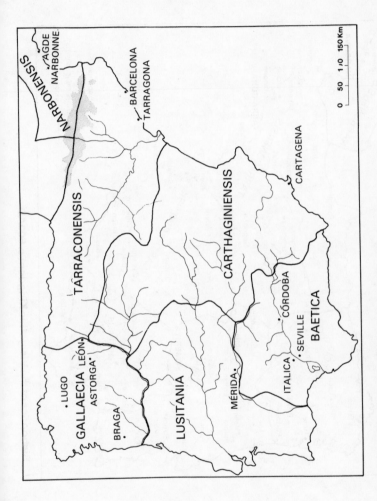

1 The Roman Provinces of Spain c. 400AD

MAPS

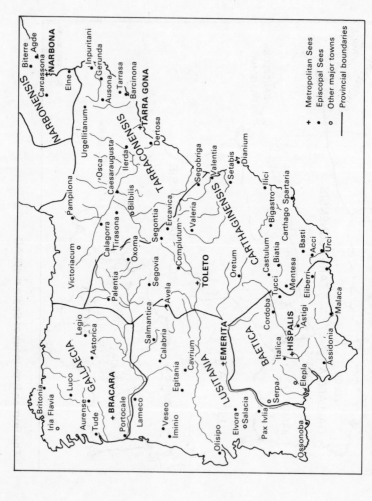

II   Bishoprics of the Visigothic Kingdom c. 600AD

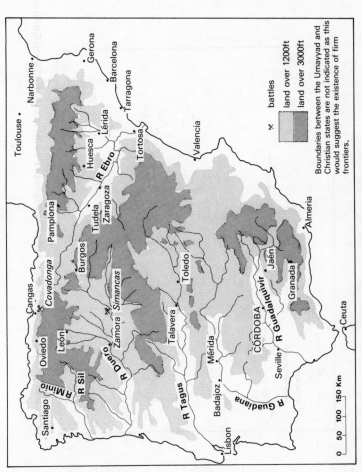

III   Al-Andalus and the Christian States in the Tenth Century

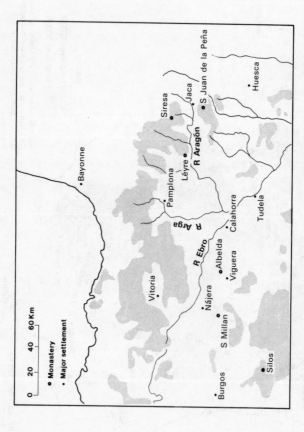

IV   Castille, The Upper Ebro and the Kingdom of Pamplona in the Tenth Century

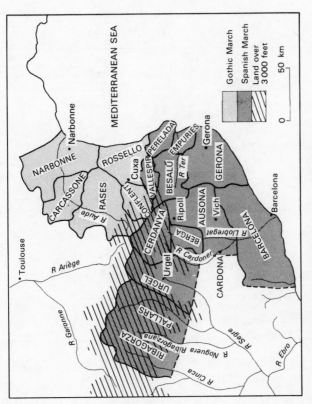

V   The Frankish Marches in Catalonia c. 900AD

For Judith
and in Memory of Denis Bethell

Introduction

The Roman Achievement

EARLY in the year 376 demoralised and frightened bands of people, in flight from their homes and deserting many of their former leaders, began to gather on the northern bank of the river Danube. They were the Theruingi, later to be called the Visigoths, a Germanic people whose origins and earliest history now survive in little more than legendary form. For over a century their tribe had dominated the flat and fertile lands between the rivers Danube and Dneister, where they had posed a continuous threat to the security of the frontiers of their southern neighbour, the Roman Empire. Even within the last decade the reigning Emperor, Valens (364–378), had been forced to take the field against them. But now they were fugitives, some taking refuge in the Carpathian Mountains to the west, but perhaps the greater part congregating on the Danube as humble suppliants of their former enemy and victim, petitioning the emperor to receive them into his territories and give them new lands upon which to settle.[1]

The reasons for this dramatic change in the fortunes of a once proud and powerful people are complex and far reaching. They have to do with an alteration in the social and economic structure of a vast area stretching northwards from the Danube along the shores of the Black Sea into the steppes of southern Russia. Most overtly this was represented by the rise to eventual dominance of the whole of this region of the nomadic confederacy of the Huns, before whom the power of the Theruings' northern neighbours, the Greuthungi or Ostrogoths, had foundered. But the emergence of the Huns was more symptom than cause. This region was a marginal zone between the fixed area of settled agricultural life around the shores of the Mediterranean and the aridity of Central Asia, which could only support a nomadic pastoral population. Conditions, that we can now only speculate about, changed gradually during the course of the fourth century, and, with a dramatic suddenness that probably concealed a longer and quieter growth, brought the nomad to the frontiers of the settled. The marginal region, balanced upon an ecological knife-edge, proved unable any longer to sustain the settled agricultural economy of the Goths and their resulting size of population, and hence their collapse and migration.[2]

Once inside the Empire a new identity was forged by the Theruingi

1

out of times of humiliation and hardship. Initially settled between the southern bank of the Danube and the Balkan Mountains, they were exploited so severely by local Roman officials and military commanders that within two years they were driven into revolt. In battle at Adrianople in 378 they routed the imperial army, killing the Emperor Valens. Although his successor Theodosius I was able to bring them to terms by 381, this was to establish them more firmly inside the Empire and to give them an important role in the emperor's fighting forces. Their crucial involvement in the two civil wars of 388 and 394 during Theodosius's reign served further to unify them, and on the emperor's death in 395 they elected a king, Alaric, to rule over the whole people, the first in its history.

It was in this same period of the entry into the Roman Empire that the new Visigothic people adopted Christianity as its religion, deserting a previous paganism of which virtually nothing is known. The earliest Christian missionary activity amongst the Theruingi had taken place in the middle of the fourth century, when the Arian heresy, that subordinated the Son and the Holy Spirit to the Father in the Trinity, had been receiving imperial support, and it was as Arians that the Visigoths became Christians. They now had the scriptures translated into their own language by Ulfilas, the first Gothic bishop. The year 381, however, had also seen the final defeat of Arianism in the Church inside the Empire, and thus these new converts were to find themselves at odds in religion with their numerous Roman subjects in the centuries to follow.[3]

The necessities of feeding and supplying the people, if their new-found unity were to be preserved, together with the confused politics of a divided Empire, caused Alaric to take an active role in the events of the subsequent decades. Eventually, in 408, he led his followers into Italy to coerce a hostile but indecisive administration into honouring promises made of payment and supply. The xenophobic intransigence of the emperor Honorius, secure behind the marshes of Ravenna, drove the Goths firstly into supporting the pretensions of a usurper in Rome and then, when he proved as unwilling to accommodate them as his rival, into sacking the former imperial capital in 410. Alaric died in the same year and his successor, thwarted of imperial recognition and driven by the constant need for secure and regular supplies of food to keep the confederacy in being, led them out of Italy into southern Gaul. Established in Aquitaine by treaty in 418 with a now more flexible imperial regime, the future masters of the Iberian peninsula were, within half a century, drawn by events over the Pyrenees into what was to be their final home. Spain, however, had other tribulations to undergo in the early fifth century before the Visigoths made themselves masters there, but before considering those it will be necessary to turn back to an earlier and more tranquil period of the peninsula's history.

Roman Spain is surprisingly little known to modern scholarship. Of all the major provinces of the western half of the Roman Empire those of Hispania, five in number after reorganisation by the emperor Diocletian (284–305), are amongst the least studied and understood. This is largely due to the limitations of the available evidence, especially the archaeological. Much that will aid the future study of Roman Spain still remains hidden in the ground. But in the last few years important work has been done, principally by Spanish scholars, on such questions as the success or failure of the imposition of Roman civilisation on the different regions of the peninsula, and the activities of the Roman army in Spain.[4] Answers to these and other problems are clearly of great importance for the better understanding of the society that was to develop in the late Roman period and to influence so many features of what was to follow.

That Roman Spain is still largely obscure does not imply that it was unimportant. To take the most obvious example, in the literature of the Empire the Spanish provinces produced more than their fair share of the writers of the 'Silver Latin' age of the late first and early second centuries AD. Thus the two Senecas and Lucan came from Cordoba, Martial from Bilbilis and Quintilian from Calahorra. Equally, in the late Empire, less studied but just as important, we find a flourishing tradition of Christian Latin poetry in the peninsula, that reached its culmination in the writings of Prudentius (*fl. c.* 400), but also includes those of Iuvencus (*fl. c.* 330), author of a metrical version of the Gospels, and of the panegyricist Flavius Merobaudes (*fl. c.* 440), testimony to the literary culture of the provinces even in the troubled times of the fifth century.

Spain also produced its quota of emperors for the Roman world: Trajan (98–117) and Hadrian (117–138) in the early Empire, Theodosius I (378–395), founder of a dynasty that lasted until 455, and Magnus Maximus (383–388) in the late.[5] The rise of emperors from Spain often led to the prominence of some of their fellow provincials under their patronage. Theodosius I drew a coterie of Spaniards with him to Constantinople, the most famous of whom was the Prefect Maternus Cynegius, noted for his destruction of pagan temples in the eastern provinces in the 390s.[6]

At a lower level but more consistent than the periodic provision of emperors and administrators was the role of Spain as a source of manpower for the Roman army, especially in the early Empire. Inscriptions relating to Spanish units and individual soldiers can be found all over the confines of the Empire, not least in Britain. Economically too Spain had much to contribute to Rome. It was particularly notable as a source of silver, mined in the mountains of the north, and of horses from the valleys of the south.[7]

In return Rome gave the Spanish provinces a measure of internal order and freedom from external aggression. Only in the middle of the third century did 'Barbarians' in the form of Germans from across the Rhine, who forced their way through Gaul, and Berbers from Africa, succeed in breaking through the adjacent provinces and briefly troubling the tranquillity of Spain. Internally too the peninsula was little disturbed by wider political upheavals in the Roman world. It was from provincial governorships in Spain that the short-reigned emperors Galba (68–69) and Otho (69) rebelled to replace the Julio-Claudian dynasty in Rome, and the province of Tarraconensis in the north-east of the peninsula briefly belonged to the Gallic Empire of the usurper Postumus (263–270). Otherwise the order of the Roman Empire was untroubled by happenings in Spain before the fifth century.

The prosperity and tranquillity of Roman Spain, up to the end of the fourth century, is still well illustrated in many of its surviving monuments, such as the great public buildings of cities like Mérida (Emerita Augusta) and Italica, the palatial private villas of the valleys of the Ebro, Guadiana and Guadalquivir, the system of roads and the impressive bridges and aqueducts that still existed and functioned when barbarians again broke into the Spanish provinces, late in 409.[8] As in other parts of the West, Roman culture, in the form of language, art, religion, education, architecture and government, was established in Spain through a network of towns interconnected by roads. There were indigenous settlements, such as Numantia, which had put up prolonged resistance to Roman conquest but these lacked the size and sophistication of the new urban foundations of the victors. In a number of cases Roman cities were built in close proximity to earlier towns, as Italica was to Hispalis (Seville), to serve both as a cultural model and as a means of control.

At first these settlements were Roman enclaves, as in the case of Emerita Augusta (Mérida), founded to serve the needs of retired veterans of Augustus's Cantabrian war, who received their pension by being established as colonists. The former soldiers were granted land in the vicinity of the city, which itself was adorned with all of the necessities and most of the luxuries of Roman urban life. Such foundations were centres from which Roman ideas and methods could permeate outwards into the countryside and local indigenous settlements, attracting emulation and ultimately assimilation. They could also, with their veterans, serve as military centres should Roman rule be opposed, although in practice indigenous resistance ended with the conclusion of the wars of conquest. There was no Spanish Boudicca or Vindex.

Distinctions in origin, appearance and character between Roman and Celt-Iberian settlements were eroded in the period of the early Empire, which is less surprising when it is considered that some of the former, such as Italica, had already existed for over two centuries. Roman styles of country life and the villa economy also clearly established themselves over older forms throughout most of the peninsula at the same time. Compared to those effected by Rome the transformations that resulted from the subsequent history of early medieval Spain are, however turbulent, less fundamental and all-embracing.

Perhaps though the most significant contribution of the Roman period to the history of Spain came in the form of the introduction of a religion. Although in the *Epistle to the Romans* St Paul had expressed a desire to go and preach in Spain, little more can be said about Christianity in the peninsula before the third century.[9] It is thought that the influence of the African Church played the greatest role in spreading the new religion into the Spanish provinces. By the middle of the third century bishoprics can be found in Mérida, Leon and Zaragoza, and it was to the Church in Carthage they turned for guidance rather than Rome.[10]

Even after the conversion of Constantine in 312, which fundamentally altered the status of Christianity inside the Empire, it is uncertain how rapidly the classical paganism of the Roman cities and surviving pre-Roman cults of the Iberian population gave way before the imperially sponsored faith. At the end of the century a small group of Spanish Christians around the emperor Theodosius I are notable for their uncompromising and even violent hostility to paganism and to heresy, but whether this indicates a complete triumph or a hard struggle in the peninsula is unclear.

Spanish bishops had begun by then to play an important role in the internal disputes of the Church. In the fourth century Arian controversy over the equality and coeternity of the Father and the Son in the Trinity, Potamius of Lisbon and Gregory of Elvira were amongst the principal Western proponents and opponents of the heretical doctrine. Bishop Hosius of Cordoba was one of the leading ecclesiastical advisers of the emperor Constantine (306–337) and is also suspected of influencing the emperor in favour of Arius's teachings. In addition Spain produced a heresiarch of her own in the person of Priscillian, Bishop of Avila, who was executed by a fellow Spaniard, the emperor Magnus Maximus, in 385, in the first use of secular punishment for a purely ecclesiastical offence.[11]

While the impression of Roman Spain is one of unity, and indeed in terms of architecture, engineering, art and religion, almost of uniformity with the rest of the Empire, it is essential to appreciate how fragile this was. It was an artificial imposition that negated much of the geography and past history of the peninsula. A full appreciation of the civilisation of Spain, not only in Antiquity and the Middle Ages but for every stage of its history up to the present, is dependent upon some understanding of its geography.

Despite being a peninsula and cut off from the rest of Europe by one of the highest mountain ranges in the continent, it is far from having a natural unity. In terms of the average height of the landmass, Spain is the highest country in Europe except for Switzerland, largely due to an impressive series of mountain ranges that divide the peninsula into a number of discrete areas with very limited possibilities for communication between them in several cases. Thus distinct regions appear.

Starting in the north-east, the area of modern Catalonia, with the Ebro valley that runs into it, is largely cut off from the rest of the peninsula by a chain of mountain ranges. In fact the most natural lines of communication of this region are to the north, and throughout the Middle Ages the areas immediately to the north and to the south of the eastern end of the Pyrenees were politically and culturally linked. Moving west from the Ebro valley, across very difficult terrain, the next major area of settlement will be found on the Meseta, a high plateau land, less fertile and habitable than the Mediterranean coast and entirely ringed by mountains. This was to be the nucleus of the medieval kingdoms of Leon and Castille. To the north of the Meseta are found the mountains of Cantabria, which effectively shut off the plateau from the Bay of Biscay. It was against the inhabitants of these mountains that a string of legionary fortresses had to be erected in the time of the early Empire. The indigenous peoples of this area and of the only slightly less rugged region of Galicia to the west received very little imprint of Roman civilisation and retained some features of their early Iron Age culture until as late as the eighth century.[12]

To go south from the Meseta is to enter the old Roman provinces of Lusitania and Baetica. Here the dominant features are the great river valleys of the Tagus, Guadiana and Guadalquivir, each with its notable cities: Toledo, Mérida, Cordoba and Seville, and a relative abundance of evidence of prosperous Roman rural life. The valleys were fertile and their towns, with the exception of Tarragona (Tarraco) and Barcelona (Barcinona) in Catalonia, the most important in Roman Spain. But even here substantial problems were imposed by local geography, as the valleys are divided one from another by mountain ranges and are less easy of access than might appear.

In the extreme west the land flattens out into an extensive coastal plain, almost identical with the area of modern Portugal, which represents the results of the silting action of those rivers previously mentioned. In the Roman period, due to the limitations on sea transport beyond the comparative safety of the Mediterranean, this region was particularly remote from the rest of the Empire and its towns, such as Lisbon (Olissipo) of relatively little note. Finally the south-eastern quarter of the peninsula is a rugged and desolate region and was probably sparsely populated at any period; the only exception being the thin coastal strip, largely cut off from the rest of the landmass and looking instead towards Africa.

The peculiarities imposed upon the peninsula by its geography were reinforced in the period before the Roman conquest by its history. Its Janus-like qualities of looking simultaneously northwards towards western Europe and south to Africa meant that waves of migrants with very different cultures were able to enter the peninsula from opposite directions. In the middle of the first millennium BC virtually simultaneous waves of Celts, coming south across the Pyrenees, and Iberians, crossing the straits from Africa, settled in Spain. As a result they gave distinct cultural differences to north and south, and also created a hybrid Celt-Iberian civilisation in the centre of the peninsula. Later the Carthaginians began to colonise the south-eastern coasts and the Greeks, subsequently replaced by the Romans, the north-eastern ones. This clash of interests was a major contributory cause of the Punic Wars, which in turn led ultimately to the Roman conquest of the whole peninsula. This process took some two centuries to complete and was often marked by bitter fighting. It was finally completed during the reign of the first Roman emperor Augustus (27BC–AD14). Not until another four centuries had passed was Spain to be subjected to another major migration or invasion.

Without minimising the Romans' achievement, it is important not to overstress the degree of cultural and administrative unity that they were able to impose upon the peninsula. Indeed some of the most interesting of modern research has concentrated upon the limitations of Romanisation. Whereas in Catalonia, the Meseta and the river valleys of the south there appears to have been a large degree of successful assimilation of Roman lifestyles both in new settlements and in the older indigenous ones, in the far north, in Galicia, Cantabria and the lands of the Basques, acceptance was much more limited. Unlike the southern and eastern parts, very few Roman towns were founded in the north, and those that were existed for military purposes. Pre-Roman tribal organisation seems to have survived in these northern regions and there are indications that nomadism, or rather pastoral transhumance, continued to flourish, despite Roman pressure for enforced settlement. The Basque language of course survived right through the Roman period, and that of Lusitania still existed in the second century, although it subsequently disappeared.[13] Again, despite some later traditions, Christianity was much slower to take root in the north and the ecclesiastical organisation of these territories was still in a rudimentary state when Roman rule came to an end.

The degree of resistance to Roman social and economic organisation seems to have varied from area to area within this northern region. The Basques appear to have been most successful in this respect, despite Roman forts in the Pyrenean passes. They probably retained a society very little different from that described by the early first century Greek geographer Strabo (c. AD15).[14] On the other hand Galicia and parts of the Asturias, where the Romans had interests in mining silver, were more affected by the imperial presence and some small villas and other traces of Romanised civil life have been found. But even here survival of pre-Roman social organisation and material culture is more striking than any marks of assimilation.

As a consequence it was these regions that created the greatest military problem for the Romans in the peninsula. Until the disappearance of Mauretania Tingitana, south of the Straits of Gibraltar, in the late third century, Hispania was not a frontier province of the Empire and might not normally have required a legionary garrison. However it did have its own internal frontier, that facing the northern mountains. Leon, Astorga and Braga were all legionary fortresses in origin and from them units of the Roman army, notably in the early Empire the *Legio Septima Gemina* (Seventh Legion), attempted to control the activities of the inhabitants of the Asturias and Galicia, who continued by their raiding and economic lifestyle to threaten the security and prosperity of their settled neighbours to the south in the Meseta and lower Ebro valley. When the Romans failed to check this, a *limes* or military frontier had to be created. This was to be one of the unsolved problems that they left to their successors.

However, Spain under Roman rule was, for over four centuries, tranquil and economically prosperous, famous for its silver, corn and horses. Its great cities were amongst the finest and most flourishing in the western half of the Empire and it was an integral part of a wider world, to which it was joined not only by administrative ties but by a common religion and a common Latin culture, towards both of which Spanish provincials had made distinguished contributions. In the fifth century a sudden and dramatic turn of events threw the peninsula into turmoil, broke the fragile internal unity created by the Romans and severed many of its ties with the outside world. When a measure of order was re-established by the Visigoths over a century later much had been lost and much was changed, but also, for good or ill, some things remained the same.

None of the later conquerors of the peninsula were to have such advantages as the Romans. The Visigoths and the Arabs were themselves the beneficiaries of Graeco-Roman culture, both material and intellectual, and in both cases had less that was clearly and attractively superior to offer the conquered populations. The effective disappearance of virtually all features of pre-Roman social organisation, religion and language from most of the peninsula by the time that the Empire came to an end is testimony to the Romans'

achievement. However much modern scholars might search for and
detect elements of survival of earlier cultures in Spain and elsewhere,
this should only be seen against the background of the revolutionary
changes that Roman rule and cultural impregnation did bring about.
The formidable inherent difficulties that had to be faced and the
vulnerability of some of that achievement make it more, not less,
remarkable.

1.   The Emergence of a New Order

The Roman Twilight

THE 'Fall of the Roman Empire', in the sense that a coherent and unified system of military and civil administration covering most of western Europe and North Africa, which was in being at the beginning of the fifth century had ceased to exist by its close, was a process scarcely perceived by those who lived through it. In place of the universal dominion of the emperor, Germanic kings and their followers, partly by force and partly by agreements, set up realms having a rough correspondence to the military divisions of the former Empire. These kingdoms were in some cases, notably that of the Franks in Gaul, to last for centuries and help to mould the future political and social geography of western Europe. Although the process of transition was at times and in places violent and destructive, reactions to it were generally limited and localised, and more often marked by co-operation between the Roman provincials and their new masters, than by resistance.

The sack of Rome by the Visigoths in 410 created a considerable stir amongst those for whom the city was the symbol not just of a form of society, but, more importantly, of a cultural tradition. But the event itself was, in material terms, transitory, and of no long-lasting significance, beyond giving occasion for Augustine's writing of *The City of God*.[1] When Rome was again sacked, by the Vandals in 455, it created no literary repercussions. As for the gradual dismembering of the Empire that took place throughout the first half of the fifth century, and which really marked its fall, this aroused remarkably little comment and no real meditation upon the nature of what was happening. Some have seen moralising treaties by contemporary Christian authors, such as the *On the Governance of God* by the Gallic priest Salvian, as reflections of an awareness of malaise and decline.[2] However, this is to misinterpret the interests and intentions of authors whose concern was with the spiritual reformation of men held to be too absorbed by the transitory and illusory ties of the secular world. That emphasis on the heavenly society, the true counterpart to the fleeting earthly one, and the rise of interest in asceticism and the monastic life in the West, were unconscious reactions to the disintegration of the social and political structures of the Roman

11

Empire is not a perspective that fifth-century men would have understood nor is it necessarily a true one.

A moralising sense of decline had been a feature of certain strands of Graeco-Roman intellectual life for over five centuries, and was reinforced by recent tendencies in Christian thought.[3] Neither tradition had any close correspondence with the realities of material decline. In fact, they were at their most strident in periods of prosperity, which threatened to undermine the pursuit of other than hedonistic values. A safer guide than Salvian to the realities of life in the fifth century may be found in the Gallic senator, and later bishop, Sidonius Apollinaris (d. c. 480), who has left us some impression of his public feelings on passing from under the administration of the emperor to that of the Visigothic king. But, for all of his regrets, he proved able to collaborate with new masters, and he and his descendants preserved much of their local influence and lifestyle.[4] There is no comparable evidence from Spain to put alongside the letters and poems of Sidonius, but what can be made out of reactions in the peninsula suggests that attitudes were not dissimilar. The local aristocracies of towns and provinces, who are the only stratum of society of whom we are given a real glimpse, proved capable of co-operating effectively with the regimes of the Germanic kings, and moulding them more closely along Roman and Christian lines.

This may have been partly due to the almost casual nature of the way in which certain events occurred that were to be of the greatest long-term significance. Those units of the Roman army that were still in Britain were removed in 407 to Gaul to take part in the brief bid for power of a usurper whom they themselves had created. After his fall, they were not returned and thus the Empire in practice abandoned any responsibility for the protection of its British provinces, which soon had to turn, with fatal consequences, to the employing of Saxon mercenaries. Likewise, the garrisons in Africa were led into Italy in 430 by their commander in an attempt, that proved fatal to himself, to seize dictatorial power in the heart of the Empire. These troops were not replaced either, and in 442 the imperial government had to recognise the authority over their North African provinces of the Vandals, already established de facto for a decade. The fate of Spain, as will be shown, was similar.

The removal of troops answerable to the imperial régime in Ravenna and their replacement under a series of voluntary or forced agreements, by the armed followers of Germanic tribal leaders meant that thenceforth the emperors, or rather the military dictators who controlled them, lacked the power to enforce their will in those provinces, although their theoretical suzerainty over them was not overtly challenged. Much of the civil administration remained, and not just at a local urban level. Germanic kings, invested with military authority in the provinces, may have filled not only the roles of the former Roman Masters of the Soldiers, but also those of their civilian counterparts the Praetorian Prefects.

In terms of constitutional theory the Empire remained alive, even when the last of the western emperors were deposed and murdered, in 476 and 480 respectively, in the course of civil war in Italy; for the two halves, divided since 395, were reunited under rule from Constantinople. That the eastern emperors could only reimpose their authority on North Africa and Italy, and that not until half a century had passed, made the transition from the fiction of imperial rule in the fifth century, to the reality of independent Germanic kingdoms in the sixth, all the easier. Furthermore, much as the Roman intelligensia may have despised the Germans as 'Barbarians', outsiders denied and incapable of the benefits of the Empire's culture, they could appreciate the benefits conferred by their new masters' military skills, which were quickly employed in the defence of frontiers and the maintenance of internal order. The Germans too, from centuries spent on the fringes of the Empire, had come to share much of the material culture of Roman provincials and some proved willing to master some of its intellectual heritage as well. The Church in particular was quick to assess the ways in which the new rulers were open to guidance, and notions of the duties and obligations of kings within a Christian context were developed under the impetus of these opportunities. Thus Romans who had consented to serve the Germanic kings as delegates of the emperor, were, in the passing of generations, able to see them instead as rulers in their own right, defenders of justice and of the Church, who could take on some of the symbolic significance of the emperors, not as representatives of a universal empire, but as the embodiments of the cultural self-consciousness of its individual former provinces. Such a process led to the emergence of the remarkable Romano-Gothic kingdom in Spain in the late sixth century, but its roots lay in a decade of violence and destruction. The unclear, and also highly controversial nature of the events in the period of transition from Roman to Visigothic rule makes some detailed consideration of them necessary.

The sequence of events that led to the entry of the Germanic barbarians into Spain on either 28 September or 13 October in the year 409 is hard to determine, not so much owing to a lack of evidence, as to the existence of many contradictions in the surviving accounts. For Spain the years 407 to 418 are, by fifth-century standards, surprisingly well documented. The nearest thing to a contemporary eye-witness account of some of the principal events may be found in the *Seven Books of History against the Pagans* of the Spanish priest Orosius, who was born at Braga, probably in the 380s, and left Spain in 413–14 for Africa. He wrote his *History* in 418 at the request of Augustine, taking his account from the Creation up to the time of his writing.[5] Unfortunately, his description of the events of his own lifetime is disappointingly brief and lacking in detail. For one thing, the whole didactic purpose of his work militated against his giving a substantial account of recent happenings. His intention was to show that the Romans had suffered worse disasters under the previous pagan dispensation than in the new Christian one. Another contemporary *History* is that of Olympiodorus of Thebes, covering the years 407 to 425.[6] Only fragments of his most valuable work survive and, as an Easterner, his information on events in the far west was received at second hand, most likely from a now lost account which he probably read during a visit to Rome in 425. However, his account is often fuller and more circumstantial than that of Orosius, and the lacunae in his text can be reconstructed to some extent from the writings of the Byzantine historians Sozomen (*fl. c.* 440) and Zosimus (first half of the sixth century), who both used Olympiodorus's work. Zosimus's *New History* is itself damaged, its account terminating abruptly in the year 410. Another excellent source is to be found in the *Chronicle* of Hydatius, which covers not only the events of the early years of the century, but is the principal fount of information on the history of the peninsula thereafter, up to the conclusion of its entries in 469. Hydatius himself was Bishop of Iria Flavia in Galicia, probably being born in the last decade of the fourth century in the small town of Ginzo de Limia (Civitas Limicorum) in that province. He intended his chronicle to be a continuation of that of Jerome, whom as an adolescent he met on a visit to Bethlehem, probably around the year 410. He seems to have begun writing fairly late on in his life, for whereas the quantity and detail of the information that he provides for the 430s to the 460s is considerable and of unimpeachable value, his references to earlier years are relatively scant and not as informative as for the later ones.

On the last day of the year 406 a confederacy of various Germanic peoples, of whom the two branches of the Vandals, the Silings and the Hasdings, together with the Sueves, are named in the sources, with the non-Germanic nomad Alans and other unspecified tribes, crossed the frozen Rhine into the Roman Empire. These peoples spent the next three years moving from the area of their crossing, on the middle Rhine around Mainz, firstly northwards to the Channel and then south-west towards the Pyrenees, finally reaching them at their western end by the autumn of 409. Difficulties of obtaining food sufficient for their needs and lack of the secure possession of land on which to settle kept them thus constantly on the move. Living off the land as they passed, they are reported to have caused much destruction and hardship in Gaul. Political disorder followed in their wake.

Why these tribes united, however briefly and loosely, and broke into the Roman Empire, deserting their former homelands and religious cult-sites, is more of a mystery than may appear at first sight. It was by no means a natural development, long anticipated, but was clearly the product of unusual circumstances. Not the least striking feature is that the Alans were previously reported, in the 370s, living to the east of the river Don and north of the Caucasus. A considerable migration was required to bring them to the Rhine in 406. Nor did such apparently Uralo-Altaic nomads make natural allies for small western-Germanic tribes such as the Vandals and the Sueves, who had lived on the frontiers of the Roman Empire for the previous four centuries. Whatever its origins may have been, the breaking of the Rhine frontier in the winter of 406–7 initiated the final disintegration of the western Roman Empire, and with it the end of Roman rule in Spain.

To this end other events within the frontiers also had a part to play. Just prior to these happenings on the Rhine, sometime earlier in 406, the units of the Roman army that were stationed in Britain rebelled. They set up, and for little apparent reason then murdered, two emperors before fastening upon a third, called Constantine, either late in 406 or more probably early in 407. This Constantine, chosen, Orosius tells us, because the soldiers thought that his name, that of the first Christian emperor, would be lucky, immediately crossed the channel with his army to Boulogne, and benefiting from the chaos of the barbarian incursion, made himself the master of Gaul during the course of 407.[7] As it had been usual in the fourth century for Spain to follow the lead of Gaul in terms of political adherence, it is no surprise to find that by 409 the peninsula had also become attached to Constantine's new empire, and that its magistrates had voluntarily accepted his authority.

The immediate lack of resistance to the usurper in Spain proved, however, to be short-lived. The legitimate imperial dynasty, the Theodosians, represented at that time in the west by the emperor Honorius (395–423), was Spanish in origin, and members of the family still lived in the peninsula. Two brothers, cousins of Honorius, determined to oppose Constantine and, raising an army from the slaves on their estates, they attempted to seize the passes over the Pyrenees, cutting Spain off from the rest of the usurper's empire. This probably occurred early in 409. Constantine sent his son Constans, a former monk whom he had elevated to the rank of Caesar, or junior emperor, together with his British general Gerontius and an army of barbarian mercenaries, to suppress this resistance. The revolt of the two brothers, Didymus and Verinianus, was crushed, though not without difficulty.[8]

Constantine and Constans, who became co-emperor with his father in 409 or 410, seem to have had little faith in the regular units of the army stationed in Spain, who appear to have taken no part at all in the struggle with Didymus and Verinianus, and they decided to replace them in guarding the crucial Pyrenean passes with units of barbarian troops of unspecified origin known as the *honoriaci*. This was clearly resented, as the regular troops petitioned Constans to change his mind, albeit unsuccessfully. Their subsequent revolt against him and his father may well stem from this episode. However, even more momentous consequences were to follow. In September or October 409 Constans's barbarian guards on the Pyrenees, either through deliberate treachery or just negligence, allowed the confederacy of Alans, Vandals and Sueves to come through the passes. Orosius records that the *honoriaci* then joined forces with them in the destruction that was to follow.[9]

In the meantime it seems that Constans had returned to Gaul, probably to deputise for his father, who was proposing to invade Italy in the spring of 410. In his absence, and taking advantage of the discontent of the Spanish soldiery, the general Gerontius rebelled. Rather than take the throne himself, he proclaimed as emperor a friend of his, Maximus, a former member of the 'domestics', or corps of honorary imperial bodyguards. This took place in Tarragona, probably early in 410. Maximus soon began issuing coins from

Barcelona, whilst Gerontius went straight on to the offensive, and invaded Gaul with the army units under his command. He seems to have had little difficulty in capturing Constans at Vienne, and there he had his former master executed. As a result of this revolt, Constantine was forced to abandon his ambitions in Italy, and after his son's death was himself beseiged by the rebel general at Arles. This siege was still in progress, when in 411 an imperial army from Italy invaded Gaul to dispose of the rival usurpers. At its approach, Gerontius fled back towards Spain, whilst Constantine in Arles was soon forced to surrender to the imperial forces. Gerontius's career too was soon terminated. His soldiers, impatient at his failure, attacked him, and despite an epic resistance, he was forced to kill his wife, his Alan bodyguard, and himself, when the mutineers were able to set fire to the house over their heads. His creature, the emperor Maximus, fled to take refuge with their barbarian allies, whilst the army that had once supported him and Gerontius made its peace with the generals of the emperor Honorius.[10]

Meanwhile, what had the barbarian invaders of 409 been doing? The sources are vague, but both Orosius and Hydatius refer to widespread destruction and violence as having resulted from their entry. Olympiodorus cites a case of cannibalism in one Spanish city as a result of the ensuing famine. In his account, Hydatius is deliberately apocalyptic, drawing on images from the prophecy of Ezechiel.[11] But whilst disorder and starvation probably did result from the unrestrained presence of the confederate barbarians in 409–10 in the peninsula, no details exist as to which regions in particular were affected, nor what the movements of the invaders were precisely. But at some point, put chronologically by all of the sources before the overthrow of the usurper Constantine in 411, they ceased their wanderings and, dividing up the peninsula between them, settled in different regions. They were still occupying those lands when Orosius wrote his account of recent years in 417–18. It seems that the southernmost province, Baetica, was occupied by the Siling Vandals, Lusitania and Carthaginiensis by the Alans, whilst the Hasding Vandals and the Sueves were crowded together into Galicia in the north-west, the smallest province of all.

Not surprisingly, argument exists as to how this division took place, and who was responsible for initiating it. One view is that it was entirely the product of a treaty between the barbarians and one of the rival Roman regimes that then existed, and that they were therefore established in those provinces as federates. The contrary opinion is that the barbarians seized lands for their own use without Roman approval, and that they drew lots amongst themselves for which portions of the peninsula each tribe would receive.[12] This latter argument suffers from several weaknesses: why were two partners in the confederacy squeezed into one not very desirable province, without apparent protest, and why was the province of Tarraconensis entirely omitted from consideration? On the other hand, when it is appreciated that the area allotted to the Hasdings and the Sueves was previously the principal military frontier zone of the peninsula, and that the towns they are subsequently found occupying are the military foundations of Leon, Braga and Astorga, it seems not at all unreasonable to suggest that they were there in the capacity of federates, military allies of the Empire, replacing units of the Roman army in Spain along a vulnerable frontier. In view of the timing, 410–11, it is most likely that this was done in order to free those troops for use in the war being fought by Gerontius against Constantine in Gaul. Thus the treaty of federation will have been made with the barbarians by the regime of Gerontius and Maximus. It was to these very barbarians that Maximus was to flee in 411 after Gerontius's death.

Orosius tells us that the Roman troops who had formerly supported the rebel empire in Spain were not returned to the province after their renewal of allegiance to the legitimate emperor. Instead, they were sent to Africa, possibly as part of the expedition to suppress the revolt there of the count Heraclian in 413, and subsequently they were transferred to Italy.[13] In effect, the imperial government gave up the maintenance of a permanent military presence in Spain, except for the province of Tarraconensis, in the year 411, and with it, in practice, its authority in those regions. For most of the peninsula, the end of Roman rule can be dated to 411. Military and political power was in the hands of the barbarians, former partisans of the defunct regime of Maximus and Gerontius. But in the aftermath of the events of 411 they were left alone, and nothing is heard of their doings for the next five years, apparently a time of some peace in the peninsula.

However, during these years a new power was developing along the frontiers of Spain, that of the Visigoths. After the sack of Rome in 410, and under a new king, Ataulph (410–416), this people, unable to make any headway in Italy, had moved on into southern Gaul. There, although thwarted in an attempt to seize Marseille, they established themselves in Arles and Narbonne. After some initial hesitation they became allies of the Romans and Ataulph a collaborator with the new Roman military dictator, the Master of the Soldiers Constantius (*d.* 421), who was trying to restore imperial authority in Gaul in the name of the emperor Honorius. Ataulph had married Galla Placidia, half-sister of the emperor, who had been carried off from Rome after the sack of 410. With the new *rapprochement* with the imperial government and the birth of their son Theodosius, the possibilities of a close working relationship between the Romans and the Goths became very real, the more so as the emperor's half-sister was his closest heir. However, the optimistically-named infant Theodosius died at Barcelona (*c.* 415), recently occupied by the Visigoths, and his father, King Ataulph, was murdered there in 416 in an act of private vengeance. His successor Sigeric only lasted a week before being murdered in turn, conceivably an act of revenge for Ataulph, whose killing he probably instigated. The new king Wallia (416–419) maintained Ataulph's alliance with Rome, but the personal ties with the imperial family were at an end, and at Constantius's insistence Galla Placidia was handed back, to marry him in 418.[14]

It was acting in the imperial interest that the Visigoths were let loose in Spain to eliminate the barbarians established in the southern provinces, the former allies of the regime of Maximus and Gerontius. In the course of the years 416 to 418 the independence of the Alans and the Siling Vandals was extinguished by the numerically superior Visigoths. Their kings were killed and the remnant fled to the Hasding Vandals in Galicia, with whom they merged. Whether the Visigoths also intended to obliterate the Hasdings and the Sueves is uncertain, for by 418 there was a clear danger that they were proposing to transfer themselves to Africa, as they had vainly attempted in 410. By withholding their food supplies and denying them access to shipping, Constantius forced the Visigoths to return northwards to Gaul instead, and in 418 they were settled as federates in Aquitaine, with a new capital at Toulouse. Their brief hold on Barcelona and the coast of Tarraconensis was probably also terminated at this point.

A False Start: The Kingdom of the Sueves

INTO the vacuum in southern Spain caused by the removal of the Visigoths and the elimination of the Silings and the Alans, the Hasding Vandals now moved. Their need for new lands, with their ranks swollen by the influx of the survivors of the slaughter of the two

tribes, was clearly great, and the increase in their numbers raised
them to dominance in the peninsula. After an abortive attack on the
Sueves, perhaps to force them into their confederacy, the Hasdings
moved south, and in 421 established themselves in Baetica. It was
against them here that an expedition was sent in 422 under the
Master of the Soldiers Castinus, one of the generals struggling for
power after the death of Constantius. However, the Roman army was
defeated by the Vandals and forced to withdraw, apparently as a
result of treachery on the part of their Visigothic auxiliaries.[15] As the
Empress Galla Placidia, formerly their queen, is known still to have
had a considerable following amongst the Goths and to have
supported Castinus's rival Boniface, the Count of Africa, this act of
treachery on the field of battle may have had its origins in Ravenna.
In practice, the defeat of 422 meant that the Romans made no further
attempts to curb Vandal power in southern Spain. However, they
themselves appear to have felt insecure there, and after the
experiences of 416 and 422, with some justification. Thus in 429,
under a new king Geiseric (428–477), they crossed the Straits of
Hercules to begin to conquer a new home for themselves in North
Africa.

   With the removal of the Vandals, only the Sueves remained of the
original invaders of 409, and they were quick to take advantage of
their former comrades' departure. Unfortunately for themselves, they
were rather too quick, as the Vandals clearly intended to retain
possession of southern Spain, at least until they were secure in Africa.
In 430 the ravages of a Suevic leader called Hermigar in southern
Lusitania led to the unexpected return of Geiseric and a Vandal
army. Hermigar was defeated at Mérida, and drowned in the
Guadiana, whilst the Vandals went back to Africa, never to return.[16]
But after this initial setback the next quarter of a century saw an
uninterrupted rise of Suevic dominance over the southern and
western regions of the peninsula under their kings Hermeric
(abdicated 438), Rechila (438–448) and Rechiarius (448–456). In
439 Rechila captured Mérida, the principal city of Lusitania, which
he made his own capital, and in 441 he obtained control of Seville. All
three of the southern provinces, Lusitania, Baetica and
Carthaginiensis were added to Galicia under his rule. His son
Rechiarius attempted to add Tarraconensis, but with results that
were to be fatal to himself and to the Suevic monarchy.[17]

   Little is known about this short-lived Suevic domination of the peninsula but clearly it did not go unresisted, even at a local level. The chronicler Hydatius was himself involved in 431 in an embassy to the Master of the Soldiers, Aetius, in Gaul, to beg military assistance for the Galician towns trying to keep free of Suevic control.[18] The appeal was effectively rejected as Aetius only sent a single count as an envoy to the Suevic king and to help the Galicians organise themselves. In 440, this count, Censorinus, fell into the hands of the Sueves and was subsequently strangled in Seville. Although the imperial government was prepared in the 440s to fight to retain Tarraconensis, it was unwilling or unable to protect its subjects elsewhere in the peninsula.

Whilst the evidence of Hydatius shows that the Galicians at least were not prepared to submit their towns voluntarily to Suevic control, perhaps too much has been made of the violence and disorder of this period. Hydatius records Suevic ravaging in Galicia in the years 430, 431 and 433, but not subsequently. Attacks on the upper Ebro valley and Lérida are only reported in 448 and 449, and the annexations of Lusitania and Baetica appear to have occurred in 439 and 441 without any recorded resistance.[19] Only in the confused years following the removal of the Vandals, and in the campaigns of conquest, is fighting and looting of towns recorded. Otherwise the existence, by the late 430s, of unitary royal authority over the Sueves, exercised by Hermeric and his two successors, must have prevented much of the disorder created when the tribe was divided under rival war-leaders, such as the ill-fated Hermigar. Little can be known of the exercise of that royal authority. We hear nothing of Suevic counts, nor of the existence at this period, or indeed later, of written codes of law, produced either for the Sueves or their Roman subjects. But this does not necessarily imply that the Suevic rule was no more than a military domination. One interesting sign is that whilst King Rechila was a pagan, his son and successor Rechiarius was a Catholic Christian.[20] He was indeed the first barbarian king to convert to Catholicism, considerably preceding the Frankish Clovis (c. 507), whilst his Gothic and Vandal peers were Arians. For the Suevic king and some of his people to embrace the Catholic Christianity of their Roman subjects must argue a substantial measure of co-operation and mutual acceptance between them.

What might have developed from this can be a matter for no more than speculation, for the Suevic ascendance in the peninsula was dramatically cut short in the middle of the century. Since the defeat of its army in 422, the imperial government made no attempt to interfere in the affairs of the Spanish provinces other than Tarraconensis, except by some slight diplomatic activity. But the rise of the Sueves to unchecked supremacy over Baetica, Lusitania and Carthaginiensis was clearly watched with some apprehension. Only in the 440s, when the position in Gaul was more stable and also the Vandals in Africa had temporarily been neutralised by the treaty of 442, was resort to military action again possible. In 446 a newly appointed Master of the Soldiers called Vitus invaded Carthaginiensis and Baetica. However, faced by the approach of the Suevic king and his army, and with his contingent of Gothic allies defeated by them, Vitus retreated in ignominious haste.[21] He is the last Master of the Soldiers reported as having campaigned in Spain. A formal peace was concluded between the Romans and the Sueves in 452. Conceivably the restitution of Carthaginiensis was one of the conditions of this, as when Hydatius reports the Sueves' ravaging of that province in 455, he also records that they had previously returned it to the Romans.[22] The cause of this cession to the imperial government of territory which it had failed to take by force in 446, may have something to do with the increasing Visigothic interest in the peninsula, which rapidly accelerated under a new king, Theoderic II (453–66).

The Visigoths' influence over the Roman court was radically increased in 455 when, as a result of negotiations between the Roman senate, the Gothic king, and members of the southern Gallic aristocracy, the Arvernian noble Avitus (455–7) succeeded the defunct Theodosian dynasty to the western imperial throne. It can hardly be coincidental that the following year was to see a massive Visigothic intervention in Spain, and it is quite conceivable that a free hand in this direction may well have been the price exacted for their support of Avitus. The emperor was apparently a personal friend of Theoderic II, and the new alliance between the Visigoths and the Gallic aristocracy necessitated the maintenance of a status quo in Aquitaine. Thus the obvious direction for the Visigothic king to channel his ambitions was southwards into Spain, where the breaking of the peace by the Sueves in 455 meant that any intervention there would be with the support of Rome. Even the deposition and mysterious death of Avitus in 457 was not to strain these new ties between the Empire and the Visigoths, for the effective ruler of Italy for the next fifteen years was to be the German Master of the Soldiers, Ricimer, who was related to the Gothic royal dynasty.

Although it was not immediate, the long-term consequence of their invasion in 456 was to be the Visigothic domination of the peninsula. The Suevic king Rechiarius (448–56), who was clearly ambitious to regain Carthaginiensis, and finally wrest Tarraconensis from the Romans, was Theoderic II's brother-in-law, having married his sister in 449. However, such a family tie and old alliance, made when the Visigoths under Theoderic I (419–451) and the Romans were less friendly, would not save him. Rechiarius and his army were defeated on the river Orbigo, twelve miles from Astorga. In the aftermath, the Visigoths marched on Braga, the Sueves' earliest capital, and sacked it. By the end of the year the fugitive Rechiarius was discovered in hiding, and executed on his brother-in-law's orders. In the events of 456 the strength and the unity of the Suevic kingdom were broken.[23]

The royal dynasty that seems to have ruled the Sueves, at least since their entry into the Empire in 406, disappeared and was succeeded by a number of rival petty kings or war-leaders. Maldras (456–60), Agiulf (457), probably a renegade Goth, Framtane (457), Rechimund (c. 460/1), Frumarius (460–465) and Remismund (465–c. 469), are all recorded in Hydatius.[24] But with the termination of that chronicle in 469, we lose sight of these ephemeral Suevic rulers altogether, and it is not until the middle of the sixth century that we know of the name of another Suevic king, by which time, although unity of rule had been recovered, the territory over which it was exercised had shrunk to the remote north-west of the peninsula. In the aftermath of the events of 456 the Sueves lost all of their recently acquired territories in the south. Although the chronology is uncertain, they were clearly driven back by the Visigoths into the area of their original settlement in Galicia. The process was doubtless a violent and destructive one for all concerned. The last entries of Hydatius, for the years from 456 to 469, are, as in the early 430s, full of references to sackings and massacres. With the end of stable rule, the rival Suevic leaders were forced to support themselves and their followers where and with what they could seize, with results principally disastrous for the Galician provincials. Although the Sueves managed to retain their political independence until 585, Visigothic influence on them became very strong. Their last effective king in the fifth century, Rechiarius, had died a Catholic, but when his successors emerged into view in the sixth century it was as Arians, fellow-believers with the Visigoths.

Theoderic II did not pursue his victory in 456 to the fullest advantage. After passing the winter at Mérida, seat of the last Suevic kings, he returned to Gaul to pursue affairs there, mainly in the interests of Ricimer. He left those parts of Spain over which he had secured some hold, that is Baetica, southern Lusitania and Carthaginiensis, to the care of various military commanders.[25] No settlement of Goths in the peninsula seems to have occurred at this point. In 466 Theoderic II was murdered by his brother Euric, who replaced him as king (466–484). In the reign of Euric, Visigothic control over those parts of Spain wrested from the Sueves was firmly established, and a functioning administration restored. What is more, Roman control of Tarraconensis was finally terminated. This was brought about, probably in the mid 470s, by a two-pronged invasion of the province by Visigothic armies from Gaul. One under-count Gauterit crossed the Pyrenees by one of the western passes, probably Roncesvalles, and proceeded down the Ebro valley, occupying Pamplona, Zaragoza and other unspecified towns. Another column led by Heldefred and Vincent the 'Duke of the Spains' besieged and took Tarragona and other coastal cities.[26] This Vincent, to judge by his title, was formerly a Roman imperial military official. There must have been several others like him who, in the final disintegration of the Western Roman Empire in the 470s, and the extinction of its theoretical existence in 480, threw in their lot with the Germanic rulers.

New Law and Old

IN the years from 456 to the final decade of the century, the Visigoths, although they administered and garrisoned most of the peninsula, did not seek to settle on its land. Whether the system of 'hospitality' whereby a proportion of the lands and slaves of the local Roman landowners were assigned to the occupying Germans, which had been employed in the Visigothic settlement in Aquitaine in 418, was extended to Spain in this period is unknown. Had the system, Roman in its devising, been used in relations between Romans and Sueves, it is most probable that the Visigoths would have taken over the holdings of the dispossessed Sueves, rather than return them to their former owners. However, nothing is known of this either way, nor is it certain whether in the system of 'hospitality' the assigned lands were handed over to leading Germans and their followers for settlement and direct exploitation, or whether this was essentially a fiscal measure whereby the revenue from the allotted estates went to the barbarian 'guests'. Thus the economic basis upon which future relations between the Romans and the Visigoths in Spain were to be built is far from clear.[27]

Before the 490s the greatest concentration of Visigothic population was probably still to the north of the Pyrenees. But the royal administration kept the recently acquired territories in the peninsula firmly attached to Euric's Empire, which stretched from the Loire and the Rhone to the straits of Hercules. Gothic counts were appointed to supervise the principal Roman towns, command and administer justice for the Visigothic garrisons, and act as intermediaries between their charges and the royal court at Toulouse. An extant inscription testifies to the benefits conferred by the restoration of order by the Visigoths after the troubles of the middle of the century. It relates to the repairing in 483 of part of the Roman bridge over the Guadiana in Mérida, carried out by the Gothic official Salla, and Zeno, bishop of the city, on the authority of King Euric.[28] In such practical ways the inhabitants of the peninsula had much to gain from Visigothic rule. The reigns of Euric, and of his son Alaric II (484–507), mark the highest point in the peace and prosperity of the Spanish provinces between the great barbarian invasion of 409 and the re-establishment of a strong and united Visigothic kingdom by Leovigild and Reccared in the late sixth century.

This period of Euric and of Alaric II is also notable as a time of considerable law-making by the Visigothic kings and their largely Roman advisers. These years saw what is held to be the first promulgation of written law for the Visigoths, the *Code* of Euric and subsequently in 506 the production of a revised body of Roman law for their subjects, in the *Breviary* of Alaric. As the individual laws, especially those of the *Code*, have occasionally been drawn upon as evidence for particular features of Romano-Gothic society at this time, and as the nature of law-making and the legal standing of the two components of the population of the kingdom can only be understood in the light of an appreciation of the nature and mutual relationship between the two law-books, some consideration of them is necessary.

The *Code* of Euric only survives in a fragmentary state, and in no more than one manuscript, the erased part of a palimpsest at that.[29] So its physical survival into the modern world has been little short of the miraculous. But its poor showing in terms of manuscript survival should not be seen as detracting from its importance in its own day:

the reason for the limited manuscript transmission is that the *Code* was superseded, first by a revised version issued by King Leovigild (569–86) in the late sixth century, and then by the promulgation of Reccesuinth's *Lex Visigothorum* in 654. This latter laid down the ruling that all previous law books extant in the kingdom were henceforth deprived of their validity. With this, Euric's *Code* lost any remaining practical value, and would have ceased to be copied.[30]

Unlike the later codes of Leovigild and Reccesuinth, that of Euric was applied over a wider geographical area than the Iberian peninsula and Septimania: it had force in the Visigothic territories in Gaul, and it was in all probability first promulgated at Toulouse. It also clearly had influence over the thinking of other legislators: this is indicated by the borrowings from it in the *Code* of another contemporary German king, the Burgundian ruler Gundobad (474–518), who controlled parts of the Rhone valley and Switzerland. There is also clear dependence upon Euric's *Code* in another 'barbarian' law book, harder to date than that of Gundobad, and that is the *Law of the Bavarians*. So clear is the relationship between Euric and the Bavarian law in areas where direct comparison is possible, that legal historians have been able to use the latter for hypothetical reconstructions of the missing parts of the former.[31] In fact, only those parts of the sections of Euric's laws relating to boundaries, deposits, sales, gifts and inheritances have survived, but on the basis of the *Law of the Bavarians*, and an analysis of those parts of the *Code* of Leovigild believed to have derived from that of Euric, it has been possible to deduce the existence of titles on judges, accusations, sanctuary in church, fugitives, thieves, woundings, doctors, violations of sepulchres, foreign merchants, rape, fires (arson), various divisions of land-law and much else beside. As well as the nature of the titles, it has also proved possible for informed guesses to be made about some of the lost laws that once went into them.

The *Code* of King Leovigild (569–86), which, as Bishop Isidore of Seville in his *History of the Goths* (625/6) tells us, was intended as a revision and expansion of Euric's work, has its own peculiar problems.[32] For it too was superseded and rendered obsolete by Reccesuinth's law book of 654. It was less fortunate than Euric's *Code* in that it failed to survive, even partly intact, in any manuscript at all. It is now extant only in the form of individual laws embedded in the titles of Reccesuinth's *Code*, marked out by the epithet *antiqua*. An attempt is currently being made to reconstruct Leovigild's *Code* as a whole.[33]

Thus the principal line of the legislation of the Visigothic kings partakes rather of the character of a Russian doll: the *Code* of Euric is inside that of Leovigild, which is inside that of Reccesuinth. In fact the chain extends back one stage further: Euric in his *Code* makes a number of references, in the surviving sections, to the laws of his father Theoderic I (419–451).[34] No attempt has yet been made to isolate the elements of this 'Code of Theoderic' from that of Euric, but it is important to note that these laws of Theoderic, whatever form they took, represent the earliest known act of legislation by a Germanic ruler inside the Roman Empire. This also invalidates the current argument that the *Code* of Euric can only have been issued after 476, when there was no longer an emperor in the West whose monopolistic prerogative of legislating might be infringed.[35] Thus no certain indication exists as to the date of the issue of Euric's *Code* and therefore of the identity of those Roman advisers who, in all probability, compiled it for the king.

What, then, was the purpose behind Euric's law-making, and to whom was his *Code* intended to apply? The answers to these questions, if determinable, are likely equally to apply to the earlier laws of Theoderic I and the later ones of Leovigild. Unfortunately, no real agreement exists as to what these answers might be. One school of thought would argue that the content of Euric's *Code* is essentially Germanic, and that it represents the writing down under Roman influence of elements of the oral customary law of the Visigoths. This theory presupposes the answer to the second question. Such a code was intended for use by the Goths and it gave them their own *lex*, distinct from that of the Romans, which was to be found in the *Theodosian Code*, promulgated by the emperors Theodosius II and Valentinian III in 438. Such a view may be supported by the statement of Isidore in his *History of the Goths* that Euric was the first king to put the Goths under written law.[36] This, of course, seems to ignore the existence of the previous laws of Theoderic, and is the view of a seventh-century commentator, rather than of an exact contemporary.

Another question arises. If an oral customary law existed amongst the Goths, why would successive kings care to have parts of it put into writing? That the *Code* of Euric was far from comprehensive is clear enough, for, although it is believed to have contained thirty-one titles, with about 360 separate enactments in them, only certain legal topics, those previously mentioned, are considered, and these by no means in full. So some have seen this royal legal activity as little more than an

aping of imperial practice, in the interest of emphasising some of the
Roman roots of their authority.[37] A more concrete notion is that the
king's intentions were purely practical, in providing a written
statement of Gothic custom and perhaps some new law based on it for
use in cases involving both Roman and Gothic participants, where
their two systems of law might thereby come into conflict. This idea
could be strengthened by reference to the *Law of Gundobad*,
contemporary with Euric's *Code*, where such a purpose does seem to
be at least one of the specific aims of the royal legislator.[38]

There is, however, another school of thought that takes a
completely different starting point. This is the view that the essence of
Euric's *Code* and other similar law books lies not in Germanic custom,
but in late Roman vulgar law.[39] By this is meant a kind of common law
that regulated the mundane workings of society, and was quite
different in character and subject-matter from the statute law of the
imperial edicts and rescripts. Land law, sales and exchanges,
inheritances and so forth were the stuff of this legal area, as they were
of the *Codes* of Euric and Gundobad. Unfortunately, in the present
state of knowledge the Roman vulgar law is almost as mysterious and
intangible as original Germanic custom. But there are a number of
remarkable parallels between some of the enactments of the seventh-
century Byzantine code, the *Farmers' Law*, and some of those of the
codes of various Germanic peoples, principally of the Visigoths, the
Burgundians, and the Lombards.[40] Parallels with the Visigothic *Code*
of Reccesuinth are in all cases with laws in that book that are marked
antiqua, that is to say, come from the lost *Code* of Leovigild. In all cases
these individual laws can be shown to be Eurician in origin, or to be
from that earlier *Code* but slightly altered by Leovigild. Now as no one
is going to argue that the Byzantines borrowed their law from the
Germanic kingdoms, a common grounding of the legislation of both
in the vulgar law of Rome is surely the most sensible explanation.
This also makes more sense of the striking similarity between a
number of common features of the various codes of the different
Germanic peoples. Thus the search for the legal origins of the
contents of Euric's *Code* and those of his fellow kings is probably better
directed towards the area of late Roman vulgar law than towards the
nebulous realm of Germanic custom.

There still remains the question for whom the law was intended. If
the basis of this law is Roman, there is less likelihood that the purpose
of the *Code* was to give the Goths a law book of their own. This

impression is reinforced by some of the laws from the *Code*, such as that relating to the inheritances of monks, that make little sense in the context of purely Gothic society.[41] Likewise, allowing the Roman nature of some, if not all, of Euric's laws, they can hardly have been intended principally to resolve conflicts between the Roman and Gothic legal systems in the courts. Thus the arguments in favour of the *Code* of Euric being, like that of Reccesuinth in 654, a 'territorial' one, that is to say, applying to all inhabitants of regions under the authority of the Visigothic king, are strong ones.

What, then, was the purpose of this legislation? In many respects it was intensely practical: conflicts existed in the vulgar law and Roman statute law was contradictory. Also the problem of what was and what was not current practice in such vital areas as inheritance, injury and landownership was a very real one, in an age when it was hard to know where to have recourse for authoritative law. Thus the production of a code containing rulings on many of these vital issues was a matter of practical value. Euric's Roman legal advisers, who may have included the Gallic aristocrat Leo, can hardly have viewed it otherwise. It is conceivable too that the context of Euric's legislating is less novel than might appear. His father Theoderic I had done something similar, and other late fifth- and early sixth-century German kings such as Gundobad (474–518) and Clovis (481–511) did likewise. The controversial *Edict of Theoderic*, probably an Italian product of the same period, is also similar in several respects.[42] By the traditional view, Euric broke new ground, and the others imitated him, even in the case of Gundobad's borrowing laws directly from his *Code*. But is is more reasonable to suppose that precedents existed for both the form and the nature of this legislation, perhaps in the legal activities of the late Roman Praetorian Prefects, whose functions the German kings now exercised.

This is uncontrovertibly the case with the next product of Visigothic royal law-making, the *Roman Law of the Visigoths* or *Breviary* of Alaric II, issued in 506. This consisted of the issue of a considerably abbreviated version of the *Theodosian Code* of 438, the principal codification of Roman law before that of Justinian I (529, revised 533), with new 'interpretations' appended to the individual laws to amend them in the light of local or altered circumstances. Previously Praetorian Prefects had had the right to issue their own 'edicts', in the form of 'interpretations' added to the statute laws of the emperors, to make them more relevant to the particular conditions of the provinces

for which they were responsible.[43] Thus Alaric II's treatment of
Roman statute law was directly in the tradition and following the
lines of known praetorian prefectural legislation. It is quite
conceivable, that the late Roman officials had similar powers and
responsibilities in respect of the vulgar law. Thus the activities of
Euric in his *Code* may well have been as much within a recognisable
Roman legal context as those of Alaric II with his *Breviary*.

These detailed considerations of the legal work, particularly of
Euric but also of Alaric, have been necessary in order to suggest how
closely within a continuing late Roman governmental tradition the
early Visigothic kings of Spain and Gaul were working. Their powers
and their responsibilities, which, under the guidance of Roman
advisers, they took seriously, derived from the way they had fitted
themselves closely into the pre-existing structures. They governed
as delegates of an Empire, that, in the west at least, no longer existed.
But it was on the basis of treaties and agreements made with that
Empire, and titles granted by it, that they exercised authority over
their Roman subjects. Having subsumed the roles and fulfilling the
functions of both Praetorian Prefect and Master of the Soldiers, their
rights and their duties were clear. Amongst these the provision and
maintenance of good law were clearly not the least, certainly in the
minds of Euric and Alaric II.

There are many features of the Romano-Gothic society of this
period that it would be pleasant to know more of, but the evidence is
limited. Certain features that will be discussed in the context of the
sixth and seventh centuries, such as royal finance, the natures of the
Roman and Gothic aristocracies, and so on, could be relevant to this
period too, but the absence of documentation prevents this being
more than speculation. However, one thing is clear, and that is that
the Church benefited from the relatively benevolent rule of the
Visigothic kings in the late fifth century, even though they themselves
were Arians, and Euric has something of an undeserved reputation as
a persecutor of Catholics, at least in Gaul. The Goths as a whole were
Arians, divided from the Catholics by their lack of belief in the
co-eternity and equality of the Son and the Holy Spirit with the
Father. But they had their own places of worship in their separate
settlements, and it is likely that the Arian liturgy was still conducted
in the Gothic language. The Visigothic court at Toulouse in the late
fifth century has been considered a possible place of origin for the
extant fragmentary Gothic manuscripts of the Gospels, although the

claims of Ostrogothic Italy are also strong.[44] Thus contact between Arians and Catholics in the Visigothic kingdom seems at this time to have been limited, and as a result, conflict was limited too. On the Catholic side it became possible, when stability had been re-established in Gaul and Spain by Euric, once again to contemplate the holding of large-scale Church councils. Thus the bishops of the sees in Visigothic territory north of the Pyrenees were able to meet in council at Agde in 506, where a plan was drawn up for the holding of regular councils thereafter, at which the Spanish bishops would also be present.[45] These would have been plenary and truly 'national' councils of the Visigothic kingdom, of the kind later to be held in Toledo in the seventh century. The Council of Agde, important also for its disciplinary canons, thus promised something of a new development for the Catholic Church under Visigothic rule, and perhaps something of a speedier resolution of the religious differences that divided Romans and Goths. However, this was not to be. In 507 the ambitious Frankish king Clovis invaded the Visigothic kingdom, and in the ensuing battle at Vouillé Alaric II was killed. In the aftermath, all the Visigothic possessions in Gaul, excepting only the region of 'Septimania' around Narbonne, fell into Frankish or Burgundian hands, and it was to take the monarchy almost half a century to recover from the effects. In view of what had already been achieved by the Visigothic kings, and what their laws and the Council of Agde gave promise of, their defeat by the more primitive Franks may justly be termed a disaster, from which the Visigothic monarchy at least was to take several generations to recover.

2.   The Imposition of Unity

Divisions and Defeats

THE series of demoralising defeats that they suffered in the years 507–31 at the hands of the newly emergent Franks and their Burgundian allies led directly to the disappearance of the Balt dynasty which had ruled the Visigoths with little interruption since the time of Alaric I (395–410), if not longer. The first disaster was that of Vouillé in 507, which saw the death of Alaric II and the loss during the ensuing year of most of the Visigothic territory in Gaul.[1] The losses might have been greater, but for the intervention from Italy in 508 of the Ostrogothic king Theoderic (493–526), whose army forced the Franks and Burgundians to lift their siege of Arles. As a result, the whole Mediterranean coastal region of southern Gaul remained in Gothic hands, mainly Ostrogothic. Although Arles and other towns of the lower Rhone valley had been in Visigothic hands in 507, they now passed into Ostrogothic control, the price of the rescue. While the kind of pan-Gothic sympathy that is hinted at by the Ostrogothic historian Jordanes (c. 551) may have had a part to play, Theoderic's interests were also involved in preventing the rapidly expanding Frankish kingdom from gaining access to the Mediterranean, or coming too close to Italy.[2] Hence the intervention in 508, which was to initiate a period of considerable Ostrogothic involvement in the affairs of the Visigoths and in Spain.

With Alaric II dead and his capital, Toulouse, fallen to the Franks, the problem of succession asserted itself. Although the automatic right of inheritance by members of the Balt dynasty was by no means guaranteed, as the successions of Sigeric and Wallia in 416 show, so long had been their tenure of power that they were likely to be the first recourse of the Visigothic nobility in electing a king. For most of the fifth century such election had been a customary formality, with the succession passing from father to son, or brother to brother, in the ruling family. However, this was possible because all of the kings had succeeded in their full maturity, and had proved themselves competent, especially militarily. In 508 the legitimate heir of Alaric II was a child, Amalaric, his only son by his wife Thiudigoto, daughter of the Ostrogothic king Theoderic. As their marriage probably occurred only in c. 500, Amalaric was clearly a long way from adulthood, so the Visigothic nobility elected instead Gesalic, an illegitimate son of Alaric II, of full age. The new king established his capital at Narbonne.

Now as the succession of Gesalic inevitably threatened the inheritance of Theoderic's infant grandson Amalaric, it is little of a surprise to find Theoderic the Ostrogoth taking the earliest possible opportunity of disposing of him. The Franks and the Burgundians continued their efforts to expand their kingdoms into Provence and to take advantage of the prolonged weakness of the Visigoths. In 511, the Burgundian king Gundobad and his army attacked and sacked Narbonne. Driven from his capital, Gesalic fled south of the Pyrenees to Barcelona, where he was deposed at the instigation of Theoderic, whose generals appear to have gained effective control of the Visigothic forces by this time. Gesalic did not give up easily. After being expelled from his kingdom in 511, he attempted unsuccessfully to enlist the aid of the Vandal king Thrasamund (496–523), himself an ally of Theoderic. Instead, Gesalic established himself in Aquitaine, and in 513 attempted an invasion of Spain. He was defeated near Barcelona by Theoderic's general Ebba, and being captured in flight over the river Durance, was immediately executed.[3]

After Gesalic's deposition in 511, power had passed in name to the child Amalaric, possibly contrary to the wishes of the Visigoths, but in practice the kingdom passed under the regency of the Ostrogothic monarch, whose authority was enforced by his commanders. Little is known of this period, which lasted for some fifteen years, until Theoderic's death in 526. Visigothic reaction to this Ostrogothic hegemony is unclear, as is how the government of the latter in the peninsula actually worked. The practical difference between Ostrogoths and Visigoths, except in terms of their separate past histories, is equally obscure. They had collaborated closely in the past, as in the years 376–8, when a band of fugitive Ostrogoths and their king Videric had joined the Visigoths in their entry into the Roman empire, and then in the subsequent great victory over the Romans at the battle of Adrianople (378). Interestingly, the Visigoths seem to have taken the legitimate line of the Ostrogothic royal dynasty, the Amals, with them in the years of wandering that followed: Theoderic discovered an Amal called Eutharic, probably a descendant of the child king Videric, living quietly amongst the Visigoths in c. 508, and married him to his daughter Amalasuntha.[4] Isidore of Seville, in his *History of the Goths*, suggests that Theoderic came to Spain in person at some point in his reign, and this was probably the starting point for a fantastic medieval legend that makes Isidore the Ostrogothic king's grandson.[5] However, no contemporary evidence survives to substantiate such a visit by Theoderic to Spain at any stage of his career.

The effective reign of Amalaric that was initiated by the death of Theoderic in 526 was brief and inglorious. It is likely that his grandfather's Ostrogothic viceroys, of whom the principal was a man called Theudis, still exercised much power and influence, as the sequel showed. Amalaric married a Frankish princess Clotild, daughter of Clovis. His ill-conceived and violent attempts to force his wife to renounce her Catholic beliefs in favour of Arianism gave her Frankish relatives an excuse for intervention. In 531 her brother Childebert I (511–58) invaded the Visigothic realm. Once again Narbonne was taken, and the king fled before his enemies across the Pyrenees to Barcelona. There trying to escape by sea Amalaric was murdered, probably by his own men, and with him died his dynasty.[6] In his place the Visigothic nobility chose the Ostrogothic general Theudis, who may have had a hand in killing Amalaric.

Why had the Visigoths proved so consistently weak before successive Frankish onslaughts from 507–531? Although many of the factors that would go to explain this cannot now be known, there is one feature of the period leading up to this era of defeat that may make the failure of the Visigoths to do more to hold on to their lands in Gaul less incomprehensible. This is the Visigothic migration into Spain during the last decade of the fifth century. The Visigoths had been established in Aquitaine since 418, and even after their conquest of the Iberian peninsula under their kings Theoderic II and Euric, their principal interests seem to have still lain to the north of the Pyrenees, and the royal capital remained at Toulouse. However, in the 490s a southward movement into Spain of substantial numbers of the Visigoths appears to have occurred. This is known from two entries in the fragmentary *Chronicle of Zaragoza*. This brief work has a remarkably complicated textual history, and now only survives in a sixteenth-century copy of two lost medieval manuscripts, which themselves only contained extracts from the chronicle as marginalia to other historical texts. It has been argued and generally accepted that the original chronicle was the work of a seventh-century bishop of Zaragoza, Maximus (*c.* 599–621). However, it is possible to show that Maximus probably never wrote a chronicle, and that the extant extracts derive from not one but two sixth-century annals.[7] The passages relating to the Visigothic settlement come from the earlier of the two chronicles, which can have been compiled no later than the middle of the century. The greater precision now possible in respect of this source means that greater reliability may be accorded to its information. Thus, when it tells us in relation to the year 494 'In this consulship the Goths entered Spain' and for 497 'In this consulship the Goths received dwellings in Spain', there is little cause for doubt.[8] This movement of Goths from Aquitaine into the Iberian peninsula a decade before the battle of Vouillé may well have caused an important alteration in the balance between the two halves of the kingdom, and have left the Gallic territories vulnerable to the subsequent Frankish attack. What prompted this movement of population, whether insecurity in Gaul or better prospects in Spain, is never hinted at in any source, and so remains a mystery, but that it had some part to play in the Visigothic loss of Aquitaine seems likely.

The losses of 507–31 included not only lands but also a dynasty. The long and relatively little-interrupted rule of the descendants of Alaric I has created something of a false perspective on Visigothic kingship in the fifth century. Dynastic succession was not as secure as is sometimes assumed. Although the evidence is difficult to evaluate, there appears to have been no system of hereditary succession before the entry of the Visigoths into the Roman Empire in 376, and there seems to have been no permanent royal office. Roman commentators on the Goths, such as the fourth-century historian Ammianus Marcellinus (c. 380/90), refer to at least two different types of ruler, kings and judges, with the latter apparently the more powerful.[9] No single figure seems to have exercised authority over the whole of the Visigothic people. This distinguishes them from the Ostrogoths, who, by the time of the destruction of their realm by the Huns (c. 370), had developed a unitary dynastic kingship that could accommodate the succession of minors. For the Visigoths, this was only to occur after their entry into the Empire, when their difficulties in the period 378–410 made the acceptance of a single permanent war-leader a necessity. Before 376, such military leaders appear to have been elected by different groups amongst the Visigoths, and only for limited periods, sufficient to cover the immediate offensive or defensive purposes. Judges may have been permanent, and fulfilled superior priestly and judicial functions.

These origins set the basic character of Visigothic kingship for the centuries to follow. The kings were essentially the war-leaders of their people. The office of 'judge' did not survive the entry of the Visigoths into the Roman world, and the concurrent abandonment of their pagan religion in favour of Christianity. So, for the Visigoths there could be no tradition of loyalty to a dynasty as occurred in the cases of the Ostrogoths and the Franks. They were thus unable to contemplate the succession of a minor, as the Ostrogoths did in 376 and 526. The king had of his very nature to be a warrior, and no dynastic loyalty could outweigh this. Further, should a king prove unsatisfactory in his principal task, that is war-leadership, he might be deposed or killed, as happened to Gesalic and Amalaric. There was thus no guarantee that a new king would be chosen from the same family as his predecessor, though as long as the late monarch's heir looked a credible choice he would be likely to be elected. For one thing, the intrusion of a new ruling family could unsettle the status quo and adversely affect the interests of those who benefited from the previous regime. Sigeric (416) was not of the family of Alaric I, and there is no evidence that Wallia (416–419) was either. Indeed the link between Theoderic I (419–51) and his descendants with Alaric is dependent upon a single reference, and is by no means certain.[10] The dynastic succession of the Visigothic kingdom in the fifth century is more tenuous than is allowed, and depended entirely upon the competence and continuing military success of the individual kings. All of them succeeded in the full vigour of their years, and they led their forces in person. Two of them, Theoderic I in 451, and Alaric II in 507, died on the field of battle. Several kings were also murdered, Ataulph and Sigeric in 416, Thorismund in 453 and Theoderic II in 466, though the reasons are not always clear. Thus there is little to distinguish the Visigothic kingship of the fifth century from that of the more troubled periods of the sixth and seventh.

The first successor of the defunct Balt dynasty was the Ostrogothic general Theudis (531–548). His nephew Ildibad was briefly king of the Ostrogoths in Italy (539–40), but there appear to have been few close ties between the two branches of the Goths at this time. The final destruction of the Ostrogothic kingdom in 552 seems to have made no mark on the Visigothic one. Much of Theudis's power in Spain seems to have come, according to the Byzantine historian Procopius, from a marriage he contracted with a Roman heiress, the slaves of whose estate he formed into a private army.[11] In this period, a generation after the Visigothic settlement of Spain, the problem of military manpower must have presented a serious difficulty for the royal administration. No system existed to replace the permanent military establishment of the late Roman Empire. Obviously in periods of migration the Germanic kings had effectively all of the able manpower of their people at their disposal, but after a settlement on the land, however conducted, the difficulty of raising armies became extreme. The Visigothic kings, like their other early medieval counterparts, relied upon their *comitatus*, a body of young nobles of fighting age, and their followers, in permanent attendance upon the monarch. They would require maintenance for their services, and in due course grants of land, but they would serve as the permanent nucleus of the royal army, to be supplemented in times of need by the resources of local landowners. Theudis's use of his wife's slaves, and Didymus and Verinian's arming of theirs in 409 make it clear that the servile populations of the great estates were a principal source of military manpower in the peninsula. As well as his private resources, Theudis would have had those of the royal estates, principally lands once belonging to the imperial treasury, to augment his *comitatus* and armed slaves. As a result he proved militarily more successful than his immediate predecessors. For the first time the Franks were defeated. One of their expeditions was forced in 541 to buy a safe retreat out of the peninsula from the king's general Theudisclus. However, a Visigothic army was defeated by the forces of the Byzantine Emperor Justinian (527–565), at Ceuta, probably in *c.* 544.[12]

This defeat, referred to by Isidore, raises an interesting problem. What were Visigothic forces doing in North Africa? From the brief account that Isidore gives, it seems that the Visigoths were in possession of Ceuta at the time of the Byzantine attack. They were expelled from the town, and finally came to grief in making an unsuccessful counter-attack. The Vandal kingdom in North Africa, with which the Visigoths had enjoyed reasonably close relations earlier in the sixth century, was destroyed by Justinian's army in 533. It is possible that Theudis, who refused a Vandal appeal for aid, took advantage of this to annexe the African shore of the Straits of Hercules to the Visigothic kingdom, and occupy Ceuta. After their expulsion in 544, the Visigoths were not to return to Africa until the very end of the seventh century.

Theudis's reputation is mixed. Isidore, who displayed a fervent Romano-Gothic patriotism, criticised him bitterly for the failure in Africa, and implied that it was for this he deserved his eventual violent end. However, he also praised Theudis for the toleration that he extended to the Catholic Church, although he himself was an Arian. One law of Theudis has survived, relating to voluntary gifts to judges.[13] The king was assassinated in 548, apparently by a personal enemy, who pretended madness until in a position to perform his deed. When dying, Theudis pardoned his murderer on the grounds that he too had once slain his own ruler, perhaps referring to complicity in the killing of Amalaric.

The next king, Theudisclus (548–9), was no doubt chosen for his military achievements. It was he who in 541 had forced the Frankish kings Childebert I and Chlotar I, who had sacked Pamplona and were besieging Zaragoza, to buy their escape from Spain. However, his reign was brief, for after a year he was murdered at a banquet in Seville, apparently by a cabal of outraged husbands, whose wives he had interfered with.[14] The antecedents of his successor Agila (549–54) are unknown, but his reign is principally notable for its failures.[15] In about 550 the city of Cordoba rebelled, apparently the result of some insult the king offered to the cult of its patron saint, the martyr Acisclus. When Agila attempted to suppress the revolt by force, his army was defeated, his son killed, and the royal treasure lost. Cordoba was not restored to the authority of the Visigothic kings until 572. After so humiliating a defeat, it is not surprising to find Agila being challenged by a member of his own nobility. In 551 Athanagild rebelled, probably in Seville. He also appealed to the Emperor Justinian for assistance, with fateful consequences. The imperial expedition that was despatched in answer to this appeal rendered little assistance to either side in the Visigothic civil war, but instead busied itself with establishing a narrow enclave of Byzantine territory along the south-eastern coast of the peninsula, with its centre at Cartagena. Agila failed to make any headway against Athanagild, who probably gained control of most of Baetica, and in 554 he was murdered by his own men in Mérida.

The Byzantine control of the south-eastern coast that resulted from the appeal for their aid was to last for over seventy years. They were finally expelled in 624. Their authority never extended very far inland, certainly not to Cordoba and the valley of the Guadalquivir, as has sometimes been thought.[16] For one thing, their aim never seems to have been one of substantial conquest inside the peninsula, even were this possible. The principal purpose of their establishment seems to have been the greater security of their recently reconquered North African provinces. The activities of the Visigoths under

Theudis around Ceuta may well have made the fear of their expansion into Africa a real one. Certainly the Visigoths had twice been prevented from invading the African provinces in the fifth century, in 410 and 418. Now, with the Vandal kingdom removed and the Byzantine forces deeply embroiled in conflict with the Berbers, renewed Visigothic ambitions in that direction presented a serious threat. Whether the Visigoths were still capable of and willing to uproot themselves from Spain to move into Africa is more problematic, but from their point of view Byzantine concern was justified. So they took the opportunity of establishing a military presence along the coast from which previous invasions of Africa had come. Their principal strongholds were Medina Sidonia, Malaga and Cartagena, the last of which was the seat of the governor and the probable site of a small mint that operated in the early seventh century.[17]

With the removal of Agila, the way was opened for a general acceptance of Athanagild (551/554–568) as king by the Visigoths. His reign is perhaps more significant than our sources may care to let us believe. He is generally credited with the responsibility for inviting the Byzantines into the peninsula, on the explicit testimony of Isidore in his *History of the Goths*, written in the mid 620s. However, it is interesting to note that in both of the emperor Justinian's other western interventions, Africa in 533 and Italy in 535, he came in ostensibly to uphold the rights of legitimate monarchs against usurpers. Now the account of the Gothic historian Jordanes, probably writing in Constantinople in 551, the year of the despatch of the expedition to Spain, suggests that this was what Justinian was doing again, and that it was the legitimately elected ruler Agila he was aiding against the rebel Athanagild.[18] Conceivably Jordanes is merely repeating the distorted version of imperial propaganda, but it is equally possible that Isidore's later account reflects the hostility towards the dynasty of Athanagild felt by subsequent Visigothic rulers. However, whether or not Athanagild was responsible for the summoning of the Byzantines, he was the first Visigothic ruler to take the offensive against them. He was also involved in diplomatic relations with the Franks. His two daughters, Brunechildis and Galswintha, were married to Sigebert of Austrasia (561–575) and Chilperic of Neustria (561–584) respectively. The subsequent murder of Galswintha by her husband initiated the great blood feud in the Merovingian dynasty that lasted for three generations and claimed at least ten royal lives.[19] Brunechildis played an important role in Frankish politics throughout her life in Gaul, and was probably the dominant figure of the years 592–613, when she was viciously executed. It is quite likely that many of the difficulties the Visigothic kingdom faced in dealings with the Franks in this period were of her devising, and hence perhaps the apparent denigration of her father Athanagild in seventh-century Spanish sources. Athanagild himself died in 568 without male heirs, and so his line in Spain was extinguished with him. Claims that the subsequent king Leovigild was related to him are based upon spurious later medieval genealogies.

On the death of Athanagild, a Gothic noble called Liuva (568–571 or 573) was elected king at Narbonne, the first occasion on which we have a reference to a king in this north-eastern region of the realm since the death of Amalaric in 531. Mention of the intermediate kings has placed them all in the south: Theudisclus at Seville, Agila at Mérida and Athanagild at Toledo, his principal residence. The making of the new king at Narbonne may reflect renewed danger of Frankish attack. The Franks had been quiescent on the Visigothic frontier since the 540s, but under a new generation of kings, particularly Guntramn (561–92) the danger was revived. With the considerable threat presented by the Franks at many stages throughout the sixth century to Visigothic Septimania and also to the Ebro valley, it is likely that the greatest concentration of military strength and with it of the Gothic nobility will have been found in this region. Certainly Liuva found it sufficiently important and demanding to delegate royal authority over the rest of the peninsula to his brother Leovigild (569–586) a year after his own election, reserving only the provinces of Narbonnensis and probably Tarraconensis for himself. Subsequently in about 580 Leovigild gave his second son Reccared responsibility for this vital frontier zone, though not as an independent kingdom. When Liuva I died, either in 571 by the implication of Isidore's account or more probably, following the *Chronicle* of John of Biclar, in 573, the whole kingdom was reunified under the rule of Leovigild.[20]

Despite both the unsettled state of the realm throughout most of the sixth century and the persistence of its rulers in their Arian beliefs until 587, the condition of the Catholic Church in this period was by no means unhealthy. The limitations of the evidence make it difficult to assess how serious a challenge Arianism presented before the reign of Leovigild, as no documents of the Visigothic Arian Church in Spain have survived. It is not known at what point after the mid fifth century its liturgy and scriptures ceased to employ the Gothic language. The nature and extent of its organisation is obscure, and before 589 there are no references to named Arian bishops at all, with the exception of Sunna of Mérida in the 580s.[21] It seems clear that the hold of Arianism on the Goths was weakening during the course of the century, and that it was Catholicism if anything that was presenting the active challenge. The monk John of Biclar, later Bishop of Gerona, was a Gothic convert to Catholicism and the best known Catholic bishop of the metropolitan see of Mérida in this century was the Goth Masona. One of his Gothic successors, the bishop Redemptus, may also have been a pre-589 convert. The names of other converts, though not their careers, may be gleaned from dated inscriptions. Whatever the percentage of the population this represented, and it was probably a relatively small one, a movement of Gothic conversion from Arianism to Catholicism was taking place gradually throughout the sixth century, prior to the accession of Leovigild.

Periods of open conflict between the proponents of the two theological systems, as occurred in the second half of that king's reign, were previously rare. The Arian king Theudis (531–548) was praised by Isidore of Seville for the degree of tolerance that he extended to the Catholic Church. Of the few provincial councils that are known to have taken place in Spain before 589, nearly half were held during his reign: I Barcelona in 540, Lérida in 546 and Valencia also in 546 (this last is wrongly dated in some manuscripts to 549).[22] It is interesting to note, on the authority of the preambles to the acts of the latter two councils, that the king was probably officially named Theodoric rather than Theudis, as he was known to Isidore. After the holding of these two councils in 546 there occurs a gap of forty years before the next recorded council, that of III Toledo in 589. This has been interpreted by some historians as indicating royal prohibition of such assemblies of Catholic bishops. However from the reign of Agila to the middle of that of Leovigild conditions inside the peninsula deteriorated in respect of internal order and security.

Leovigild

IT was the career of Leovigild that really altered the standing of the Visigothic monarchy in the peninsula. He restored it to a position of strength that it had not enjoyed since the days of Euric and Alaric II. It is fortunate that the literary evidence for Leovigild's reign, whilst by no means considerable, is at least fuller than that for his immediate predecessors. In particular, the whole period of his rule is covered in the *Chronicle* of John of Biclar, the most substantial work of its kind produced in Visigothic Spain.

John, as Isidore tells us in his *On the Lives of Famous Men*, was of Gothic origin, born at Scallabis in Lusitania.[23] Whilst still a youth he went to Constantinople, where he was to spend seventeen years. The reason for this journey and protracted stay are nowhere explained. He may have commenced work on his *Chronicle* during this visit, as the earliest sections, covering the years 568 to about 577, are remarkably well informed on Byzantine events, and his writing is one of the principal sources for the history of the Empire in those years. The *Chronicle* itself was conceived as a continuation of that of the African bishop Victor of Tunnunna.[24] This latter work was written in Constantinople, where its author was long detained for his opposition to the religious policies of the emperor Justinian I. John returned to Spain during the reign of Leovigild, and was subsequently exiled by the king to Barcelona. It is usually believed that this was due to his being a Catholic at a time when Arian-Catholic conflict was bitter, and the king was especially hostile to Goths who had deserted their traditional Arianism. However, this is nowhere stated explicitly, and chronologically the exile may have occurred before the outbreak of religious hostilities. John's Byzantine contacts and lengthy sojourn in Constantinople may have more of a part to play in this than his theological beliefs. Isidore mentions that John suffered from the hostility of the Arians for ten years, and this gives something of a chronological starting point for reconstructing his life. Arianism was not finally suppressed in north-east Spain until 589/90, which suggests that John's exile in Barcelona began *c.* 579 and thus the stay in Constantinople might fall into the years *c.* 562 – *c.* 579, though there is no indication as to how long an interval there was between his return and his exile. After the final elimination of Arianism in Tarraconensis, John founded a monastery at a site called Biclar, probably close to Tarragona, for which he composed a *Rule*, now lost. Soon after, at some point between 589 and 592 he was consecrated Bishop of Gerona. It was probably in the same period that he completed his *Chronicle*, which ends in 590. As bishop, John signed the acts of several councils, II Zaragoza in 592, the Synod of Toledo in 597 and II Barcelona in 599. He was probably still living at the time of the Council of Egara in 614, as the signature of a Bishop John to its acts is probably his.[25] Isidore records the writing of the *Chronicle*, which he himself used extensively in composing his own *Chronicle* for the years 568–590, and he also refers to the existence of other unspecified works by John, which, however, he had not read and are not known today.

It is from John's *Chronicle*, supplemented by the brief biographical notice on the king in Isidore's *History of the Goths*, that we know as much as we do about Leovigild. There are also occasional references to him in other sources, such as the contemporary *History* of Bishop Gregory of Tours (573–594), and in hagiographical works, such as the *Life of St Aemilian* and the *Lives of the Fathers of Mérida*. The account of the king in the last of these works, probably written *c.* 630, is composed out of direct borrowings from the *Life of Desiderius* by the Visigothic king Sisebut (612–21), and as such intended as a literary set piece description of an impious ruler.[26] By contrast, the picture that emerges from the works of both John and Isidore is that of a most able warrior, whom the writers admired for his achievements, despite the difficulties of his last years and the sufferings of the Catholics at his hands.

The division of the kingship in 569 was a new development in Visigothic history. There had never been other than a single king ruling since the time of the first emergence of the institution under Alaric I. But the division was sensible: in the north lay the threat of resurgent Frankish aggression and the Basques and Cantabrians in the upper Ebro valley were always open to the opportunities of raiding the settled areas to the south of them, and at the other end of the peninsula in Baetica were the Byzantines in their coastal fortresses. Although after their initial seizure the Byzantines seem to have made no effort to extend the region under their control, the possibility that they might initiate a full-scale war of reconquest doubtless seemed a real one to the Visigothic kings. As well as these external threats, within the peninsula there were other areas that had either succeeded in denying or had thrown off royal overlordship. Cordoba had not been recovered since its revolt in 550. Most of the mountainous zones of the northern coastal regions were beyond the king's control, and perhaps had always been, even in the late fifth century. Also there was still the kingdom of the Sueves up in the north-west.

This people, who disappear from historical view with the ending of Hydatius's *Chronicle* in 469, re-emerge in the middle of the sixth century. The small Galician realm had lapsed into Arianism in the meanwhile, but in *c.*560 the kingdom formally reverted to Catholicism, probably under Frankish influence, for miraculous intervention on the part of Martin of Tours, the principal western Gallic saint is recorded, and also the translation of some relics of Martin from Tours to the Suevic capital of Braga. The principal human agency in this conversion was a man, also called Martin, from the former Roman province of Pannonia in the western Balkans. After a period of training as a monk in Egypt, he sailed to Galicia, probably in 556, and was permitted by King Charraric to establish a monastery at Dumio near Braga. A considerable account of his life and writings is to be found in the *History* of Gregory of Tours and also in his *On the Miracles of St Martin*, further evidence of the communication between Gaul and the Suevic kingdom.[27] Under Martin's influence the return of the Sueves to the Catholicism they had once accepted under their king Rechiarius (448–456) was completed, certainly by the time of the holding of the first council of Braga by the Catholic episcopate in 561. Such rejection of the religious beliefs of their once dominant Visigothic neighbours was only possible at a time when the kingdom of the latter was relatively weak. But such action with the attendant closing of links by sea to the Frankish realms and possible openness to Byzantine political influence inevitably made the Suevic kingdom an object of justifiable suspicion to reviving Visigothic power under Leovigild.

However, the Visigothic king's first attention was devoted to the Byzantine forces in the south. In 570 he sacked but apparently did not reoccupy Malaga. The following year he did recover Medina Sidonia, the most westerly of the Byzantine fortresses, which was betrayed to him by one of its Gothic inhabitants. In 572 he finally terminated the independence of Cordoba, twenty-two years after Agila had lost the city. After these opening campaigns, Leovigild turned his attention to the north, probably as the consequence of his brother Liuva's death in 573. In that year he invaded a region called 'Sabaria' by John of Biclar, and devastated the lands of its people, the 'Sabi'. Unfortunately the exact location of this district is unknown, but it has been reasonably conjectured that it was an area in the eastern Pyrenees. Also in the same year Leovigild made his two sons by his first wife joint rulers with him, perhaps in pursuance of the idea of divided rule that had existed between Liuva I and himself. However the two princes, Hermenigild and Reccared were not yet given separate territorial responsibilities. Further campaigns in the north followed, moving in geographical succession from east to west. Cantabria, which probably included the Rioja, was invaded and added to the kingdom, perhaps for the first time in 574. Its former rulers, the 'Senate of Cantabria' were massacred. In 575 the 'Agregensian mountains', on the frontiers of Galicia, where the Sueves and the Vandals had once fought each other in 421, was the next region to be annexed and its former autocrat and his family were imprisoned. This had brought the Visigoths right to the borders of the Suevic realm and its king Miro (570–583) sued for peace in 576. He thereafter remained an ally of Leovigild until his death. A final campaign in this sequence, in 577, gained the Visigoths control over 'Orospeda', another region whose location is unknown, but may be in Galicia.[28]

After this, as John of Biclar records: 'King Leovigild having everywhere destroyed the usurpers and the despoilers of Spain, returned home seeking rest with his own people and he built a town in Celtiberia, named Reccopolis after his son (Reccared), which he adorned with walls and suburbs and by a decree he instituted it as a new city.' It is believed that the site of this town of Reccopolis is to be identified with a place called Zorita de los Canes, now in open country some thirty miles east of Madrid.[29] It is by no means clear what its purpose was to be, or whether or not Leovigild proposed to make it his capital instead of Toledo, which was his principal residence, at least during the second half of his reign. At all events Reccopolis was not to come to much, as it never became the site of a bishopric and coins are recorded from its mint only for the reigns of Leovigild and of Egica (687–702). However, if the identification is correct, archaeological excavation may reveal more of the king's intentions in this foundation, the first of its kind in the Visigothic period.

The tranquillity and restored unity of most of the peninsula achieved by Leovigild, after nearly a decade of campaigning, were broken almost immediately by the revolt of his son Hermenigild. In 579 Leovigild negotiated a marriage for this his eldest son, with Ingundis, the sister of the Austrasian Frankish king Childebert II (575–596). As well as the diplomatic implications of this, in respect of a Visigothic-Austrasian alliance in relation to the other two Frankish kingdoms of Neustria and Burgundy, there are some interesting genealogical ramifications. Leovigild had married, doubtless as his second wife, Gosuintha, the widow of his predecessor Athanagild, immediately upon his accession in 569. She was by her first husband the mother of the Austrasian queen-dowager Brunechildis and grandmother of both Childebert II and Ingundis. Thus the marriage of 579 further united the previous and the present Visigothic royal families. Hermenigild and Ingundis named their only child Athanagild. However, the effects of this may not have been what Leovigild envisaged, when he then established his son as subordinate king in the south of the peninsula, with his capital at Seville. For in that same year Hermenigild rebelled. According to John of Biclar, this was at the instigation of his step-mother Gosuintha.[30]

In practice, this rebellion of Hermenigild was no more than a repudiation of his father's authority over Baetica and southern Lusitania, where it is clear that at least the cities of Cordoba, Italica, Mérida and Seville gave their allegiance to the new king. Why Gosuintha had a part to play in this is by no means obvious. According to Gregory of Tours the queen had treated her granddaughter Ingundis, Hermenigild's new wife, very badly upon her arrival at the Visigothic court, attempting forcibly but unsuccessfully to make her renounce her Catholic beliefs in favour of her ancestral Arianism.[31] As a result some scholars, following the traditional association of Hermenigild's conversion with his revolt, have interpreted John's words as meaning it was in reaction to Gosuintha, rather than as a consequence of her prompting. However, the chronicler is clear enough, and, as it can be shown that Hermenigild continued an Arian after his revolt, an alternative explanation is necessary. It is conceivable that Gosuintha urged Hermenigild to rebel in order to set up an independent kingdom for the heirs of Athanagild.

Whatever may have been the cause of the revolt, there was to be no violence between father and son for three years. Leovigild appears to have accepted the situation with apparent equanimity and in 581 went to campaign against the Basques in the north-east of the peninsula. Here he founded another new town, Victoriacum, the modern Vitoria.[32] At no stage after his initial declaration of independence in 579 does Hermenigild seem to have made any further move to increase his territories at his father's expense. As has been mentioned, this rebellion has always been seen as a Catholic reaction to Leovigild's attempts to impose Arianism as the norm for religious unity within the kingdom. However, a close examination of the evidence reveals that Hermenigild, whose death as a Catholic is

rightly recorded in both Gregory of Tour's *History* and in the
Dialogues of Pope Gregory the Great (written in 593) probably did not
convert from Arianism until about 582.[33] He was known to be a
Catholic by the time Gregory wrote Book VI of his *History*, almost
certainly in 584, but was not one when Bishop Leander of Seville
parted from the future pope in Constantinople in the opening year or
two of the decade. Leander had been in Constantinople when
Gregory arrived there as papal *Apocrisiarius* or envoy in 579 and
returned to Spain after a protracted stay in the imperial capital, early
in the 580s. According to his brother Isidore, it was the influence of
Leander that brought about the conversion of Hermenigild. This
cannot have occurred before Leander and Gregory first met in 579, as
the latter recalled that he heard the news of the conversion from
Spanish travellers whom he encountered in Rome, so it must be after
Leander's return to that city in 585. Therefore to see Hermenigild's
rebellion in 579 as relating to Arian-Catholic hostility is misguided. It
is also possible to question whether Leovigild's attempts to impose or
promote a general acceptance of Arianism had really got under way at
this period.

Now if the rebellion of Hermenigild was effectively an effort on the
part of the southern regions of the peninsula to secede from the
authority of the King in Toledo, under a ruler of their own, how did
the religious element come to play so large a part in it, at least in the
minds of such external commentators as the two Gregorys? For one
thing the conversion of Hermenigild in *c.* 582, and his subsequent
violent death, did alter his standing. Gregory the Great included
Hermenigild in his *Dialogues* as an example of one who had suffered
persecution and eventually death at the hands of Arians: he became a
Catholic martyr. Interestingly, for his Spanish contemporaries, even
after the formal establishment of Catholicism in the kingdom in 589,
Hermenigild was never more than a failed usurper and certainly no
martyr. This again argues against the notion of the revolt as a
Catholic reaction against Arian tyranny. It was only in the late
seventh century, probably as a result of the popularity of Gregory's
Dialogues, that the cult of Hermenigild was to become established in
Spain.[34] For Romans and for Goths in the late sixth and early seventh
centuries, Hermenigild's attempt to redivide the recently united
kingdom was unwelcome, and his precocious effort to make a
Catholic king of himself was no compensation for the dangers
threatened by his actions.

If a motive beyond that of personal conviction is to be sought for Hermenigild's conversion, it may lie in the increased possibilities of rapprochement with the Byzantine Empire that this opened up. It is not inconceivable that Leander acted as diplomatic intermediary between Hermenigild and the Emperor Tiberius II (578–582). If there is a foundation in this, it may explain why, after three years of peaceful co-existence, Leovigild finally reacted to crush the ephemeral kingdom of his son in 582, the probable year of Leander's return from Constantinople and of Hermenigild's conversion. In that year, as John of Biclar records, Leovigild began to raise an army to move against his son. In campaigns in 583 and 584 he reduced city after city that Hermenigild proved powerless to hold. The brief account in John of Biclar can be supplemented by the triumphal coinage that Leovigild issued in those cities to record his taking of Seville and Italica.[35] During the siege of Seville in 583 his ally Miro, King of the Sueves, who had been brought down by Leovigild willingly or otherwise to assist, died. Gregory of Tours suggests that Miro and his Sueves were there to help Hermenigild, but the contemporary Spanish testimony of John of Biclar to the contrary is to be preferred.[36] Finally Hermenigild himself was captured in 584 when Cordoba fell, and he was exiled by his father to Valencia. By this time his wife and son were in Byzantine hands, either as hostages or for safety – explicit testimony to the rebel king's imperial links. The Queen Ingundis died at Carthage *en route* for Constantinople but their son Athanagild survived the journey to the Byzantine capital. There, despite attempts by his grandmother Queen Brunechildis to have him sent to her in Francia, he remained and disappears from view.[37] As for the exiled Hermenigild, he was killed in 585 at Tarragona by a certain Sisbert. The reasons for this, and the degree of his father's involvement in his death, are unknown. Certainly outsiders such as the two Gregorys blamed him, and his second son and successor Reccared had Sisbert put to death, but the matter remains obscure.[38] It has sometimes been thought that John of Biclar and Isidore failed to do justice to Hermenigild in their works out of deference to Reccared, whose succession was only made possible by his brother's death and whose own conversion to Catholicism might lose lustre if overmuch was made of the earlier one. However, it is more likely that the political instability that resulted from the frequent revolts and contested successions which plagued the Visigothic kingdom, together with their own convictions of the sinfulness of rebellion, prevented John and Isidore from being able to see Hermenigild as anything more than an unsuccessful 'tyrant' and usurper, and certainly not as a Catholic martyr.

With the final suppression of his son's rebellion in 584, one last achievement remained for Leovigild. This was the extinction of the Suevic kingdom and its incorporation within the Visigothic realm. The Suevic king Miro, who had died in 583 outside Seville, was succeeded by his son Eboric. The new king was probably lacking in military experience and may have been a minor, for the next year he was overthrown by a Suevic noble called Audeca and consigned to a monastery. This deposition of the son of his ally gave Leovigild an excuse to intervene in the Suevic kingdom, which had probably been in large measure under Visigothic tutelage since 576. In 585 he deposed Audeca, having him ordained priest, to render him incapable of holding the royal office, and exiled him to Beja. Leovigild seized the Sueves' royal treasure and added their kingdom to his own. There was a rebellion immediately after he left Galicia, led by one Malaric, seeking to restore the Suevic realm, but this was easily suppressed by Visigothic generals left in the province. With this, the Suevic kingdom disappears from history forever. Whether the memory of it lingered on throughout the seventh century, and whether its former inhabitants and territory remained consciously Suevic in any sense after its passing, cannot be determined. Certainly no attempts were made to take advantage of the periodic weaknesses of the Visigothic kings in subsequent decades to try to revive it. Even artistically it is not possible from the scanty surviving remains of the region's material culture to identify what may be distinctively Suevic styles and traditions. But it is hard to believe that a kingdom that lasted for one hundred and seventy-five years can have left no memories.[39]

The conquest of the Suevic realm was Leovigild's last campaign. Much still remained to be done: the Byzantines retained their hold on most of the south-eastern coast and the Basques, if temporarily quiescent, were by no means pacified. However, Leovigild had achieved much in a relatively short time, ending the independence of most areas of the peninsula from the Visigothic monarchy, and defeating most of the external enemies of the kingdom. As well as by his military conquests, the king had transformed the position of royal authority in other ways. He was the first of the Visigothic kings to employ Byzantine or late-Roman regalia in the form of a crown, a sceptre and the use of a throne. He also began the process that was to transform Toledo into the ceremonial centre of the kingdom. It was his reign, too, that saw the introduction of a distinctive Visigothic coinage, stylistically different from the late-Roman and Byzantine ones that had previously been imitated, and now bearing the king's name and title and the place of minting. It has been argued that the first experimental versions of this coinage were initiated by Hermenigild, but even if this be so, the distinctive type of Visigothic coin for the next half-century, with the facing bust of the king on both the obverse and the reverse, was the creation of Leovigild.[40] But, however much the king may have achieved in all of these respects, when he died in 586 he left one crucial problem unresolved for his successor to face: that of the continuing division in the kingdom between the Arian and Catholic creeds.

The religious distinction between Arian and Catholic had not been an area of conflict during the reigns of most of Leovigild's predecessors since the time of Euric, but with the effective political unification of most of the peninsula achieved, the issue became more acute. Religious uniformity became the prerequisite of the ideological unity necessary to support a strong and centralised kingdom. There were limits to what could be achieved in this direction by force alone. Leovigild, with his hostility to Byzantium and its Frankish Catholic allies, retained his adherence to the traditional Arianism of the Goths and took active steps to promote this creed, although, with the exception of the newly created Lombard realm in Italy, Visigothic Spain remained isolated as the only surviving Arian state. Leovigild first offered gifts and then used threats, both without avail, to win over Bishop Masona of Mérida to Arianism.[41] He may well have tried the same with other Catholic bishops, and in one case at least was clearly successful. Bishop Vincent, of the important see of Zaragoza in the Ebro valley, apostacised and became an active polemicist in the Arian cause.[42] Although the chronology is far from clear it seems unlikely that Leovigild began his Arian offensive before about 578, since the first decade of his reign was devoted to virtually continuous campaigning. It has been suggested that the exile of John of Biclar, which may well have occurred in that year, was part of the king's anti-Catholic measures, and that these were primarily directed against Goths who had converted to Catholicism, breaking from the traditions of their race. However, it is equally possible that John was exiled due to suspicions aroused by his long stay in Constantinople.

The first clearly dated event, and the one that might have initiated the whole process, was the holding of an Arian synod at Toledo in 580, recorded in John's *Chronicle*, at which a significant modification in doctrine was proclaimed, whereby the equality and co-eternity of Father and Son were conceded, whilst that of the Holy Spirit continued to be denied.[43] This council also permitted the admission of renegade Catholics into the Arian fold without the necessity of rebaptism. Both of these measures must have considerably increased the potential popularity of Arianism, for few of the laity can really have understood, let alone have been prepared to suffer for, the role of the Spirit in the Trinity, unlike that of the Son. Likewise, rebaptism was always a stumbling block in conversion, both as a matter of pride and because it threatened the status of the dead, for in accepting that your own baptism had not been a true sacrament you implicitly condemned that of departed friends and relatives, which in a post-Augustinian theological age was effectively to believe in their damnation. Thus a serious intellectual offensive was being mounted by the Arians in the 580s, which may well, with active royal support, have led to a disturbing number of defections from the Catholic ranks. It certainly prompted a Catholic counter-offensive, with Bishops Severus of Malaga and Leander of Seville writing polemical anti-Arian treatises in the course of that same decade, particularly to parry the attacks of their apostate colleague Vincent of Zaragoza.[44] Unfortunately, none of these doubtless bitter exchanges has survived.

It is easy, on such a basis, to categorise Leovigild just as a persecutor of Catholics, but a closer look at the methods he is found employing may modify this view. Only in one city, in the pages of the *Lives of the Fathers of Mérida*, can we get a glimpse of the Arian-Catholic conflict of this period at a local level. On his failure to win the support of Bishop Masona by threats or bribes, the king turned instead to building up the power and standing of the practising Arians in the city. A bishop called Sunna was sent to them. Whether there had been an Arian episcopate previously in Mérida or whether Sunna was its first incumbent is not made clear, but with that bishop's arrival, and by royal command, the Arians were able to take over some of the basilicas in the city, formerly in the hands of the Catholics. With that the struggle to control the cult of the city's patron saint, Eulalia, and with it effective dominance of the religious life of the city and its province, really began. Whichever side could control the basilica where the saint's body was buried, and could possess the more mobile relic of the martyr's tunic, would be able to monopolise access to the patron saint and thus acquire spiritual supremacy in the city and region. Masona resisted royal commands to surrender both basilica and tunic. In the case of the former, a tribunal was set up to judge the merits of the Catholic and Arian claims, before which Masona appears to have emerged triumphant. This is a rare example of the practical workings of the restrictions of the law on the arbitrary use of royal authority that existed in the Visigothic kingdom, and it is important to bear in mind that the whole episode can be seen as much in terms of the defining of the limits of royal power over local autonomy, as in those of religious conflict.

In the matter of the tunic different procedures were employed, perhaps as a direct consequence of the thwarting of the royal initiative by local power on the previous occasion. This time Masona was summoned to the king in Toledo, and there commanded to hand over the tunic of Eulalia, not to the Arians of Mérida but to those of the capital city. The bishop refused the king to his face, and in consequence was exiled. Although the account in the *Lives of the Fathers* is often vague and probably overly dramatic, it is important to note that the king, whatever his personal inclinations might have been, was unable to act in a totally arbitrary fashion. In the cases of both the basilica and the tunic, legal processes were involved: a tribunal in Mérida and a trial before the king. Masona is exiled, rightly or wrongly, for his refusal of a royal command, and not just because he was a Goth who had converted to Catholicism. He represented a more serious threat by his challenge to a novel extension of royal authority at a local level. For what was also at issue in this Arian-Catholic confrontation was the extension of the king's power into the ecclesiastical sphere and his attempt to impose his authority far more directly than hitherto on the cities and regions of the kingdom by taking an active part in local struggles for control and influence.[45]

None of Leovigild's predecessors had sought to involve themselves in struggles for dominance at a local level, nor had they sought by means of their royal power to alter the balance in favour of one side or the other in the religious disputes. This was the threat the Catholics faced in Leovigild and naturally enough they resisted, although this could bring them within the range of secular penalties or lead them to support a usurper such as Hermenigild against the lawfully

constituted authority of the king, his father. The real significance of
the reign of Leovigild in the religious sphere lies not so much in the
fate of individuals or in short-lived political upheavals, as in that it
finally brought the issue of Arian-Catholic differences to a head in the
open and made its final resolution imperative. After Leovigild a
return to the *modus vivendi* that seems to have existed between Arians
and Catholics earlier in the century was impossible. For one thing, the
kind of monarchy that was created in the course of the reign made
such a final settlement necessary in the interests of a unity of the
kingdom that was based on consent rather than force. Thus it was
imperative that the conflicts in the different regions of the peninsula
caused by royal involvement should be resolved as speedily as
possible. The power of the Arians, who were probably in the minority
throughout most if not all of the peninsula, had been artificially
increased. As in Mérida, the results must have been intense local
conflict. But the new strength of the Arians was essentially
ephemeral, depending as it did upon active royal support. When this
was removed with the death of Leovigild in 586, they were left
defenceless before a Catholicism reinvigorated by intellectual
conflict.

The end of Visigothic Arianism was rendered inevitable by the
personal conversion of King Reccared (586–601), announced in 587,
soon after his accession. Theologically the position of the two sides
had grown closer since the Arian synod of 580. The modification of
the Arian stand on the Trinity and the abolition of the necessity for
rebaptism for converts, which had probably won over several
Catholics in the last years of Leovigild, could also facilitate a move in
the opposite direction away from Arianism, so long as the Catholics
did not prove too doctrinaire over the requirements for readmission to
the fold. As has been explained, the division between the two creeds in
terms of the racial separateness of Roman and Goth had long since
broken down. What remained at issue was power at the local level. In
towns and cities such as Mérida, Arian parties had been strengthened
or even created during the reign of Leovigild, on royal initiative. The
combination of an Arian bishop and various Gothic nobles, together
with influential converts from Catholicism, may well have become the
politically dominant one, with royal backing, in many Spanish towns
in the early 580s, overshadowing the Catholic bishop and his
supporters. This is the picture that emerges from the account of the
Lives of the Fathers of Mérida. There must have been sharp regional

variations, for in some areas the Arian groups may have been powerful for considerably longer, whilst in others they may not have emerged at all, despite royal promotion. There is insufficient evidence to provide a full perspective on this.

The weaknesses of the Arian position in the sixth century, and the rapidity with which it disappeared after 589, suggest that it was on the wane and its short-lived flourishing under Leovigild largely an artificial growth. Possibly more would have come of it had his successor been of the same persuasion. However, for reasons of personal conviction, but which may also have taken into account the virtual isolation of the Visigothic kingdom by reason of its Arianism, Leovigild's son and successor was converted to Catholicism under the guidance of Bishop Leander of Seville.[46] With this change in royal attitude, the local strength of the Arians was undermined.

It took two years from the conversion of Reccared for the assembling of the Third Council of Toledo in May 589. The summoning of a council took time, with communications in the peninsula as bad and as slow as they must have been, but time was also spent in other ways. By the time the council met on 8 May it had been made clear that those Arian bishops who were prepared to anathematise their former beliefs and accept those of their Catholic colleagues would be confirmed in possession of their sees, even if this meant having two bishops in one diocese. The Arian bishops of Barcelona, Valencia, Viseo, Tuy, Lugo, Oporto and Tortosa all publicly renounced their former beliefs at III Toledo, and went on subsequently to sign the acts of the council with the other Catholic bishops. Thus two bishops of Lugo came to be amongst the signatories. The subsequent careers of the former Arian bishops are unclear, as too few councils were held between 589 and 633 for us to be able to detect them from their signatures. One of them, however, Bishop Ugnas of Barcelona, continued to hold his see until some time after 614, as in that year he signed the acts of II Barcelona.[47]

It is notable that all of these Arian bishops who appear at III Toledo come from only two regions: Galicia and Catalonia. It has been suggested with much plausibility that as the Suevic kingdom in Galicia had converted from Arianism to Catholicism (c. 560), these Arian bishops from that region were ones imposed by Leovigild after his conquest of the Sueves in 584. Why Catalonia should be so well represented, having two Arian bishops recorded contemporaneously in Valencia, is not so clear. Ugnas in Barcelona may have had no

Catholic rival, as he is the only bishop to sign for that see in 589, but both Tortosa and Valencia had Catholic bishops as well as Arian, thus giving the last named city three prelates.

Other Arian bishops were not prepared to submit in the way those present at III Toledo had. It is possible that the Arian bishops were required to undergo a period of penance before being admitted to the fellowship of the Catholics and restored to their offices. This was certainly expected of Sunna, the Arian bishop of Mérida, who refused. Being involved in a plot against his Catholic rival Masona and probably the king, he was banished and went to try to preach Arianism in Mauretania, where ultimately he came to a violent death.[48] Unfortunately we know little about the fate of Arianism in Mauretania in the 590s.

Another Arian bishop who refused to compromise was Athalocus of Narbonne, who instead involved himself in an unsuccessful rebellion.[49] It is notable that both Sunna and Athalocus were bishops of metropolitan sees, and it is unlikely that the compromise worked out by the Catholics would have envisaged these men retaining their special authority, particularly over suffragan bishops who had been loyal Catholics. Of other Arian bishops we know nothing. Apart from those who formally renounced Arianism there, a number of other bishops with Germanic names are found amongst the signatories of III Toledo, but whether, like Masona of Mérida, they were Goths who had always been Catholics, or whether they were recent Arians who had made a more timely conversion than their fellows, cannot be ascertained. The fate of the notorious apostate Vincent of Zaragoza is unknown. His see was represented at III Toledo by a Bishop Simplicius, but whether this was because Vincent was dead or had been deposed is uncertain.

The acts of III Toledo say little about the mechanics of the transition from Arianism to Catholicism. It was more concerned with correct definitions of faith. It reiterated the creeds of the councils of Nicaea (324), II Constantinople (381), and Chalcedon (451), which were then formally recited by King Reccared and Bado, his Queen, and it went on to promulgate a creed of its own and issue a list of twenty-three anathemas on points of Arian belief. It also produced an impressive number of canons on matters of church discipline, but of these only the eighth, which laid down that the churches of the Arians should now pass into the control of the bishops in whose dioceses they stood, related to the problems of the transition.

We do learn more about the process from the acts of a subsequent provincial council, that of II Zaragoza, held under Bishop Artemius of Tarragona in 592.[50] There it was decreed that former Arian priests and deacons who had converted to Catholicism and had led a blameless life should be reordained and maintained in their offices. It also makes clear, which III Toledo had not, that former Arian bishops were likewise to be reordained, as it decreed that Catholic churches consecrated by those bishops who had not received the benediction of a Catholic bishop were to be reconsecrated. It seems possible that some of the episcopal converts from Arianism had resisted the requirement of reordination. The most fascinating canon is the second one, which lays down regulations concerning what is to be done with relics found in Arian churches. They were to be taken to the bishop and tested as to their validity by being put into a fire. This is an interesting and unusual example of relics being subjected to ordeal. Anyone found concealing such relics, a natural enough temptation in the circumstances, would be excommunicated.

At the level of the local priests and deacons the transition of the kingdom from Arianism to Catholicism may have had little practical effect and was clearly made as easy as was compatible with correct canonical observance. Some formerly cherished relics may have perished in the flames, but as there were no cults of peculiarly Arian saints the effects on popular devotion were probably slight. In this way no real realignments of spiritual allegiances were called for.

However, there were some for whom the changes threatened a real eclipse of their political fortunes. These were the Arian bishops who, for whatever reasons, were not prepared to compromise, together with those Gothic nobles who had supported them during Leovigild's reign and might now expect to see a transfer of royal favour to their Catholic rivals. Reccared's conversion made some form of political upheaval unavoidable, for, however willing to compromise the new régime might be, the polarisation of local societies into opposing factions that Leovigild had encouraged meant that a change in the direction of royal support would completely alter the previous balance of power. Scores remained to be settled and inevitably the supporters of the new king and his religious affiliation would expect the balance of local power to be redressed in their favour. For their formerly dominant rivals one option was rebellion. This occurred in Mérida even before the holding of III Toledo. There are two complementary accounts of this, one in the *Lives of the Fathers of*

Mérida and the other in John of Biclar's *Chronicle*. In 587 or 588 Bishop Sunna, together with a group of Arian Gothic counts, including the future king Witteric (603–610), hatched a conspiracy involving both the murder of Bishop Masona and the setting up of a certain Seggo as king. The plot was betrayed by Witteric and the conspirators seized by Claudius, the *dux*, or provincial military commander of Lusitania. Sunna ended by being exiled to Mauretania, whilst Seggo had his hands cut off, rendering him militarily incapable and therefore ineligible for the royal office, and was banished to Galicia. Witteric survived to have Reccared's son King Liuva II (601–603) deposed, mutilated and then murdered in 603, thus ending the dynasty of Leovigild.

In 588, another plot was uncovered, involving a Bishop Uldila, possibly of Toledo, and Reccared's stepmother the Arian Queen Gosuintha, who had already had a mysterious hand in the rebellion of Hermenigild back in 579. Uldila was exiled and Gosuintha conveniently died, from causes John of Biclar does not record. Another Arian revolt that probably preceded III Toledo was that already referred to of the Bishop of Narbonne, Athalocus, in league with two Gothic Counts, Granista and Vildigern. They applied to the Franks for assistance and set about trying to massacre as many Catholics as they could. Although Catholics themselves, the Franks were quick to take advantage of the opportunities offered, and King Guntramn of Burgundy (561–592) sent an army into Septimania under his duke Boso. Claudius, the Duke of Lusitania, who had recently suppressed Sunna and Seggo's conspiracy, was sent against the Franks by Reccared and catching them besieging Carcassone, he routed them. Of the fates of Athalocus and his friends we are not informed.

One final conspiracy that took place immediately after III Toledo may have had Arian overtones, but no bishops are named as being implicated in it. Instead it was headed by Argimund, Duke of an unspecified province, and it proved as unsuccessful as the rest. Argimund was scalped and had his right hand amputated at Toledo in the aftermath.[51] With this, if they were even involved, all Arian resistance appears to have come to an end. It used to be believed that there was a short-lived Arian revival in the reign of Witteric (603–610), but this is merely based upon knowledge of his involvement in the plot at Mérida in 587/8, and there is no evidence that he attempted to restore Arianism in any way when king.

Certainly he was not popular with some of his bishops, notably
Isidore of Seville, but this was for other reasons of personal and
political character. Arianism in Visigothic Spain, as in the
Burgundian kingdom, but unlike Lombard Italy, is notable for the
relative ease with which it was replaced, and the rapidity with which
it disappeared. In the 580s it was more of a matter of party and of local
power, and the events of 587 to 590 saw the elimination or the
reconciliation of those who had something to lose by the conversion of
the kingdom from Arianism to Catholicism.

3. A Church Triumphant

THE intellectual vigour of the Spanish Church in the late sixth and seventh centuries must owe much to the challenge presented to it by Arianism in its final development under Leovigild. To combat the arguments of Arians and Catholic apostates, such as Vincent of Zaragoza, and the blandishments offered by the Arian Synod of Toledo of 580, the Catholics had to look for assistance from beyond the confines of Spain. Naturally enough it was to Africa that they turned. The links between the two churches had always been strong. It has been argued that Christianity was first introduced into Spain from Africa, and the African liturgy may have had a formative influence on the development of that of the peninsula; unfortunately all too little of the former has survived for this to be established definitively. In the third century, when the Spanish churches needed advice on matters of doctrine or of discipline, it was to Carthage rather than to Rome that they turned. In the sixth century the ties had been strengthened by the flight of African monks into Spain, escaping either imperial religious persecution over the issue of 'The Three Chapters', or the depredations of Berber tribes. Nanctus, who settled near Mérida, and Donatus, who founded the monastery of Servitanum, are but two of those involved in this exodus. Such refugees must have brought some of the considerable learning of the African Church with them.[1]

The experience to be gained from Africa in the late sixth century was particularly pertinent to the problems facing the Spanish Catholics under Leovigild. The African Church had existed under Arian rule for just over a century, from the time of the death of Augustine in 430 to the imperial reconquest by Justinian I in 533. For much of this time it had suffered active persecution from the Vandal rulers, and many of its foremost bishops had spent long periods in exile. The threat posed to the Catholics by the establishment of a rival Arian clergy throughout the towns of Africa had been a very real one, and in contests with their heretical opponents for local dominance, and in periodic debates held at court before successive kings, the Catholic bishops acquired considerable fluency in countering the arguments of Arianism. The most prominent of the Catholic bishops of the Vandal period was Fulgentius of Ruspe (d. c. 525), who spent most of his episcopate in exile.[2] However, he was once permitted to

59

engage in open debate with the Arian bishops in the presence of King Thrasamund (498–523), and he wrote an important treatise outlining the Catholic position for the same monarch. It is not surprising to find this work and some of his other controversial pieces, and expositions of the Catholic doctrine on the Trinity and on predestination, being available in the episcopal library in Seville. Isidore refers to these and other works by Fulgentius in his *On Famous Men*, and it is not unlikely that the books were available in Leander's time too.[3]

The writings of other Africans also featured in the library at Seville. Amongst others, Possidius, the biographer of Augustine and author of a collection of homilies, the Christian poet Verecundus, the deacon Ferrandus, disciple and biographer of Fulgentius, Victor of Tunnuna, the chronicler, and Facundus of Hermiane, the leading opponent of the religious policies of the Emperor Justinian, were represented.[4] In addition, manuscript evidence shows that some of the short anonymous writings produced in Africa during the Vandal period, dealing with such important controversial issues as the nature of the Trinity, were also circulating in Spain.[5] However, the strongest evidence of the influence of African theology on the Spanish Church is to be found in the credal formulations of successive councils from III Toledo onwards, and in the writings of the leading intellectual figures of the Visigothic kingdom.

The African debt was not the only one incurred by Seville, and through that see the rest of the Spanish Church, in the late sixth century. Sometime between 579 and 582, Leander of Seville went to Constantinople where he encountered the resident papal envoy or *Apocrisiarius*, Gregory. The mutual influence of the two men upon each other was enormous. The encouragement of Leander contributed to Gregory's undertaking his exegetical exposition of the Book of Job, which he later wrote up as his *Moralia*, one of the most substantial and most influential of all of his works. The lasting friendship that developed between the two men, which persisted after Leander's return to Spain and Gregory's to Rome, where he became Pope in 590, opened an important channel of communication. This meant that most of Gregory's writings very quickly became available in the Visigothic kingdom and they came to exercise, with the sole exception of the thought of Augustine, the greatest single influence upon the learning of the Spanish Church in the seventh century.[6]

Surprisingly little, by contrast, was to come during this period from Gaul. The greatest debt owed in this direction was to the sermon collections of Caesarius of Arles (502–542), one of which became the basis of the homiliary used by the Church of Toledo in the seventh century.[7] But as the Spanish Church itself produced writers of the calibre of Isidore of Seville and Ildefonsus and Julian of Toledo, so it became increasingly closed to outside influences beyond those privileged ones of Augustine, Fulgentius and Gregory the Great. The *florilegia* of the Visigothic period are made up of extracts from the writings of these authorities. This is not just a matter of isolation or of self-satisfaction. A brief glance at the intellectual landmarks of the seventh-century Mediterranean world in general is sufficient to show both how unusually vital the Spanish Church of that time was, and how little anywhere else, even the Byzantine Empire, had to offer it. With its own products, and the heritage of the writings of some of the best minds of former centuries, whose like was no longer to be found, it could remain justifiably proud, even into the period of Islamic domination.

In Isidore of Seville, the Church of the Visigothic period had its most distinguished and most prolific author. His debt to his brother Leander is hard to determine, for the latter's surviving works only comprise a brief treatise on aspects of the monastic life for women, addressed to his sister Florentina, and the sermon he delivered at the third Council of Toledo in 589. Isidore also refers in his *On Famous Men* to Leander's liturgical compositions, but these are now lost. However, Leander's influence was important. It was probably he who built up the resources of the episcopal library at Seville, and was Isidore's principal teacher. Their father's name was Severianus, and the family apparently moved from Cartagena to Seville sometime in the mid sixth century. Both Leander and Isidore are Greek names and are most unusual in a western context, so it is quite conceivable that the family was of Byzantine origin, like the episcopal dynasty of Paul and Fidelis at Mérida. Isidore also had another brother Fulgentius, who became Bishop of Ecija and who signed the acts of II Seville in 619, and a sister Florentina, a nun.[8]

It has been conjectured that Isidore was born in the 560s, but nothing is known for sure about his career before he succeeded Leander as Metropolitan Bishop of Seville in 599 or 600.[9] It used to be thought that he had been a monk during much of the intervening period, but there is no evidence that any regular monastic establishment existed in Seville at this time. Rather it is probable that he and his brothers lived a life of self-imposed ascetic discipline in their family household, along the lines of the aristocratic house-monastery that had been fashionable in Rome and other parts of the West in the late fourth and fifth centuries. Isidore comes into view for the first time upon his ordination to succeed his brother, although it is possible that at least one of his works, his *Differentiae*, or *Differences*, was composed before 600. If Isidore also inherited any of Leander's influence at court with Reccared and his dynasty, it may well have gone into eclipse with the violent deposition of Liuva II in 603, for it is not until the reign of Sisebut (612–621) that he appears as the regular adviser and confidant of a king in matters concerning the Church and learning. Thereafter, Isidore appears consistently as the foremost intellectual figure in the realm, and is usually presented as exercising possibly the greatest single influence over successive kings right up to his death in 636. However, in this last respect it is important to bear in mind that although they have left us no writings, and may have been in no sense scholars, the bishops of Toledo at this same period were by no means negligible figures, and as Toledo remained after the reign of Leovigild the principal formal royal residence, their access to king and court remained more constant than that of Isidore, with his responsibilities in Seville. His principal contemporary as Bishop of Toledo, a see whose metropolitan status was confirmed by a special synod in 610, was Helladius, a former high court official and then abbot of the foremost monastery in the capital, that of Agali.[10] In the absence of evidence either way it is idle to speculate, but considering the standing and career of such a man it is perhaps unwary of modern historians to write as if Isidore enjoyed a monopoly of influence at court, even just in matters concerning the Church.

At least Isidore's intellectual pre-eminence was real and assured. He dedicated books to both kings Sisebut and Suinthila, and for Sisenand he presided over IV Toledo in 633, which first introduced the use of ecclesiastical penalties in defence of the life and security of the king.[11] As metropolitan of the province of Baetica, Isidore also directed II Seville, the most substantial of all the Spanish provincial councils of which the acts are preserved, and which concerned itself with a wide range of issues of church discipline and of theology. Its most notable feature was a lengthy discussion of the two natures and single person of Christ, which in its scriptural and patristic erudition would seem to show the hand of Isidore. The chronology of his writings is by no means clear, and further difficulties exist in the form of a number of works attributed to and for a long time accepted as being by him, whose authenticity has now been called in question or even disproved. There is guidance as to the basic corpus of Isidoran writings in the list drawn up by his friend and former pupil Braulio, Bishop of Zaragoza (631–651), which, with a brief memoir on their author, he appended to Isidore's own *On Famous Men*.[12] Braulio, however, saw little of Isidore in the last two decades of the latter's lifetime, as their mutual letters makes clear, and thus his knowledge of Isidore's work may not have been comprehensive. So controversy still exists concerning the authenticity of some minor works attributed to Isidore in their manuscript transmission, but not featuring in Braulio's list.

The assured writings fall into a number of different categories. There are historical writings such as the *Chronicle*, completed in 615/6, and the *History of the Goths, Vandals and Sueves*, written in 625/6. Both of these may have been royal commissions, and they put the Visigothic kingdom into the scheme of the history of the world as it was then conceived. The book *On Famous Men* was a continuation of that of Jerome (*d.* 419) and Gennadius of Marseille (late fifth century), and it concentrated principally on the writings of African and Spanish ecclesiastics of the fifth and sixth centuries. Their lives are described hardly at all, but Isidore lists those of their books he had read, and those of which he had heard but had not seen. A second group of his writings comprise his aids to the study of scripture. In this area he followed in the footsteps of such masters as Jerome and Gregory the Great. These works were principally handbooks intended for those who had to expound the scriptures in public or for monks, for whom its regular study was an obligation, as, for example, laid down in Isidore's own monastic rule. Some of these exegetical writings of Isidore's were devoted to the explanation of problematic passages in the Old and New Testaments, again for the same readership. Isidore's scriptural knowledge and interest also lay at the heart of much of his other writing that was not overtly exegetical. His book *On the Christian Faith, against the Jesus* is concerned with controverting Jewish beliefs and arguments against Christianity, on the basis of passages from the Old Testament used to show that the Jews were confounded by the authority of their own scriptures. Likewise his *On the Order of Created Things* is also dependent upon the Bible for the substantiation of its arguments.

Isidore's most substantial work was his encyclopedic *Etymologiae sive Origines* (Etymologies or Origins), in the course of which, in twenty books, he attempted to offer a conspectus of all branches of knowledge. He provided his readers with illumination of the individual topics considered by studying the etymology of the terms used and of words related to them, not always with a great deal of accuracy. To take a typical example, in the section 'On Astronomy' in Book III, Chapter 29 is devoted to 'the world' (*mundus*) and it reads: 'The world is what endures in the heavens and on earth, in the sea, and the stars. It is called the world (*mundus*) because it is always in motion (*motus*); no rest is ever allowed it.'[13] This illustrates both the principles on which Isidore organised his materials, and the far-fetched nature of some of the etymologies that he and his contemporaries relied upon. His work was fundamentally serious, for all its flaws, and it provided an enormous storehouse of knowledge for his contemporaries, remaining extremely popular and influential throughout the rest of the Middle Ages, as the enormous number and variety of the surviving manuscripts of it testify.

Isidore sought to attain knowledge through the understanding of words. His *Etymologies*, commissioned by King Sisebut but probably not completed until the early 630s, represent but one of his approaches, albeit the most sustained, to the problem of the meaning of words. Previously he also employed the techniques, long known to Roman rhetors, of 'differences' and of synonyms. In his work *Of Differences and the Meaning of Words*, possibly his earliest composition, he looked at the meanings of words that were either similar in form but very different in meaning, or those which were dissimilar in form but identical in meaning. Thus, for example, the difference between *auspicia* and *auguria* (*Differentiae* I.6): 'Auspices are things which are incoherent and come from beyond, whilst auguries are things which may be consulted and followed.'[14] It is typical and perhaps to his credit that when he deals with subjects long condemned by the Church and by civil law, Isidore introduces no Christian gloss into his text. His approach through synonyms was quite differently conceived. This, because of the nature of its material, is a highly rhetorical piece cast as *The Lamentations of a Sinful Soul*. The author, in confessing his faults, repeats each key statement or lament as many times as he has synonyms available to do so. Thus the work opens: 'My soul is in anguish, my spirit is agitated, my heart unquiet ....' (I.5) Even in this short passage, two sets of three synonymous nouns and verbs have been employed. This particular style was to have a considerable vogue in Visigothic Spain after Isidore and was developed to its greatest extent by Bishop Ildefonsus of Toledo (657–667), in his book *On the Perpetual Virginity of the Blessed Virgin Mary*. It is also to be encountered in parts of the Visigothic liturgy, where its use is particularly appropriate in rhetorical invocatory prayers.

Isidore has also left an important work *On the Offices of the Church*, which describes the different services of the Church and their subdivisions as they existed in his day in the first book, and the functions of the different grades of the clergy in the second. The value of this work for modern canonists and liturgical scholars has been considerable. Of a different kind of interest is Isidore's *On the Nature of Things* (or *The Divisions of Nature*), dedicated to King Sisebut (612–621), which studies, in a way that is reminiscent of the later *Etymologies* and may well be the inspiration for Sisebut's commissioning that work, the various phenomena of nature, such as rain, clouds and earthquakes, and also the divisions of time. Sisebut used the omission of the subject of eclipses from Isidore's book to write a poem of his own on that theme by way of a reply.[15]

Finally, some of Isidore's letters have survived, but included amongst them are a number of forgeries, ranging in date from the later seventh and eighth centuries to the twelfth. The great reputation and authority of Isidore, both in Spain and beyond, notably in Ireland and in Gaul, meant that the spurious addition of his name to texts that were innovatory, but sought the respectability of antiquity or recognised status of authorship, proved irresistible to forgers. best known example of this is the great canonical compilation of the Carolingian period known as the Pseudo-Isidoran Decretals. As so many of the letters of the early medieval period take the form of replies to enquiries concerning issues of Church discipline and order, it was relatively easy to produce pseudonymous epistles making apparently authoritative pronouncements on points of canon law. When the spurious ones are removed, the few genuine letters of Isidore that survive are surprising for their extreme brevity and are very formal in character, even when addressed to his particular friend Braulio of Zaragoza. By contrast, the latter's replies are long and effusive. The greater part of the extant letters of Isidore are exchanges between himself and Braulio on the subject of the *Etymologies*, which the latter was most anxious to read, whereas its author was apparently most reluctant to let him do so. In reply to one pressing request, Isidore claimed ingenuously that he was interrupted when beginning to read

Braulio's letter, and when he returned from his summons to the king it had mysteriously disappeared.[16]

This is indeed one of the few human touches that can be given to the portrait of Isidore, who for all of his prolific literary output, remains curiously concealed from us. Unlike Gregory the Great and quite unlike his own contemporary Braulio, Isidore's personality remains firmly closed to view. The great variety of his writings, and the different literary styles that he employed, obscure rather than clarify our impressions of him. In this way he was a master of the art of Late Antique rhetoric, in being able to mask his own character behind the conventions of the literary forms with which he was working. For these reasons Isidore has never enjoyed the scholarly and lay popularity that has attached itself to Augustine or to Gregory, which is regrettable, since he was a real polymath within the limitations of the learning available in the Mediterranean area.

Isidore died in April 636, and a brief account of his last days was written by one of the deacons of Seville, called Redemptus.[17] According to this, Isidore, realising his impending end, adopted the state of canonical penance and had himself carried to the Basilica of St Vincent where he was to die. This is the first account to be found in Visigothic Spain of the practice of formal renunciation of office and the adoption of the penitential state prior to death that became standard practice for kings by the time of Wamba (672–680), and remained so for several centuries to come. It may have been common for bishops also to follow Isidore's lead in this. Of course, there is a possibility that this work of Redemptus's was not composed at the time of Isidore's death but was written subsequently to give authority to this practice, perhaps later in the seventh century. Isidore's name did remain the most potent source of authority in matters of canon law and of learning for the rest of the Visigothic period, and, for the Spanish Church, for many centuries thereafter. But with his death the scholarly and possibly political pre-eminence of Seville, that had been developed and maintained by Leander, and then his brother Isidore, came to an end. None of their successors is known either for their lives or their writings, and by 693 it was possible for a bishop of Seville to be translated to the see of Toledo by way of a promotion. Not until the ninth century was the Church of Seville to regain some of the independence and authority that it had enjoyed under Leander and Isidore. In the seventh century, the mantle of Isidore, at least in the sphere of learning, fell firstly upon the shoulders of his friend and pupil Braulio of Zaragoza, and passed thence to a series of outstanding bishops of Toledo. But before reviewing their achievements, it is worth pausing to consider the career of Isidore's most remarkable and surprising collaborator.

Of all the Spanish kings before Alfonso X 'the Wise' (1252–1284), the Visigothic ruler Sisebut (612–621) was the most learned and has rightly been depicted as 'the most sophisticated of all the barbarian kings'.[18] Of his origins and education nothing is known, nor how he came to succeed Gundemar (610–612) to the throne, but he must have been a prominent member of the Gothic aristocracy with enough of a military reputation to make him an acceptable king. His reign, like that of most of his successors, was dominated by warfare. He himself is recorded by Isidore, our sole source for the history of the kingdom in the years from 589 to 625/6, as having conducted a series of campaigns against the declining Byzantine outposts in the southeast, preparing the way for their final elimination by his successor in 624.[19] At the same time successful campaigns were being conducted by his generals against the Asturians who were in rebellion, and against the mysterious Ruccones, last heard of being defeated by the Suevic king Miro (570–583). The command of this expedition was entrusted to the duke Suinthila, who was to succeed Sisebut as king in 621. Despite this considerable military activity and the necessary administrative tasks that came the way of a king, Sisebut, in a short reign, still found time to act as a patron of learning and to write works more substantial than any produced by a monarch before the time of Alfred of Wessex (871–899).

One of Isidore's more important works, *On the Nature of Things*, was dedicated to the king, and the composition of the monumental *Etymologies* was instigated by him, although it was not completed during his reign. Another work of Isidore's produced at this time was his *Chronicle*, of which the first version finished in 615/6 may have been commissioned by the king. Its author subsequently continued it in a second version about a decade later. In response to the first of these works, *On the Nature of Things*, Sisebut produced a composition of his own, a verse epistle of some sixty-one hexameters' length on the subject of eclipses. In the poem, Sisebut refers to the military burdens of his office and the campaigns against the Cantabrians and the Basques. Technically the king's verses are more than just competent, and their contents display a considerable breadth of reading on his part, especially in Lucretius and the astronomical poetry of antiquity.

Sisebut's other work in verse is a hymn, and there is also a corpus of prose of considerable interest. The most remarkable of these pieces is a *Life* of Bishop Desiderius of Vienne, who had recently (*c.* 605) been murdered at the instigation of the Frankish king Theoderic II (596–613) and his grandmother, the infamous Queen Brunechildis (*d.* 613).[20] It is surprising to find a king writing hagiography, and that his subject should be a contemporary from a neighbouring kingdom makes it more so. But Brunechildis, herself the daughter of the Spanish king Athanagild, had been an implacable foe ever since the overthrow of the ephemeral kingdom of her son-in-law Hermenegild in 584, and it has been thought that Sisebut's aim was to discredit that Frankish régime most hostile to the Visigothic monarchy by depicting its persecution and killing of a saintly bishop. However, both Brunechildis and Theoderic II were probably dead and their line ended by the time of the work's composition. Moreover, as can be seen from its substantial use by the author of the *Lives of the Fathers of Mérida*, it was to be in Spain rather than in France, where another *Life of Saint Desiderius* was already circulating, that the work became best known. It is more probable that Sisebut's version was intended rather as a consideration of the nature of the royal office in respect of its obligations to the Church and in particular bishops and men of proven sanctity. For in his portraits of Theoderic II and Brunechildis he created literary models of tyrants and unjust rulers, directly borrowed by the author of the Méridan *Lives* for his description of Leovigild. The principal influence on Sisebut's thinking in this respect may well have been that of Isidore.

The king has also left us the remains of a collection of letters, that must once have been more extensive. Those that survive, and they are remarkable enough, were preserved together with a number of other letters of roughly the same period in a single manuscript, brought from Cordoba to the Asturian kingdom in the ninth century. Other items in the collection include a letter of complaint from an otherwise unknown monk called Tara to King Reccared, complaining about conditions inside his monastery, and also part of the diplomatic correspondence of a Count Bulgar who served on the frontiers with Francia in the reign of King Gundemar (610–612), and played a part in that monarch's unsuccessful attempt to create an alliance with the Lombards and the weaker Frankish kings against Theoderic II and Brunechildis. Sisebut's letters in the manuscript are especially striking for their variety and their contents. There is a polite formal exchange of letters between himself and his principal opponent in the peninsula, the Byzantine Patrician Caesarius, governor of the dwindling Imperial enclave centred on Cartagena. More surprising are the letters of spiritual or pastoral guidance. One of these is addressed to Bishop Cilicius of Mentesa, who wished to resign his see in order to become a monk, a decision over which the king sternly remonstrated with him for the sake of his responsibilities towards his flock. Another letter is addressed to one Teudila, who is thought to be the king's own son. If this be so he must have been illegitimate as Sisebut's successor Reccared II (621) was a child when his father died, whereas this Teudila, as the letter makes clear, had just become a monk. A final letter is directed to the young Lombard king Adaluald (616–626), urging him, albeit unsuccessfully, to renounce his Arian beliefs.[21]

Limited as the remnants of this collection are they leave very firmly the impression of a humane man, interested in a wide range of subjects and with an unusual and highly developed sense of the obligations of his office. This led him on occasion to taking some striking initiatives, as in his letter to Adaluald. Some of these may have been ill-conceived, the product of a desire for speedy results. Thus the fourth Council of Toledo, held in 633, twelve years after his death, rebuked him posthumously for his having imposed baptism on the Spanish Jews, irrespective of their willingness or preparedness to receive this sacrament. But Sisebut has left a more endearing image in the brief note on his reign given by the Burgundian chronicler known mistakenly as Fredegar, who, in relating his victories over the Byzantines, wrote: 'The slaughter of the Romans by his men caused the pious Sisebut to exclaim: "Woe is me, that my reign should witness so great a shedding of human blood". He saved all whom he could from death.'[22] His own death in 621 is veiled in obscurity. Not even Isidore knew, or was perhaps prepared, to reveal the causes, merely relating three conflicting contemporary opinions, that it was due to natural causes, was the product of an overdose of medicine, or was the result of poison.[23] If it were the last of these, such a king surely deserved a kinder fate.

Braulio is one of the most immediately likeable characters to be found in the history of Visigothic Spain. Of course, this may be due in part to the fact that he is one of the few of whom even the outline impression of their personality may be formed, owing principally to the survival of his collection of letters, which is the only one to survive intact. That of Isidore is diminutive and clearly truncated, and those of Eugenius II, Ildefonsus and Julian, the great seventh-century bishops of Toledo, the existence of whose letters is confirmed by contemporary accounts, have disappeared without trace, save for a few dedicatory epistles prefixed to some of their writings. However, it is not the survival of his letters alone that gives the firm impression of Braulio's personality – those of Isidore show how unrevealing Late Antique letters can be – but it is the prolixity and warmth that comes out in the literary style of everything that he wrote that gives the reader so firm an assurance of the writer's essential amiability.

Braulio, like his master Isidore, was a member of virtually a clerical dynasty, something that was not uncommon in the western Church at this time. His father Gregory was a bishop, possibly of Osma. It was quite permissable canonically at this period for a bishop to have children, as there was no formal ban on married clergy, and, as in fifth century Gaul, it was possible for a man of high social rank to abandon secular life and marriage in middle life to take up an ascetic or clerical career. Various of the Spanish councils did come increasingly to advocate the creation of a purely celibate clergy and certainly a married cleric was expected to lead a totally chaste life after he had been ordained. Braulio's elder brother John was Bishop of Zaragoza, the foremost see in the Ebro valley, from 619 until his death in 631. His predecessor Maximus was compiler of a brief work of history, which, as has been previously mentioned, is now entirely lost and may not be identified with the so-called *Chronicle of Zaragoza*, the original two parts of which may have been sources for the Bishop's missing work.[24] Braulio succeeded John at Zaragoza, holding the see until his death in 651. Another brother, Fronimian, became abbot of St Aemilian's monastery in the Rioja, as is known from Braulio's dedicatory introduction to the *Life* of the saint that he wrote. The bishop is also said to have had two sisters, Pomponia, an abbess, and Basilla, who married and was widowed. Both of these appear as correspondents in Braulio's letter collection, but as there is no evidence there, or in any other contemporary source, the suggestion of a family relationship may well be unsound.

Braulio's career prior to his episcopate is somewhat vague. He certainly passed some time with Isidore in Seville, as the latter refers to it in a letter. Subsequently he became an archdeacon. Most reasonably this may be assumed to be in Zaragoza, and it has been suggested that this may have occured in 619/620 upon his brother's

promotion to the episcopate in that city. During this time, at Bishop
John's request, he began preparations for writing his *Life of Saint
Aemilian*, but he stopped and did not resume work on it until his own
episcopate, when he completed it for their brother Fronimian.[25] All
three brothers were deeply devoted to the recently developed cult of
Aemilian (*ob. c.* 580), with Bishop John dedicating a basilica to him in
Zaragoza. This suggests that the family originated in the area of
Aemilian's activities, in the Rioja, and the growth of the cult must
have owed much to their impetus.

After the death of Braulio in 651, Toledo emerged as the dominant
intellectual centre of the kingdom, and it was there in the *urbs regia*, the
royal city, rather than in Seville or Zaragoza, that the traditions of
Isidore were to be perpetuated. Links of master and pupil were clearly
of the greatest importance in the Spanish Church during the seventh
century. Braulio had commemorated Isidore, and in the second half
of the century successive bishops of Toledo did the same for their
predecessors and teachers. Ildefonsus wrote a continuation of
Isidore's *On Famous Men*, concentrating on the recent masters of the
Spanish Church, Julian added a section to this on Ildefonsus himself,
and finally Felix (693–700) did likewise for Julian, his own teacher.
This tradition, the extending of the *On Famous Men*, demonstrated the
intellectual pedigree of the Toledan Church.[26]

Bishoprics had been created, from the fourth century onwards, in
most of the major centres of population, and they were divided under
the authority of metropolitan bishops (in Spain not called
archbishops until the twelfth century), into ecclesiastical provinces
that coincided exactly with those of the Roman civil administration.
The principal cities – Tarragona, Cartagena, Seville and Mérida – all
became the sites of the metropolitanates. However, this pattern was
disturbed by the rise to prominence of Toledo as the centre of royal
government, and at the same time the loss of Cartagena to the
Byzantines.

The bishops of Toledo appear to have pressed for a special
recognition of their see from the early sixth century onwards, but it
was only raised to primacy in the province of Carthaginiensis in 610,
when Cartagena was consequently downgraded. The acts of the
synod, held under King Gundemar, at which this decision was taken
are, in the manuscripts of the Spanish Councils, appended to the
proceedings of XII Toledo of 681.[27] The same twelfth Council gave
Toledo pre-eminence over the whole Church in Spain, allowing its

metropolitan to consecrate bishops to sees in any of the other ecclesiastical provinces of the kingdom, with royal consent.

By this same period Toledo had secured for itself a monopoly on the right to perform the ecclesiastical consecration of the kings and added an ecclesiastical dimension to what had probably previously been a purely secular ceremony. This took the form of royal anointing or unction. Bishop Julian (680–690) made it clear that the performance of the ceremony in Toledo marked the distinction between legitimate and illegitimate initiation into rule.[28] At a time when a king such as Wamba (672–680) might be challenged by a rival and both claim to be anointed monarchs, such a further distinction was clearly important. The Toledan church developed a royal liturgy that provided sophisticated ecclesiastical ritual not only for such events as royal consecration but also for the initiating and concluding of military expeditions and also for the way by which, through the formal adoption of the penitential state, a king should end his reign.[29]

Toledo may not have been the permanent royal residence and centre of government, but its church made sure that it was the heart of the kingdom, where all major undertakings had to be seen to begin and end. In such ways and through its position as the only place where councils of the whole Church of the kingdom might be held, Toledo acquired a unique and apparently unchallenged pre-eminence and prestige, which even survived the Arab conquest and the ensuing decline in the secular importance of the city.

There are no exact parallels to the position achieved by the Toledan Church to be found in other parts of western Europe. Rome is a special case, and even its authority inside Italy did not always go unchallenged. No Frankish archbishopric ever secured pre-eminence, although individual bishops such as Hincmar of Reims (845–882) might. The nearest comparison may be with Canterbury, but even its authority continued to be disputed by York on into the twelfth century, and there were only the two ecclesiastical provinces in England. On the other hand, Toledo's rise in the sixth and seventh centuries was unchallenged and its lead, in terms of definition of doctrine and attempts to impose uniformity of practice, especially liturgical, was accepted without recorded demur.

Toledo was not an ancient city. Its ecclesiastical past was obscure and its patron saint, Leocadia, less widely venerated in the peninsula than St Eulalia of Mérida.[30] The peculiar achievements of the Toledan church in the seventh century must be linked firmly to the special relationship of the city with the Visigothic monarchy, and the strong degree, as clearly evinced in most of the councils, of ecclesiastical support for the kings. However, the status of the city as royal residence was not of itself enough. That the Lombard kings made Pavia their centre of government did not significantly affect the ecclesiastical standing of that city. The previous obscurity of Toledo may have made it a more acceptable focus of authority for the Spanish Church than one of the older rival metropolitanates, but much of the responsibility must rest with the activities of a remarkable series of bishops, true heirs of Isidore.

The Isidoran connection came to Toledo in the person of Bishop Eugenius II (646–57). Like all of these men, his family antecedents are unknown, but in early life he was a member of the Toledan clergy. He moved to Zaragoza, apparently out of a personal devotion to St Vincent, that city's patron martyr, at whose basilica he gave himself up to an ascetic life. However, he seems soon to have been drawn back into the ranks of the clergy, becoming archdeacon of the city and the closest friend of Braulio, its bishop. As is clear from one of his letters, Braulio clearly intended Eugenius to succeed him, but in 646 he was recalled to Toledo on the specific order of King Chindasuinth, to fill the vacancy caused by the death of Eugenius I (636–646).[31] Some letters of entreaty from Braulio to the king asking that Eugenius be allowed to remain at Zaragoza, are to be found in his collection, together with the definitive royal rejection of his plea. As a result, Eugenius went to take up his new post in the capital and Braulio came in due course to be succeeded by the former priest Taio (651–post 656), with whom, as we also learn from the letters, he had not always been on the best of terms. This Taio had previously been sent to Rome by King Chindasuinth, to find and bring back copies of works by Gregory the Great that were not then known in Spain, or at least in Toledo. He also, doubtless as the result of this trip, produced a corpus of *sententiae* or extracts, all drawn from the various writings of Gregory, thus providing a useful abridged edition of an author, the influence of whose work on the Spanish Church at this time cannot be minimised. However, of Taio's episcopate nothing is known, and really with the death of Braulio, as far as the evidence goes, Zaragoza, like Seville before it, disappears from the intellectual map of Visigothic Spain.[32]

Eugenius II of Toledo, disciple of Braulio and thus heir to Isidore, was himself the teacher of his eventual successor Julian (680–690).

He is best known for his poetic works, the largest corpus of attributed verse to have survived from the Visigothic period. At the instigation of King Chindasuinth who, for this and his despatch of Taio to Rome, ranks second only to Sisebut as a royal patron of learning, Eugenius revised the *De Creatione Mundi* (On the Creation of the World) of the African poet Dracontius (*c.* 490), and he completed it by adding a new section on the Seventh Day of Creation. He also produced a version of the same poet's *Satisfactio* (Satisfaction) originally written to appease the Vandal king Gunthamund (484–496). The alterations to the original texts made by Eugenius appear to have been made to improve, in his view at least, his predecessor's vocabulary and poetic structure, rather than to make any ideological points or theological distinctions. As well as undertaking these revisions, he also composed poetry in his own right, including a series of metrical epitaphs, amongst which were ones for King Chindasuinth (*d.* 653) and for his son Reccesuinth's wife Queen Reciberga. A large part of Eugenius's minor poems are a series of versifications of short sections from Isidore's *Etymologies*, probably intended as examples for instruction in poetic composition in the episcopal school known to have existed in Toledo at this time. Eugenius's verse influenced the work of subsequent generations of poets in Visigothic Spain, including his own pupil Julian, whose own corpus of poems is now unfortunately lost. His work continued to be cited and to have influence on both form and content after the fall of the kingdom, and beyond its frontiers, as can be seen in its use by the Cordoban Paul Albar (*c.* 850) and by the foremost poet of the Carolingian Renaissance, himself of Spanish origin, Bishop Theodulf of Orléans (*d.* 821).

Eugenius's other writings may, however, have been of more consequence to him personally. He composed a lost work on the Trinity, which according to the account in Ildefonsus's *On Famous Men*, was going to be sent to the East, doubtless to the Byzantine Church.[33] Being composed in the mid seventh century, it is most probable that it was principally concerned with the Monothelete controversy, which dealt with the problems of the nature and 'operations' of Christ, which was currently arousing much passion in Africa and the rest of the Byzantine Empire. What may be a fragment of Eugenius's treatise has been detected by the Spanish scholar José Madoz in the credal formulation of XI Toledo (675).[34] Eugenius himself attended and may well have composed the acts of the four Toledan Councils held during his episcopate (VII–X), including the very important eighth Council of 653. This dealt with the political problems created by the recently ended reign of Chindasuinth, and also promulgated a substantial creed. The early years of Reccesuinth's reign (649–672) were particularly difficult ones, and however little we may be able to see of the period due to the lack of narrative historical sources, it is likely that Eugenius's role at this time was a prominent one. What part, if any, he played in the creation of Reccesuinth's famous law book, promulgated in 654, can only be a matter of conjecture.

Like his successors Ildefonsus and Julian, Eugenius was responsible for the composition of liturgical pieces, that went to swell the growing corpus of the Visigothic liturgy, the greatest product of the Spanish Church of the Early Middle Ages. While it is likely that a surviving hymn to St Aemilian is the one that he composed while still a deacon in Zaragoza, at the request of Bishop Braulio, his other contributions to the liturgy, the existence of which we are assured by the account in Ildefonsus's *On Famous Men*, cannot be identified in the vast anonymous body of the surviving texts.[35] However, we do know, from the same source, that he was responsible for a reform of the chant used in the Visigothic Church. Also, most unusually, Ildefonsus, who as his contemporary knew St Aemilian well, gives us a terse physical description of this, the most shadowy of the great Fathers of the Spanish Church: 'He was thin, and weak in body and constitution, but truly radiant by virtue of his spirit.'[36]

Attempts have been made to suggest that a conflict existed within the Church of Toledo in the seventh century between those bishops and their supporters who were drawn from the ranks of the clergy and those who came from the monastery of Agali.[37] This institution, the most important monastic establishment in the vicinity of the capital, was built in the suburbs of the city in the early seventh century, and from the ranks of its abbots were drawn a number of the bishops of Toledo, including Helladius (615–633), Justus (633–636), who had been Helladius's successor in the abbacy, and Ildefonsus (657–667). Bishop Sisbert (690–693) may well have been the abbot of that name who signed the acts of XIV and XV Toledo (684 and 688), and if so was possibly from Agali too. Also drawn from a monastic environment, although which one is nowhere specified, and as Ildefonsus wrote about him it is unlikely to be Agali, was Bishop Eugenius I (636–646), who was made a member of the city clergy by Helladius. On the other hand, other bishops – Eugenius II

(646–657), Julian (680–690) and Felix (693–700) – were clerics, members of the secular clergy, before their elevation to the episcopate. The only other bishop of note, Quiricus (667–680), is harder to place as he has left us no written works, nor did he receive an entry in the continuations of *On Famous Men*. It is conceivable that he is to be identified with the bishop of Barcelona of the same name (*c.* 656), and was transferred to Toledo on the death of his friend and correspondent Ildefonsus.[38] Such an origin might explain his being ignored in the Toledan tradition epitomised in the *On Famous Men* and its continuations.

To argue, as some have done, that a fundamental divide and indeed hostility existed between monastic and clerically derived bishops, and that the kings might alternate between what were virtually two parties in their choice of successive bishops, is in fact patently nonsensical. 'Clerical' bishops such as Eugenius II and Julian are recorded as having deep involvements in monastic life, both having spent long periods under self-imposed ascetic discipline prior to their being ordained to the clergy, whilst a 'monastic' bishop, Eugenius I, joined the ranks of the clergy of the city after passing several years as a monk. Likewise a 'monastic' bishop, Ildefonsus, could write the entry in his *On Famous Men* on Eugenius II, whilst it was a 'clerical' one, Julian, who did the same in turn for Ildefonsus. There is no serious indication that the bishops drawn from Agali were the promoters of a consistent line of policy, let alone that they were antagonistic to royal authority. What is striking about the Toledan bishops of the seventh century is their awareness of continuity in the see and their maintenance of a firm sense of tradition and the importance of the chain of master-pupil relationships.

Eugenius II's successor Ildefonsus shared his interest in the liturgy, and despite its anonymity some of his contributions to the development of the corpus can be detected by reason of the very distinctive nature of his literary style. He was peculiarly fond of that synonymous style first developed by Isidore, and he employed it in his most famous work, *On the Perpetual Virginity of the Blessed Virgin Mary*, which begins thus: 'O, My Lady, my Queen, my Ruler, Mother of my Lord, Handmaiden of your Son, Bearer of the Creator of the World, I beg you, I pray you, I beseech you, that I may have the spirit of your Lord, that I may have the spirit of your Son, that I may have the spirit of my Redeemer, that I may truly and worthily know you, that I may truly and worthily speak about you, that I may truly and worthily say things about you that ought to be said. . . .'[39] As well as being the first great outburst of Marian devotion in the Spanish Church, this work represents the furthest and most extreme development of the synonymous style. We know from Julian's *Elogium* on Ildefonsus that the latter composed a number of masses, sermons and hymns. As some of the masses in the surviving Visigothic Sacramentary are written in this developed and very florid synonymous style peculiar to Ildefonsus, it is not unreasonable to assume that these may be some of the pieces referred to by Julian.[40] Unfortunately no sermons and hymns can now be so safely ascribed to him, although the Toledan homiliary contains a number of pseudo-Ildefonsine pieces.

Ildefonsus's greatest distinction lies in the impetus that he gave to Marian devotion in the Spanish Church, and the influence of his work may have some responsibility for its further spread into other parts of the West in the seventh and succeeding centuries. His book, in its unusual style, was couched in the form of a violent and indeed abusive attack upon those who doubted the perpetual virginity of Mary and the arguments on which they based their scepticism. The popularity of his writing, both within and without the peninsula, is confirmed by the survival of a substantial body of manuscripts.[41] His other two surviving works were clearly less highly regarded. They are both treatises on baptism, basically composed of selected extracts from writings of Augustine, Gregory and Isidore. The second of them, the *Book of the Desert Journey*, only survives in one manuscript. Other works recorded in Julian's account of Ildefonsus, such as his treatise on the differences between the persons of the Trinity, have disappeared entirely.

Ildefonsus was succeeded by Quiricus (667–680), who, despite a slightly longer than average pontificate, has left remarkably few traces of himself. Neither he nor Ildefonsus before him were engaged in much conciliar activity. During his pontificate the only synod to be held in the capital was XI Toledo of 675, attended only by bishops from the province of Carthaginiensis. The reign of Wamba (672–680) was, as we know from the complaints voiced at XII Toledo, a trying time for the Church. One of the complaints then made was that the king had erected a new bishopric in the suburbs of Toledo, in defiance of canonical injunctions against having two bishops in one city. How Quiricus reacted to this and other royal acts that contravened the canon law is unknown. It may be that his compliance with royal wishes also explains his being omitted from the continuations of the

On Famous Men tradition. He died in 680, just prior to the deposition of Wamba, which possibly might not have occurred if it were he, rather than Julian, who had been the one faced with the problem of a king in the state of canonical penance.

Julian (680–690) is probably the most striking and most versatile of the seventh-century bishops of Toledo. As is the case with his predecessors, we know all too little about his early life and antecedents, but at least the account written of him by his successor Felix (693–700) is fuller than any we have of the others. Interestingly he was of Jewish descent but this is all that is revealed of his family. Some of Julian's writings are now lost, including collections of hymns, masses, poems and letters, although some of his compositions doubtless rest undetected in the great anonymous corpus of the Visigothic or 'Mozarabic' liturgy. Of his extant works the *Prognosticum Futuri Saeculi* (Sign of the Future Life), composed in 688, had the greatest impact, at least in succeeding centuries. Its most recent editor lists one hundred and eighty-six manuscripts of the work.[42] This is a prodigious rate of survival, matched, in early Spanish texts at least, only by certain writings of Isidore.

The contents of the book are not original in themselves, in that the three sections in which the *Prognosticum* was composed are comprised almost entirely of quotations from earlier patristic authors. However, it was the selection and organisation of the material that gave Julian's compilation its value. He treated themes of central importance to Christian thought, but which in several cases had not previously received full and coherent coverage. By combining the thoughts of several writers, Julian produced a single treatise that dealt, in three easily comprehended parts, with the questions of the origins of death, the fate of souls after death and the final resurrection of the body. Julian's main source was Augustine, whose treatment of these topics in the *City of God* he principally drew on, but he also included passages from Jerome, Ambrose, Gregory the Great, Isidore and others. Amongst Julian's other works are *Antikeimenon* or *De Contrariis* (On Conflicts) which sought to reconcile apparently contradictory Biblical texts, and his *Liber de Sextae Aetatis Comprobatione* (Book on the Proving of the Sixth Age), dedicated to King Ervig. Julian's *Libellus de Divinis Judiciis* (On Divine Judgements) was dedicated to the same monarch, possibly prior to his accession. The book on the 'Sixth Age' was a work of anti-Jewish polemic, aimed at refuting their arguments that the age of the Messiah had not yet arrived.

Julian is probably better known now for his activities as bishop than for his writings. In particular his involvement in the mysterious deposition of King Wamba in 680, and the succession of Julian's friend Ervig, have earned him some harsh words from modern commentators.[43] It has been suspected that he deliberately induced the appearance of fatal illness in the king who, then accepting the penitential state but subsequently recovering, had to be removed from office and be replaced by a more pliable successor. Such an interpretation is quite unnecessarily Machiavellian. A serious canonical problem was created by the recovery of one who had in penance renounced all secular involvements. It is possible that Julian, with the subsequent support of the bishops assembled at XII Toledo in 681, was not displeased to be able to get rid of Wamba by uncompromising adherence to the letter of canon law, but at worst he can be accused of taking advantage of an unexpected occurrence.

Another affair in which Julian can be seen taking a strong line was in the controversy with the papacy that arose from the terminology he used in condemning the Monothelete heresy. This latter had been troubling the Church in the Byzantine Empire since the early seventh century, and the emperor Constantine IV (668–685) sought to end it by a conciliar condemnation. Pope Agatho promised to add those of the Western Church and sought decrees from Spain amongst others. In replying for the Spanish Church, Julian used certain expressions about the nature of Christ that were misunderstood by the new pope Benedict II (684–685). Julian wrote a vigorous defence of his ideas in 686 in the *Apologeticum de Tribus Capitulis* (Defence of the Three Chapters), and his views were approved by XV Toledo in 688. Some have gone so far as to see this as a prelude to a schism between Rome and the Spanish Church, but there is no justification for this. The whole issue died with its participants and was never referred to again.[44]

In Julian the Church of Toledo had its most colourful and vigorous bishop, who advanced significantly both the claims and the prerogatives of the see. Even if some of his writings have made no mark and others offer little of originality, he could, as in his *History of Wamba*, use neglected classical literary genres to break new ground. With his death in 690 the great age of Toledo in the Visigothic period came to an end, but the position that he, probably more than any of his predecessors, had achieved for the Church of the *Urbs Regia* was to survive the difficult centuries of Islamic domination.

His successor Sisbert (690–693) appears in our sources only in retrospect, in the acts of XVI Toledo of 693, where his previous deposition and excommunication for plotting rebellion against King Egica are confirmed. He was sentenced to perpetual exile (within a monastery?) and denied communion until upon his deathbed.[45] This conspiracy has been linked with the existence of a unique coin of the Toledan mint in the name of an otherwise unknown king Sunifred. The style of the coin would put it into the late 680s or the 690s, and thus it is held that Sisbert's plot led to this brief and unsuccessful usurpation. However, the name of Sunifred does not appear in the list of the bishop's fellow conspirators given in the acts of the council, nor is there any indication there that this plot ever went beyond words.[46]

A former Toledan cleric and pupil of Bishop Julian called Felix, who had been elevated to the see of Seville some time after 688, was translated to the office left vacant by Sisbert's deposition. He has left us the final continuation of the chain of *On Famous Men* in his eulogy of Julian, but no other work of his is known. He died *c.* 700, and his successors Gunderic and Sindered, the last bishops of Toledo of the Visigothic period, are even obscurer. The latter fled Spain during the Arab invasion, a desertion for which he was posthumously castigated in the Toledan Chronicle of 754 as the hireling who abandons his sheep. He retired to Rome, where he signed the acts of a council in 721.[47]

It is regrettable, in view of its important formative influence on so many of the leading figures of the Spanish Church in the Visigothic period, that so little is known of the monastic life of the peninsula at that time. The province of Tarraconensis is notable as the only part of the peninsula for which there is evidence of the existence of monasticism in the period before the reign of Leovigild. Monastic institutions appear to have been much slower in developing in Spain than in most other parts of western Europe in the fifth and sixth centuries. Although individual Spaniards with an interest in the growing ascetic movement are known from as early as the fourth century, such as the Lady Egeria who went on a pilgrimage to the Holy Places and Egypt in 383–4 and wrote an account of it, there is little evidence of monasteries being founded in Spain, as they were in Gaul, during the next two centuries. The conditions inside the peninsula during the lengthy period of the invasions may help to explain this. But in the south it was only the influx of ascetics from Africa in the 550s and 560s that seems to have led to the establishing of monastic institutions in

Baetica, Lusitania and probably Carthaginiensis. The cause of this movement of monks, who seem to have brought some of their books and their learning with them, was probably the Emperor Justinian I's attempts to impose unacceptable theological views on the African Church in those decades. It is in this period that we first hear of the Cauliana monastery at Mérida, and then the establishment of the African hermit Nanctus near that city under the patronage of Leovigild. At the same time the African Donatus founded his monastery of Servitanum, the exact whereabouts of which are uncertain, but are believed to lie in the south-eastern region of the peninsula. Donatus, we are told by Bishop Ildefonsus of Toledo (657–667) in his continuation of Isidore's *On Famous Men*, was the first to introduce the use of a monastic rule into the peninsula. If this be true, and we possess no grounds for doubting Ildefonsus's word, this is a surprisingly late date for such a development. Donatus's successor as abbot of Servitanum, Eutropius, later bishop of Valencia, was to play a distinguished part at III Toledo in 589.[48]

The introduction of monasteries and of monastic rules in the south of the peninsula may well have been as slow as the evidence indicates, but the picture from Tarraconensis is rather different. There contact with the Mediterranean coast of Gaul was close and direct, and that was an area of considerable monastic activity ever since the establishment of Cassian at Marseille and the foundation of the island monastery of Lérins, both *c.* 410–420. Later, too, the great sermon-writer and monastic founder Bishop Caesarius of Arles (502–542) had close contacts with various Spanish bishops, probably from the north-west. As a result monastic influences were probably transmitted fairly rapidly from southern Gaul to Visigothic Septimania, the Catalan coast and the Ebro valley.[49] Unfortunately no evidence survives from the fifth century but in 517 the Council of Gerona devoted some of its time to the issuing of regulations concerning monks, something the assembled bishops were unlikely to have done if there were not sufficient monastic activity already underway in the region to warrant their trying to bring it under their control.

Slightly fuller evidence for some aspects of monasticism in this province in the sixth century has survived. Braulio, bishop of Zaragoza (631–651) in his *Life of Saint Aemilian* has described the activities of a monastic recluse of the upper Ebro valley, who lived in the second half of the sixth century. There are likely to have been several others like him whose lives have gone unchronicled, and the penetration of Christianity into the still heathen Basque regions of the western Pyrenees has been attributed to their work. A number of cave churches in the Cantabrian area have been dated to this period or to the early seventh century.[50] One of Aemilian's own hermitages developed into an important monastic community in the opening decades of the seventh century, taking its later name San Millan de la Cogolla from his. This monastery indeed grew in importance after the collapse of the Visigothic kingdom and was a major centre of learning for several centuries. Another foundation of roughly the same period, probably exceeding San Millan in contemporary importance, but which seems to have disappeared with the Visigoths, is Asan, whose location is unknown but probably in the Pyrenees. Its founder was Victorianus. Unfortunately no early *Life* of this monk survives, unlike the case of Aemilian, and all we have is a fourteenth-century one written in the vernacular.[51] Although this may be based upon or even be a translation of an earlier Latin original, the peculiarities of the work suggest that it is of no earlier date than the tenth or eleventh centuries. Indeed the very existence of Victorianus might be doubted but for the survival of a contemporary poem by Venantius Fortunatus dedicated to the abbot.[52] This certainly proves his existence and is further evidence of the contacts that took place between northern Spain and western Gaul in the later sixth century, but tells us little else. It certainly does not establish Asan as the 'nursery of bishops' that some have seen it to be, very much along the lines of the monastery of Lérins in the fifth century. Such a view, deriving as it does from the anachronistic *Life*, cannot, unfortunately, be substantiated for Asan. But the poem at least shows Victorianus as a figure of some substance, at least in the eyes of some of his contemporaries.

Another important figure in the monastic history of the peninsula in the sixth century, who is also attested to in Gallic as well as Spanish sources, is Martin of Braga. Born in the province of Pannonia in the Balkans in the early sixth century, Martin experienced monasticism in its original home in Egypt, spending several years there amongst the solitaries and the cenobites or ascetics who dwelt in communities. Subsequently, *c.* 550, he made his way to Galicia. His intentions in going to a place so remote by the standards of his own day are unknown. However, he arrived at a peculiarly crucial time, as soon after his appearance there the Suevic kingdom renounced the Arianism it had held to for the past century and reverted to the Catholicism of its fifth-century king Rechiarius. Some responsibility for this has been attributed to Martin, but in the Gallic tradition recorded by Gregory of Tours in his hagiographical writing it is also explained by the arrival at Braga, the Suevic capital of relics, of his namesake, Saint Martin of Tours. At any rate, Martin of Braga did have a crucial role to play in helping shape the Church in the Suevic kingdom after the conversion, with effects on the special characteristics of the Galician Church lasting well into the Visigothic period. Martin was originally granted land at Dumio, near Braga, by the king, probably Charraric, and he set up a monastic community there, most likely along the lines of monastic life as he had experienced it in Egypt. There the norm was for groups of aspiring ascetics to gather around a spiritual guide and leader, the 'abba' or father, to receive direction and teaching. The intention of this was the furtherance of the spiritual development of the individual, and the communal life was not regarded as an end in itself; ideally the aspiring ascetic should be strengthened by his experiences, not so much of living with others as of the spiritual direction of his 'abba', to be able to go on to the higher life of the solitary, even if only for a time. The charismatic abbots were often figures of considerable power and influence in Egypt in these centuries, sometimes coming into conflict with the established hierarchy of the Church in the form of the bishops. On the other hand in Gaul, especially in the south where monastic ideas and institutions from Egypt and Syria had been making themselves felt since the late fourth century, it became increasingly common for bishops of aristocratic descent to be drawn from amongst the ranks of those who had spent some time leading the monastic life in a community. Interestingly, the role of the communal life in monastic formation came increasingly to be emphasised and more vigorous episcopal control of monasteries was exercised in the West than in the East. Galicia, however, was somewhat unusual. It was an area penetrated by Roman civilisation at effectively little more than the military level, and it is unclear how developed the ecclesiastical organisation of the province was by the end of the Roman period. It was certainly still subject to the metropolitan authority of distant Mérida in southern Lusitania. With very few towns, and a greatly under-Christianised countryside, it looks as if established urban bishoprics were relatively slow in coming into existence, whereas in most other parts of the Roman world they were created, often at an early stage, around the pattern of the provincial centres employed by the civil government.[53] But in odd under-urbanised and under-Romanised areas such as southern Numidia in Africa, or Galicia in Spain, alternative forms of organisation had to be sought. It seems that there were more of the 'country bishops', so much a cause of contention in the African Church, in Galicia, than has been recognised. Certainly in Martin and his successors at Dumio there existed a line of bishops whose seat of authority was a monastery rather than a city.

Martin, like his namesake of Tours, is often considered to have been an active opponent of rural paganism. This is quite possibly true, but it cannot rest, as is usually assumed, upon the evidence of his book *De Correctione Rusticorum* (Reforming the Rustics). This took the form of a letter in reply to a request from Bishop Polemius of Astorga, which contains a sermon that Martin composed. The work is largely modelled on a treatise by Augustine, and the gods, or rather for Martin demons, that it sought to oppose were those of classical paganism. There are no points of contact with what little is known of the indigenous pre-Christian cults of rural Galicia. Despite superficial appearances this is a model composition, rather than a work intended for practical application.

The peculiarities of Galicia are held to have produced a distinctive form of monastic regulation, known as 'pactualism'.[54] This stems from the survival of a small number of agreements made between bodies of monks and their abbots, and take the form of a simple contract by the former to accept the authority of the latter. They lay down certain regulations that all agree to follow, as for example the procedures to be followed should the community be dispersed by war. Although no manuscript of such agreements survive from before the ninth century, it has been argued that the origins of the practice go back to at least the mid seventh century.

This is quite a reasonable probability, but the attempt to make of them a distinctively Galician feature is less seductive. Such pacts are not incompatible with existing monastic rules of the same period, such as that of Fructuosus, which are generalised and theoretical. Pacts could have been employed to supplement regular observance with special conditions. They are not especially egalitarian or deleterious to the authority of the abbot. Surviving examples from the ninth and tenth centuries come from Galicia, Castille and the Rioja, but general problems of the survival of evidence make the lack of such texts from Leon and even more the Arab-held south less surprising.

'Gallegan pactual monasticism' as distinct from other forms of regular observance may be a fantasy.

The development of monasticism in seventh century Spain is not easy to assess. Compared with Gaul in the same period, the sites of very few monasteries can be recorded with any degree of certainty. Some of the major urban monasteries, such as Agali at Toledo and Cauliana at Mérida, are known from literary sources, but although the possible situations of both of these have been the subject of antiquarian conjecture, no excavation has revealed their actual sites. The location of those rural monasteries that are encountered in the sources is usually equally uncertain.

A relative lack of hagiography, as in contemporary Lombard Italy, makes the task of studying Visigothic monasticism much harder. For the sixth century there is only Braulio's *Life of Saint Aemilian*, which gives some glimpses of ascetic life in the Rioja. The *Lives of the Fathers of Mérida*, written *c.*630, contains some references to monastic practices in that city in the mid sixth century, whilst for the seventh century proper the only work of monastic hagiography is the anonymous *Life of Saint Fructuosus*, probably composed in the 690s. This recounts features of the career of the most famous founder of monasteries in Visigothic Spain.

Fructuosus, a member of the Gothic nobility, spent much of his early life in founding communities in two regions, the Bierzo on the frontiers of Galicia, and in the south around Cadiz. He subsequently became Bishop of Braga and Metropolitan of Galicia *c.*656. For his principal northern monastery, at Compludo, he wrote an extant rule of remarkable severity: his monks were required to reveal all their thoughts, visions and dreams to their superiors, and the prior, second in charge to the abbot, was instructed 'silently to pass the bed of each one' as they were going to sleep, so that 'by observing the actions of each more closely, he may learn how to treat the character and merits of each'. This inspection was repeated before the monks were awoken for their midnight prayers. They were forbidden to look at each other or anyone else. Certain offences were punished by flogging and imprisonment within the monastery on a diet of six ounces of bread a day and 'a small amount of water'. Such confinements could last for three or six months.[55]

This rule is more purely practical than, say, that of St Benedict (*c.*525), in that it restricts itself to the making of regulations for the leading of the common life and omits any more general considerations as to the ends of that life. But the obligations laid upon the officers of the monastery show that they were expected to lead by example, and to be even more rigorous than their charges in self-discipline and the carrying out of their duties. However, it is hard to escape the impression of unnerving surveillance that pervades this rule: the abbot or prior had to change the allocation of the monks' beds twice every week and 'shall carefully watch to see that no one possesses anything unnecessary or hidden'.[56]

As well as in monasteries proper, in which groups of monks lived communally under the direction of a hierarchy of seniors, aspiring ascetics could be found leading solitary lives as hermits. The Bierzo, in western Leon, where Fructuosus established some of his monasteries, was famous for its hermits, who, like Aemilian in the Rioja, lived in caves and sought their own spiritual salvation in isolated contemplation and rigorous mortification of their bodies. Although basically solitary, groups of such men could have an overall spiritual director. Because they were not as regimented as the monks in monasteries, and therefore harder for the ecclesiastical hierarchy to oversee, conciliar decrees were directed to keeping them under episcopal supervision, and some were forcibly co-opted into the ranks of the clergy.

One such late seventh-century ascetic, Valerius of Bierzo, briefly forced to become a priest against his will, has left a fascinating if eccentric corpus of short writings. This includes three brief accounts of visions of the afterlife and of celestial rewards and punishments seen by the monks Maximus, Bonellus and Baldarius. Valerius also wrote a précis of the late fourth-century ascetic Egeria's story of her pilgrimage to the Holy Land, and he composed some short works of monastic instruction and a small body of poetry. His most peculiar writings are three short autobiographical pieces describing certain difficulties and persecutions to which he was subjected, particularly at the hands of the local clergy and populace. The inmates of a nearby monastery, whom he designated 'pseudo-monks', were apparently another source of malevolence, but his greatest enemy was a priest called Justus—'a weakling of puny stature, and with the colour very black to behold of the barbarous Ethiopian race; for outwardly on account of his skin he was ugly in his sallow appearance, but in his secret heart he was absolutely blacker than a crow.'[57] As his robust language shows Valerius clearly lacked a temperate disposition, and his many quarrels may not have been unprovoked, as he would have us believe. Justus was certainly driven, for whatever reason, to attack him with a sword during the celebration of mass, but was apparently too drunk to do any damage. Valerius viewed his varied literary *oeuvre* as a unity, and in its few extant manuscripts it is kept together and the whole dedicated to his fellow hermits in the Bierzo and their spiritual director Donadeus.[58]

Despite the limitations of the evidence, it is clear that it was in the Visigothic period that asceticism took a firm hold on the peninsula. The signatures of abbots appended to the act of the councils, the enactments of some of those councils concerning monastic practices and discipline, and the clear interest of individuals such as Bishops Eugenius II and Julian of Toledo in the ascetic life and its aims all clearly indicate the hold that it was gaining on the Spanish Church. Later references too, as for example in Catalan charters of the ninth and tenth centuries, to the existence of earlier monasteries or churches on sites such as Montserrat, may suggest that monastic institutions were more numerous in Visigothic Spain than strictly contemporary evidence can establish. In its monastic life, as in its strong if idiosyncratic intellectual traditions, the Church of the Visigothic period created a distinctive personality for itself that proved quite capable of standing up to the challenges of the centuries that followed the Arab conquest.

4. The Seventh-Century Kingdom

Local Society in Town and Countryside

IT would be interesting to know something of the social and economic life of the peninsula during the Visigothic period. Some indications can be drawn from the regulations of the law codes but these provide at best an abstract and generalised impression. The peculiar and probably largely localised circumstances that caused the promulgation of particular laws cannot now be known, and insufficient wariness has been displayed in looking out for the presence of anachronistic rulings preserved from the Roman past to fill out the Visigothic written codes. As will be shown, the circumstances of the issuing of the seventh-century codes suggest that their functions were intended to be other than primarily utilitarian. However, despite the pitfalls to be encountered in attempting to use this class of evidence for a picture of life and society in the Visigothic centuries, it is possible from other sources to get more penetrating and particular glimpses of local conditions.

This is especially the case with the important city of Mérida, provincial capital and seat of the metropolitan bishop of Lusitania. Thanks for this must largely be given to the survival of an unusual work of hagiography, the *Vitas Patrum Emeritensium* (sic) or *Lives of the Fathers of Mérida*. The author is anonymous, but he describes himself as being a deacon attached to the Basilica of Saint Eulalia, the city's principal patron saint. It has been conjectured with good reason that he was writing around 630, and he explicitly stated that, following the lead given by Gregory the Great in his *Dialogues*, his aim in writing was to show from recent and local examples that miraculous happenings could still occur.[1] His principal interest was in miracles relating to departure from the body by the soul, either in a vision or at death. After three short accounts of the experiences of a boy in a monastery, of a gluttonous monk and of an African ascetic who came to Mérida, the author devotes the rest, by far the larger part, of his work to the lives of some of the sixth-century bishops of the city. Although retaining his special interest in aspects of the miraculous, he describes the origins and careers of three of these bishops in considerable detail, thus incidentally providing substantial accounts of their secular involvements and of the city in which they lived.

88

The wealth of information concerning town life and the activities of bishops within their sees given in this work is quite unparalleled in the evidence for the history of early medieval Spain and for most other regions of Western Europe. Its value is also enhanced by the fact that Mérida is unusually rich in archaeological remains of the Roman and Visigothic periods, thus permitting the making of some comparisons of the literary evidence with the material.[2] Of course Mérida, as a metropolitan see and provincial capital, cannot be assumed to be typical of other Spanish towns of the time. Nor may it be assumed that what is true of the sixth century is necessarily so of the seventh. However, as evidence relating to virtually all other towns and regions of the peninsula in both centuries is lacking it is necessary to make the fullest use of what little is available.

The impression created by the *Lives of the Fathers of Mérida* is that the city was still enjoying a period of some prosperity in the sixth century, and the wealth of the architectural remains that have come to light seems to confirm this. The city, which had been founded as a 'colonia' for veteran legionaries of Augustus's Cantabrian wars, had been lavishly endowed with public buildings such as theatre, amphitheatre, temples and baths by Augustus's chosen successor Agrippa. In the second century, possibly by the Emperor Hadrian, these had been restored and augmented.[3] During the Early Empire the city had been made the provincial capital of 'Hispania Ulterior' and numbered the future Emperor Otho (AD69) amongst its governors. Little more than a few inscriptions have been found from the third century, but the traces of town walls that survive may date from this period when southern Spain was occasionally threatened by raids from Berber tribes across the Straits of Hercules. The fourth century, however, saw another time of intensive building activity. After the conversion of Constantine I in 312, churches began to be erected and small shrines marking the burial places of local martyrs were transformed by the erection on their sites of full-scale basilicas. At Mérida, we know from the *Lives of the Fathers* of the existence of a basilica dedicated to St Eulalia, which was outside the city walls and erected over the place of her burial in one of the cemeteries. This basilica and other churches dedicated to Saints Faustus, Lucretia, Cyprian and Laurence, together with that of St Mary, also called the Church of Holy Jerusalem, which was the principal episcopal church inside the city, may well have been first erected in the fourth century. The same might be true of the adjacent Baptistery of St John and the nearby episcopal palace. The city was also enriched by the restoration of some of its earlier secular buildings. The amphitheatre was repaired and used for a naval display to celebrate the accession of the emperor Constantine II (337–340). The hippodrome, which enjoyed a much greater vogue in the Later than in the Early Empire for political as well as sporting purposes, may have been built or restored at this time. Some very fine private villas also appear to have been erected in this period, one of which contains the finest Roman mosaic yet discovered in Spain, possibly a product of the fourth century and related to contemporary North African work. This villa might prove to have been an official residence, such as that of the governor of the newly created province of Lusitania, which together with Baetica replaced the older and larger unit of 'Hispania Ulterior' in the reign of Septimius Severus (193–210).[4]

Mérida may not have suffered much in the fifth century, for there are no references to its ever having been sacked, and it was the residence of the Suevic and then Visigothic kings for nearly a decade. An inscription survives from the year 483, recording the repair of the Roman bridge over the river Guadiana by the Visigothic count at the request of the Catholic bishop. A mosaic has also survived from this period depicting Bacchus; it seems to have been made locally and bears the name of a workshop, indicating that the manufacture of such luxury items continued, although aesthetic standards or the quality of craftsmanship may have declined.[5]

Continuity from classical antiquity into the sixth century is strikingly recorded in Mérida. Of course, it had been a thoroughly Roman city, an important administrative centre and fortunate in its fate in both the third and fifth centuries, but the experience of other major Roman cities of Spain, especially in the south and the east, may not have been dissimilar. Ultimately only archaeology may be able to tell. Obviously Galicia, Cantabria and northern Lusitania, where urban development was small and the degree of Roman cultural penetration limited, whilst the amount of fighting and destruction recorded in those areas in the fifth century was considerable, will have presented a very different picture. However, in Visigothic Spain the elements of physical continuity with antiquity were greater than is often appreciated. Thus the very distinctive Méridan style of sculpture of the sixth and seventh centuries, which seems to have spread to other parts of western Baetica and southern Lusitania, appears to owe more to the conscious imitation of the models of the earlier Roman past, many examples of which will still have been visible in the city, than, say, to the influence of contemporary Byzantium. As with the mosaic workshops, there may have been more continuity in the stonemasons' yards than can now be appreciated.

Recent excavation has shown that the urban centre of Mérida did remain in use in the Visigothic period and that, unlike some of the former towns of Roman Britain, it did not become a deserted or semi-rustic area. The principal change lay in the way Christian buildings replaced the former secular public ones in the city centre. Traces of what appears to be a substantial civic basilica, now obscurely described as a triumphal arch, survive beside the site of the early Roman forum. Adjacent to this structure were erected the Church of St Mary, the Baptistery of St John and the bishop's palace. At least one other church was built across on the other side of the forum in the sixth century. It is interesting to note that as well as the probable former secular basilica, a pagan temple survived more or less physically intact in the same area until the sixteenth century, when it was incorporated into the structure of an aristocratic mansion. A similar and indeed better-preserved survival of the shell of a pagan temple may be found in the Portuguese town of Evora. It would be of interest to know to what use, if any, such buildings were put during the Christian centuries of the Visigothic period and after.

During the episcopates of Paul, Fidelis and Masona, whose deeds are described in the *Lives of the Fathers of Mérida*, the city underwent yet another period of substantial building activity and public work. Unfortunately the chronology of these three bishops is imprecise. The author gives no indication beyond putting some at least of the episcopate of Masona in the reign of Leovigild (569–586), and the absence of conciliar acts from Lusitania in the sixth century rules out any chance of precision in respect of his two predecessors. Indeed, with very few exceptions, it is only the survival of episcopal signatures appended to the rulings of councils that has enabled historians from the time of Fr Enrique Florez in the mid seventeenth century onwards, to draw up their far from complete and roughly-dated lists of the incumbents of the Visigothic sees and their successors after 711.[6] Masona of Mérida was the first signatory and therefore probably the senior metropolitan at III Toledo in 589. He must have presided. The third senior in the list was Leander of Seville, who probably held his see by 579, the year of Hermenigild's revolt. Previous to the achievement by the Metropolitan of Toledo of automatic priority over his fellows in the later seventh century, it is believed that seniority in the two ranks of the episcopate (the metropolitans – later called archbishops – and the ordinary bishops, who were subordinate to them) depended strictly upon date of election. Thus Masona's consecration must have preceded that of Leander, therefore at least it cannot be later than the 570s. This should put his two predecessors into the 550s or 560s. The first of these, Paul, was a Greek and a former doctor. As an outsider, coming to the peninsula in the middle of the sixth century for reasons unknown and acquiring a bishopric, his case has some points of comparison with that of Martin of Braga, described in the previous chapter. The author of the *Lives of the Fathers of Mérida* without naming him, refers to the period of Paul's predecessor in the see as being disturbed. This may be a reference to the time of the civil war between Agila and Athanagild and the former's murder in Mérida in 554.

The episcopate of Paul is notable for the considerable increase in the wealth of the see that was to come from a legacy the bishop received in rather peculiar circumstances. Paul was able, because of his medical training, to perform a delicate surgical operation on the wife of a Lusitanian senator, or local aristocrat, said to be the wealthiest in the province, and save her life. The bishop was made this family's sole heir and inherited an enormous personal legacy from them. It was probably on the strength of this that the building and charitable activities of his successors were made possible. The story of the 'caesarian section' performed upon the senator's wife is also important as being the sole reference to a surgical operation in the literature of the early medieval West, and in addition some evidence of the high level of skill of Byzantine doctors in this period.[7]

Paul's successor, Fidelis, was also a Greek and, what is more, his predecessor's nephew, apparently brought by chance to Mérida when travelling in the company of a group of eastern merchants. Although the story sounds suspiciously like something from the *Arabian Nights*, the incidental details that the merchants came by ship, therefore up the river, and that such visiting merchants were expected to call upon the bishop on their arrival to give him gifts, show that foreign traders were not unknown in Mérida and that commercial contact was being maintained with the eastern Mediterranean. It is likely that such merchants docked at the Roman river port attached to the bridge over the river Guadiana, which is still visible today.

Fidelis was trained by his uncle and took over his functions as bishop when the latter was too old to fulfil them. Such hereditary succession of a bishopric, although uncanonical, was not uncommon in the western Church at this period. A more famous Spanish example is the succession of Isidore to his brother Leander in the see of Seville (*c.* 600). In the case of Fidelis there was some opposition from the local clergy, and he offered to stand down, taking with him the fortune he had inherited from his uncle and which had previously been put to the service of the Church. The threat of this great financial loss proved sufficient to still all opposition and a compromise was reached whereby Fidelis retained the bishopric on condition that his personal wealth became the property of the see of Mérida upon his demise. This is not an isolated incident of financial motivation affecting ecclesiastical appointments, as local churches were very largely dependent upon the wealth of their clergy, both to pay for the erection or restoration of buildings and for the financing of a wide range of charitable activities, such as those soon to be described in the case of Bishop Masona. Priests as well as bishops could be expected to contribute and in many cases, as the clergy were generally, though not necessarily, required to be celibate, their personal wealth might well be bequeathed to their church to become its institutional property on their deaths. As the Church from the fifth century onwards became increasingly important for the economic as well as the spiritual well-being of local communities, and with the system of ecclesiastical financing by way of a tithe on the incomes of the laity still no more than a pious wish, the acquisition of a wealthy clergy became a matter of considerable importance. Thus unsuitable or otherwise unpopular candidates might be elected if financial considerations proved paramount. This could also lead to the effectively forcible ordination of wealthy laymen by local congregations. This happened to the enormously wealthy Aquitanian aristocrat Paulinus of Nola in Barcelona, and Augustine describes the narrow escape of the Roman Senator Pinianus from a similar fate in Africa, when he was taking refuge there after the sack of Rome in 410.[8] Of course, the Church could and did rely for its funds upon the charitable offerings or legacies of members of the laity, as some of the sermons that have survived from the fourth and sixth centuries make clear, but these can at best have been irregular and unreliable. So, however sordid the episode of Fidelis's election may now seem, it makes sense in the light of the problems of church financing of his day, all the more so as receipt of Fidelis's legacy made Mérida into the wealthiest episcopal see in the peninsula.

Fidelis himself used some of his resources for rebuilding the episcopal palace, which collapsed one Sunday morning – miraculously, as our author points out – just after the bishop and his attendants had left it. The palace built to replace it was sumptuously decorated: the walls and floor were completely faced with marble. Fidelis also restored the Basilica of St Eulalia and erected two towers over it, an interesting if rare glimpse of architectural detail.[9] His successor Masona was a builder on an even more lavish scale. He erected a number of monasteries, an episcopal activity later strongly advocated at III Toledo over which he presided, and also several new churches. The monasteries were endowed with farms to make them economically self-supporting. So too was the *xenodochium*, a cross between a hospital and a pilgrim's hostel, that he erected in the city. It was intended to accommodate the sick and travellers, many of whom may have been pilgrims to the shrine of St Eulalia, whose cult was widespread in the peninsula by this time. Physicians were attached to the institution and were required to visit all parts of the city to find and bring in the sick of all religious persuasions. Such a system is unparalleled in the evidence for urban life in the West at this period, but it may not have originated entirely with Masona, as there is a reference to doctors being attached to the Church in the time of the Greek bishop Paul, himself a former physician.

Our source provides evidence of the enormous range of philanthropic activities that a bishop such as Masona could indulge in. As well as building his hospital, he arranged for a free distribution of wine and oil and honey to any in need, a service available both to the citizens of Mérida and to those who came in from the countryside. He also deposited two thousand gold *solidi*, a fairly substantial sum from what comparisons can be made, to be available in interest-free loans. This service was administered by the clergy of the Basilica of St Eulalia. With sufficient funds at his disposal, a bishop could make a considerable impact on the lives of his fellow citizens, not only in respect of their economic and bodily needs but also upon the physical appearance of the city in which they lived.[10] Of course Mérida was exceptional, even in comparison with other metropolitan sees, in respect of the wealth that its bishops had at their disposal. Other bishoprics, less well endowed and more dependent upon the chance offerings and legacies of poorer congregations, must have presented a far less impressive display of episcopal opulence.

However, it was not on secular wealth alone that the status and local influence of a bishop in his town depended. Their spiritual standing was also important. This depended principally on the effectiveness, in local eyes at least, of the bishop's relationship with the patron saint of the city. Spain was particularly well endowed with these, mostly martyr saints of the Decian (249–251) or Diocletianic (303–311) persecutions. Modern scholarship has revealed the existence of some of these saints to be spurious or highly dubious, but that is irrelevant to the important position they occupied in popular devotion from the fourth to seventh centuries, the highest point in the cult of martyrs in early Spanish history. Virtually every town of any note could claim its own particular martyred saint, whose relics would be preserved and venerated, usually in a basilica erected over the supposed site of burial. As well as indigenous saints, with the growth of the traffic in relics from the early fifth century onwards, other non-Spanish cults came to be introduced into the peninsula, especially of Roman and southern Gallic martyrs such as Laurence and Maurice.[11] As small relics of these more 'international' saints came to be acquired, subsidiary basilicas were erected in the Spanish towns to house them, and a series of secondary cults would thus develop alongside that of the central indigenous saint. Such additional cults and their churches distributed in and around the cities and towns may also have catered for refinements in local particularism, with different districts of the towns or surrounding regions being able to focus their loyalty on the saint whose relics and basilica they had in their midst, whilst still reserving a general veneration for the patron saint of the city as a whole. It was possibly to emphasise the cohesion of the whole against the centrifugal tendencies that such secondary cults might encourage, that from the later fifth century onwards liturgical processions come into being in most parts of the western Church. These took the form of ceremonial processions, usually starting and ending at the principal patron saint's basilica, but taking in most of the other churches of the city *en route*. Obviously each town that employed such processions varied them to fit local requirements, and it was possible, as in the City of Rome, to have more than one type of procession. There, as in some of the cities of southern Gaul, special penitential processions came into existence to implore divine assistance in times of plague or war. In Mérida, as doubtless elsewhere, processions seem to have been principally connected with the great feasts of the liturgical year. They manifested the respect of the city for all its cults and highlighted the dominant role of the principal one. The distinction is also mirrored in the miracle stories of the *Lives of the Fathers*, where we find the principals of some of the subsidiary cults, such as Saints Cyprian and Laurence, engaged in performing such homely miracles as enabling a widow to get her bond for a debt cancelled by the bishop, whereas the city's main patron St Eulalia only features in matters of major concern for the community as a whole, as in the quality of harvests and the avoidance of epidemics.[12]

Processions around the city's basilicas, originating in the fifth or sixth centuries, are recorded in both the accounts of Bishops Fidelis and Masona, and the description of an Easter procession conducted by the latter indicates just how magnificent they could be and how central to the city's self-esteem the bishop had become: 'Not only to his bretheren and friends but also to the slaves of the Church did he show himself generous beyond belief. So enriched were these in his time that on the holy day of Easter, when he went in procession to the church, many attendants walked before him as before a king, clothed in silk robes ... a thing no one at that time could do or presumed to do, (they) went ahead of him giving him the homage that was his due.'[13]

The explicit comparison with the king and the unique, indeed presumptuous, nature of Masona's magnificence is particularly striking, and testifies to the wealth and social standing of the bishop in his see. The author's emphasis that such episcopal magnificence was unique 'at that time' suggests that such ostentation was more common at the time of his writing (*c.* 630). Indeed, after some forty years or so of Visigothic royal and aristocratic adherence to the Catholic Church, and consequently of ecclesiastical endowment on their part, this seems probable. However, before the conversion of 589, in periods of weakness of the royal power, a bishop as well-endowed as Masona, with local popular support behind him, could prove a formidable rival to the king, at least within his own see. Such indeed Masona showed himself to be in his encounters with King Leovigild in the latter's attempts either to win over the bishop to the Arian cause, or at least secure possession of the prized relic of St Eulalia's tunic for the Arian congregation in the city. Even exile failed to end the bishop's resistance or to undermine his popular following in Mérida.

Masona's great strength and hold over the mind of his Catholic congregation lay in the apparent power of his ties to St Eulalia. The role of the bishop was to act as intermediary on behalf of the city with the principal patron saint, and the success or failure of his intercession was held to depend upon his own personal character and devotion. The relationship was one of patron and client in the traditional Roman manner. The bishop sought benefits from the saint, who was his peculiar patron, for the good of the community over which he exercised his episcopal authority. Masona was particularly successful in this. For one thing he had been in the service of Eulalia for many years prior to his elevation to the episcopate and had lived in the basilica dedicated to her, probably either as deacon or lay-ascetic. Thus his relationship with the martyr was held to be unusually strong. This and the personal sanctity of Masona's own life made his intercession especially powerful. It is described in the *Lives of the Fathers* thus: 'In his time the Lord in answer to his prayers and because of the merits of the holy virgin Eulalia drove far away and banished from Mérida and all Lusitania the pest of disease and want due to scarcity of food and bestowed upon all the people such good health and so great an abundance of all good things, that no one, even though poor, ever lacked anything or was harassed by any need; but the poor, like the wealthy, abounded in all good things and all the people rejoiced on earth with a sort of celestial joy at the merits of so great a bishop.'[14]

The influence of the saint and the work of the bishop were in no way restricted to the city itself, although this was the main focus of their activity. Lusitania as a whole was encompassed within the bounds of Eulalia's authority, while the bishop's spiritual influence as well as his charity was extended to the countryside. Unlike Baetica, where Cordoba might match Seville, or Tarraconensis, where Barcelona might rival Tarragona, in Lusitania and Galicia there was no other city that could equal Mérida in size or economic and political importance. All too little is known of the relationships between the metropolitan bishops in Mérida and their suffragan bishops in the other sees of the province or of the strength and distribution of other saints' cults, but it is unlikely there was any serious challenge to the dominance of the provincial capital and its patron saint before the Muslim invasion of 711.

Precise details of the interaction of town and countryside, not only for Lusitania, but for Visigothic Spain as a whole, tend to elude us. Clearly there was much interpenetration and the horizons of most social classes must have been highly localised. As can be seen from the *Lives of the Fathers* and a few inscriptions, there were powerful

aristocratic families with landed wealth to be found in southern
Lusitania, some older, of Roman origin, others, more recently
arrived, of Visigothic. One such family was probably based at La
Cocosa, not far from Mérida, where a substantial villa of Late Roman
foundation, with evidence of occupation continuing into the
Visigothic period, has been unearthed.[15] Relations between the
aristocracies, Roman and Gothic, and the local bishops could be
close, as evinced in the case of Mérida in the support given by
Claudius, the *Dux* or Duke of Lusitania, to Masona, matched by the
aid of various Visigothic *comites* or counts to his Arian rival Bishop
Sunna. However, the limitation of our evidence means that we lack
any real indication of the power and influence of these men in their
localities, or of their wealth. Our view is an essentially clerical, indeed
episcopal, one.

Unlike fifth-and sixth-century Gaul, where the existence of a
considerable number of aristocratic episcopal dynasties can be easily
shown, the scantiness of information makes it impossible to assert
that the bishops were or were not largely drawn from a limited
number of aristocratic families, who thereby continued to exercise
some of the local influence of their secular forebears. However, the
antecedents of so few of the Spanish bishops of these centuries are
known that no such deductions may be made. Fructuosus, Bishop of
Braga (*c.* 650) and a noted monastic founder, is known from his *Life* to
have been the son of a Visigothic duke, but such a detail is a rarity.[16]
There are a few episcopal dynasties to be found: Braulio of Zaragoza
(631–651) succeeded his brother John (*c.* 619–631) in that see and
their father appears also to have been a bishop, though of a different
city. However, the previous social standing of the family is completely
unknown. What is fairly striking are the number of aliens who come to
acquire bishoprics. We have already encountered Paul and Fidelis in
Mérida and Martin in Braga, but it is also worth noting that Leander
and Isidore of Seville were members of a family of refugees from
Byzantine Spain. Indeed the fact that they both had Greek names
might suggest that the family originally came from much further east
than that. All of this suggests that, in the sixth century at least,
southern Spain was still functioning as part of a much wider Mediterranean world and that the local aristocracies had not obtained the
virtual monopolies on episcopal office that may be found in the
Auvergne and other parts of southern Gaul at this time.[17]

As has been pointed out above, power at the local level was in a large measure manipulated and articulated through the cult of the patron saints. But exactly how and why devotion to the martyrs and other saints came to be so passionate and generally accepted a part of the religious life of the period is not clear. In the case of Eulalia of Mérida, it has been suggested that the strength of devotion to her in southern Lusitania rests upon the previous existence of the local cult of the goddess Atacaina, an Iberian divinity who in the Roman period was identified with Proserpina. There are apparent similarities between the pagan goddess and the Christian martyr: Atacaina or Proserpina was invoked in the interests of agricultural fertility and she did undergo an act of immolation, albeit involuntarily. However, such comparisons are superficial and the whole explanation simplistic. The real growth of the cult of the martyrs occurred later than, and not as an integral part of, the large-scale conversion of the mass of the population to Christianity. Veneration of Eulalia of Mérida was certainly underway by *c.* 400 when the Spanish Christian poet Prudentius devoted one of the twelve sections of his *Peristephanon* to her.[18] The cult had spread even beyond the confines of Spain to Africa where Augustine in Hippo (395–430) wrote a sermon for her feast-day. But the growth of the ceremonial already referred to, and the development of her cult to its special significance within the city, seem to be more products of the sixth century than of those that preceded it. From this time, and related to the development of ceremonial, comes the writing of liturgy for the feasts of the saints, in the form of masses and prayers and also the composition of passions for liturgical recitation. The sixth century was a particularly rich period for all of these, and in hymn writing too.[19] The *Passion* of St Eulalia was most probably composed at this time and much else of her particular liturgy. Fortunately, just as the Iberian peninsula is peculiarly rich in the number of its venerated martyrs, so is the historian fortunate in the survival of much of the liturgy written to honour them.

Place names and church dedications also provide some indication of the spread of devotion to Eulalia inside the Iberian peninsula. However, this is not quite as straightforward as it may seem, in that the relics of the saint were carried off to the kingdom of the Asturias, in the course of a Christian raid on the Muslim territories, probably in the eighth century. The relics today repose in a side chapel in the Cathedral of Oviedo. As a result, the cult of Eulalia enjoyed something of a new vogue in the north, until finally eclipsed by the devotion to St James and the development of Compostela in the tenth and eleventh centuries. There is an interesting though possibly spurious letter of Alfonso III (866–910), to the community of the monastery of St Martin of Tours, requesting further information about the miracles of their saint and offering to send in return a book describing those of St Eulalia. This must be a reference to the *Lives of the Fathers of Mérida*, indeed the only such reference we have in the literary sources. The difficulty of tracing the spread of the cult of Eulalia of Mérida is complicated by the existence of devotion to a second saint of the same name in the peninsula: St Eulalia of Barcelona. Not surprisingly, much scholarly and partisan controversy has been aroused by this, with some arguing that the cult of Eulalia of Barcelona was no more than a mistaken transformation in the north-east of the peninsula of that of Eulalia of Mérida. However, the surviving liturgical evidence does at least prove that both Eulalias were separately venerated in the Visigothic period.[20]

The account of town life and religion that has been given has inevitably been centred on bishops and martyr saints, because that is the central perspective of the author of our principal source of evidence. We have to see Mérida through his eyes, not forgetting that he was writing over half a century after the period with which he was concerned. The rapid decline of the city after the invasion of 711 and its subsequent neglect has made of it, unlike most other Spanish towns that were in existence in the Roman and Visigothic periods, a potentially rich hunting ground for the archaeologist, with little modern building to hinder access to the sites. Unfortunately, although much work has been done, it has been directed principally at the Roman rather than the later levels, and few of the findings have yet been published. Some deductions can be made by the informed visitor to the sites but a definitive archaeological survey has still to be undertaken. All too many questions remain to be answered and we must for now remain content with the perceptions, however idiosyncratic they may be, from our sole literary source, and in view of the lack of anything comparable for other cities of this period in Spain, be thankful for the little we have. Also the particular importance of the cult of Eulalia in the peninsula in the Visigothic and to some extent Asturian periods makes the information we are given on its workings in its own place of origin of especial interest, and again is something that cannot be paralleled in the surviving evidence before the rise of the cult of Santiago or St James, which will be treated later.

Before parting from the *Lives of the Fathers* and the glimpses it has given of at least some aspects of sixth-century Mérida, it is worth noting the brief *aperçu* of another leading figure in the ecclesiastical hierarchy of the city that it offers: that is the archdeacon. After the bishop this was the most important church office-holder. As can be seen from a number of Gallic examples to be found in the pages of Gregory of Tours's *History* and elsewhere, bishops in the early Middle Ages often had trouble with their archdeacons. For one thing the archdeacon, effectively the bishop's lieutenant and controller of his household, with also a significant role to play in the performance of the liturgy, might in many cases expect to succeed to the episcopate – this was often the case in Rome – and thus would be foremost in opposing a hereditary succession, such as that of Fidelis to Paul. Further, where the succession of the archdeacon was likely or even inevitable, he would have a vested interest in ensuring that the present incumbent did not disperse too many of the goods of the church under his control. Some bishops, for both worthy and unworthy motives, were quite capable of doing this. Pope Agapetus (535–536) had to turn down a request by Caesarius of Arles (502–542) to be allowed to give away all of the wealth of his church in charity.[21] Instead Caesarius handed over complete control of his church's material resources to his deacons to administer, leaving himself free for the pastoral responsibilities he felt distracted from. Similarly Gregory of Tours records how Sidonius Appolinaris of Clerment-Ferrand (*c.* 470–480) was deprived by his archdeacon's gaining of an injunction from continuing to exercise control over the wealth of his church.[22] A story about Masona makes sense when seen in this context. On his deathbed the bishop manumitted, that is to say gave legal status of freedom, to some of the slaves owned by the church, who had served him particularly well. Such gestures were not uncommon. Fidelis had cancelled all debts owing to the church of Mérida prior to his death. However, the archdeacon Eleutherius, who clearly expected to be elected to the bishopric once vacant, warned the freed slaves that they would be made to return the money and other property given them by Masona when the bishop died and he had succeeded him. He showed his hand too soon, as the freed slaves told Masona of the archdeacon's threat. The sick bishop then prayed in the Basilica of St Eulalia that Eleutherius should predecease him and refused to be persuaded to retract his plea despite the frenzied appeals of the unfortunate archdeacon's mother. Clearly the whole proceeding was a public and awesome occasion. Not surprisingly, within a few days Eleutherius fell ill and died. In due course Masona came to be succeeded by Innocent, the youngest of the Méridan deacons, who, like his predecessor, was peculiarly efficacious in ensuring the continued agricultural prosperity of his province by virtue of his great spiritual merits.[23]

Just as we know all too little about ordinary civil life in the city in the period, albeit plentifully informed about its religious affairs, so too does the *Lives of the Fathers* fail to tell us about the civil and military administration, whilst being most forthcoming on aspects of the ecclesiastical. Our author does refer to various Gothic counts who opposed Bishop Masona. One of these, interestingly, is named as the future king Witteric (603–610). It is unlikely from what we do know of Visigothic administrative practices that more than one of these officials was permanently resident in Mérida. This was the *Comes Civitatis* or Count of the City, appointed by the king as the principal royal representative and civil administrator in the city. He was also responsible for the overseeing of the running of local lands belonging to the royal fisc and doubtless for forwarding at least a proportion of their revenues to the officials in charge of the king's treasures. The counts, drawn from the upper strata of Gothic society, also had responsibility for the local Visigothic population and controlled what garrison there might be in the city. They also acted as judges in law suits involving purely Gothic participants, whilst another official, the *iudex* or judge, did the same for the Roman population. This was more likely to have represented a distinction between military and civil jurisdiction than one between rival systems of national laws, as is sometimes made out.

This of course raises the crucial questions of the nature, extent and whereabouts of the Visigothic settlement. Unfortunately only hypothetical or negative answers can be given. If it is accepted that the cemeteries excavated by the German archaeologist Zeiss in the 1930s do not necessarily represent Visigothic necropolises but are just as likely to be those of indigenous Ibero-Roman communities, then the notion of the Meseta – the high plateau land of Leon and Old Castille – as the principal area of Gothic settlement must be given up.[24] This view has not been sufficiently forcibly challenged, as archaeologists have remained content enough with it not to look for alternatives, and it has led historians to interpret many facets of the history of these centuries in terms of conflict between a Gothic north and a Romanised south and east. However, Visigothic garrisons must have been established in the major urban centres of the peninsula from the fifth century onwards, leading to a diffuse settlement, with lands all over Spain being distributed and redistributed to their particular followers by successive kings. They, in turn, are likely to have settled their own supporters and families on the newly acquired lands. Such Goths will have retained a military potential, to be used in service in the cities under the *comes* or on a larger scale under the provincial *dux*. Along the frontiers with the Franks and in the Basque regions a permanent military presence will have been needed, whereas in other parts, once the internal disorders of the sixth century had passed from memory, the military functions of the counts must have declined, and in the course of the seventh century a far greater degree of integration between those of Roman and those of Visigothic descent in the population become possible, leading to the breaking down of the functional and administrative distinctions that had previously existed.

It would be valuable to know if, and to what degree, the Visigothic settlement created a moderately stable local Gothic aristocracy to exist side by side with the longer-standing Roman one that we know was still in being. If so, mutual co-operation between sectors of both in the furtherance or protection of their local interests against the outside interference (that might be represented by the king, or even the Church) may be a reasonable surmise, and a better guide to an understanding of the intense local particularism that marks the whole history of early Medieval Spain than any explanation based upon ideas of fierce racial disharmony. In the Visigothic period it would be interesting to know where the counts fitted into such a context. Were they largely drawn from the ranks of the local aristocracy or were they principally Palatine officials sent from the court or another part of the kingdom? In Merovingian Gaul the local nobility was trying by the early seventh century to obtain something of a monopoly on such offices, but there is no knowing if a parallel development occurred in Spain.

We are no better informed about the administrative staff and procedures that the counts had available to them. However, it does look as if the practice of issuing charters to grant or confirm possession of land was being employed by the king by the late sixth century, in a way very similar to that we shall find in use in Catalonia in the ninth. It also seems likely, as is certainly the case in that later period, that the local count had a role to play in the process. There is a reference in the *Lives of the Fathers of Mérida* to Leovigild granting an estate together with the slaves attached to it to the African hermit Nanctus. Interestingly, this is described as being done by the issue of a written deed, despatched to the local official in charge of the lands belonging to the royal fisc.[25] Unfortunately no complete charter survives from the Visigothic period, but in view of such references as this, and the need for some antecedents to the later procedures that can be documented, it is not unreasonable to suspect their existence.[26]

One story in the *Lives of the Fathers of Mérida* provides a unique insight into the obligations of social status in Visigothic Spain. It is clear, from such evidence as laws which lay down different penalties for offenders of higher and lower social class, that society was stratified. Emphases on lineage and prerogatives may also suggest that distinctions of class were fairly rigid. There is no evidence of social mobility and the upper levels of society were clearly expected to display a magnificence and probably a munificence that not only reflected their own status but also shed lustre upon their dependants and clients.

The story in question shows what could happen when such conventions, which imposed restrictions on the behaviour of all levels of society, were flouted. The African hermit Nanctus, invested with royal estates in the vicinity of Mérida by Leovigild, preserved his original unkempt appearance and pastured his own sheep. His new slaves, those tied to the estates, were so horrified that they murdered him, proclaiming that it was better for them to die than to have to serve such a master. Of course, they all came to a bad end, which for the author was the point of the story, but it does also provide us with a brief glimpse of social attitudes and expectations in Visigothic Spain, to lay alongside less personal and immediate impressions to be gleaned from the laws.[27]

The conclusions to be drawn from studying Mérida in the Visigothic period, slight and partial as they may be, suggest that we are looking at a city that had changed surprisingly little from its Late Roman past. Buildings remained and new ones were erected within a tradition recognisably linked with earlier centuries. The commercial importance of the city, as in Roman times, was still considerable, as may be seen from the distribution of its artistic products over a wide area of south-western Spain. Its coinage was plentiful throughout the later sixth and seventh centuries and examples of it have come to light in most parts of the peninsula.[28] In the sixth century at least, merchants could visit it from as far away as the eastern Mediterranean, and Greek doctors and African hermits could take up residence there. Such openness to the wider world must have continued into the seventh century, as the author of the *Lives of the Fathers of Mérida* found nothing strange or untoward in these events in themselves in his incidental recording of them. Of course, considerable changes in the population had occurred with the coming of the Visigothic nobility and their followers, but these seem to have fitted relatively easily into the pattern of local alliances and loyalties. The division by race can have mattered little if a Goth could be as devoted to the patron saint of the city as Masona was, and rise to become its bishop and Metropolitan of Lusitania. Why not, seeing that his two predecessors had been Greeks? Some aspects of administration and government may have changed from Roman days, but not substantially, and in these areas the Visigoths were merely building upon Roman foundations. A better understanding of the military and governmental procedures of Late Roman times, especially of the fifth century, might make some features of the Germanic successor kingdoms less different from those of their great predecessor than they now appear. On the basis of what has been seen in Mérida, and most of it must be true of the other major cities of the south, the notion of the isolation of Spain in the Visigothic period needs to be drastically revised. Certain parts of the peninsula remained, particularly in the light of continued Byzantine political and commercial interest in the West, very much part of a wider Mediterranean world.

All of that may be true of some regions, particularly the south and the eastern seaboard, but there certainly were parts of the peninsula that were, and in some cases still are, remote from not only the world beyond the frontiers but even from the rest of the kingdom. Also, however cosmopolitan some aspects of the cities might be, to go outside of them into the countryside was to enter a zone of rapidly diminishing horizons, as indeed it had been in previous centuries. Little as we may really know about the cities, it is much harder to gain any impression of those other parts of the peninsula, especially where there was little urbanisation and where Roman tradition had a weak hold. The *Life of St Aemilian* written by Bishop Braulio of Zaragoza (631–651) for his brother Fronimian, abbot of the monastery that grew around the site of Aemilian's former hermitage, does give some glimpses of life in the upper Ebro valley in the later sixth century. The work itself is further evidence of that considerable process of liturgical composition that was carried out in Spain in the sixth and seventh centuries. The *Life*, which is basically a collection of miracle stories put in roughly chronological setting, was composed for recitation during mass on the feast day of the saint. Braulio also had his archdeacon, Eugenius, later to be Bishop of Toledo (646–657) write the prayers for the mass. The probable text of these has survived, as has a hymn in honour of Aemilian, which may also be the work of Eugenius.

In the *Life* various local aristocrats are mentioned, qualified by the titles Senator or Curial, a term in Late Roman usage equivalent more or less to town councillor. Some of these men are named and some of these, such as Sicorius or Tuentius, appear to be indigenous; that is to say of neither Roman nor Gothic origin, and this may hint at the survival of a continuing Cantabrian nobility. Other senators have Roman names, such as Honorius and Nepotianus. The latter is of especial interest, as there appears to have been an important Roman aristocratic family that bore this name living across the Pyrenees in southern Aquitaine, one of whose members was Master of the Soldiers in Spain in 461.[29] The curials mentioned, such as Maximus, may have been members of the urban senates of the few towns, such as Calahorra, that existed in the region, but it is possible that both titles, of senator and of curial, were by the later sixth century basically honorifics retained by families that had once formally been of those ranks in the Roman local government structure. Such titles have already been encountered in the pages of the *Lives of the Fathers of Mérida* in stories that refer to senators in Lusitania, and there has been much unresolved argument as to what extent, if at all, Roman urban senates still survived in a period when most of their former functions can be found being exercised by Visigothic counts and others.[30] The balance of probability favours the disappearance of the institutions but the survival of the titles. However, from the *Life of St Aemilian* we do learn of the existence in the sixth century of a most unusual body that was actually functioning, called the Senate of Cantabria.[31] Whether such an institution existed in the Roman period or whether it was the peculiar creation of the disturbed times of the fifth and sixth centuries, a form of local self-government established by the senatorial and curial families of the region, is unknown. Its nature and functions are unclear, as are the geographical limits of its authority. The term 'Cantabria' is now used to refer to the area of the Cantabrian mountains, in central northern Spain. However, there are indications in the *Life* that in Braulio's day the word could also be used of parts of the upper Ebro valley. Whatever the answers to these questions might be, the existence of the institution and the lives of some of its members were terminated violently by Leovigild, during the course of his campaigns in the north in the 570s.

Whilst the stories in the *Life* often refer to such local aristocrats and their servants and, less frequently, to clerics and monks, they tell us nothing of the lives of the country people, who led a largely transhumant pastoral existence, and whose social organisation must have been very different from that of the town dwellers, even in the same region of the peninsula. A little more about them may be learnt or guessed at from the early history of the Basques. In the pages of Braulio's *Life of St Aemilian* these and other essentially tribal and unassimilated peoples such as the Ruccones, do not appear, although many of them must have lived in the area of the saint's activities in the Rioja. This, however, probably reflects more on the author's interests or those of the work's monastic recipients, as Aemilian, who, apart from a brief and enforced period spent as a priest, lived most of his life in the fastnesses of the countryside. At this time the Basques were almost certainly still pagan, and others might well have been likewise. It has been conjectured most sensibly that the real penetration of Christianity into this north-west Pyrenean area only began with the establishment in it of ascetics like Aemilian who lived and made churches in caves, and may in due course have come to exercise considerable influence over the inhabitants of the surrounding mountainous countryside.[32] The wider reputation of Aemilian and others like him, whose names are now lost, meant that others would come after them and communities of monks grow up around them in their lifetimes or develop in their former dwelling places and around their relics. In this way, Aemilian having died (*c.* 580), a monastic community had come into existence at the site of his death at Berceo by the early seventh century.

The process of the penetration of the northern Spanish and Pyrenean countryside continued from at least the late sixth century throughout the seventh. Certain figures stand out, such as Aemilian, Fructuosus of Braga (*fl. c.* 650/660) and Valerius of Bierzo (*fl. c.* 680/690), either because of their own writings or because of what was written about them. However, there were many other solitaries, monks and monastic founders whose names are lost to us. These are the men whose cumulative responsibility it was to have ensured the Christian penetration of the Rioja, Alava, the Bierzo and Montserrat, all later to be the sites of important monasteries. It was in the monasteries of the later Visigothic period, that such men founded or inspired, rather than in the few towns of these regions, that so much that was to be found of importance for the future was developed. For their Christianising of those mountainous regions, virtually untouched by Rome, prepared the way for their transformation from being the most backwards parts of the peninsula into becoming the bastions of resistance to Islam and the birth places of the new Spanish kingdoms of the *Reconquista*.

The Rulers of the People

ONE of the most disappointing features of the study of Visigothic Spain is the lack of available detail on so many aspects of the history of the kingdom. So little is known about the personalities of the kings, their policies, the lives and preoccupations of the nobility, to say nothing of the daily round of their social inferiors, that the whole of the seventh century tends to look uniform and frustratingly intangible. The only individuals who stand out are those few bishops who are known from their writings, and the subjects that can be most satisfactorily studied, from the relative abundance of their surviving evidence are law, both civil and canon, and theology. The secular activities of the Visigothic kingdom can best be seen as mirrored in the law codes, but these are not necessarily accurate guides to practical reality. However, for all of the difficulties raised by the lack of certain kinds of evidence, notably historical writing, some assessments of the activities and interests of the Visigothic kings and their principal subjects can be made. The lower strata of society in this period unfortunately hardly emerge from behind the impersonal legal classifications of the codes.

Visigothic kings and their successors in the Christian states of the next three centuries in the peninsula never emancipated themselves from being principally the war-leaders of their people. They were hardly unique in this, for it is equally true of their fellow Germanic kings and of most of their Roman and Byzantine imperial predecessors and contemporaries. Thus the prime interest of the king was in war: either in defending the frontiers of his realm from external enemies, or in extending them at the expense of neighbours. Possibly an even more important and frequent call upon the king's time and energies was the conduct of military operations inside the kingdom for the maintenance of internal order and the making effective of royal authority over local subordinates. The threat of force was the only practical sanction of that authority, although supernatural ones were increasingly invoked through the employment of oaths of loyalty.[33]

Much hinged upon a king's success, or lack of it, in the conduct of his military undertakings, not least his own survival. Warfare was intimately connected with the political stability of the kingdom, and also in some measure to its economic prosperity. The Visigothic rulers, like their Frankish and other Germanic contemporaries, inherited various rights and powers from the Roman emperors whom they had replaced. These included limited rights of legislation, which it took them some time to exceed, but may not have comprised the kind of comprehensive powers of taxation once exercised by the emperors. Taxation can only be raised effectively where a right to levy it is recognised, however grudgingly. The Visigothic monarchy received revenue from the lands belonging to the royal fisc, which included all of the former imperial possessions in the peninsula, together with others that successive kings may have confiscated. Whether they inherited residual rights to tax their Roman subjects is unclear, and whether they could have had any such powers over their free Gothic ones, who had never been subject to Roman taxation, is most doubtful.

At the same time the demands made upon a king's generosity by the more powerful men in the kingdom, particularly at times of political crisis or in the aftermath of a royal succession, must have been considerable. Unless the possessions of the fisc were to be alienated, thus further depleting the principal source of the royal revenue, land and property acquired by conquest was necessary to maintain political loyalty. In the period that stretches from the beginning of the campaigns of Leovigild in 570 to the final expulsion of the Byzantines in 624, the wars of the Visigothic monarchy served to strengthen royal authority by providing a fairly ready source of supply of lands, goods and offices to reward the king's friends and to increase their number. That this period of expansion, which ended when the peninsula was effectively pacified and unified, should be followed very rapidly by the political upheavals of the 630s is hardly surprising. However, during those decades the Visigothic monarchy had, through the conversion of Reccared I, gained a new and valuable ally that proved a staunch friend in the difficult times to come.

The kingdom united, in its religious convictions at least, by the decisions of III Toledo and the extinction of Arianism, was potentially much stronger than it had ever been before. The major ideological rift that had divided the population and provided opportunities for the polarisation of local struggles and tensions had disappeared and, as was made clear at III Toledo, this opened the way for the Catholic Church to rally actively around the Visigothic monarchy. The Church realised well enough the benefits that could be conferred by the existence of a strong central authority, but was unable to accept them at the hands of an Arian king. However, for all of the new spirit of co-operation and harmony, certain basic problems still faced the kingdom and would continue to do so throughout the course of the succeeding century.

The difficulty of imposing a single centralised authority on all parts of the peninsula, with its rich diversity of local cultures and the immense problems of communication and enforcement posed by its geography, remained as formidable as ever. The Catholic kings, from Reccared onwards, at least had the advantage of a greater will to co-operate on the part of many of the leaders of local society, especially the bishops, than had previously existed. But this benevolence needed to be actively maintained and the parts kept continuously involved in the concerns of the whole. Some of the most difficult areas of the peninsula, as far as authority based in Toledo was concerned, were the northern regions of Galicia, the Asturias and Cantabria. However, as a result of Leovigild's campaigns and the penetration of Christianity, these regions were now more open to Romano-Gothic culture and with it royal power. The Basques, however, remained virtually untouched and presented the greatest military demands to the Visigothic kingdom in the seventh century. The Basques showed no signs of being affected by the civilisation of their Visigothic and Frankish neighbours and attempts, initiated by Leovigild, to control their transhumant nomadism appear to have been to no avail. Two Visigothic kings founded towns in the Basque regions: Leovigild erecting Victoriacum (Vitoria) after his campaign in 581 and Suinthila (621–631) persuading some Basques to form a settlement at an unspecified site in the course of his reign. In this respect the kings were following precedents set by their Roman predecessors in their attempts to pacify and Romanise Cantabria through a programme of urbanisation. If this was their intention the effects were clearly limited. The Basques appear to have retained their paganism, although there was a bishopric at Pamplona, and were quick to take advantage of any Visigothic military weakness to raid the settlements of the upper Ebro valley, even penetrating as far south as Zaragoza. Both kings Sisebut (612–621) and Suinthila (621–631) undertook substantial campaigns against them. This may have been a contributory factor in the simultaneous migration of some of the Basque tribes out of the Pyrenees into southern Aquitaine, where they came to pose a considerable problem for successive Frankish kings.[34] However, this by no means solved the problem for the Visigothic monarchy, and on at least two occasions would-be usurpers in the north-east of the peninsula sought Basque assistance in their schemes (653 and 672).

Whilst the difficulties posed by the failure of the Visigothic kingdom to assimilate or control the Basques remained as considerable for the seventh-century kings as for their predecessors, the danger to be anticipated from other external enemies was in practice greatly reduced. The Franks were generally embroiled in their own difficulties for much of the time, and after the death of Theoderic II in 613 the threat of Frankish royal expeditions against Visigothic territories was small, except when their aid was actively solicited, as in the case of the assistance given by Dagobert I (629–636) to the rebel count Sisenand in 631, which enabled the latter to overthrow King Suinthila and take his throne.[35] But Frankish involvement in the affairs of the Visigothic kingdom was slight and with the exception of the support given to Sisenand in 631, which cost him 200,000 gold solidi, unsuccessful. In 672, when the Franks came to the assistance of a local usurper, Paul, in Narbonne, they were easily driven out again by the forces of the legitimate ruler as in 588.[36] But, although in practice limited, the potential menace of the Franks may well have weighed more heavily on the minds of the Visigothic kings than our meagre sources can now reveal. The last details we are given on features of the diplomacy carried on between the two peoples are to be found in an exchange of letters dating from the reign of King Gundemar (610–612).[37] The silence of the sources should not make us ignore the possibility of more pacific commercial and cultural contacts between the kingdoms. A letter of introduction and recommendation to the ecclesiastical and secular authorities was given by Bishop Desiderius of Cahors (d. 652) to a cleric who

proposed to make a journey into Spain.³⁸ Such chance survivals do at
least give credence to the possibility of wider contacts than has
usually been allowed by those wedded to a belief in the essential
isolation of Spain in the Visigothic period.

Another old enemy of the realm whose menace may have pressed
more heavily on the kingdom than its practical potential to interfere
would have warranted was the Byzantine Empire. After the death of
the emperor Maurice in 602, the Empire underwent crisis after crisis
throughout the course of the seventh century, facing enemies on two
fronts: in the east the Persians and then from 634 the Arabs, and in the
Balkans the Avars from beyond the Danube and the Slavs attempting
to settle south of it in imperial territory. The Empire was also riven by
serious internal religious and social divisions. In general it was in no
condition to launch the kind of expeditions against the Germanic
kingdoms that had been possible in the sixth century. Even when
Constans II (641–668) moved the imperial capital from
Constantinople to Syracuse he was unable to make any headway
against the Lombards in Italy. Nor could Byzantine Africa pose an
independent threat to the Visigothic kingdom. Indeed by the very end
of the century, if the unanimous testimony of the Arab historians is to
be believed, the Visigoths had returned to Africa for the first time
since they were evicted in the reign of Theudis (531–548), and gained
control of at least Ceuta on the continental mainland. However, for all
of the relative weakness of their formerly threatening neighbours and
the final expulsion of Byzantine forces from the peninsula by
Suinthila in 624, the Visigothic kings remained acutely sensitive to
the dangers of external aggression, and to the possibility of
discontented groups within the realm conspiring with hostile powers
beyond the frontiers. Several laws, both civil and ecclesiastical, were
passed imposing secular and spiritual penalties upon those who either
plotted with or fled for refuge to any of the kingdom's enemies.³⁹

The almost obsessive fear of the kings and their advisers of the
dangers to be apprehended from the actions of inimical powers had its
roots not so much in their active hostility towards their neighbours, as
in the inherent weaknesses of the political structure of Visigothic
society. Royal authority was still very fragile. The difficulties of
internal order and external vigilance meant that the essentially
military character of Visigothic kingship went on unchanged into the
seventh century. The kings had to be able to fight, and fight
successfully. Unlike the Franks, the Visigoths had never adhered to a

single royal dynasty; in this they were like the Lombards, whose history is marked by frequent dynastic changes and even a ten-year interval when they had no king at all (574–584).[40] Visigothic kings had to be visibly and successfully warriors, thus the succession of minors created insoluble problems of credibility and in every case child rulers fell victims to aristocratic *coups d'état*. Despite the achievements of his father Reccared and grandfather Leovigild, the infant Liuva II (601–603) was deposed, mutilated and murdered by the Gothic nobility, led by Witteric. In 621 the child king Reccared II died suspiciously within a month of succeeding his father Sisebut (612–621), and in 642 the brief rule of the boy king Tulga (639–642) was terminated by the usurpation, with aristocratic backing, of Chindasuinth (642–653).

The principal effect of the need for efficient war-leadership in Visigothic kingship is that it did make dynastic succession impossible in the long term. Just as the dynasty of Theoderic I (419–451) had foundered due to its military incompetencies in the face of Frankish aggression, so the various successor dynasties failed to establish themselves securely enough to be able to carry off successfully the transmission of power to a child, or to survive military disaster. In theory the kingship of the Visigoths was, from its earliest appearance in our sources, purely elective; in practice though, from the time of Alaric I onwards it appears that when the reigning monarch had a male heir of age, son might be expected to succeed father automatically, with the process of election no more than a formality. Even those child kings who so quickly came to be deposed, were initially accepted because they were the direct heirs of the former ruler and only on their subsequent inability to perform their functions were they disposed of. If election had been the serious and fundamental part of the process of kingmaking that it is often claimed to be, how do we explain the Visigothic nobility voluntarily choosing children as kings? The point is that it was only in the most exceptional circumstances that election played a crucial role in the choosing of a new king. This occurred in 672 after the death of Reccesuinth (648–672), who seems to have had no male heirs and, as we are told in Julian of Toledo's *History of Wamba* (written in the 670s), the army then elected Wamba (672–680).[41] Even in this case it is hard to credit that we are talking of an open election. Much negotiation and prior planning must have preceded the spontaneous unanimity of Wamba's selecting. In reality, direct dynastic succession was the norm in the transmission of royal power in the Visigothic kingdom, but this was tempered by the occasional natural failure of a line to produce an heir and by successful conspiracy or revolt.

Only when a dynasty failed, as each did in turn, and left no heir or only a minor, did serious problems arise in relation to the succession. For then election did become of crucial importance. An elected king, drawn from the ranks of the Visigothic nobility, would have to command a substantial body of support amongst the rest of the aristocracy. Those who were currently holding office at court were particularly influential in this respect. Obviously the choice of a new king was not an easy one to make. Factions must have existed amongst the aristocracy, the details of which we are now ignorant. As well as divisions in the palatine nobility, elections to the kingship sometimes created upheavals in the provinces. Powerful groups of nobles with military authority occasionally rebelled, either, as in the case of Paul in 672, to create independent regional kingdoms, or to seek to reverse the decision by force of a centrally made election. This latter might be caused by fear of replacement by the new régime or be in order to test the capabilities of the new king, who if unsuccessful might be deserted by his own followers. Even a king who succeeded in effect by family inheritance, such as Reccesuinth, would not necessarily be immune from such a challenge. In 653, Reccesuinth, although already king in asssociation with his father Chindasuinth (642–653), for four years was faced by the rebellion of Froila in the north-east.[42] A king's authority was frail until proved in war.

It was not just kingship that was affected by this potential flaw at the heart of the Visigothic political system: power throughout the whole of the kingdom was influenced by the changes in the ruling families. For with the ending or overthrow of a king or dynasty the position of all office-holders and supporters of the previous régime would be called into question. In the case of a usurpation those who had brought the new king into power would expect to be rewarded with the offices and influence of those who had benefited from the previous ruler. Some of the latter might succeed in changing sides in time, but it is unlikely that the majority would. In view of the general difficulties of royal finance and the dangers inherent upon the excessive alienation of the king's own properties, the confiscation of the estates of the supporters of the overthrown dynasty provided an obvious means of enabling the new king to reward those to whom he was indebted or whose goodwill he wished to ensure. Thus a change in dynasty could have far-reaching consequences for the aristocracy and significant effects upon the relative local power and influence of rival noble families. Indeed a change of dynasty could provide occasion for quite a violent upheaval. Thus according to the Frankish *Chronicle of Fredegar* (mid seventh century) the succession of Chindasuinth in 642, which involved the replacement of the dynasty of Chintila (636–639) and Tulga (639–642), was followed by the execution of seven hundred members of the Gothic aristocracy.[43] From the Law Code it is fair to assume that this would have been accompanied by the expropriation of their estates. Even allowing that the anonymous but contemporary author of this part of the *Chronicle* may have grossly exaggerated the numbers involved, this particular usurpation was clearly the occasion for a major change in the distribution of power in the kingdom.

In view of this it is hardly surprising to find that changes in ruler were frequently accompanied by violence and revolt in Visigothic Spain. The friends and dependants of a former king, and this could extend down into relatively low levels of society, as all those with any ties to the ruler and his more important followers would be affected, clearly stood to lose a great deal in both status and office if the new monarch was inimical to them or was able to dispense with their services. For such men, as for the Arian supporters of Leovigild in 587–590, revolt could be the only way to alter the new balance of power. Conversely, such men's interests lay in ensuring the maintenance of the dynasty to which they were committed, and this could involve attempting to secure the succession of a minor, as in 601, 621 and 639. If this proved impossible or unworkable, then the alternative was to bring about the election of one of their own number to ensure the maintenance of the status quo. This is the likeliest explanation of the apparently peaceful transfers of power that occurred in 612 and 636. But if thwarted, or if the consensus amongst the ruling group could not be maintained, then rebellion might prove the only alternative to prosecution and deprivation under a new and unsympathetic régime that needed to recover what had been given away by its predecessor in order to reward its own adherents.

Attempts were made by the Church to deal with this problem. V and VI Toledo (636 and 638) legislated to protect the family and dependants of former kings, trying to ensure reasonable security for them.[44] Whether this had any effect in practice is unlikely as the enactments were essentially part of an over-optimistic attempt by

King Chintila (636–639) to ensure the future protection of his own family and followers. These, however, are likely to have been the very people to have borne the brunt of the violent changes attendant upon Chindasuinth's usurpation in 642. The sharp distinction drawn between the personal and inheritable family lands and property of the king and those that he held temporarily and in trust by virtue of his office, expounded by VIII Toledo (653) and enshrined in a contemporary civil law, may also have served to protect the interest of the royal family, when dispossessed of the kingship.[45] Again we cannot know if this worked in practice, and it was not necessarily the primary purpose of the legislation.

Thus it was not just the Church, as is so often thought, anxious for the stability and protection that strong kingship could offer, but also substantial sections of lay society that had a firm interest in ensuring hereditary succession or at least the smooth transfer of royal power with the minimum of upheaval. This can be illustrated by the letter of Bishop Braulio of Zaragoza, written in conjunction with Celsus, probably the local count, urging King Chindasuinth in 649 to make his son Reccesuinth co-ruler, and thus obviate the problems of succession.[46] They were probably not alone in their feelings, as this is precisely what the king did. Political instability was not in the interests of any except those suffering or excluded under the present régime. Indeed a king who achieved power through usurpation could make his own role as ruler harder thereby. Thus when Sisenand deposed Suinthila with Frankish aid in 631, he initiated, by exposing the weaknesses of royal authority, over a decade of political insecurity and upheaval. One of the consequences of this was that the monarchy came to lean more heavily on the Church, in a fashion unprecedented since 589, and thereby initiated a period of intense conciliar activity. It was the problems of this period, not the precedent of III Toledo, that gave the church councils held in Toledo so special a place in the political and judicial life of the kingdom in the seventh century.

Royal interest in Church councils was made clear from III Toledo onwards. The kings frequently attended in person those councils of the whole Spanish Church held in Toledo, and some of the business conducted there overlapped the borders between the secular and the clerical. On occasion the ruler was armed with spiritual weapons to use against his temporal enemies, as in the decreeing of excommunication for those who conspired or rebelled against him.[47] To the king, too, was reserved the right of pardoning such offenders.

Certain secular laws were also quickly paralleled by ecclesiastical legislation.

The practice developed whereby the king began the deliberations of a council by delivering a tome, or written speech, which laid down certain themes and issues that the monarch wished the bishops to discuss. The first of these appears at the beginning of the acts of III Toledo. No more are known until that issued by Reccesuinth to VIII Toledo in 653, but from XII Toledo of 681 onwards they become a standard feature. It is possible that the texts of other tomes have been lost, but if not, the responsibility for making them a regular part of conciliar procedure must rest with Bishop Julian and King Ervig. This may in practice represent greater control over the councils by the bishops of Toledo, who by their access to the monarchs might influence the contents of the tomes.

The acts of some of the councils were terminated by a royal decree confirming the proceedings and giving them force as law. These are found more frequently than royal tomes, and it has been suggested that those councils, such as VII or X Toledo, that lack such 'laws in confirmation' had incurred royal disapproval and that their acts were possibly thereby invalidated.[48] However, this is unlikely; it is more sensible to assume that, as with the issue of the tomes, the procedure became standardised in the later seventh century and that previously the practice was followed when some special force needed to be given to the acts, as for those of the sixth Council of Toledo which considered the protection of the monarch. Councils that lack such laws may be found to have concerned themselves exclusively with matters of internal ecclesiastical order.

Our knowledge of the councils of the Spanish Church, from the earliest held at Elvira (Granada), around the year 300, up to XVII Toledo of 694, comes from a series of collections of conciliar acts compiled at various stages in the seventh and early eighth centuries. The first of these, it has been argued, was put together by Isidore of Seville between 619 and 633, who added the Spanish canons to earlier collections of African and Gallic ones. Later in the seventh century, the acts of the subsequent Spanish councils, from those of IV Toledo in 633 to those of XV Toledo in 688, were added to the initial compilation of Isidore. This second version has been attributed with some justification to Bishop Julian of Toledo (680–690).[49] The whole corpus, known from its place of origin as the *Hispana*, passed into Gaul in the eighth century and became one of the principal sources of canon law in western Europe in succeeding centuries. In Spain however, sometime between 694 and 704 a final version of the collection was prepared incorporating the acts of councils subsequent to XV Toledo (688) up to those of XVII Toledo (694). These never became part of the fundamental corpus of the *Hispana*, and the last council of the Visigothic kingdom, that of XVIII Toledo held in 704, according to a reference in an eighth-century chronicle, has left us no written acts at all. The Muslim invasion of 711 put an end to this chain of canonical compilation.

Thus our knowledge of the existence of councils depends principally upon the awareness of those, notably Isidore and Julian, who incorporated their acts into collections. That some provincial councils, particularly of the sixth century, were unknown to these compilers and hence have left no trace of their existence, is confirmed by the case of a Baetican provincial synod, held probably in Seville *c.* 625, known from the correspondence of Isidore and Braulio of Zaragoza, but without extant acts.[50] Incidentally there is another theoretical danger that may be raised here: that seventh century and later compilers or copyists deliberately altered or falsified the acts of the earlier councils in order to give an appearance of spurious antiquity to relatively recently developed claims and regulations. There are certain features about the acts of II Toledo of 527 that give rise to such suspicions.

The canonical legislation of a particular council can often look haphazard and erratic. An apparently random selection of topics may be treated with little or no obvious connection between the consecutive enactments. However, the nature of canon law was intended to be cumulative. Thus the new legislation of councils supplemented the existing body of law, at least in so far as it was known. Hence the importance of such great canonical collections as the *Hispana*. What was discussed at particular councils was determined by the disciplinary cases brought before the bishops or by the need to reform prevalent local abuses. These issues might then be decided on the basis of authoritative decisions of earlier councils or, if these were lacking, new regulations propounded to deal with the circumstances which in turn, when incorporated into collections, might serve as precedents for the future. There is in this respect an unnoticed and striking similarity between the functioning of canonical and royal secular law codes of these centuries.

One common approach to this conciliar material which is unsound is the taking of individual laws, removing them from the particular context of the time and place in which they were promulgated and treating them as having relevance to the history of the kingdom as a whole. Thus, in condemning the supposed weaknesses of the Visigothic state, some historians have taken laws or canons issued for example in the 630s and treated them as being symptomatic of the condition of the kingdom in the 690s or 700s. Obviously such laws were still valid at the later time but the circumstances, possibly no more than a single case that required adjudication, that had called them into being belonged to the past, and there is no justification for assuming widespread or continuing survival of the offence thus condemned. Assessments of several apparently prejudicial features of the society of Visigothic Spain tend to be made without sufficient awareness of the need for a chronological context for the evidence used.

This can be illustrated by the relationship between the kings and the Church as mirrored in the legislation of the various councils held in Toledo in the course of the seventh century. In the conciliar acts may be found a number of striking gestures made towards the enhancement of royal authority. The king was given the power to use ecclesiastical sanctions on his own initiative, and similarly the threat of excommunication was wielded by the bishops against any who might seek to overthrow or conspire against the monarch. The future security of members of the royal family and the protection of the king's *fideles* after his death was also legislated for on more than one occasion.

Now whilst the overall impression that this gives of the existence of close ties between monarchy and Church, and the interest of the latter in maintaining strong and stable kingship is certainly not erroneous, the individual enactments make most sense when fitted into their proper chronological context, which also highlights the fluctuations in the relationship, which tend to be obscured when it is taken as a generalised whole.

The conciliar enactments relating to the kings and to their families and followers come from only two periods: the 630s and the 680s, products of deliberations at IV, V and VI Toledo (633, 636 and 638) and at XIII and XV Toledo (683 and 688). One or two other royal references are to be found, such as the third canon of the Council of Mérida of 666 which regulated ecclesiastical observances to be followed when the king undertook a military operation, but these were not enactments issued at the ruler's behest or concerned with his powers. Both the 630s and the 680s were periods of political instability, probably the worst that the kingdom suffered.

In 631 Suinthila was overthrown by the count Sisenand, with the assistance of the Frankish king Dagobert I. Although both Sisenand (631–636) and his successor Chintila (636–639) survived brief reigns to die of natural causes, both may have been challenged by usurpers. One of these was almost certainly Iudila, known only from a few coins issued in Cordoba which may be dated stylistically to this decade.[51] Chintilla's son Tulga (639–642) was successfully overthrown by a conspiracy in 642 led by Chindasuinth (642–653), with whose accession some stability was restored.

In the 680s changes of dynasty may have been less violent, but the strength of royal authority was no more certain. Wamba's deposition in 680 was distinctly unsettling. His reception of penance when apparently mortally ill prevented him from resuming his secular functions, as theoretically it did for the Frankish emperor Louis the Pious in 833, and he was forced to abdicate and enter a monastery. To what extent this was an unplanned coup is uncertain, but the circumstances of Wamba's departure and his continued survival clearly did not leave his successor Ervig (680–687) in a strong position. The first ecclesiastical council of his reign had to try to justify the steps that had been taken.[52]

The succession of the next king, Egica (687–702), was equally confused. He is reported as having been chosen as his heir by the dying Ervig in return for marrying that monarch's daughter and promising to maintain the former ruler's family after his death. However, immediately on taking the throne Egica repudiated both promises, dismissing his new wife and dispossessing his predecessor's family of their property. Later chronicles attribute his actions to the advice of the former king Wamba, who thus avenged himself upon his supplanter. Whatever the truth of that, Egica's breaking of his oath was justified for him by the bishops at XV Toledo in 688, despite the existence of the earlier regulations of V and VI Toledo relating to the protection of royal widows and their families.[53]

Looked at strictly from the point of theory, the behaviour of many of the councils appears cynical or pusillanimous, in that existing regulations or principles seem to be on occasion ignored or flouted. The great Isidore of Seville presided over IV Toledo in 633. He had already formulated his views on the duties of the royal office and upon the illegitimacy of opposition to a king, however tyrannical, in both his *Sententiae* and his *Etymologiae*. Thus it comes as little of a surprise to find the last and longest of the canons of this council devoted to this very subject.[54] It three times reiterates its prohibition, on pain of excommunication, on anyone conspiring against the king, seeking to kill him or reduce his power, or seizing the throne tyranically and by force. But Sisenand, the king under whose authority the council was being held and at whose protection the canon aimed, had come to power in just such a fashion three years previously, having conspired against his predecessor and dethroned him by force.

This, however, was but a start. In the two councils held under his successor Chintila, V Toledo (636) and VI Toledo (638), the greatest part of all the canonical legislation relating to kingship was issued. What relationship Chintila had to his predecessor, if any, is not known, nor how he came to succeed him, but his position was insecure. V Toledo, presided over by Eugenius I, was concerned exclusively with matters pertaining to the king and to royal authority. The second canon refers to the decree of IV Toledo relating to the defence of the king, and goes on to promise protection for the ruler's heirs and their descendants, and the preservation of their property. Further canons again threaten excommunication for any who might seek to obtain the throne by any means other than election, for attempting to divine a future succession by fortune-telling, or for cursing a reigning monarch. The king's *fideles* are also guaranteed undisturbed possession of properties received from him.

Two years later another council, VI Toledo, was held, which, whilst the range of its proceedings was wider than those of V Toledo, repeated virtually all of the enactments of the previous gathering, with only some differences of expression. The explanation for this substantial repetition lies in the respective sizes of the councils. V Toledo was attended by only twenty-four bishops, of whom only one was a metropolitan, whereas VI Toledo attracted forty-eight bishops, including all six metropolitans under the presidency of Bishop Sclua of Narbonne. Clearly V Toledo was not held to be weighty enough and a second meeting was required at which all of the metropolitans had to be present. Chintila expected that the greatest possible ecclesiastical sanction would strengthen his position and ensure the security of his family and supporters should his reign be terminated prematurely.

If this were his hope, he would have been posthumously

disappointed. He died in 639, and after a brief reign his infant son
Tulga was deposed by Chindasuinth and despatched to a monastery.
Chindasuinth had thus conspired against a recognised king, deposed
him, and as far as we know never submitted himself to an election. To
our eyes he had done almost everything forbidden by the canons of V
and VI Toledo. Yet the church never stirred. The threatened
excommunication of the canons was not employed. Why not? This
acquiescence by the Visigothic Church in the apparent flouting of its
canons was not due to political cowardice. For one thing the bishops
had a genuine interest in maintaining a strong monarchy, and child
rulers were thus as much of an embarrassment to them as to the lay
aristocracy. But there were other reasons for their acceptance of
successful usurpation.

On the one side lay the acts of the councils against conspiracy and
rebellion, whatever its outcome, but on the other was a powerful
tradition of thought, most recently enunciated by Isidore but
stretching back to the New Testament, of obedience to the secular
ruler and acceptance of his authority, however exercised. The notion
of the divine pre-election of the monarch, developed in the Christian
Roman Empire in the fourth century, was explicitly accepted in
Visigothic Spain, as witnessed for example in Julian of Toledo's
description of the elevation of Wamba.[55] But the problem lay in the
detection of the operation of the divine will. At what point did the
victorious usurper become the legitimate ruler? Although elevation
by means of election might be preferred, the dominant political
ideology of the Visigothic kingdom required submission to the ruler
once established, however he may have acquired the power. For he
was ultimately chosen by God, either for the good of the people or for
their chastisement. Only the unsuccessful usurper might expect to
feel the weight of ecclesiastical sanctions. Nor do we ever find these
being applied until after a rebellion was suppressed and the issue thus
decided. The Church in Visigothic Spain was a redoubtable
supporter of kingship, which it sought to mould to its own
requirements, but it did not commit itself to the fortunes of individual
kings.

It is thus possible to modify or give greater precision to general
assertions about the relationship between church and monarchy by
taking more account of the context of ecclesiastical legislation. The
same principle can be applied to the secular law-making of the kings,
not only in terms of individual decrees but also the promulgation of

the codes. An example of the former is the legislation in respect of fugitive slaves, a subject that has given occasion for those ill-disposed towards the Visigothic kingdom to make sweeping criticisms of the state of its society in the late seventh century. However, before looking at that, it is worth considering the purposes of royal legislation and the circumstances surrounding the issuing of the codes.

The earlier history of the law-making of the Visigothic monarchy has already been outlined in a previous chapter. After the issue of Leovigild's revision of the *Code of Euric*, at some unspecified point in his reign, a period of nearly three-quarters of a century elapsed before further codification was undertaken. This time, however, it was not just a question of revision and amplification of an existing corpus, but rather the production of a completely reorganised code to which a substantial body of new law had been added.

This process was carried out in the reign of Reccesuinth, and the resulting code, entitled the *Liber Iudiciorum* (Book of the Judges) was probably promulgated in 654. It consisted of twelve books, divided as to subject-matter. It was further refined by the division of the books into subsections called 'titles', into which the individual laws were grouped and classified. This system was retained in the subsequent revision by King Ervig in 681. It has been suggested that the choice of dividing the code into twelve books was intended deliberately to reflect the founding collection of Roman legal tradition, the Laws of the Twelve Tables. However, the precedent of Justinian's code of 534, the similarly divided *Corpus Iuris Civilis*, may have been a weightier one.[56] Although Reccesuinth's version of the *Liber Iudiciorum* is the earliest form in which we now have it, it has been questioned whether or not a prototype of the code was issued in the reign of his father Chindasuinth.[57] However, the evidence in favour of such a view is not strong, especially when the mistaken belief that the Visigoths and the Romans had previously existed under entirely separate rules of law is abandoned. It is clear enough from the code itself though that Chindasuinth was a substantial legislator, and ninety-nine of his laws are included in his son's great compilation.

A few manuscripts have survived, one possibly contemporary with the initial promulgation, of Reccesuinth's version of the *Liber Iudiciorum*, but within thirty years it was replaced by the expanded edition undertaken for Ervig.[58] To this in turn were added new laws of his successors Egica (687–702) and Wittiza (698–710). Although this did not lead to a third official codification Egica made clear his intention of revising his predecessor's work, and manuscripts of Ervig's version and of that version with Egica's additions do not exist as two distinct classes.

The significance of the *Liber Iudiciorum* for the society of Visigothic Spain has generally been assessed in the light of its specific prohibition of the continued use of any codes of law other than itself. For those who believe that the Goths and the Romans had hitherto existed under the jurisdiction of two independent systems of law then the effect of this regulation was to abolish the Romans' law. The *Liber Iudiciorum* thereby appears as the first territorial law code, that is, the first code to apply its rules equally to all inhabitants of a region irrespective of racial or cultural differences.

However, it has already been suggested that the *Codes* of Euric and of Leovigild were enforced upon Romans and Goths alike. Some of their regulations were preserved in the *Liber Iudiciorum*. Thus what was really affected was the continued standing of the *Lex Romana Visigothorum* or *Breviary* of Alaric II. This still had a considerable future ahead of it in the Carolingian Empire in Francia, whence many of its extant manuscripts have come, particularly from the region of Burgundy.[59] However only one manuscript of it is known from Spain, and it is possible that even that was written elsewhere. This manuscript, now in Leon Cathedral, is a palimpsest made up of sections of two seventh-century manuscripts, one of the *Breviary* and the other of a Bible, put together and written over in the ninth century with a text of Rufinus's *Ecclesiastical History*. Thus Alaric's *Breviary* was possibly still being copied in Spain in the seventh century but had ceased to be of interest by the ninth.[60]

Its continued application in the first half of the seventh century is also confirmed by a few citations of secular laws in the acts of some of the church councils, notably II Seville of 619, which appear to be references to the *Breviary*.[61] Interestingly the individual laws in question are described by the bishops as coming from *lex mundialis* or *lex publica* (the universal or the public law), which would seem most inappropriate if this law were not common to all sectors of society.

However, some of what was contained in the *Breviary* had already been supplemented or amplified by the legislation of Leovigild's code. For instance the two laws relating to rape in the former were more than matched by the six to be found in the latter, which also paid much greater attention to the divisions and conventions of contemporary Romano-Gothic society. As well as laws that had in practice been replaced by more recent legislation, the *Breviary* contained rules that had ceased to have much relevance, as for example the law relating to 'Free-born men who were enslaved in the times of the Tyrant', which interpreted an enactment of the emperor Constantine I, issued in 314 and referring to his defeated rival Maxentius (306–312).[62] The impression that the *Breviary* needed revision and that it was better for the Visigothic rulers to abandon it is hard to resist.

The codifications of Leovigild, Reccesuinth and Ervig represented important stages in the functioning of a working legal system that sought to affect*and enhance the operations of justice by means of royal law-making. The very title of the code of Reccesuinth, attested to in the earliest manuscript, calling itself 'The Book of the Judges', seems to indicate that, as in the case of earlier Roman equivalents, the intention was to provide the administrators of the law with a systematic statement of it. Such an aim was paralleled in the royal edicts of the Lombard kingdom, but alien to Frankish and Anglo-Saxon conceptions.

However, even in the heyday of the Roman Empire, the workings of the legal system were never as coherent and uncomplicated as some critics of the subsequent Germanic law codes seem to imply. Contradictions existed in the laws and little effort was made to bring new legislation to the knowledge of those required to administer it. The first official codification of Roman law was not undertaken until 438. Nor can we be certain that the promulgation of this the Theodosian Code or of its successor, that of Justinian, implied that thereafter a copy might be found in the hands of every judge in the Empire. So, too, in Visigothic Spain, it is not necessary to assume that the existence of codifications was essential to the working of the legal system, although their value in practice was considerable.

In fact, there are strong indications that the codes of Reccesuinth and Ervig were as much the products of political necessity as of disinterested concern for legal reform. Strikingly, both were directly preceded by trenchant criticism of royal government in church councils. This is only elsewhere found in the disparagement of Sisebut's attempt at enforced conversion of the Jews by the bishops at IV Toledo. VIII Toledo of 653, held the year before the first issue of *Liber Iudiciorum*, took the remarkable step, unique in the Visigothic period, of systematically defining its conception of the qualities required of kings. This went far beyond the limited statements of

Isidore in his *Etymologiae* and *Sententiae*, although clearly deriving from his definitions. The bishops at VIII Toledo held that kings should be the protectors of the Catholic faith, its defenders against the 'perfidy' of the Jews and the injuries that might be inflicted by heresy. Kings should be moderate in their making of laws and giving of judgements, and modest in their own lives. They were warned against using force to extort property from their subjects or making fraudulent claims about agreements. Most remarkably the distinction between property held by the king by virtue of his office in trust for the people and that which he owned as his personal family property was firmly outlined: '... gifts presented to him by way of thanks should not be regarded as his private property, but as being in custody for the people and land (*gens et patria.*). Of all the things acquired by the kings, they may only claim those parts which royal authority has enriched, but the rest shall be inherited by their successors in (royal) glory, without it being disposed of by testament, and leaving aside those personal goods justly acquired before their reign, which will be received by their sons or legal heirs'.[63]

Although the significance may not be fully clear to us, this seems to be allowing monarchs to take certain profits from their activities but strictly preventing them from treating royal property, doubtless in the form of treasure and fiscal lands, as their own. Conversely, it does also guarantee their own personal possessions from being absorbed into the fisc. That this law is to be binding on all future monarchs is made clear: '... it will remain in permanence, immutable, and none shall ascend the royal throne before having sworn to obey it in all its parts. This law (*lex*) and episcopal decree (*decretum*) shall not only be complied with in the future, but shall be obeyed in the present, and any detractor or one who is not a venerator of this law and decree, be he lay or cleric, shall not only be excommunicated but also be deprived of his secular office.'[64]

This was the first time that a council issued a decree limiting the autonomy of the holder of the royal office, and is evidence of the strength of feelings aroused by recent excesses in the employment of royal authority, notably by Chindasuinth. There are other indications. The same council lifted the excommunications imposed on the authority of a canon of VII Toledo of 646 on conspirators, and the bishops justified themselves for breaking an oath they had there been required to take. They used biblical and patristic citations, including some from Isidore, to support their decision that an unjust and unmerciful oath could not be binding. The effect of this was to pardon the political opponents of the late king Chindasuinth who had been penalised by his council of 646. Further evidence of the reaction to the severities of that king after his death came in the form of a letter of Fructuosus of Braga to King Reccesuinth urging him in very forcible language to pardon former offenders and to free captives, and also a civil law of 654 that provided an amnesty for offences committed against the king since the time of Chintila (636–639).[65]

The most vivid manifestation of the feelings that swept over the clerical establishment on the death of Chindasuinth comes in the epitaph composed on the king by Bishop Eugenius II of Toledo: 'I Chindasuinth ever the friend of evil deeds; committer of crimes Chindasuinth I, impious, obscene, infamous, ugly and wicked; not seeking the best, valuing the worst.'[66] This is the bishop who, if anyone, was the motivating force of VIII Toledo, and it is not overfanciful to suspect that he had a role to play in the preparation of the subsequent law code.

These features which had come out so strongly from the deliberations of the bishops are also found in the secular laws. Some of these, such as one intended to 'curb the greed of rulers' (i.e. the king) preceded the holding of the council, and probably represented a response to pressure from the nobility, the principal sufferers under Chindasuinth. The *Liber Iudiciorum* contained the new laws that sought to contain the king's abuse of power in extortions from his subjects, that defined the distinctions between the royal and personal property of the monarch, and that explicitly stated the subjection of the ruler to the law.

This last was a particularly striking concept, especially when contrasted with such notions of the sovereign as the fount of law as existed in Byzantine jurisprudence. It is equally alien to the ideas of contemporary Lombard law-makers, who, for example, ruled that murder at the command of the king was no crime 'for since we believe that the heart of the king is in the hand of God, it is inconceivable that anyone whose death the king has ordered could be entirely free of guilt.'[67]

While Byzantine and Lombard lawbooks commence with statements of the will and intention of the royal legislators, that of the Visigothic kingdom starts with a whole book devoted to the nature and purposes of law and the duties of the law-maker. This has occasionally been denigrated or neglected by modern commentators, wrongly so, as it was of fundamental importance to the minds of the devisers of the code. Although in practice the king's power was very great and often unchecked, the evidence of the *Liber Iudiciorum* indicates that the law was greater than the king, and that he was seen as the custodian of an office to be exercised on behalf of the *gens* and the *patria*, answerable at least to God.

The linked terms of *gens* and *patria* make frequent appearances in the civil and ecclesiastical texts of the later Visigothic period. Their significance as terms implying 'people' and 'homeland' is important. The lack of qualification in racial distinction seems further evidence of the breaking down of division between Romans and Goths, and the aspiration towards a common homeland for a single people is suggestive of the advances that the society was making.

In the later part of the reign of Reccesuinth, and for the whole of that of Wamba, no full councils of the whole Visigothic Church were held, possibly a reflection of the unpalatable features of VIII Toledo. When the next plenary session was held it was that of XII Toledo of 681, at which the dominant personality was that of Bishop Julian, the former pupil of Eugenius II. Once again criticisms of a ruler were voiced, now directed against the recently deposed Wamba. The bishops criticised him for his uncanonical actions in creating new bishoprics, notably one in the suburbs of Toledo, while the new king Ervig repealed his predecessor's law ordaining loss of legal status for those who failed to attend the mobilisation of the army when summoned or who deserted from it.[68]

Once more an attack on what were regarded as arbitrary and excessive uses of royal authority was swiftly followed by promulgation of a new law code, Ervig's revision of that of Reccesuinth. It can hardly be coincidental that the only two major outbursts of public criticism of the monarchy recorded in Visigothic Spain should be so closely linked in time with the issue of codes. Laws could be and were made without requiring the labour of a full codification, as the substantial corpus of those of Chindasuinth shows. But the codes were more than systematic handbooks; they were also statements of principles, and it is hard not to see those of Reccesuinth and Ervig as products of hard thinking about the limitations and obligations of the royal office. Such an approach to the contemporary significance of the codes is perhaps confirmed by the case of the subsequent confirmation, not only of the civil but also of the ecclesiastical laws by the late tenth-century king of Leon Vermudo II, whose succession, like that of Ervig, was contentious and divisive.[69]

The evidence of the laws and councils, difficult as it sometimes is to interpret, indicates development rather than stagnation in the Visigothic kingdom in the later seventh century. Far from declining from the age of Isidore, the Church was building on his legacy and, as in the case of VIII Toledo, groping towards fuller definition and resolution of problems on which he had touched. From both sides the relationship between the Church and the monarchy was changing, and while many of the basic difficulties of maintaining unified and centralised rule in the peninsula remained, unity became a more fully expressed hope, and possibly more of a practical reality. Mythical or not, this was a time to which later generations in a divided peninsula looked back as to a golden age.

Outsiders and the Law

ASPIRATIONS towards unity of the people under the aegis of Visigothic monarchy and Catholic Church, in a society where every tendency was centrifugal, inevitably created greater hostility towards those who would not or could not conform. If the rhetoric of the kings and the bishops was to have meaning, then there was little room for toleration of those who could not be fully integrated into the new society they sought. The principal sufferers from this were the Jews.

Jewish communities had probably existed in the peninsula from at least the first century AD. That St Paul had intended to go to Spain is itself indicative of the existence of a substantial body of Jews, at least in some parts, prior even to the destruction of the Temple and the beginnings of the Diaspora. Evidence concerning the Spanish Jews during the Roman period is slight, but the unusual degree of attention devoted to them in the legislation of the Visigothic kingdom may be a further indication of a relatively sizeable Jewish population in the Iberian peninsula, in comparision with most other western Mediterranean regions. Unfortunately, but for the existence of a handful of inscriptions, some in Hebrew, the Jews of Spain in the Visigothic period have left little record of themselves outside of the regulations that their Christian rulers sought to impose upon them.[70]

The treatment of the Jews by both the secular power and by the Church in the Visigothic kingdom is the most reprehensible feature of its history. From the reign of Reccared onwards a series of laws and conciliar decrees were enacted inhibiting the rights and liberties of Jews, even on occasion requiring them to abandon their own religion and convert to Christianity. Although this legislation was originally only directed against Jewish practitioners of Judaism, those who, willingly or otherwise, converted to Christianity soon came under the suspicion of the lawmakers and came to be supervised and restricted almost as fiercely as their former co-religionists. What began as a process of law-making aimed at the practitioners of a religion ended as one directed against a race.

Just as the scope of this legislation grew during the period of the kingdom, so too did its scale. It increased in its comprehensiveness, its frequency and the violence of its tone as the years of the kingdom passed, though its beginnings were by no means small. The earliest series of laws from the Visigothic realm relating to the Jews may be found in the *Breviary* of Alaric II, his interpreted abridgement of the Theodosian Code, promulgated in 506.[71] A number of regulations that become increasingly familiar as they were reissued time and again in the councils and law codes of the kingdom make their first appearance in Visigothic legislation here. Intermarriage of Jews and Christians was banned. Jews were forbidden to hold public office, as they were not to be permitted to possess positions of authority which they could employ to inflict harm upon Christians. They were also prohibited from building new synagogues, although they might repair their old ones. Conversion of Christians by Jews was forbidden on penalty of death and they were prevented from owning Christian slaves. These last two laws are somewhat contradictory, as whereas the latter regulation prohibits Jews from having slaves who were Christians, the former forbids their Christian slaves being converted to Judaism. Such ambiguities are fairly typical of all late Roman and Early Medieval legislation, both in relation to Jews and in general. Here it is important to note that the Visigothic monarchy in the *Breviary* is taking over Roman imperial laws concerning the Jews, with only very slight modifications of its own introducing: much of the seventh-century legislation is also little more than a repetition of the earlier Roman injunctions. In such cases it is impossible to know to what extent these laws were still enforced and held to be of value and to what extent they had in practice become anachronistic. On the other hand, especially in the second half of the century, much new legislation relating to the Jews in the kingdom is introduced and this, whatever the uncertainties about the practicalities of enforcement, clearly had contemporary significance.

The third Council of Toledo of 589, that marked the end of Visigothic Arianism, also saw the promulgation of the first laws of the

Catholic monarchy in respect of the Jews. At III Toledo, paralleling civil legislation that was probably issued at the same time, the fourteenth canon decreed that Jews were not to have Christian wives or mistresses, that they were not permitted to buy Christian slaves and that those they had who had been made to accept Judaism must now be freed without indemnity. Finally Jews were again, as in the *Breviary*, forbidden from holding public offices. The aim of these rulings, as with the earlier ones of Alaric II, was to prevent Jews from having any powers over Christians, either in their family, their household or in the business of state. To what extent Jews had previously been employed in public office is unknown, but the restrictions on slave-owning, if fully enforced, may well have proved particularly hard, for it was necessary, because of the requirements of Jewish religion, for the servants and slaves in a Jewish household to have been practitioners of Judaism. However, the number of Jews of such classes was probably small and therefore the purchase of Christians or others, prepared to convert to Judaism, would have been a necessity.

Reccared's immediate successors did not add to his laws relating to the Jews, and indeed were later accused of having relaxed them. With Sisebut (612–621), however, there came a renewal of activity, culminating in a royal decree ordering all Jews to accept Christian baptism.[72] This was probably never fully implemented, as the actual enforcement of this and other laws was by no means as easy as their promulgation. The spirit of this one was clearly out of step with the feelings of the Church at that time, and Sisebut's misguided enthusiasm was posthumously deprecated at IV Toledo in 633. However, his initiative had created serious practical problems which the council had to resolve. For there now existed a body of former Jews who had been converted to Christianity against their will. Some of them practised their imposed new faith outwardly, without believing in it, whilst others openly lapsed back into Judaism in defiance of their enforced baptism. Therefore the council decreed in a series of canons, that those forcibly converted during Sisebut's reign should not be permitted to return to their former religion because they had partaken of Christian sacraments. As for those who had already apostatized, they were to have their children removed from them, doubtless to be brought up as Christians, their slaves were to be liberated, and being, it was held, forsworn, they were deprived of the right to give evidence at law. This last ruling will have left them incapable of initiating litigation and vulnerable to legal attack by others.[73] So the long-term effects of Sisebut's activity was to drive some Jews into Christianity and to further weaken the status and legal standing of others. IV Toledo went on to reiterate at greater length the inhibitions placed on the Jews by III Toledo. VI Toledo of 636 also confirmed those decrees, in even more grandiloquent terms, speaking of the ardent desire of the new king, Chintila (636–639), not to allow anyone who was not a Catholic to dwell in his realm. VIII Toledo of 653, held under King Reccesuinth, did likewise.[74]

Whilst the rhetoric of these pronouncements grew in its intensity in the denunciation of the 'abominable and impious faithlessness of the Jews' (VIII Toledo), and in the statements of the aspirations of the rulers, no new laws were introduced to further restrict or coerce the Jews during this period. Their position probably deteriorated little between the death of Sisebut in 621 and the beginning of the reign of Reccesuinth in 653. Some have seen the conciliar decree of IV Toledo concerning the removal of children from their parents as applying to all Jews, but if so it can hardly have been enforced as otherwise there would have been no Jewish communities left.[75] It is more likely that Sisebut's original decree was never fully implemented and that the council's ruling was only dealing with the families of those who had been forced to convert but had later returned to their original faith. Any other view would make of IV Toledo a cataclysm for the Jewish community that it clearly was not.

Thus, with the exception of IV Toledo, the conciliar pronouncements of the period 621–653 seem more designed to keep the kings from lessening the disabilities of the Jews, rather than increasing them. Canon three of VI Toledo, opening with its grandiose statement of Chintila's desire to see a kingdom united in its religion, is really devoted to his promise not to show favour to the Jews, nor to permit any compromise that might strengthen the position of their faith. In the first half of the seventh century it is the Church that clearly took the initiative over the question of the Jews. With the exception of Sisebut, the kings appear luke-warm on the issue. The bulk of the legislation was promulgated, admittedly with royal assent, in the Church councils. Only three civil laws exist from this period relating to the Jews: one from the reign of Reccared and two from that of Sisebut, all concerned with the matter of Jewish ownership of Christian slaves.[76] Up to the early 650s, all of the legislation dealt solely with the legal standing of the Jews in relation to the Christians. If they were prepared to accept the disabilities involved, Jews could continue to practise their religion, officially disapproved of, but in practice unmolested by their Christian rulers.

The reign of Reccesuinth changed all of this. By the time of the promulgation of his law code in 654, the king had issued a series of decrees that sought, for the first time, to outlaw some of the fundamental practices of Judaism. Thus the celebration of the Passover was prohibited, the performance of Jewish marriage ceremonies was forbidden, as was the rite of circumcision, and the Jews were commanded to abandon their dietary laws. As well as these proscriptions of many of the essential practices of Judaism, all Jews now lost the right of initiating legal action against Christians or to give evidence against them. What had previously been applied only to converted Jews who relapsed, by the acts of IV Toledo, was now thus enforced upon them all.[77] At this same time another significant development occurred, and this is the first official suspicion of the reliability of Jewish converts to Christianity. IX Toledo of 654 decreed that baptised Jews must spend both Christian feast days and also those that they would previously have observed under Jewish law in the presence of their local bishop, who could thus ensure their participation in the one and their avoidance of the other.[78] These developments, the proscription of Jewish religious practices and the increasing use of royal law and the supervision of converted Jews, set the tone for the second half of the seventh century.

Reccesuinth's successor Wamba (672–680) added nothing to this growing body of royal legislation concerning the Jews, and indeed he may have relaxed the enforcement of it. For when Ervig (680–687) came to reissue the law code, the *Forum Iudicum*, soon after his accession, he included a whole new title to Book Twelve of laws relating to the Jews.[79] Some of this was merely a restatement of the earlier laws of Reccesuinth, but in his own new laws he went much further. As well as the Passover, already banned, the observance of the Sabbath and the celebration of all other Jewish rites were forbidden. On the other hand the Jews were required not to work on Sundays and Christian feast days. They were commanded not to read books of scriptures not accepted by the Christians. They were not permitted to defend their own faith in argument, let alone to dare to traduce Christianity. Jews who were travelling were ordered to report to the bishops in the towns which they visited, so that they could be observed, and all Jews were required to deposit written confessions of

their errors and agreements not to revert to them with their local
bishop, who was to keep them in the archives of his church. In order
that no Jew could claim to be ignorant of these new laws, a copy of the
book containing them, probably just title three of Book Twelve of the
code, was to be given to each of them by the bishop or local priest,
which they were then required to keep permanently on their persons.
Also these laws were to be read out to them publicly in church on
various occasions. The penalties to be inflicted for the infringement of
these regulations were severe in the extreme. Thus a Jew practising
circumcision or following his dietary laws might receive one hundred
lashes and be 'decalvated' – whether this means scalping or just
head-shaving is a matter of doubt. Possession of books denying the
truth of Christianity or the teaching of this to their children was also
punishable by a hundred lashes. There were in addition monetary
penalties, such as the fine of one hundred gold *solidi* for using Jewish
marriage customs. Most horrifyingly of all, Jewish children over the
age of ten became liable to receive the same punishments as adults for
breaches of the laws.

These new laws of Ervig must have been issued immediately after
his accession in 680, for they were formally confirmed by the bishops
assembled at XII Toledo in January 681. It is reasonable to believe
that much of the responsibility for the conceiving and drafting of this
set of laws must lie with the Church, and in particular with the new
bishop of Toledo, Julian (680–690), himself of Jewish descent. But
the king can hardly have been indifferent on this subject. Ervig was
the dedicatee of Julian's *On the Proof of the Sixth Age*, a work written to
combat Jewish arguments, and the two men had been personal
friends prior to their elevations to monarchy and metropolitanate in
680. If, as has sometimes been argued, Ervig was a tool of the Church,
he was a very willing one.[80] There is insufficient evidence to determine
whether Reccesuinth, who was under considerable pressure from the
Church on other scores, acted against the Jews out of personal
conviction or in response to the demands of the episcopate, but in the
case of Ervig no such possibility of a conflict of motives existed. In
this, and perhaps in his patronage of the learned Bishop Julian, he
was something of another Sisebut.

From the reign of his successor Egica (687–702), a monarch whose
reputation is rather sinister, we have almost our last surviving secular
and ecclesiastical enactments, and with them further laws concerning
the Jews. In 693 Egica issued a decree, which was reiterated by the

bishops at XVI Toledo the same year, freeing all Jews who had converted to Christianity and had followed its precepts without equivocation, from the taxes they owed as members of the Jewish community to the royal fisc. It is interesting to note that previously converts had laboured under the same burden of special taxation – when introduced we do not know – as was imposed upon other Jews. Now, however, the fiscal obligations of the latter were to be increased by the amount formerly paid by the converts. So, for the first time, a financial incentive to conversion was being offered, and one that cost the royal treasury nothing.[81]

The following year, 694, marked the most dramatic royal initiative against the Jews since the attempt at forcible conversion carried out by Sisebut. Apart from those living in the vulnerable frontier province of Narbonnensis, who were temporarily exempted, the entire Jewish population of the kingdom was reduced to slavery. This is the startling implication of the *Tome* of Egica presented to XVII Toledo in November 694 and the eighth canon of that council, issued in response to it.[82] The language of both is somewhat elusive until the practical injunctions are reached: the Jews are to be deprived of the ownership of their own property, and they and their families are to be reduced to servitude and given into the possession of whomsoever the king chose, condemned never again to recover their free status. Their Christian slaves are to be liberated and some of them may be entrusted with the property of their former masters. If so, they would be expected to continue the payment of the special taxes that had been imposed on their previous owners. It is interesting that after two centuries of reiterated legislation against Jews owning Christian slaves, this decree still expected them to be existing and in significant numbers. This might warn us against assuming that these, and indeed any of the laws, were necessarily enforced in full, or even in part. The final part of Egica's decree concerned the children of the enslaved Jews. They were to be taken from their parents once they had reached the age of six, to be brought up as Christians. Whether they regained their legal status of freedom is left unmentioned.

This notorious canon and its lengthy justification in the *Tome* really offer little clear explanation of the causes of this unprecedented move. There is much of the standard abuse of the Jews for their perfidy and unfaithfulness, but the principal justification for this measure appears to lie in a very generalised accusation that the Jews inside the Visigothic kingdom had been in league with those from without to carry out some kind of concerted action to overthrow the Christian population and to subvert their religion. This is linked to rumours, described as coming from 'other parts of the world', of Jewish revolts against their rulers and their violent suppression in consequence. The bishops imply in their canon that they had only heard about this alleged conspiracy during the course of the council, in other words from the king himself. For the first time since the reign of Sisebut, then, we seem to be dealing with an unequivocal royal initiative that was not the result of ecclesiastical pressure. This is clear, too, from the nature of the penalty involved, which, except in the case of the children, has little to do with the hoped-for conversion of the Jews.

In fact, the effect of this law must have been to transfer the persons and properties of the Jews into the hands of the royal fisc. They became possessions of the king, who could dispose of them and their goods at will. The opportunities that this presented for the exercise of royal patronage and the refurbishing of the royal finances must have been considerable, all the more so as the king ensured that the former Jewish properties would continue to be subject to special taxation even under new Christian owners. It is difficult when contemplating the enormous enhancement of the fisc that the acquisition of such considerable resources in lands, goods and slaves must have provided, and given the evidence of the instability of Egica's régime at the time with the consequent need to buy or reinforce support, to resist the conclusion that the whole operation was more concerned with the restoration of the financial position of the monarchy than with any material or spiritual threat to the kingdom that the Jews were held to pose.

As this is the last glimpse that we catch of the Spanish Jews under Visigothic rule, only seventeen years before the Arab invasion, this decree of Egica casts a lurid glow over the declining years of the kingdom. However, it is possible that the laws of 694 were never enforced or only partially so, as was clearly the case with many of their predecessors. The Jews may, by timely submissions or payments, have alleviated the full rigour of it, or Egica's successors may have abandoned it. On the other hand, the Jewish population may have remained disposable royal property until the fall of the kingdom.

This, then, is the history of the Jews in Visigothic Spain as exposed in the acts of the councils and in the royal laws. The impression thus formed is one of severity, even of savagery and of a persecution of a religion that at times becomes one of a race. However, the frequent repetition of injunctions and the warnings against compromise and prevarication, and the threats issued against those who fail to implement the laws, suggest that in practice the enforcement of these decrees was quite another matter from their promulgation. It seems clear, too, that it was the Church that was most active in the process of law-making, and that the kings were not always willing to co-operate: with the exception of Sisebut, the two kings most responsible for wide-ranging and savage anti-Jewish legislation were Reccesuinth and Ervig, who were most dependent on the good will of the Church at the outset of their reigns. Reccesuinth was faced by rebellion and bitter criticism of his father's régime as well as demands for reform, whilst Ervig owed his throne entirely to the strict enforcement of canon law that had incapacitated his predecessor. Both kings conceded to restrictions on their royal authority in the opening councils of their reigns and both produced law codes within a year of their accession. On the other hand, those monarchs, such as Chindasuinth or Wamba, most censured by the Church after their deaths, are not associated with legislation against the Jews.

Kings were not the only members of Romano-Visigothic society who were not uniformly hostile to the Jewish communities in their midst. Lay nobles are known to have patronised them. Bishop Aurasius of Toledo (c. 603–615) denounced the Gothic noble Froga for his support of the Jews.[83] This episode probably occurred during the reign of Witteric, himself implicitly criticised by Sisebut for his leniency towards the Jews. Even bishops were possibly not averse to protecting their local Jewish communities from the full rigour of laws that they themselves periodically enacted in their councils. It is likely that the Jews who suffered most were those of Toledo.

Petitions made by the Toledan Jews to some of the kings have survived and provide one of the few additional sources available to supplement the laws and conciliar acts. The earliest of these 'professions' comes from the reign of Chintila, and was signed by the converted Jews of Toledo in the Basilica of St Leocadia on 1 December 638.[84] In it they formally renounced their previous beliefs and the rites of the Jewish faith. They also promised to surrender their 'apocryphal books'. It is not possible, unfortunately, to be certain what is implied by this term. Does it refer to the Mishnah or other post-Biblical Hebrew texts, or to actual apocrypha of the Jewish Biblical tradition such as IV Esdras or Baruch? The signatories of the document bind themselves to expel from their number and stone to death any who subsequently broke with these undertakings.

The declaration of the Toledan Jews made to Reccesuinth on 1

March 654 was very similar.[85] In it those members of the Jewish community in the capital who had converted to Christianity promised that they would not associate with the other unconverted Jews, that they would use Christian marriage customs and not observe the Passover, Sabbath or any other Jewish festival, and that they would abandon circumcision and all Jewish rites as well as their dietary laws. Anyone who broke one of these undertakings would be expelled from their community to be stoned to death or burnt alive.

Depressing as this document may be, it is interesting to note that whilst the Toledan Jews promised to accept all of the laws of Reccesuinth requiring the abjuration of their former religion, they were permitted to punish any transgressions within their own community in the first instance, and perhaps to employ their own distinctive forms of punishment. Neither stoning nor burning feature elsewhere in the judicial practice of Visigothic Spain. It is quite possible that a greater degree of latitude was practised than if bishops or Gothic judges had been given jurisdiction. It seems likely that despite the apparent ferocity of the laws, the individual Jewish communities were able to retain a considerable measure of autonomy. From the evidence of the 'professions' it is clear that they had their own leadership and exercised at least some measure of judicial independence.

There may also have been quite a degree of intellectual vigour in the Spanish Judaism of this time. It would be wrong to think that conversions from Christianity to Judaism were possible on any scale at this period, even if they had been sought. The laws and the local power of the bishops would have seen to that, although conversions inside a Jewish household were more likely to be ignored. However, the intellectual arguments of the Jews against Christianity did exercise an influence on the thoughts and writings of the leading Christians in the kingdom, and a corpus of polemical literature thus developed. Of this we have today Isidore's *Two Books on the Catholic Faith against the Jews*, Ildefonsus's *On the Perpetual Virginity of the Blessed Virgin Mary* and Julian's *On the Proof of the Sixth Age*. Of the three, Isidore's work is perhaps the most interesting, as it is the most far-ranging. The other two are restricted to specific points of controversy, on the Virgin birth, and on rival Jewish and Christian views on the spiritual chronology of human history, respectively.

Isidore, however, considered a range of issues on which Christian and Jewish ideas differed, and although abusively, he did include some Jewish arguments.[86] The first book is divided into sixty-two short chapters, each devoted to one of the principal features of the life and work of Christ, and in every case his arguments consist of passages from the Latin Old Testament employed to show how each item was there prophesied or mystically prefigured. His general thesis was that the Jews' lack of belief was clearly condemned by their failure to see and accept that which their own scriptures had foreseen. The second book considered the differences between Jews and Christians in a more general way, and again using the Old Testament Isidore sought to controvert Jewish beliefs and practices. He argued that the Christians had become the heirs of the promises made by God because of the unbelief of the Jews, and that it was the Christians that were 'the New Israel'. He attributed the ruin of Jerusalem and the dispersal of the Jews to the same cause. Whilst his arguments are rarely new in themselves, being mostly the stock ones of earlier patristic anti-Jewish polemic, their extended treatment and systematic organisation give his work particular value.

Unfortunately no writings of Spanish Jews of this period have survived to enable us to determine to what extent Isidore and his fellows were writing to combat arguments currently being advanced in controversy by their Jewish contemporaries, or whether they were rather producing set-pieces intended principally to display the forensic and exegetical skills of their Christian authors. The legal prohibitions on Jews arguing against Christianity and the demands that they surrender their books would, however, suggest that the Jews had available the intellectual equipment to debate with the Christians, were they permitted so to do. A further possible indication of the dissemination of Jewish ideas in Visigothic Spain is the parallel efforts that were made by the ecclesiastical and secular rulers to suppress what were seen as Judaising innovations amongst Christians. The unprecedented frequency with which these are encountered throughout the Visigothic period suggests that this was not a trivial problem.

An early example of this tendency comes from Ibiza in the Balearic Islands, where the bishop Vincent wrote (c. 590) to Licinianus of Cartagena to solicit his advice on a document then circulating in the island, which was widely held to have fallen from heaven.[87] This text enjoined the strictest observance of the Lord's Day, even forbidding walking or cooking, rules reminiscent of sabbath observance. Licinianus was rightly sceptical of its divine origin and denounced it as both a forgery and a piece of Judaising. In the Visigothic kingdom proper, attacks on similar attempts to introduce Jewish practices into Christian observances are found incorporated with the laws against the Jews themselves in both the secular and ecclesiastical collections. But the most extreme stand was taken by Chindasuinth, who issued no legislation against the Jews themselves, in decreeing the death penalty for any Christians convicted of using Jewish rites, a punishment, it was stated, that would be inflicted slowly.[88]

What really did lie behind the ill-treatment of the Jews in Visigothic Spain, when allowance is made both for the probable gulf between theory and practice, and the intellectual threat that Judaism presented to the teachings of Christianity? The canonical and civil legislation of the first half of the seventh century did little more than perpetuate the regulations of the later Roman Empire as far as the Jews were concerned, although Sisebut's venture into mass-conversion indicates that some individuals, at least, wished to go further. But although the level of rhetoric rose, the principal concern still lay with the legal standing of the Jews, and there may well have been an acceptance of the belief expressed by Isidore that the Jews could not be converted to Christianity before the end of the world. Indeed their conversion was to be a sign of the imminence of that event. However, such relative restraint ended in the 650s, and thenceforth, on paper at least, a concerted effort was made to extirpate Judaism as a religion in the kingdom.

In part this was a question of ideology: only a realm fully united in the practice of the Catholic faith would be acceptable in the eyes of God, and in this respect the continued existence of Judaism within its frontiers threatened the peace and material prosperity of the kingdom. The fragility of the Visigothic state, that became increasingly apparent from the 630s on, made this a consideration of growing significance. The rise in repression directed against the Jews is also paralleled by the development of penitential litanies, and the more sombre features of the liturgy, through which the Christian populace were urged to atone for their own sinfulness.[89] The survival of the Jews became, as much as the prevalence of conspiracy and usurpation, a sign of the spiritual unhealthiness of the realm.

It would be unwise to suggest that opprobrium was directed against the Jews as a means of distracting attention away from the real weaknesses of the kingdom or the strength of regional loyalties. For one thing, there is no evidence of any deep-felt popular hostility towards the Jews, or attacks on their communities by force, as occurred in Spain on many occasions in the later Middle Ages. The complaints against the support and protection afforded to the Jews suggest there was little popular malevolence towards them. Opposition to them was conceived and expressed in terms of theory and came principally from the Church, speaking through the councils. In these Bishops Ildefonsus and Julian of Toledo appear most active and their pontificates coincided with the two most intense periods of legislation.

Looking more widely, the seventh century in general was not a good time for the scattered communities of the Mediterranean Jews. It was the period of the greatest Byzantine persecution of its Jewish citizens, and legal disabilities were also imposed upon them in Lombard Italy and Merovingian Gaul.[90] For one thing, these were dramatic and frightening times. The sudden emergence of the new religion of Islam, and the attendant military conquests of the Arabs, gave rise to a whole range of Apocalyptic and Messianic speculations amongst Christians and Jews alike.[91] The Jews, too, had found irresistible the opportunities afforded by the Persian and then Arab campaigns in the eastern provinces of the Byzantine Empire to take local revenge on their Christian former overlords and tormenters, and as a result their political loyalty became widely suspect.[92] As the Arab advance into Byzantine North Africa developed in the 680s and 690s, bringing them closer to Spain, this may have become a forceful consideration in the minds of the Visigothic rulers, ever prone to distrust.

Such fears may also lie behind the promulgation of a law by Egica that prohibited unconverted Jews from engaging in overseas trade.[93] The same king alluded to Jewish opposition to their Christian rulers in other states in his *Tome* addressed to XVII Toledo, and was probably thereby referring to the experiences of Byzantium. Thus, by the end of the century there were, rightly or wrongly, very material reasons, as well as spiritual ones, for the Visigothic kings to look askance at their Jewish subjects. With the Arab conquest of 711 the lot of the Jews in Spain was considerably alleviated and they were relatively little troubled for the next three centuries. Roman and Visigothic law were replaced by that of the Koran, and under Arab rule there occurred one of the most important periods of the literary and intellectual flourishings of Diaspora Judaism.

The treatment of the Jews in Visigothic Spain, particularly in the second half of the seventh century, is the clearest and most fully documented symptom of the changes going on in the society as a whole. In some respects it looks thoroughly anarchic: conflict can replace co-operation between king and Church; bishops seem capable of defying their own rulings, the increase in law-making, both civil and ecclesiastical, reveal stranger and stranger abuses and malpractices, attacks on the Jews reach quite hysterical proportions.

Obviously personality played a role that we cannot now easily detect and the inner workings of politics are totally obscured. However, it seems that this was a society with a sense of direction. It was not drifting and out of control as some modern commentators believe. On the contrary, it was subjected to a degree of supervision unparalleled since the fall of Rome. Lay and clerical lawmakers were concerned to regulate minutiae, and the development of centralised government of the Church was matched by that of the state. The mass of legislation is a symptom of vigilance, not of neglect. There is something here of the unsleeping supervision of the monks that Fructuosus of Braga enjoined upon the officers of his monastery.

This is all the more remarkable as being on the part of a government that lacked the massed bureaucracy of its Roman predecessor. Much had to be done through bishops, who might supervise the Jews, oversee the local officials of the fisc, undertake judicial responsibilities and quite possibly act as a source of local information and intelligence. Much of the ill-founded criticism of the late Visigothic state has been based upon a mistaken belief that a sophisticated administrative machinery existed, which in the late seventh century was in the process of breaking down. As an instrument of central government any such machinery had disappeared in the fifth century, whilst most of those features of local administration that survived that period of cataclysm continued in being up to the Arab conquest, and in some cases, under new titles, even beyond.[94] However, this is only to talk of a small handful of officials, with local responsibilities towards justice or the revenues of the fisc or military supervision. The Visigoths did not inherit a complex administration.

The issue of fugitive slaves well illustrates both the aspirations and the limitations of late seventh-century royal government in the peninsula. The existence of several laws in the codes relating to the problems of the apprehension and return of fugitive slaves has been interpreted as a symptom of the breakdown of internal order in the kingdom.[95] The very existence of fugitive slaves is not in itself surprising. Slaves had existed in the peninsula at least since the beginnings of Roman domination and were a fundamental feature of the rural economy, especially of the large estates. This is equally true of the other Germanic kingdoms and of the Byzantine Empire.

There are no grounds for supposing that slaves in the fifth or sixth centuries were happier than their successors in the seventh, or that the latter were more prone to flight. Of the laws relating to the flight of slaves and the harbouring of fugitives and related offences treated in the ninth book of the Code, only five out of twenty come from the seventh century, the rest date back to the times of Leovigild or Euric. Two of the laws belong to Chindasuinth, two to Ervig and one to Egica.[96] This last, issued in 702, puts increased onus on local communities to check the identity and legal status of dubious outsiders.

This should not be seen as indicating that the royal administration was no longer able to guarantee owners secure possession of their slaves. No Early Medieval government, not even that of Rome, could do that. The problem in Spain was made even more difficult by the nature of the terrain, and the threat posed to public order by banditry on the part of such fugitives was all the harder to combat. What Egica did was to provide means of redress in disputes over ownership and legal status when possible escapees were found, and, more strikingly, to place responsibility on local citizens to co-operate in detecting fugitives. This was a far from impractical measure, and similar in character to subsequent developments in medieval judicial practice, that placed responsibility for local good order on the community.

Christian slaves were not outsiders in the society developing in late Visigothic Spain in the way that the Jews were, though the final state of the two was equated by Egica's act of enslaving the Jewish community. Even without legal status or privilege both groups still needed to be regulated and watched. So too did foreign merchants, grave robbers, bee thieves and many other categories of suspicious or iniquitous persons: Visigothic Spain was not a comfortable place in which to live, particularly in its final half-century of existence. But it is important not to let its subsequent fate, as the result of unexpected invasion, cast an apocalyptic glow over those decades. The incapacitating of the state in 711, as a result of the death of the king and the fall of the capital, is, if anything, evidence of how successful the Visigothic kings and their episcopal advisers had been in their centralising of authority. It was not moral crisis or demoralisation that made the kingdom so vulnerable. Paradoxically it was rather the achievement of that very aim of central control of political authority, that its rulers had so long sought to bring about. Nor should it be forgotten just how much survived, or how much later centuries in Spain were to owe to this period, and particularly to the achievements of its Church and its law-makers.

In conclusion it is striking, although it has hitherto gone unremarked, that the last three major legislative acts of the Visigothic kings prefigured similar but subsequent developments in Medieval Europe. The first of these was the enslavement of the Jews by Egica, the possible fiscal motivation for which has just been discussed. Jews outside of Spain suffered similar losses of legal freedom and endured bondage to the state in later centuries. Those in France were made royal serfs, and in 1205 Pope Innocent III declared the Jews to be property of the Church. Secondly, as has been referred to, Egica's ruling on the responsibilities of local communities in respect of fugitive slaves mirrors such later developments in legal practice as the Frankpledge system and the Jury of Presentment, that were important features of the maintenance of public order in Anglo-Norman England. In these and related developments the onus of responsibility was placed firmly on the local community. Finally, what appears as the last recorded secular law of the Visigothic kingdom, promulgated by King Wittiza, relates to the administration of the ordeal. It is matched by contemporary liturgical compositions for its performance.[97] Although anachronistically denounced as the nadir of Visigothic legal thought and practice, in the eighth and ninth centuries the ordeal became the standard means of determining guilt in judicial processes throughout most of western Europe. It left the decision to God, in that the accused could, by voluntarily submitting to an ordeal, usually in the form of carrying a heated iron bar or plunging a hand into hot water to extract a stone, appeal to a divine verdict, manifested according to whether or not he then sustained visible injury.

It would be quite unjustified to claim that the subsequent history of Christian-Jewish relations, jurisprudence or the ordeal were in any way directly affected by these precedents in late Visigothic Spain. The fall of the kingdom and the limited subsequent dissemination and use of its civil laws would show that. However, what is important to note is that ideas and practices seen to be coming into being at the end of the Visigothic period are remarkably congruous with developments elsewhere in the West. The society of Visigothic Spain was heading in a way that others would soon unwittingly follow. It was not declining or decaying: it was evolving. However, as with the Germanic invasions, the Arab conquest of the peninsula in 711 cut across purely internal developments in the society, and by introducing new elements of culture and population required the whole process of assimilation and the search for unity to be begun anew.

5.   The Arab Conquest: The New Masters

THE sources for the history of Islamic Spain, or Al-Andalus as the Muslims called it, are incomparably richer than those available for the preceding Roman and Visigothic periods. Although much that once existed has now been lost, their bulk alone is impressive. Even more immediately striking to the historian accustomed to the alusive brevity of Latin annals is their wealth of incidental detail, such as information about the hair and eye colours of the rulers. Such minutiae of description, allied to confident assessments of character and a wealth of anecdote appear to take us more profoundly into the heart of this society and into the minds of some at least of its citizens than is possible for earlier periods. Not since the demise of classical historiography in the late Roman Empire do literary historical sources seem to offer so much, and in themselves compensate for the lack of most other forms of evidence.

However, alluring as this material undoubtedly is, it does present its own peculiar problems. For one thing, all of the extant Arabic historical writing concerned with Al-Andalus in the period it was ruled by the Umayyad dynasty (756–1031) is later in date than the times described. In some cases this is very considerably so, as with the *History of the Islamic Dynasties of Spain* written *c.* 1628–32 by Ahmed ibn Mohammed al-Makkarī, from Telensin in North Africa. Somewhat closer to the period in question is the *Al-Bayān al-Moghrib* or *The Astonishing Explanation of the History of the Kings of Spain and North Africa* of Ibn 'Idhārī or Marrakeshi ('the man from Marrakesh') compiled in the thirteenth century. From two centuries earlier, and from Spain itself, comes the *Muktabis* of Abu Marwan ibn Ḥayyān (*d.* 1076), possibly the most valuable of all the extant texts.

In the western historical tradition it is highly unlikely that much credence would be given to a seventeenth-century account of events in the eighth to tenth centuries, although the Irish *Annals of the Four Masters* is an exception. However, the character of Islamic historiography gives even quite late sources considerable value, sometimes more than that of others closer in time to the periods described. This is due to the deliberate and open inclusion by Muslim writers of history of substantial fragments of their predecessors' works in their own accounts. Thus Al-Makkarī's seventeenth-century book, written in Cairo and Damascus, is amongst the most important extant accounts of Umayyad Al-Andalus. This is due entirely to his inclusion of lengthy quotations from earlier writers, and especially from works of theirs not now elsewhere available. In particular he incorporates much of an otherwise lost book by Ibn Hayyān. Such borrowings were made explicit, fortunately for us, due to the Islamic tradition of citing recognised earlier authorities which would give stature to a book, and also enable its readers to know how much credence might be given to any anecdote or episode, by revealing the quality of its source.

This system of authority lies at the very heart of early Islamic historiography, which derives principally from the concern for collecting the sayings and teachings of the prophet Mohammed supplementary to the Koran. Such collections began to be formed within about a century of his death in AD632, and the strength and validity of the stories and apothegms, which were potentially important guides to religious and social beliefs and actions, had to be gauged from the chain of authorities cited by the compiler, who, in each case, might say from whom he received the account, how his informant had heard it and so on back to its source. The status of the originator gave the tradition or *hadīth* its standing, as more weight would be given to the testimony of a contemporary or a companion of the Prophet than to that of one whose relationship was less close or who might never have known him personally.[1]

From such an origin Islamic historiography developed in its own unique way, tending to be anecdotal and laying especial emphasis on the provision of explicit reference to the sources of information.[2] The latter feature might have given it a marked advantage over contemporary Latin and Byzantine historical writing, but Muslim historiography has its own peculiar pitfalls as well as strengths. For one thing, its anecdotal qualities give it a particular immediacy, and the wealth of incidental detail a sense of reliability, that are frequently at variance with reality. Thus Muslim historians in giving figures, be it of the composition of armies or of the revenues of states, often presented statistics of daunting but quite spurious precision.

Further difficulties were caused by the tendency to judge information more by the informant's known religious or moral status than by his demonstrable veracity as a witness of events: also as in the compilation of *hadīths*, falsification or the linking of names of recognised authority to fabricated stories was a danger appreciated by authors, but one which they were not always able to avoid. Often, when faced with contradictions or variations between authorities, Muslim historians presented the alternatives to their readers and left the conflicts unresolved. However, when their suspicions were not aroused they could prove uncritical in their acceptance of their sources. This in itself is hardly surprising, and their Christian counterparts were rarely more rigorous, but we must be less than credulous in our treatment of their accounts.

In the centuries following their rise to domination of the southern and eastern shores of the Mediterranean that began in the 630s, the Arabs became increasingly exposed to, and receptive of, the literary culture of Antiquity and its extension in Christian form into contemporary Byzantium, but their attitude to history and the aims of historical writing remained distinctive. Unlike the general run of their Christian counterparts, Muslim historians were secular men, usually not *qadis*, or authorities on the law, which being that of the Koran was religious in its origin and in its hold on society. Because, however, Islam never produced or sought a professional religious caste, as existed in medieval Christianity, and because of the particular religious penetration of society that is distinctive of Islam, most of its historical writers intended their works to be edifying, hortative and expressive of Muslim ideals.

Thus the extremely valuable historical work of Ibn Ḥayyān, the *Muktabis*, is fully entitled '*The Imparter of Information or the Fire Striking Steel on the History of the Eminent Spanish Muslims*'. The aim of his writing was to illuminate the lives of prominent Muslims of Al-Andalus rather than to compose narrative or annalistic history in the way that a Christian contemporary or Roman predecessor would have conceived it. Indeed the Christian narrative historical tradition, deriving from that of late Antiquity, has no exact counterpart in Islam. Muslim historiography tends to be biographical, and indeed there exists a *genre* of biographical encyclopedias that is unique to Islam and provides some of the most valuable historical sources. Of particular interest for Al-Andalus is the *Lives of the Qadis of Cordoba* written by Al-Kushanī for the caliph Al-Ḥakem II.[3] That a developing chronological structure is employed by Muslim historians, and the reigns of monarchs used to provide a skeleton for their works, gives a deceptive impression of similarity between their tradition and that of Christianity. This can just serve to obscure fundamental differences between the two. There was also a secondary but valuable annalistic strand in Muslim historiography, perhaps deriving from Byzantine practice. Such works are more limited in their information and inevitably duller in character than the anecdotal histories, and are not necessarily more reliable. In respect of the history of Al-Andalus this tradition is best represented by the works of Ibn al-Athīr (1160–1233) from Mesopotamia and the African *Bayān al-Moghrib* of Ibn 'Idhārī (thirteenth-century).

It is from these and other Islamic sources that our understanding of the Arab conquest of Visigothic Spain mainly derives. The narrative history of the late Visigothic kingdom is virtually non-existent. From the conclusion of Isidore's two historical works in the 620s to the aftermath of the Arab invasion only one contemporary history survives, Julian's *History of Wamba*, which only deals with the events of a single year. This lack is probably not due to the disappearance of other sources, for the *Chronicle* written anonymously in 754, probably in Toledo, which covers the history of the peninsula since 611, provides little information that we are not already aware of concerning the period up to 711.[4] Its sources appear to have been the law code and the acts of ecclesiastical councils. For the conquest and its aftermath it does have considerable independent value, but its annalistic character and brevity make it allusive and frustratingly elusive.

The same is basically true of the only other Spanish Christian accounts, to be found in some short chronicles composed in the Asturian kingdom in the late ninth and early tenth centuries. These also suffer from legendary accretions and give few grounds for confidence in their reliability. Attempts to establish that parts of one of them, the *Chronicle of Alfonso III*, are genuine eighth-century entries, composed by a bishop of Toledo driven to take refuge in the Asturias, are purely fanciful.[5]

Unfortunately the account of the conquest of Visigothic Spain given by the Arabic sources, although far more substantial in bulk than the Christian equivalent, is every bit as much the repository of later legendary elaborations, which severely curtail its value as a description of the actual events. As with the Christian authors, the conquest represented an occurrence of overwhelming significance to the Islamic historians, but it was one far removed from their own times. The earliest extant historical source relating to Al-Andalus only dates from the tenth century, and survives solely in a thirteenth-century Portuguese translation.[6] But it is not just a question of chronological perspective, for the same sources provide a sober if not always accurate picture of events in the decades succeeding the conquest. The episode of the invasion and its rapid triumph clearly took on an apocalyptic quality not only for the conquered but also for the conquerors.

Thus, as well as a common story about a certain Julian, supposedly the governor of Ceuta, aiding the Arabs to cross the straits into Spain out of a desire to revenge himself on King Roderic, the seducer of his daughter, the Muslim accounts describe premonitory signs that heralded the invasion and also the fabulous treasures that fell to the victors in its aftermath. Amongst the latter is usually included the 'Table of Solomon', part of the treasures of Jerusalem.[7] The stories of supernatural warning relate to a palace or tower that none of the Visigothic kings ever entered, but rather, on their accessions, added more locks to its gate. Roderic, however, despising the entreaties of his advisers, insisted instead upon removing the padlocks and entering the sealed building, only to be terrified by painted images of the Arabs on the walls within and an inscription stating that in his day his kingdom would fall to these men.

Variations of this story, which has interesting parallels with certain Jewish ones, and related ones about a chamber in which successive Visigothic kings hung up their crowns, have rightly never been taken as descriptions of reality. However some historians, while disdaining the supernatural tale, have been happy to believe in the human one, that is to say the story of Count Julian and his daughter.[8] Such rationalisations of cataclysmic political events in terms of small-scale personal dramas are not unusual in ancient and medieval sources and may well represent a typical human response to such things. This does not imply that they are to be believed in; on the contrary, they are signs that events have occurred of such magnitude as to be beyond the grasp of ordinary intelligence to comprehend. An explanation that reduces them to simpler levels of the actions of a small group of individuals, although fictional, is going to prove attractive and acceptable. Our task is to recognise such stories for what they are.

Other aspects of the accounts of the conquest have been subjected to increasingly critical scrutiny, and in some cases have been rejected. One such element is a supposed preliminary raid on Spain in 710 by Arab forces led by a certain Ṭarīf. This is now regarded as a purely literary mirroring of the probably genuine expedition of 711 led by Ṭarīk.[9] This, as far as the strictly historical record is concerned, should join the Julian stories in oblivion. Both, however, have their interest for literary and social anthropological research.

Essentially, the Arab conquest of Spain seems to have developed along the following lines: after the military subjugation of most of North Africa had been completed, but long before the cultural and religious assimilation of its indigenous Berber inhabitants can have occurred, an expedition, probably originally intended as a probing raid, was sent into Spain in 711 by Mūsa ibn Nuṣayr, the Arab governor of Ifrikiya (the new Arab North Africa), under the command of his former slave Ṭarīk. The number of the latter's forces are quite possibly minimised in the Islamic accounts. Ibn 'Abd al-Ḥakem gives a figure of 1,700 men. However, if this was only a raid rather than a full invasion, as the absence of the governor from its command, contrary to Arab practice, would seem to indicate, such a number is not unreasonable. That ascribed to the Visigothic army that encountered them is: Al-Makkarī gives it as 100,000 men.[10]

King Roderic (710–711), at the outset of his reign, was in a vulnerable position. The opening of a new king's rule was a peculiarly sensitive time, when challenges to his authority might be expected and his military capacities would have to be displayed to their best advantage. Roderic's standing may have been unusually weak due to continuing controversy over the succession. The Islamic sources, although here again we may be encountering that tendency to personalising and myth-making, refer to the existence of sons of Wittiza.[11] If this were so, they must have been deliberately excluded from succeeding their father in 710. They are described as having acted in collusion with the Arabs, and as having deserted Roderic in the course of the decisive battle in the Guadalquivir valley that ended his reign and the Visigothic kingdom. Some historians have seen a King Achila II who ruled in Narbonne and Tarragona c. 710–713 as being one of these sons of Wittiza. However, if they played the significant part in the events of 711 that is ascribed to them, their exclusion from the succession in 710 is hard to understand. The elective element in royal succession was more theoretical than practical, and in no other case are surviving sons, even children, known not to have succeeded their fathers. Reference to the traitorous behaviour of the sons of Wittiza in the Asturian *Chronicle of Alfonso III* is no additional guarantee that they actually existed, as the Christian and Muslim traditions on the conquest are clearly related, despite the brevity of the former.[12]

Even putting the sons of Wittiza to one side, it is possible that the election of Roderic had proved divisive. The absence of coinage in his name from Tarraconese and Narbonese mints suggests that his authority was challenged there.[13] His particular strength seems to have lain in the south, and Mérida was a stronghold of his partisans. His first recorded concern was with the need to campaign against the Basques, and it was from his northern expedition that the king was called to face the incursion by Ṭarīk.[14] Hastening south, he encountered the invaders only to be defeated in battle in the Guadalquivir valley, probably near to Medina Sidonia. Roderic's death is not recorded in the reliable accounts, but as he never again features it is reasonable to assume that he perished in the battle. Legends of his escape and withdrawal to penitent refuge in a monastery circulated from the Middle Ages onwards, finally taking extended poetic form in Robert Southey's *Roderic* of 1816.

The battle itself was in all probability a rather small-scale affair: Ṭarīk's forces were few in number, and with his march from the north and possibly the limited size of the threat, it is unlikely that Roderic had raised substantial levies from other parts of the peninsula. He was probably accompanied only by his household troops, the nucleus of the Visigothic army, and levies from the great estates of Baetica. The victory itself may have owed much to the unfamiliarity of the tactics employed by Ṭarīk's army. Greater armies and more powerful states had already succumbed to these conquerors. The probable death of the king and the destruction of his *comitatus*, the royal troops and the court nobility, must have given the battle its decisive character. Roderic had no clear successor and the effective elective body, the Gothic nobles in the army, were either dead or scattered in flight. No king was created in the aftermath of the battle because of the complexities involved when a son was not there to succeed his father. Ṭarīk's subsequent and speedy capture of Toledo, the only place where a king might legitimately be anointed, can only have added to the disarray.

There are remarkable parallels between the Arab invasion of Spain in 711 and the Norman conquest of England in 1066. In both cases a single battle effectively decided the issue, and in both instances the defending ruler was forced to make a rapid and lengthy march to meet the invader. The deaths of the monarchs, the scattering of their immediate and highly influential military following, and the fall of the capitals, convert battles into conquests. That these events have more to do with the social and political organisation of the defeated state

than with the supposed morals or morale of their citizenry has now
fortunately been recognised in respect of Anglo-Saxon England,
though not yet of Visigothic Spain.[15]

Unlike the Normans in 1066, the Arabs in 711 probably had not
expected to undertake a full-scale conquest. However, in the
aftermath of his victory, Ṭarīk altered his objectives, and rather than
be satisfied with the plunder of the Guadalquivir valley, proceeded
via Cordoba to Toledo, encountering no resistance *en route*. This
dramatic change, of course, brought over the governor Mūsa from
Kairouan, the Arabs' military base and centre of government in
Ifrikiya, with a large army, either later in 711 or in 712, to reinforce
but also to supersede his deputy. The tribal democracy of Arabian
society, reinforced by the egalitarianism of Islam, made it essential for
any governor, however appointed, to take the lead in person in any
major military undertaking, or risk being deposed by his own
followers.

Mūsa took Seville, provincial capital of Baetica, with ease, but was
resisted at Mérida, then full of the family and followers of Roderic.
The siege lasted for some sixteen months and was the most protracted
opposition that the conquerors had to face in the aftermath of their
victory. Only after the way across the Guadiana had been cleared by
the capitulation of the city was Mūsa able to proceed north along the
Roman road leading to Salamanca. He turned east before reaching
that city to encounter his subordinate Ṭarīk coming from Toledo to
meet him at Talavera (713). According to some of the Islamic
accounts Mūsa deliberately humiliated his freedman, ordering him to
be flogged, to underline his subordination and status and to
undermine his achievement.[16] In the same year Mūsa's son 'Abd
al-'Aziz, who had been left to hold Seville, led an expedition to subdue
Huelva and Faro in southern Portugal.

In 714 Mūsa and Ṭarīk together continued the northward thrust of
conquest, proceeding to Zaragoza, and there dividing. Mūsa
advanced via Soria and Palencia into the Asturias, reaching the Bay
of Biscay at Gijon, while Ṭarīk marched by way of Logroño to Leon
and Astorga. The last stage of this rapid and wide-ranging initial
period of conquest ended in 715, when 'Abd al-'Aziz pacified the
south-east of the peninsula. Taking Malaga and Elvira (the precursor
of Granada) he completed his expedition by coming to terms with a
certain Tudmir, probably a Gothic count who had made himself
master of much of the region in the aftermath of the invasion. The

absence of detailed sources for the Christian side denies us any knowledge of how individual towns and regions coped with the difficulties of the period between the collapse of Visigothic royal authority and their passing under the control of the new conquerors, but it is likely that conditions were not dissimilar to those that had existed in the sixth century prior to the campaigns of Leovigild.

By the time of Tudmir's submission to 'Abd al-'Aziz, Mūsa and Ṭarīk had left Spain, recalled in the winter of 714–15 by their master the Umayyad caliph Walīd I, now grown distrustful by reason of their successes. His brother Suleymān, who was ruling by the time of their return to Damascus, disgraced Mūsa and confiscated his property, leaving him to die shortly after in poverty. Ṭarīk disappeared into obscurity.[17] Like Columbus and Cortes, they were poorly rewarded by the master in whose name they had achieved so much. The caliph also ordered the arrest of 'Abd al-'Aziz, left by Mūsa to govern in his absence, but he was already dead, murdered in Seville in 716 by some of his own followers supposedly for adopting Visigothic royal practices. He had married the daughter of Roderic, and it was apparently at her instigation that he tried to make his fellow Arabs perform acts of obeisance before him and took to wearing a crown. The story as presented in the Islamic sources has certain anachronistic features, but is not improbable.[18] It is the only evidence of anything approaching an attempt to preserve direct continuity from Visigothic to Arab styles of government. Its failure is indicative of the changes that the conquest would very quickly impose upon society in the peninsula.

The rise of Islam and the creation of the Arab empire, that stretched from the Pyrenees to the Punjab during the course of the seventh and early eighth centuries, transformed the political and cultural geography of the Mediterranean and the Near East. Arguably they represent the most important developments in Europe and western Asia during the whole of the first millennium AD. However, in terms of surviving evidence, for events of such magnitude we are remarkably badly informed about them. Early society in the Arabian peninsula was pre-literate, although having strong oral traditions. With the exception of the Koran, the record of successive divine revelations to the Prophet Moḥammed in the years c. 610 to 632, and traditionally held to have been compiled in written form c. 650, there is no extant Arabic literature securely dated to before the ninth century. The accounts of even the earliest available Arabic histories of the origins of Islam and its spread have recently been subjected to severe criticism.[19]

Likewise the Byzantine Empire, which in the mid sixth century had boasted a substantial historiographical culture, has left effectively no contemporary account of itself in the crucial seventh century. For the central Greek tradition only the works of ninth- and tenth-century chroniclers are available. What does survive presents considerable problems to the modern historian. The mid seventh-century Egyptian *Chronicle of John of Nikiu*, which has an account of the Arab conquest of that province, only survives in an Ethiopic translation of 1602 of a lost Arabic translation of the Greek or Coptic original.[20] In such a transmission, that sections of the work should disappear entirely and some of the text become garbled is hardly surprising. Likewise an apparently contemporary Armenian history of the reign of the Byzantine emperor Heraclius (610–641) by a Bishop Sebeos is in large measure the work of ninth- and tenth-century interpolators.[21] The state of the evidence is, even by early medieval standards, deplorable. As a result, the detailed working of certain crucial developments cannot be seen, and features of the utmost importance can only be described in the haziest of terms.

Although the standard account of the early history of Islam and the rise of the Arab Empire given in the Islamic sources has been subjected to severe and critical scrutiny, and is probably deficient in many respects, it cannot be jettisoned, not least as there is precious little to put in its place. Attempts by the critics to construct alternative versions have failed to attain conviction, in part due to the inadequacies of the non-Arabic sources. A brief survey of the traditional account is necessary in order to put the conquest of Spain into a context of the wider developments, which should make an understanding of its cultural and social impact more comprehensible.[22]

Supposedly born in 570, Moḥammed, a lesser member of one of the leading families of the dominant tribe in Mecca in western Arabia, began *c.* 610 to receive revelations from God via the Archangel Gabriel, requiring him to preach monotheism to his fellow Arabs. In addition, particularly as his mission developed, certain ethical doctrines were revealed to him, as were various practical injunctions concerning social behaviour, law and punishments to be observed within the community of believers, or Muslims ('those who have surrendered'). At the heart of the revelations lay the five 'Pillars of

Islam': the theological affirmation that 'there is no God but God', to which was added assent to the validity of Moḥammed's message in the form of 'and Moḥammed is his Prophet'. The other four 'Pillars' are the requirements to pray five times daily at stipulated times, to fast during daylight during the month of Ramadan, to make pilgrimage to Mecca, and to distribute a fixed portion of personal income in alms to the poor. These commands and various supplementary doctrines and injunctions were revealed and elaborated upon in stages during the last twenty years of the Prophet's life.[23]

Because his religious message threatened the unity and social cohesion of the tribesmen of Mecca, once he began to attract followers, opposition developed. For one thing the town, which controlled the caravan trade between the Yemen and the Byzantine provinces of Egypt, Palestine and Syria, was a centre of religious pilgrimage, housing the shrine of a divinity called Hucbal – probably a meteorite cult – and was one of the principle centres of a developed polytheistic worship in the peninsula. Mecca's commercial and religious significance gave its leading tribe, the Quraysh, advantages and influence over other, principally nomadic, tribes in Arabia. In 622 Moḥammed, to avoid a planned assassination, was able to take the opportunity of a request by some of the tribes of Medina to move there with his followers, to act as a mediator in the current inter-tribal feuding that was dividing the town. Once there, he was able to impose his religious reforms on some of the tribes and to expel others, including some converted to Judaism. He was further able, thanks to Medina's strategic position on the caravan routes to the north of Mecca, to impose an economic blockade on the latter, cutting its trade to the Byzantine provinces. Failing in successive attempts to break his hold by force the Meccans were eventually obliged to capitulate in 630, accepting Moḥammed's religious reforms. In the last two years of his life the Prophet went on to make many of the other tribes of Arabia receive his teachings and his political suzerainty.

A reaction, called the *riddah*, set in with his death. Many tribes apostasised, while a crisis of leadership developed in Mecca. The latter was resolved when, setting aside 'Ali, Moḥammed's nearest male relative, a small group of the Prophet's closest associates selected Abū Bakr, traditionally the first disciple, to be caliph ('successor') or secular leader of the Muslim community. During his brief tenure of this new office (632–634) Abū Bakr and his advisors put an end to the *riddah* or apostasy amongst the tribes, and instead launched them into simultaneous attacks on the territories of the two great empires to the north, the Byzantine and the Sassanian Persian. This had dramatic consequences: during the rule of the second caliph, 'Umar (634–644), another former companion of Moḥammed, armies of both empires were defeated in successive engagements. Syria, Palestine and Egypt were lost by the Byzantines, Mesopotamia and western Persia, including their capital city of Ctesiphon, by the Sassanians. In 636 Jerusalem fell and 'Umar entered it, riding a donkey.[24]

The initial impetus of conquest was halted after the murder of the third caliph, 'Uthmān (644–656), who had over-endowed his own relatives with military commands and governorships of the newly conquered provinces. He had also offended Muslim opinion by laxness in enforcing the full legal injunctions of the Koran. Moḥammed's cousin 'Ali, thrice disappointed of the caliphate, was suspected of complicity in the murder and during his rule (656–661) civil war ensued between his partisans and the Umayyads, the powerful family to which 'Uthmān had belonged. When 'Ali was in turn murdered by a fanatic, the leader of the latter, Mo'āwiyah, governor of Syria, was elected caliph (661–680) and, despite subsequent civil wars, inaugurated a dynastic rule that lasted in his family until 750. Territorial expansion continued. In the course of the next eighty years Arab armies moved progressively further eastward over the former lands of the Sassanians, reaching as far as the river Oxus, modern Afghanistan and the borders of the Punjab.

Similarly, earlier tentative expeditions into North Africa in the 650s were followed by more determined expansion under the Umayyads. A permanent military base was established at Kairouān, in modern Tunisia, and in 681 an army under 'Ukba ibn Nāfki marched across the whole length of the region to arrive at the Atlantic ocean. They were ambushed by Berber tribes on their return and 'Ukba killed. It was these Berbers, rather than the residual Byzantine administration, that provided the principal resistance to the ensuing Arab conquest. In 698 Carthage, the former capital, fell and the imperial government abandoned its North African holdings, removing its forces to Sicily. However, the Berbers continued to resist, often with considerable if short-lived success. But by 711 the Arabs' Ifrikiya was sufficiently pacified for the expedition into Spain to be launched, with the unexpected results that have been seen.

There are obviously many difficulties in accepting this account of events, as it is largely an interpreted version of that given in the Islamic sources, and many problems are raised by the traditional relating of the life of Moḥammed, but for present purposes some questions concerning the spread of Islam and of the Arabs need to be considered. Some great issues, however, such as the underlying causes of the success of the conquests that covered such an enormous extent of territory and which were completed so rapidly, still remain baffling, and explanations can only remain in the realm of conjecture. It is unlikely that a single answer will fit all cases, in view of the divergencies of society, culture and geography encompassed in the area of the conquests. An approach from the point of the conquerors is more likely to prove fruitful. One problem is that of manpower. As the Arabian peninsula was clearly not depopulated in the process, what were the human resources employed in these remarkable expansions, achieved by the hardly numerous inhabitants of one of the world's most desolate regions?

A related question is that of how Islamicised the Arab tribes were by the time of the death of Moḥammed and the sudden military extension of their race to dominance over their settled neighbours. By traditional chronology eight years out of the last decade of the Prophet's life was spent in making himself master of the Hijāz – the region of central western Arabia in which Mecca and Medina were the chief settlements. Although this process must have affected most of the tribes in that area, it only leaves two years (630–632) for Islam, and the authority of Mecca, to be imposed on the rest of the peninsula, including the Persian-held Yemen. Islamic sources which imply that this happened are reticent on the means of its achievement. Even allowing that the essential tenets of Islamic belief and practice had become firmly established during the Prophet's lifetime, a notion which has not gone unchallenged, and which the history of most of the world's other religions might lead one to doubt, its hold over its original recipients was still very new, even at the time of their conquest of Spain. Further, that they were numerically very small in comparison with the populations of the areas of their new empire makes the subsequent spread of the Arabs and Islam in those regions all the more remarkable.

Culturally the Arab tribes had very little to offer. Some modern historians looking back through the great age of the cultural florescence of Umayyad Spain in the tenth century, tend to write as

if all the elements of learning, sophistication and material civilisation
that were certainly present in that period, were also features of Arab
society in the eighth century. This is patently nonsensical. Such
things were the products of protracted influence on Islamic society of
the learning and culture of the far older civilisations whose lands they
had conquered, and are hardly traceable prior to the ninth century.[25]
The cultural and commercial openness of the Islamic world, despite
various political rifts, enabled such developments to spread within it,
principally from Iraq, into all regions, Spain included.

The Arabs who crossed from Africa into Spain in 711 were then a
tiny minority in respect of the population over which they made
themselves masters. They had to make use of others, the Berbers, to
buttress their own military insufficiency. Further, only three
generations on from the time of Mohammed, they still retained the
tribal basis of their society unimpaired, with very few imprints of the
higher culture of their victims or neighbours yet made upon them. In
short, they were not unlike the Visigoths on their entry into Spain in
the fifth century.

Obviously there are many striking differences between the two
groups of invaders. For one thing, the Arabs were, despite its roots in
Christian and Jewish thought and scriptures, the proponents of a new
religion, that in their eyes sharply distinguished them from their
subjects; however it is worth recalling that the Visigoths, as Arians,
were divided from the Hispano-Romans by the barrier of heresy, and
that for centuries Christians were unable to free themselves from
thinking of Islam as being only an errant form of their own religion.[26]
In addition, however, the Arab invaders of Spain were part of a wider
Arab and Islamic community, and were thereby less isolated and
vulnerable than the Visigoths. On the other hand, the latter probably
had more points of immediate cultural contact with the indigenous
population, after their century inside the Roman Empire. By 711,
however, although some assimilation had already got underway, and
the Arabs had been despised neighbours and occasional allies of the
Romans for centuries, they must have seemed far more alien to the
inhabitants of Spain than the Visigoths had two centuries previously.

Borrowings from the Roman and Persian traditions by the
triumphant but, in terms of complex administrative skills, sorely
deficient Arabs were restricted in character and locality during the
seventh and early eighth centuries. The Umayyad caliphs, starting
with Mo'āwiyah, had moved their residence from Mecca to

Damascus, hitherto a not very important provincial city in Byzantine Syria. There their styles of life and government underwent certain modifications, borrowing various Byzantine forms of bureaucratic administration. For this continuing imperial traditions of local government were available, as were trained personnel. So too were craftsmen skilled in Byzantine or Persian styles, who could be employed in the creation of the new Islamic religious buildings, such as the Dome of the Rock at Jerusalem (687–691) and the Great Mosque at Damascus (705–715), as well as in the building of palaces for the caliphs. For craftsmanship of the finest quality though, it was necessary to borrow skilled artisans directly from Constantinople.[27]

Such contacts and borrowings were relatively rare and largely confined to the upper levels of administration and the direct artistic patronage of the caliphal dynasty. In general contacts between the conquerors and their subjects were restricted. The Arab armies, or *djunds*, were kept segregated in great military camps or garrison cities, such as Kūfa, Baṣra and Wāsit in Mesopotamia (Irāq), Fusṭāṭ (later Cairo) in Egypt and Kairouān in North Africa, which were founded in the aftermath of the conquests. At first they were kept in permanent military readiness, and of course, the process of conquest and expansion continued until virtually the end of the Umayyad period, drawing to a close in the 740s. Local communities were left by the Arabs to be largely self-governing, required only to pay land and capitation taxes that were imposed upon their non-Muslim subjects by the caliphs.[28] The proceeds were principally intended for distribution to the Arab *djunds*. As a result of this separation, the latter retained an untainted Islamic fundamentalism, their sense of superiority to non-Arabs and their own tribal identities. The members of the *djunds* thus stayed largely detached from the benefits, or seductive influences, of the cultures of their victims, whilst the Umayyad caliphs were lured increasingly, from practical necessity tempered by personal choice, into an alien lifestyle, and in some cases into disregarding the rules of the Koran. This led to a widening gulf between leaders and led, the more so as the increasing autocracy of the rulers, following Byzantine or Sassanian precedents, was at variance with the traditions of consensus government typical of the tribal sheikhs.

The isolation of the *djunds* and the Arabs' sense of racial superiority limited the initial impact of Islam on the conquered. In the periods of expansion the standard practice had been for the Arab commanders to offer simple terms of capitulation to towns that they threatened. If they surrendered without resistance then they might retain their own forms of self-government and religious observance, being subjected only to the land and poll taxes, themselves scarcely dissimilar to the fiscal obligations previously imposed by Byzantine or Sassanian administrations. The alternative offered was destruction of the town and the enslavement of its inhabitants, though in practice the general terms were usually imposed even on cities that had put up a fight. With limited local military resources, perhaps only sufficient to contain banditry, and quite possibly with fortifications in disrepair, most settlements capitulated without resistance. This is as true of Spain as of Syria, and just as comprehensible.

Religious toleration was granted to Jews and Christians, though not formally to Persian Zoroastrians, and there was little subsequent incentive to press for conversion to Islam. For one thing, by ruling of the Koran it was forbidden to tax Muslims, and thus Islamic governments had to depend largely upon the revenues derived from imposts on their non-Muslim subjects. Obviously religious coexistence was far from easy, and in due course pressures towards conversion developed within the communities of the non-Arab population. The causes and effects of this in Spain will be examined in a subsequent chapter.

By the time of the conquest of Al-Andalus in 711, three generations had passed since the death of Mohammed and already some members of the subject populations had joined the Arabs in adherence to Islam and in some cases, by attachment to tribes, had even been integrated formally into Arabic society. It is likely that such individuals were in most cases slaves or descendants of slaves taken in the initial periods of conquest and subsequently freed. It is impossible to quantify them, but their existence complicates the question of racial and cultural mix in this formative stage of the Arab Empire. It is possible that more of them were Persians than anything else, as 'the Peoples of the Book', that is to say Jews and Christians, whose scriptures had exercised some influence on Mohammed's thought, were extended a tolerance in the Koran that was denied to 'pagans', such as the Zoroastrians.

These converts, called *muwallads* ('adopted'), should in principle have enjoyed the freedoms of their Arab co-religionists, as the message of Islam was directed to a religious not a racial community. However, in practice it seems they were scorned by the Arabs and often not freed from their tax burdens by the government, which could ill spare the revenues. As the isolation of the Arabs in military settlements began to break down in the eighth century and they began to purchase lands from non-Muslims, attempts were made to preserve the tax obligations on such lands even when under Muslim ownership. Arab discontent with the increasingly less Islamic character of the Umayyad regime grew, as did that of the *muwallads* or converts, denied their full rights as members of the community of believers. These and other discontents helped to create a climate propitious to the overthrow of the Umayyad dynasty, which in turn led to the breaking of the political unity of the Islamic world, a process in which Spain had a vital part to play.[29]

That settlement of the Arabs and Berbers in the peninsula followed in the aftermath of the campaigns of conquest is made clear in the Islamic sources. However, the nature of the settlement needs to be considered. It is improbable, seeing the precedents set by the conquerors in other regions, that a real distribution of and settling on the land immediately succeeded the invasion. Al-Makkarī lists the tribes of which elements settled themselves in Spain and where they did so.[30] The genealogical materials that he or his sources were depending upon must have substantially postdated the period of the conquest, but it is striking that Arab settlements in the tenth and eleventh centuries were still clustered around certain focal points, those listed by Al-Makkarī for the eighth century. The principal areas of settlement at the end of the Umayyad period in Spain were Cordoba, Granada, Seville and Beja, and this probably represents a similar pattern to that existing at its beginning. There are a few other towns that might be added to the list from other indications, and there are some such as Mérida where, unusually, significant populations of Berbers and Arabs coexisted.

It seems possible to suggest that the first phase of occupation was a purely military one, based upon the establishing of Arab garrisons in certain strategic towns. In other cases, as with the founding of Kairouān in North Africa, wholly new settlements were created to serve as garrison towns and administrative centres. However, this was not a universal rule; existing centres could be used, as in the case of Merv in Khorāssān. Also the development of Granada, on a different site from Romano-Visigothic Elvira, conceivably represents the establishment of such an Arab fortress town. These key towns became the focal points in which most of the crucial episodes in the history of Al-Andalus were to be played out. In outline at least, this opening phase of Arab rule in Spain was not dissimilar to that of the beginnings of Visigothic rule in the peninsula in the mid fifth century. The initial impact was probably limited to those towns actually occupied; and much of the countryside remained unaffected.

The cultural impact was also probably less clear than is often assumed, in that on the new scale of empire Arab identity was still in the process of formation. Leaving aside the Berber element, it is highly unlikely that the Arabs who entered Spain were racially unified. The enormous extent of Arab expansion in a relatively short period must have produced a crisis of manpower in the conquering armies. The tribes from Arabia proper are known, from the copious genealogical information that is available, to have been supplemented by the resources of other Arab clans living in Mesopotamia and on the fringes of Syria. Even so that was insufficient, and it is clear that slavery played an important role in determining the composition of the Arab armies. Slaves captured in the wars may well have been used to fight. It is certain that freedmen were. These former slaves uprooted from their own societies, were, on their emancipation linked under close ties of patronage to their quondam owners and to those owners' tribes. Employment in tribal armies may have been a principal reason for emancipation. The freed slaves became members of the clan and tribe of their masters, to whom, as was also the case for freedmen in the Roman and Visigothic periods, they were tied in strict dependency. The role of the former slave Ṭarīk in the campaigns of 711–14 has already been mentioned. Another leading figure in the conquests of Spain was Mugeyth ar-Rūmi ('the Roman' i.e. Byzantine) who, captured in the wars in Syria, was a freedman of the former caliph 'Abd al-Mālik (685–705), and commanded the cavalry in the battle against Roderic.[31]

The converts, *muwallads*, were also, at least in the opening stages of Islamic expansion, affiliated to Arab tribes, which effectively adopted them. Mūsa ibn Nuṣayr, according to his biographer Ibn Khallikān (1211–1282), was the son of a convert of the tribe of Lakhm.[32] Such revelations might lead us to expect that, like these their leaders, many of the invaders were freedmen or converts. To complicate matters, the premium that came to be placed upon pure Arab descent, almost in itself a sign of massive adulteration, made genealogical fabrication or the obscuring of unsuitable ancestry a necessary concern in the centuries to follow. From the start in Al-Andalus interesting and varied origins were concealed behind a facade of adopted Arabism.

This is not to say that these elements, which may well have been in the majority, should not be counted as Arabs. They were in the sense that they thought of themselves as such, spoke and wrote Arabic, belonged to tribes, and adhered to a religion that had arisen in Arabia, but their connection to the real Arab past was tenuous. Two considerations arise from this. Firstly it is by no means clear how far this process had gone by 711, and our perspective through our sources writing after its completion cannot but be distorted. Secondly this dislocation of many diverse elements of population and culture and their reformation around a new Arab identity may explain the remarkable survival of the distinctively Arabic features of this civilisation, in such things as language and social organisation, when faced by the possible challenge of older or more sophisticated traditions. It was a new identity created for people of different origins uprooted from their distinct pasts in a period of upheaval.

In this respect the Berbers were different, in that, Arabised as they became in language and Islamicised in religion, both slow processes, they never sought to fit themselves into an Arab identity. They had put up the most protracted resistance of any group that the Arabs encountered, probably because they were tribally organised and mountain-dwelling. They had already, like the Basques, preserved their identity and distinct forms of society, despite centuries of contact with Roman civilisation and even the penetration of Christianity. Thanks to their already existing tribal structures there was little incentive for them to be drawn into the network of attachment to Arab tribes. Because of their independence they had to be despised and even derided as being racially inferior by the Arabs, whose own origins were much less clear cut.[33] The poet Khalf ibn Fāraj as-Samir of Almeria wrote of them (c. 1080): 'I saw Adam in my dream, and I said to him: "O, Father of mankind! Men generally agree that the Berbers are descended from thee." "Yes it is true, but none dispute that Eve was at that time divorced from me." '[34]

Berber movement into Spain occurred basically in two waves, one at the time of the initial conquest, and the other in the late tenth century. In both cases only some of them remained permanently in Al-Andalus; the others subsequently returned to Africa. It seems that the Arabs employed the Berbers as mercenaries. Some probably accompanied Tarīk and others were brought across by Mūsa. Whilst the Arabs established themselves in the principal towns of the south of the peninsula, the Berbers were sent to the more vulnerable regions of the centre and north, particularly once it became clear that a military occupation of the northern mountain zone would not be feasible.[35] Although some Berber tribes and individuals are recorded living in the south, the bulk of those brought into Spain, and no guess as to numbers can be made, were put to occupy what became the frontier region: the Ebro valley, Extremadura, Catalonia and the southern Meseta. From the account of events given by Al-Makkarī and others it is clear that they, like the Arabs, were concentrated in particular strongpoints that included Mérida, Tarragona and Talavera amongst others.[36] An attempt to establish Berbers in the north-west of the peninsula, perhaps in the former Roman military bases of Leon, Astorga and Braga, was abandoned by the middle of the eighth century when the tribes in question withdrew back to Africa. The Berbers probably remained on a military footing for longer than the Arabs in the south. This was due in large part to their positioning on a violent frontier, but the hostility directed towards them by other sectors of the population may also have contributed. In Al-Andalus the Berbers filled many of the roles of the federate German barbarians in the later Roman Empire, despised but necessary defenders of the frontiers.

Unfortunately the question of the Berber contribution to the culture of Al-Andalus has received little attention. It is often assumed that they were thoroughly Islamicised by the time of their entry into Spain in the early eighth century. However, the Arab conquest of North Africa was hardly complete by that point. What is more, evidence of the continued use of Latin there can be found for as late as the tenth century, and substantial Christian communities were still in existence in Africa in the eleventh.[37] It is thus highly improbable, particularly in view of the general indications of slow conversion to Islam on the part of the Arabs' subject populations, that large numbers of Berbers were Muslims in 711, nor in view of their role would they have been required to be.[38] A reference in Al-Makkarī to the religious practices of Berber rebels who beseiged Mérida in 742 makes it clear that they were not Muslims.[39]

All too little is known about Berber society and culture, both in the Roman and early Islamic periods of North African history. As they remained distinct from the Arab tribal organisation they were excluded from consideration in the writings on genealogy and in the biographical encyclopedias. Not until the fourteenth century and the writing of Ibn Khaldūn's monumental *History of the Berbers* was any serious study devoted to their traditions, and by then little reliable memory remained of distant centuries. The distinctive Berber presence in Al-Andalus is thus hard to delineate. The histories merely refer to events in which they participated, usually in a hostile vein, and the insights that are possible on so many features of the culture and society of this stage are generally denied us when it comes to the Berbers.

The conquered Christians will receive fuller investigation in a subsequent chapter, but in the wake of the conquest they were little disturbed, particularly those not living in towns garrisoned by the Arabs. Our Arabic sources tend to be best informed about events in the city of Cordoba, which became the capital of the Umayyad state in the peninsula, and the difficulties that the Christian community occasionally faced there are not necesarily typical of the rest of Spain. Christian worship was never prohibited and injunctions intended to prevent any expansion of Christianity may have been better observed in Cordoba than elsewhere. The effects of the conquest on the Romano-Gothic aristocracy, potentially the principal sufferers from the events of 711, are unclear. The likely lack of any substantial settlement on the land by the conquerors may have limited expropriations, and noble families of Roman and Visigothic descent that eventually converted to Islam do make occasional appearances in the pages of the Arab historians. Indeed one chronicler, Ibn al-Kūtiyya ('the Goth'), claimed descent from King Wittiza. The former royal lands of the Visigothic monarchy, and perhaps those of the aristocracy who fell in battle in 711, are likely to have become the property of the caliphs, administered for them by the governors, until 756 when they passed into the hands of the rulers (amirs) of the newly independent Umayyad state of Al-Andalus. Other lands retained by the Christian nobility would have been liable to tax, and probably served as an important source of revenue for the Muslim rulers.

As for the conquerors, despite certain doubts–the caliph 'Umar II (717–20) thought of ordering Al-Andalus to be abandoned–they continued their military expansion with unabated zest, following in the footsteps of Ṭarīk and Mūsa.[40] The almost frenetic quality of the military activity in the three decades after 711 again makes the idea of a peaceful settlement on the land at this time a virtual impossibility. After the murder of 'Abd al-'Aziz ibn Mūsa, there followed a succession of governors ruling Al-Andalus in the name of the caliph. They were generally appointed by their immediate superior, the governor of Ifrikiya. Occasionally, as when one of them met a violent death in battle, the army in Spain elected its own leader, until a replacement was appointed or sent from Africa. The most notable of these governors, whose principal role was military, include As-Samh ibn Mālik al-Khaulāni (718–721), who captured Barcelona and Narbonne, extinguishing the vestigial Visigothic kingdom there, and then, starting the long series of raids into the territories of the Franks, fell in battle at Toulouse. Another governor who met a like fate and thereby came to the regarded as an Islamic martyr was ʿAbd al-Raḥmān ibn ʿAbd-Allah al-Ghāfiki. Chosen by the army briefly to succeed As-Samh in 721, he was governor again in 731–2 before being killed at the famous battle of Poitiers, the importance of which is often exaggerated. The hold that the Arabs had already established on much of Provence was not affected by it, nor did it terminate their raids into Aquitaine. Perhaps its greatest significance lay in the resulting shifts in the balance of power inside Francia. More crucial in putting a stop to Arab expansion across the Pyrenees, and establishing the Ebro valley as the frontier of Islam, were the civil wars that erupted in Spain in the 740s.

These conflicts resulted from Berber risings in Africa. The full pacification of that region had not been achieved by the Arabs, and the indigenous tribes resumed their struggles against their new masters in 739. Several Arab armies were defeated and substantial reinforcements had to be sent from Syria by the caliph Hishām (724–42). In all the fighting lasted for nearly two decades. Meanwhile in Spain, the Arab advance into Provence had been continuing, especially during the governorship of ʿUkbah ibn al-Hejaji (734–9). However, he was deposed in an army revolt led by a former governor ʿAbd al-Mālik ibn Kattān (732–4), who had been disgraced for his excessive cruelty. Almost immediately the Berbers in Al-Andalus rebelled, whether as a result of the recent coup or because of events in Africa is not clear.

ʿAbd al-Mālik was unable to suppress the revolt, and, in serious difficulties, appealed for help to Africa. One of the Syrian relief armies, led by Balj ibn Bishr, was invited to cross the straits from Ceuta, where it had recently been beseiged by the Berbers. Lands were assigned in Spain for the Syrians' support, but they were required to agree to return to Africa once their object was achieved.[41] This would suggest a fiscal arrangement, and that the revenues of the lands were being earmarked rather than a settlement by them being envisaged. The latter is inconceivable if the Syrians were expected to leave once the fighting was done. Again this seems to provide some hint at the essentially military character of the early Arab occupation in Spain.

However, Balj and his Syrians, having by 741 quelled the Berber rebels, turned upon their paymaster 'Abd al-Mālik. He was seized and crucified at Cordoba with a dog and a pig being similarly killed on either side of him. This manner of execution, with its strange mimicry of the Crucifixion, occurs again at other points in the history of Al-Andalus, usually when there is some element of revenge or degradation involved in the killing. The consequence of 'Abd al-Mālik's death was feud. Blood feud was a traditional feature of Arab society, as it was amongst the Germanic successors of the Roman Empire.[42] However, its effects were probably far more violent and disruptive amongst the former, in that the obligation to avenge blood by blood extended beyond the limits of the small clan or family to the whole tribe. The number of possible participants, involving the members of all the tribes involved, could be substantial. Feud operated on a far greater scale than in Germanic societies, and attempts to end it by agreement and composition were thereby made all the harder. Its extent in distance and time could be considerable. In 'Abd al-Mālik's killing an extended and protracted blood feud reached Spain.

Certain traditional tribal enmities survived from the pre-Islamic past, but the conflicts in the Arab empire precipitated by the rise of the Umayyads and their struggles to establish their dynasty created a network of bitter hostilities between the tribes involved in the civil wars of 656–61 and the 680s. Whatever the outcome of the wars or of individual battles, the feuds thus created only intensified. In particular, violent enmities were created by the wars of 681–694 and the subsequent power struggles in Syria and Arabia between two great tribal confederacies, the Kais and the Yemenis. The killing of 'Abd al-Mālik of the Kais tribe of Fihri, by Balj and his Yemenis (who confusingly came to North Africa and Spain from Syria, and are often referred to as Syrians) resulted from a feud already half a century old, in which in his youth in Arabia he had played a minor part.[43]

The earlier repercussions of these tribal hostilities had not made themselves felt in Al-Andalus, probably due to careful selection of those tribes used in the conquests of North Africa and Spain. However, the death of 'Abd al-Mālik resulted in nearly twenty years of violent feuding in the peninsula. His two sons and other members of his tribe rose against his killers. Balj defeated them in 742, but was killed in the battle. As well as an ever-increasing circle of vendetta, the intrusion of a substantial body of outsiders into Al-Andalus created hostilities, and the Arab population divided into two factions: the *Shāmiūn*, the Syrians who had accompanied Balj (tribally Yemenis) and the *Beladiūn*, the earlier invaders and their descendants. The latter, together with the Berbers, defeated by Balj, lined up behind the sons of 'Abd al-Mālik.

In 743 the arrival of a new governor, appointed by the caliph, briefly stopped the hostilities, but, being of a Yemeni tribe, he was soon suspected, rightly or wrongly, of favouring the Syrians. Civil war was renewed until a strange compromise was reached in 747, whereby the two sides agreed to take turns to appoint a governor, who would rule for one year. If there be any truth in this story it certainly indicates that the authority of the caliph and of the governor of Ifrikiya had ceased to have much weight in Al-Andalus.[44]. The Banu Adnān or Kais faction had first choice, and it is little of a surprise that their governor Yūsuf ibn 'Abd al-Rahmān al-Fihri, of the same tribe as 'Abd al-Mālik, refused to surrender his office at the end of his year. Catching the Yemenis by surprise he massacred large numbers of them and then maintained an effective dictatorship until 756.

In the meantime dramatic events had occurred in the East, that were to have significant and long term consequences for Al-Andalus. In 749 a widespread revolt had broken out in eastern Persia against the rule of the Umayyad caliphs, which combined discontented converts, Shiites (supporters of the descendants of Mohammed's cousin 'Ali) and the 'Abbāsids, heirs of the Prophet's uncle. In 750 the Umayyads were routed and their last caliph, Marwān II (744–750) was killed. A massacre of the surviving members of the dispossessed dynasty was ordered by the new 'Abbāsid caliph As-Saffāh 'the Shedder of Blood' (750–4). From this only one important member escaped, 'Abd al-Rahmān, grandson of the Umayyad caliph Hishām. His own very picturesque account of his adventures is preserved in the *Muktabis* of Ibn Hayyān. 'Abd al-Rahmān managed to make his way incognito to Africa, where he took refuge with the Berbers. One of his freedmen called Badr, the companion of his flight, crossed into Spain to take soundings there.[45]

In Al-Andalus conditions were very favourable. The Yemenis, oppressed by Yūsuf, had been especially favoured by the Umayyad dynasty in recent decades. There was also a contingent of some five hundred Umayyad *muwallads* – converts attached to the caliphal family – serving in the army, whilst the Berber and possibly indigenous Spanish *muwallads* led by Abū ʿUthmān were discontented with Yūsuf's dictatorial rule. There had also been severe famine in Al-Andalus throughout the previous six years.

With such support a conspiracy was soon hatched, and while Yūsuf was absent, suppressing a pro-ʿAbbāsid revolt in Zaragoza, ʿAbd al-Raḥmān crossed from Africa in 756 and began collecting adherents in Granada, Sidonia and Seville. Yūsuf's own men were incensed by his killing the Zaragozan rebel, as he was a member of the Prophet's own tribe, and many deserted him. On his hasty return to Cordoba, he found himself with insufficient support to oppose ʿAbd al-Raḥmān and he was forced to submit. In 758 he rebelled unsuccessfully at Mérida, and was murdered while fleeing to Toledo.

ʿAbd al-Raḥmān set up an independent state in Al-Andalus, breaking the political unity of the Islamic world, an example soon to be followed by others, notably in North Africa. He took the title of Amir, basically a secular and military one, and refused allegiance to the ʿAbbāsids. However their precedence as titular heads of the community of Orthodox Muslims, as expressed in the title of caliph, was not challenged by the Spanish Umayyads until 929, when ʿAbd al-Raḥmān III, a descendant of the founder of the dynasty, established his own caliphate. Through the rule of ʿAbd al-Raḥmān I (756–788) a measure of order was restored to the peninsula, principally by the careful placing or relocation of the mutually hostile elements amongst the conquerors. It has sometimes been stated that Arab tribal distinctions declined and disappeared in early Umayyad Spain. Quite the contrary appears to have been the case. The tribal organisation of Arab society remained strong, possibly being reinforced by recruitment from the ranks of the *muwallads*, until at least the end of the tenth century.[46]

As Al-Makkarī saw it: 'Even after this monarch (ʿAbd al-Raḥmān I) had subjected the whole of Andalus to his sway, the western provinces of the Empire were still cut up and divided into districts, inhabited by tribes, clans, and families, who in case of need, clung to each other for protection, and who in time of rebellion or civil discords, were sure to stand by one another.'[47] These continuing tribal divisions, with the attendant feuds and loyalties, together with the existence of large numbers of Berbers, *muwallads* and Christians,

presented the Umayyad regime with far greater problems of order
and stability than their Roman or Visigothic predecessors had had to
face.

It is possible to know more about the government of Islamic Spain
than about those of its precursors. The accounts to be found in the
sources, notably Al-Makkarī, provide a basically unchronological
picture, but it appears that most of the standard features of the
administration developed by the 'Abbāsids in Iraq in the later eighth
and ninth centuries were also employed in Al-Andalus.[48] The resulting image may be truer of the later stages of Umayyad rule than of the
times of 'Abd al-Raḥmān I, but it is equally likely that many features
underwent little change over the centuries.

At the head of the state stood the amir. Unlike the earlier governors
or the Visigothic kings, the Umayyad amirs rarely led their armies in
person, though often entrusting commands to their many sons. They
themselves usually remained in Cordoba, the 'Navel of Al-Andalus',
which replaced Seville as the capital of the Arab state during the time
of the governors.[49] As all of the Spanish Umayyads, until the
accession of Hishām II in 976, succeeded as adults, they invariably
took a direct role in administration, making appointments and taking
all major decisions. Their life-style became increasingly magnificent,
culminating in the reign of 'Abd al-Raḥmān III (912–961), who built
the great palace complex of Medina Azahara outside Cordoba.[50] All
of the rulers were notable builders, and not just for themselves. From
the time of 'Abd al-Raḥmān I onwards, Cordoba was embellished
with a series of palaces, public baths, fountains and gardens. In
addition, and still extant, the Great Mosque of Cordoba was begun by
the founder of the dynasty, and extended and adorned by many of his
successors up to the late tenth century.[51] Such lavish programmes of
public building are recorded almost exclusively in respect of
Cordoba. Elsewhere fortifications were erected by the Umayyad
rulers, but their munificence in other and more luxurious directions
was reserved for their capital.

As a dynasty the Spanish Umayyads were remarkably successful.
Up to the late tenth century each of them without exception appears
in the sources as a distinct and forceful personality. None of them can
be accused of incompetence or of military or political ineptitude.
Anecdotes record their determined style of rulership: in 781 an
Abbāsid expedition, sent by the caliph Abū Ja'far (754–775) to
challenge 'Abd al-Raḥmān I, was easily defeated and its leaders

executed. 'In order the better to strike terror into his enemies, 'Abd al-Raḥmān caused labels, inscribed with the names of the deceased, to be suspended from their ears; their heads were then stored in sealed bags, together with the black banners of the house of 'Abbas, and the whole given to a trusty merchant, who was directed to convey his cargo to Mecca, and to deposit it in a public place at a certain time.' The caliph, then on a pilgrimage to the holy city, there discovered the gruesome remains of his commanders, and exclaimed of 'Abd al-Raḥmān: 'God be praised for placing a sea between us!'[52]

The Umayyads were very much aware of their own high descent. Thus Al-Ḥakem II (961–976) wrote of his family to Nazr, the Fātimid ruler of Egypt: 'Are we not the sons of Merwan – that favoured family upon whom Nature has poured her richest gifts, and whom Fortune has loaded with her richest favours? Whenever a birth occurs in our family, is not the entire earth illumined with joy at the appearance of the new-born child? Do not the pulpits shake to the sound of the proclamation of his name?'

The same Nazr was treated to a display of the other side of this feeling, when in a diplomatic exchange he ventured criticism of the Umayyad ruler. Al-Ḥakem replied: 'Thou hast reviled us because we are known to thee; had we been acquainted with thee in the same manner, we might have given a proper reply. Farewell.'[53]

For all their justifiable pride in their ancestry and achievements, the Umayyads in Spain never gave the kind of offence to religious sensibilities that their family had been notorious for in Syria. The individual piety of most of them is amply recorded in the histories. They did not always satisfy the more fundamentalist elements amongst their fellow Muslims. In the reign of Al-Ḥakem I (796–822) some religious teachers led the population of one of the suburbs of Cordoba into a revolt against the amir. This 'revolt of the suburb' was violently suppressed by the ruler's guard and on his order the offending portion of the city was completely destroyed.[54]

A measure of egalitarianism had always been a feature of Arab society, as a result of its nomadic origins, and this was reinforced by the teachings of Islam. Autocratic and resplendent as some Muslim rulers could make themselves, popular rebellion or at least agitation quickly developed if they were thought to have disregarded the rules of the Koran. The Muslims of Al-Andalus were particularly well known for their forthright attitude in this respect, leading to 'the pelting of judges and governors whenever the inhabitants thought that proper justice was not given to them in their trials or that they were despotically treated by their rulers. Thus 'their disobedience to their rulers and their want of submission and respect to their superiors have become almost proverbial.'[55]

Generally the Umayyads did not fall foul of their volatile subjects. As well as the positive benefits which they conferred upon Cordoba, the rulers of the dynasty cultivated the proper virtues of piety and of respect for learning. The latter in particular was made great play of. One, probably apocryphal, account of why 'Abd al-Raḥmān I chose his younger son Hishām I (788–796) to succeed him rather then the elder Suleymān describes a secret enquiry that he had made into the company that the two brothers kept: 'If thy son Hishām receives company, his hall is thronged with learned men, poets or historians who discuss the exploits of the brave, and converse about military affairs and so forth; whereas the hall of thy son Suleymān is always filled with sycophants, fools and cowards.'[56] 'Abd al-Raḥmān II (822–852) in particular brought men of learning and discrimination to his court from all over the Islamic world. The most notable of these was a Persian Mawali called 'Ali ibn Zaryāb, a famous musician and singer who was also learned in astronomy and geography. He became an arbiter of elegance to Andalusi high society, introducing a new fashion in hair style, the eating of asparagus, and the use of an under-arm deodorant.[57]

Several of the Umayyads were themselves highly cultivated men. Al-Ḥakem I and 'Abd al-Raḥmān II were noted poets, but the most outstanding of them all was the caliph Al-Ḥakem II (961–976): 'He preferred the pleasures of perusing his books to all the enjoyment which royalty can afford; by which means he considerably increased his learning, doubled his information and improved his taste. In the knowledge of history, biography and genealogy he was surpassed by no living author of his days. He wrote a voluminous history of Andalus, filled with precious information; and so sound was the criticism which he displayed in it, that whatever he related might confidently be believed to be a fact.' His library is recorded as containing four hundred thousand volumes, with a catalogue of forty-four volumes. He kept agents in most of the major cities of the Islamic world to buy books for him, and even bribe authors to delay publication of their works until an advance copy had been sent to him. The philosophical, scientific and astronomical collections were burnt publicly during a period of reaction in the reign of his son in order to please orthodox opinion, and the rest of the library was sold during the period of the collapse of the caliphate in the early eleventh century.[58]

The amirs and caliphs of the Umayyad line, despite occasional conflicts with public opinion, generally took care to present themselves as the upholder of Islamic virtues and as models of Muslim rulership. Although of genuine Arab descent and from Mecca, most of these Umayyads had mothers, wives and slavegirls of indigenous Spanish origin. Some of these were of high standing, such as the wife of the amir 'Abd-Allah and grandmother of 'Abd al-Raḥmān III who was the daughter of King Fortun Garcés of Pamplona, sent to Cordoba as a pledge of loyalty. This had its effects on the appearance of the rulers. Hishām I is described as being of fair complexion, with blue eyes, whilst his son by a slave, Al-Ḥakem I, was very dark. 'Abd al-Raḥmān III, like many of his line, had blue eyes and red hair, which he was reported to have dyed black (the better to fit the Arab racial stereotype). Details of such intermarriages and their effects only survive for the ruling dynasty. Although political advantages made such ties as those between the Umayyads and the kings of Pamplona a necessary part of the family's history, they were probably not alone in crossing racial divisions in marriage.

While they remained personally in control of their own administration the Umayyads were the best guarantee of the stability and competence of the government, and the dissolution of their regime followed within a generation of their loss of personal power, resulting from the succession of a minor. This was fully appreciated by Ibn Ḥayyān: 'It is generally known that the strength and solidity of their empire consisted principally in the policy pursued by these princes, the magnificence and splendour with which they surrounded their court, the reverential awe which they inspired in their subjects, the inexorable rigour with which they chastised every aggression on their rights, the impartiality of their judgements, their anxious solicitude in the observance of the civil law, their regard and attention to the learned, whose opinions they respected and followed, calling them to their sittings and to their councils, and many other brilliant qualities.'[59] Inevitably in the austere periods of Berber rule that were to follow in Al-Andalus, it is not surprising that nostalgia for the days of the Umayyads should develop, but this need not have been based upon a totally mistaken perception of those monarchs' virtues. Certainly in practice up to the accession of Hishām II in 976 the

achievements of the Umayyad state were essentially those of its ruling
dynasty.

The administration that functioned under the control of the amirs
was centred upon Cordoba. It was divided into departments of
finance, justice, foreign relations and 'the care of the frontiers and the
provision and equipment of the troops stationed upon them.' The
nominal heads of these four bureaux were the viziers, who corporately
formed an advisory council to the ruler. Unlike the case in the
Abbāsid state, such offices were largely honorific and ornamental, as
was that of the *Hadjib* or chief Vizier.[60] Only with the accession of the
child caliph Hishām II did the Vizirate become a route to real
power.[61] Other departments of state were the two secretariates that
looked after the drafting of documents, and the protection of
Christians and Jews. Some of the personnel of the bureaux were
drawn from the ranks of the latter. In general the government was in
the hands of what amounted to a class of professional civil servants
subject to the active control and decision-making of the rulers.
Unfortunately it is not known how large or practically efficient the
offices of central government were, although if the accounts of the
large revenues that some of the Umayyads collected have any basis in
fact they cannot have been ineffective. The extension of the power of
the administration outside of Cordoba however depended more upon
the play of local politics.

The most important cities of Al-Andalus outside of the capital had
governors appointed by the amirs, and Seville in particular was often
entrusted to a member of the ruling dynasty. Away from the
Guadalquivir valley, especially in the frontier zones, such governors
were generally selected from the ranks of men with local power and
following. They were thus tribal or sectional leaders, and as their
interests and authority were locally rooted they were not always
reliable in their allegiance to their distant overlord. They, like all
office-holders and tribal leaders, were required to take an oath of
loyalty on the accession of each new ruler.[62] The principal functions of
the governors were military, with responsibilities for public order.
Whether they, like their Visigothic predecessors, had any duties in
respect of local lands belonging to the rulers is uncertain. Perhaps,
too, they were responsible for ensuring that the latter also received
their proportion of any loot taken in war. Local tax collectors
independently transmitted the proceeds from taxes on non-Muslims
and the tolls on goods imported into the cities.

Precise details on financial administration are lacking, though late accounts report that the revenue of ʿAbd al-Raḥmān I amounted to 300,000 silver *dirhems* per annum, rising by the time of ʿAbd al-Raḥmān III to 5,480,000.[63] The coinage of Al-Andalus consisted almost exclusively of these *dirhems*, identical in style to those used throughout most of the Islamic world, though with occasional fluctuations and differences in weight, and there was no continuity with the practices of the Visigothic period, when only small gold coins had been minted and in very limited quantities.[64] In addition from the late seventh century on, as the result of developments in Islamic thinking about the sinfulness of naturalistic representation in art, a new design of coinage had to be developed to replace earlier styles that imitated Byzantine issues. The putting of the head of Christ on their coins by the latter in 692 may have played the major role in prompting this stylistic revolution, that eschewed any representative design and employed only Arabic script.[65] For economic and religious reasons a virtually uniform coinage came to be used throughout the Muslim world, which made no explicit reference to secular rulers. Early experiments with a small bronze coinage in Al-Andalus in the time of the governors were soon abandoned, and there were also some limited issues of gold *dirhems*, identical in design to the silver ones, in the tenth century.

The law that was applied to Muslim subjects of the Umayyads was that of the Koran. Although many specific injunctions and regulations were there laid down it was still necessary for them to be interpreted and for a class of professional jurists to exist to administer this law. Rival schools of Islamic jurisprudence developed. In Al-Andalus, thanks to the preference of the amir Hishām I, that of Mālik ibn Ans of Mecca became dominant from the late eighth century onwards. This was amongst the most literal and severe of the schools of thought in its interpretation of Koranic law, and its wholesale acceptance in Al-Andalus may well represent the fundamentalism of the tiny entrenched community of Muslims in a largely non-Islamic Spain.[66] Its continuing strength may also explain both the fiercely independent stand that individual judges could take in imposing the law, even against the wishes of the Umayyad rulers, and also the dichotomy between religious orthodoxy and humanistic thought that was particularly marked in Al-Andalus. Conflicts between revealed religion and philosophical speculation were a feature of many parts of the Islamic world from the tenth century onwards, but the hold of

extreme Mālikite orthodoxy in Spain may well have limited the scope
and support for the latter in the peninsula. For, despite the considerable achievements of Spanish Muslims in scientific and literary fields,
the religious orthodoxy of the intelligentsia in the Umayyad period is
especially marked, as is its avoidance of certain areas of speculative
thought. The destruction of certain sections of the caliph Al-Ḥakem
II's library to appease religious opinion is a further indication of the
strength of fundamentalism.

The judges or qadis were, at least in the main cities, appointed by
the amir or caliph. The most prestigious post was that of Qadi of
Cordoba, and the holder of that office helped to set the tone of the
regime in respect of its religious image. Thus men of outstanding piety
were frequently appointed, although their unswerving orthodoxy and
rigour might lead to confrontations with the ruler and his court. The
amir or caliph could and on occasion did dismiss a qadi, but this could
have a detrimental effect upon public opinion. Stories of the eminent
justice of certain qadis, such as Ibn Bashir (d. 813) of Cordoba
became part of popular folklore.[67] Little is known about individual
qadis outside the capital, but their influence must have had some
weight in determining the attitudes of local populations for or against
the regime in the frequent periods of disturbance and revolt. They
must also have influenced attitudes towards the non-Muslim
elements in the communities.

Other office-holders, with less general importance but with
significance within their own towns, are recorded. The mohtesib,
usually drawn from the ranks of the trained jurists, supervised
weights and measures in the urban market, and also fixed the prices
on such staple items as bread and meat. The ṣāhib al-medinah was a
magistrate, seen by some scholars as a continuation in Arab guise of
the late Roman defensor civitatis, an official who still functioned in the
Visigothic period, who was appointed only with the consent of the
local qadi and who had the responsibility for detecting and trying
offences that did not fall within the purview of the religious judge.[68]
His main concern was therefore probably with the non-Muslim
citizenry. Nightwatchmen patrolled the streets on the look-out for
nocturnal crime, but, according to one report, murder was of frequent
occurrence in Al-Andalus, although the penalties for this as for other
offences were generally severe, under the rigorous influence of
Mālikite thought. Al-Makkarī refers to the imposition of capital
punishment for the theft of grapes.[69]

The thirteenth-century author Ibn Saʿīd (c. 1230) gave some account of the dress and personal habits of the Spanish Muslims: 'They are the cleanest people on earth in respect of their person, dress, beds and in the interior of their houses.'[70] Also, in distinction to other parts of the Islamic world, they wore woollen caps or had bare heads rather than turbans. The Andalusis did not always impress their fellow Muslims. Ibn Ḥaukal, who visited Spain in 948, said of them that they were 'people of vicious habits and low inclinations, narrow-minded and entirely devoid of fortitude, courage and military accomplishments.'[71]

During the heyday of the Umayyads in the tenth century Al-Andalus was one of the greatest states in Europe, to which the Byzantine emperors and the kings of Germany might send embassies in search of favours, while the Christian realms of northern Spain were little more than its client states. As well as for its military might and diplomatic importance, it was also notable as a centre of learning, an achievement that survived into the subsequent *Taifa* period, when, with the disappearance of the Umayyads, Al-Andalus split into a disorderly mass of small states. Andalusi scholars were distinguished in many fields. Amongst the most notable and also most eccentric of these polymaths was ʿAbū al-ʿAbbās Kāsim ibn Firnas (d. 888–9), a noted musician and doctor, who invented a patent metronome and was highly regarded as a poet and astronomer. He also tried to fly: 'He covered himself with feathers for the purpose, attached a couple of wings to his body, and, getting on an eminence, flung himself off into the air. Whereupon, according to the testimony of several trustworthy writers who witnessed the performance, he flew to a considerable distance, as if he had been a bird, but in alighting again at the place whence he had started his back was very much hurt, for not knowing that birds, when they alight, come down on their tails, he forgot to provide himself with one.'[72]

The existence of other such men of many-sided talents in the Umayyad period is well recorded, but in most cases their works are now lost. A typical figure is Yaḥya ibn Yaḥya of Cordoba (d. 936/7) who was 'versed in arithmetic, astrology, rhetoric, prosody, jurisprudence, traditions (i.e. *ḥadīths*), history, scholastic controversy and the meaning of verses.'[73] Although these Umayyad scholars are not as well-known or preserved as such famous later masters as Ibn Rushd ('Averroes'), philosopher, physician and astronomer, who died in 1198, they led the way to that flowering of intellectual culture in Islamic Spain, which had such an important influence upon Christian Europe in the twelfth and thirteenth centuries. In the Umayyad period historical, religious and grammatical studies were especially prominent, together with astronomy, which was principally cultivated for astrological purposes. Interest in the natural sciences, deriving from the increasing availability of Greek writings translated into Arabic in the ʿAbbāsid Caliphate, really came to the fore after the end of the Umayyad period.

The love of poetry and an interest in books were the particular hallmarks of the upper ranks of polite society in Cordoba. Book auctions were held, although some, notably the less wealthy and more scholarly, complained that prices were raised to absurd levels by the activities of pretentious bibliophiles, anxious to be famous for the size and completeness of their libraries but uninterested in the contents of the books. Poetry had been the principal literary concern of the Arabs from pre-Islamic days, and in Al-Andalus the ability to compose complex but impromptu verses was regarded as the necessary accomplishment of a learned man. As in Celtic societies, the continued strength of traditions of oral verse composition and song was matched by the high regard with which those capable of them were received. Thus men of learning and verbal skill, many of whom were peripatetic in the Islamic world, were accorded a warm welcome in Al-Andalus. Zaryāb, in the reign of ʿAbd al-Raḥmān II, is the best example of this. However, on occasion such feted outsiders could arouse the jealousy of indigenous scholars. Abū ʿAli Saʿīd ibn al-Ḥuseyn, who came to Spain during the ascendancy of the *Hajib* Al-Manṣūr (*c.* 980–1002) incurred the wrath of the Cordoban *literati* by his pretensions, and to expose him they bound up a book of blank pages which they entitled *The Book of Lies*. When Abū ʿAli was shown it during an audience with Al-Manṣūr he instantly claimed to have read it, but when questioned about its contents was forced to prevaricate and was exposed as an incorrigible boaster.[74]

The composition of that high society in Cordoba that took such delight in feats of poetic composition, the collecting of books and the pursuit of an ever increasing sophistication is not easy to ascertain. The determining factor was the patronage of the Umayyads, themselves the supreme patrons of letters and learning, who could make or unmake their courtiers at will. The use of honorific titles, offices and emoluments created a fluctuating court nobility, in the ranks of which Christians and Jews might be found as well as

Muslims. Had we more prosopographical information, it might have been possible to detect more of the activities of families of hereditary office-holders and bureaucrats, as were to be found in other parts of the Muslim world, but which in Al-Andalus remain largely obscure. However references in Ibn al-Kūtiyya prove the existence of such dynasties of administrators in the mid ninth century.[75]

Outside of Cordoba the roots of status were different, and much less dependent upon the favour of the ruling dynasty. In the early stages of the conquest elements of different tribes which entered Al-Andalus were established in certain areas, especially in the south of the peninsula. The maintenance of tribal organisation, until deliberately challenged by Al-Manṣūr in the later tenth century, meant that the traditional ruling families in the tribes, or those who had created an ascendancy in the early period of the conquest, retained their dominance. Thus the descendants of 'Abd al-Mālik ibn Kattān, the governor executed in 741, were the lords of Al-Bont (Puente), as well as having another of their branches numbered amongst the leading families of Seville. Similarly the descendants of the governor As-Samh were still leaders of local society in the tenth century. Such dynasties, whose power was rooted in tribal tradition and loyalty, did not require patronage from Cordoba, and could take a very independent, even rebellious, stand in defence of their own interests.

The same is equally true of the Berber tribes, although their numbers probably decreased during the Umayyad period up to the time of Al-Manṣūr and their second wave of immigration, and also of the *muwallads*. Powerful factions of the latter, under secure leadership, revolted against the amirs on numerous occasions from bases in and around Mérida, Malaga and the Ebro valley throughout the ninth and early tenth centuries. Other *muwallad* families, such as the Banu Angelino, were amongst the most influential in Seville, the social and economic rival of Cordoba. Unfortunately in none of these cases is it clear how far back the traditions of these families really stretched. Whether their influence in Al-Andalus had anything to do with status in the Visigothic past is uncertain, but it seems in some cases that they claimed it. The Banu Kasī, the leading *muwallads* of the Ebro valley in the ninth century, saw themselves as the descendants of a Visigothic count Cassius, although their genealogy is not long enough to stretch them back to the period of the Visigothic kingdom and the name Cassius would there have been totally anachronistic. On both scores an eighth- rather than seventh-century origin is indicated. In general it is clear that in Al-Andalus social authority had many different roots, and that in most respects Cordoba represented the exception and not the rule.

The capital has left many memories of itself in the pages of the extant histories, but it suffered badly and many of its greatest features were destroyed in the civil war of 1009–1010. With the final collapse of the Umayyad Caliphate in 1031 its days of greatness were over and for the remaining centuries of Muslim rule in the peninsula it was eclipsed by Seville, which became the centre of government and recipient of the rulers' patronage under the dynasty of the Almohads in the twelfth and thirteenth centuries. Thus Cordoba and the memory of its departed glory came, as did Granada after 1492, to take on a symbolic quality. It became the embodiment in literary representation of a paradise, lost because of the vices and short-sightedness of the Muslims of Al-Andalus. As a consequence some of the physical descriptions of the city may have been invested with a more than objective reality, which it is unwise to take literally.

One of the fullest of these comes from the *Book of Variegated Leaves on the Ornamental Beauties of Andalus* by Ibn Sa'īd (*c.* 1230), which was much quoted by Al-Makkarī. The breadth of the city was said to be ten miles from east to west, although this includes the two completely detached palace suburbs of Medina Azahara and Medina Azahira. The royal palace inside the city was on the site of a building used by the Romans and the Visigoths. (It may be under the present episcopal palace.) As well as the walled inner city, twenty-one, or according to other writers twenty-eight, suburbs were created, which were not fortified until the time of the civil war (*c.* 1010). The whole of the city and its suburbs were supposedly lit by lanterns at night, and water was provided through aqueducts and pipes to all parts for ornamental and practical requirements. Steam baths certainly existed, one of which has been excavated, although this is a far cry from the three hundred, or by another account seven hundred, that literary sources mention. From its final Umayyad phase an estimate of the number of its buildings by an unnamed 'trustworthy writer' is given as 200,077 for private houses, 60,300 for the residences of nobility and 8,455 for shops. Archaeology has not and probably never could confirm such an impression for such figures are hardly reliable, any more than that of 490 for the number of mosques in the city supposed to have been in existence in the time of 'Abd al-Raḥmān I. In fact, it is unlikely that there was more than one mosque there in the late eighth century, not least as it was the practice in early Islam for all Muslims in a settlement to worship corporately. The gradual growth of the Great Mosque is a better indicator of the size of the capital's Muslim population. However, such literary fictions do give a vivid impression of the romance of Umayyad Cordoba in the eyes of Muslim intellectuals in the centuries after its fall.

6. The Umayyad Regime

The Government of a Divided Society

CORDOBA under the Umayyads filled many of the roles of Visigothic Toledo as royal residence, cultural centre and capital. It was, however, less strategically placed as far as the north of the peninsula was concerned, though it should be borne in mind that the Muslim rulers were more often interested in events in North Africa than in those in inaccessible Cantabria and the Asturias. The Umayyad court was not peripatetic in the way that the Visigothic one had been, although the amirs did on occasion command military operations in person in which event the entire population of Cordoba was required to evacuate the capital.[1] Thus the complexities of social and racial divisions previously mentioned, the lack of close interrelation between the government in the capital and the provinces, and the re-emergence of a frontier zone within the peninsula, made the problems of order and the imposition of authority even more difficult for the Umayyads than they had been for their Roman and Visigothic predecessors.

Best known are the conflicts that the Muslim rulers had to face in their relations with the emerging Christian states in the north. Viewed anachronistically from the hindsight of the fall of Granada in 1492 and the final expulsion of the *Moriscos*, the creation of the tiny kingdoms in the Asturias and the Pyrenees and their struggles against the power of Cordoba look like the beginnings of the long, gradual but linear process of the Christian reconquest of the peninsula, the *Reconquista*. Such a perspective is distorted in that it seems to imply dogged resistance, inevitable hostility, and religion as the motivating force of the conflict. Probably at no stage did the simple ideology of crusade really apply in the peninsula. Motives and relationships were always mixed, even more so than in the eastern Mediterranean contacts between Christianity and Islam. This was especially true of the early centuries. In particular, although there has been some recognition of the ambivalence in Christian attitudes, an impression is often given that a more uncompromising attitude existed on the Muslim side and that the Islamic rulers were unrelenting in their determination to destroy the Christian states. The Umayyads did frequently take the field against the northern kingdoms, and it may appear that, but for the demands put upon them by their own internal problems, they might have obliterated those tiny realms. This is a distortion of the real relationship that existed between north and south during these centuries.

The creation of the kingdom of the Asturias in the early eighth century is enveloped by obscuring legend, but in brief, according to the late ninth-century Asturian chronicles, for the whole episode made no impact upon Arab historiography, the region rebelled against its new Arab and Berber overlords in 718 under the leadership of a Visigothic noble called Pelagius. An overwhelming victory over an Arab army at Covadonga in the same year ended the alien rule and ensured the future independence of the Asturias. The dating of these events has been challenged and the year 722 proposed as a more likely date.[2] However, more significant is the possibility that the importance and scale of this episode are less great than the traditional account allows.

The lack of concern by the Arabs as to what had taken place in the Asturias is obvious. The reign of Pelagius coincided with a period of intense military activity by the Arab governors, launching their almost annual attacks on the Frankish possessions in Provence and Aquitaine, and yet none of them could be bothered to divert their attention to suppress him. One reason for this may be that the Arabs were unused to severely mountainous terrain and their tactics of war were not adapted to coping with it. It is notable that the Taurus mountains marked the limits of their advance against the Byzantine Empire, just as the Pyrenees were to become the effective limit of their westwards expansion. Although Mūsa and Ṭarīk had briefly campaigned in the region, attempts to garrison the Asturias and Galicia proved short-lived. The Arabs, unlike the Visigoths, did not attempt to hold even limited lines of communications and settlement in the Cantabrian mountains and the Pyrenees, nor did they seek to retain the line of the former Roman *limes*, once the Berbers planted in Galicia were permitted to return to Africa. If anything, all of this suggests that they deliberately chose to abandon these northern regions, and create a defended frontier zone much further south.

East, central and western marches were created, with their centres at Tudela, Calatrava and Mérida, and the task of garrisoning these regions was entrusted principally to the Berbers, established in them like the earlier German *foederati*. In the Ebro valley defence was, from the late eighth century on, made the responsibility of the local *muwallad* dynasty of the Banu Kasī, while a similar function was performed in Catalonia by the Berber forces at Tarragona. Once attempts to retain or expand a hold north of the Pyrenees had been given up, as the result of Frankish resistance and also the establishment of settled government under the Umayyads, the Islamic state centred itself firmly in the Guadalquivir valley. The heart of Al-Andalus corresponded roughly with the former Roman province of Baetica, with a large and frequently disturbed frontier region established to the north of it, right across the middle of the peninsula. As in the general expansion of the Arab Empire, Islamic Spain found its own limits. This was partly determined by the bounds of what it was possible to hold down effectively by force, and partly by what could be transformed by acculturation, the latter being a substantially smaller area than the former, but in neither case extending to the whole of the peninsula. Perhaps in this lay the seed of the ultimate destruction of Al-Andalus.

The Arabs were patently less successful than their Roman and Visigothic predecessors in solving the problems of the assimilation of the northern regions of the peninsula. However, their difficulties were far greater in terms of what they had to achieve in the south, where they eventually proved themselves eminently successful. Also, being at the very extremity of the Islamic world, their interests were not as greatly involved in the north, where communications over the Pyrenees were of much less importance than they had been for the Romans and the Goths. Africa and the eastern Mediterranean were the more natural areas of concern for the Umayyads.

As a result, the tiny Asturian kingdom, lodged behind the mountains, was able to expand, first by merging its ruling family with that of the dynasty of the Dukes of Cantabria to the east, and then by extending itself westward into Galicia. Similarly, at the turn of the eighth century, as a result of Frankish activity from Aquitaine, a minute independent realm was able to come into existence at Pamplona, and the Franks were able to create a march at the eastern end of the Pyrenees extending south to Barcelona, and also a county in the valley of the river Aragon. The society and subsequent history of these areas will be examined in a later chapter. For now it is important to note that the problems they represented to the Umayyads were similar to those that had faced the Visigoths, in the forms of independent mountain-dwellers and Frankish aggression;

secondly, that significant transformations had taken place in these regions. The kingdoms of the Asturias and of Pamplona were more complex societies than the earlier confederacies of Cantabrian and Basque tribes, and also the Frankish state, under its new Carolingian dynasty, posed a more serious threat than had been the case under the previous Merovingians.

The effective imposition of unitary royal authority over all of Francia, finally achieved by Charlemagne (768–814), made the threat of Frankish involvement in the affairs of the peninsula a reality for the first time since the days of Dagobert I (*d.* 636). However, after Charlemagne's fruitless expedition into the Ebro valley in 778, and the formation of the Franks' 'Spanish March' around Barcelona in the first decade of the ninth century, a relative stability came into being on this frontier. The programme of settlement and the rapid decline of Frankish royal authority in the course of the ninth century halted further expansion, and put Barcelona and the other counties of the march firmly on the defensive.

As for the states of Pamplona and the Asturias, these, by virtue of developing more sophisticated political and social organisation, became much easier for the Umayyads to control by diplomacy or force than had been possible with their tribal predecessors. On the other hand when that control was not or could not be exercised, they presented a more concentrated and coherent threat to their southern neighbours, and eventually came to expand at their expense. They took advantage of the internal difficulties of the Umayyad state, in the way that the Basques had those of the Visigoths, and also manipulated them to more concrete advantage. It is notable, though, that in this they were generally not assisted by the Christian communities in Al-Andalus. As in the Visigothic period, the defence of local interests usually outweighed any considerations of common race or religion.

The advantages or liberties that could be taken by the Christian states depended much less on their own military capabilities, than on the degree to which the southerners were embroiled in their internal disorders. Once 'Abd al-Raḥmān III (912–961) had finally quelled the many revolts and disturbances within his own frontiers, it did not take long for him to bring the kingdoms of Asturias-Leon and Pamplona-Navarre to heel. He did not, however, any more than the even more successful Al-Manṣūr, seek to terminate their existence. The complicated relationships between the Umayyads, discontented elements amongst their subjects, and the Christian states need to be examined in more detail.

It is best to look first at the difficulties that the amirs faced in maintaining their authority over their own subjects, as this determined much of their relations with the powers beyond their frontiers. The problems of imposition and maintenance of their rule on local communities were essentially very similar to those encountered by the Visigothic kings in the sixth century. Certain basic factors, such as the difficulties created by the geography of the peninsula for the maintenance of communications, remained the same. The Arab rulers had, however, increased the natural disadvantages by their choice of site for their capital, and by the limitations of their style of government. The Umayyads could not have the same kind of relationship with the provincial *qadis* that the Visigothic kings had had with their bishops, nor were the amirs willing to make their presence felt in person in the way that their predecessors had. Their style of rule was more like that of the contemporary Byzantine emperors or the 'Abbāsid caliphs, centring upon the palace. Although this had enormously beneficial consequences for the city of Cordoba, it set up unnecessary tensions between capital and provinces. As has been mentioned, the maintenance of tribal organisation, together with the limitations of the central bureaucracy, meant that authority in the ruler's name had to be entrusted to those who already had local power, as this was the only way in which it could be enforced.

Such a system could work, as for example in the Byzantine Empire, where there was a large measure of cultural cohesion, reinforced by the threat of aggression by external and alien powers. In Spain the opposite was the case: the racial and religious unity that had largely been achieved by the Visigoths was now replaced by diversity and diffusion. New racial elements, the Arabs and the Berbers, were introduced, who were not even in harmony amongst themselves. A new religion came in with the conquerors that furthered this disunity, not least by creating a class of indigenous converts who failed to be properly integrated with the Arab Muslims.

Taking the peninsula as a whole, such a mixture of diverse, and often antagonistic, racial, religious and cultural elements should have been disastrous. At the level of local communities the introduction, often in successive waves, of such widely varied types of citizen created friction and sometimes violent conflict. In addition, the power of government had to be devolved to those whose authority really stemmed from the strength of their own personal following, and who could easily disregard or defy the will of their overlord in Cordoba as well as take a partisan interest in local conflicts.

In fact the Umayyads turned the potential weaknesses of their position to their greatest advantage. The very disunity could be made a great source of strength. The destructive feuding of the Arab tribes before the arrival of 'Abd al-Raḥmān I had, as in Syria and Iraq, been brought under control by keeping the opposing parties geographically separate, and also by careful composition of armies. Conversely, the existence of adjacent groups of different racial origin or religious conviction could serve as a restraint on the ambitions of governors or the power of potential rebels. So great was the strength of local hostilities and feuds, as for instance in Mérida, that it was impossible for a rebellious *wali* (governor) to unite all elements of the population behind him.

Many of the early Umayyads proved competent in the playing off of local antagonisms in undermining revolts that they were unwilling or unable to confront directly. They could also change their support quite cynically, as best suited their interests. Thus 'Abd al-Raḥmān I came to power principally thanks to the assistance of the Yemenis, but by the late 760s he had turned against them. Likewise in 889, during a revolt that involved virtually the whole of the lower Guadalquivir valley, the amir 'Abd-Allah first depended upon the support of the *muwallads* of Ecija to oppose Yemeni rebels, but subsequently ordered his generals to execute their leader in order to gain the allegiance of the Arabs of Carmona.[3]

Particularly violent were some of the conflicts between the Berbers and the indigenous population, exacerbated by racial hostility and insecurity. In 794 a virtual civil war broke out in Tarragona, in the course of which many of the citizens were massacred by the Berbers, who in turn had to be suppressed by an Arab army. In the aftermath the city was left abandoned for seven years, only being reoccupied after the Frankish capture of Barcelona in 801, which itself may been a consequence of the dispersal of the Berber garrison of Tarragona.[4]

How far the Umayyads deliberately fostered such antagonisms is unclear, but they were certainly quick to take advantage of them. They could on occasion take particularly forceful measures to eliminate those regarded as potential rebels and to dissuade others. The most notorious of these episodes was 'the Day of the Ditch', of 16 November 806, when, on the orders of the amir Al-Ḥakem I, 5,000 of the leading men of Toledo are recorded as having been massacred at a banquet held by the city's governor. The number of those slain may be exaggerated and the effects were fairly short-lived, but Al-Ḥakem earned a reputation for this and 'the Massacre of the Suburb' as 'a tyrant and shedder of blood'.[5] Exemplary punishments could be inflicted. The heads of defeated rebels were usually displayed on the gates of Cordoba, and those of Christians killed in the Umayyads' expeditions to the north were sent back to the capital for exhibition, but the crucifixion of the father of a rebel leader with his son's head hanging around his neck was unusually savage. However, such methods failed to reverse an ever-increasing spiral of violence that reached its culmination in the reign of the Amir 'Abd-Allah (888–912), whose authority was at times restricted to just the city of Cordoba.

The problems of order that the Umayyads faced were of several different kinds. The more or less straight-forward rebellions aimed at local autonomy occurred principally in the frontier zones, where the independence and power of the governors was greatest and where the fortified cities could hope to defy the retaliation of the amirs. Toledo was one of the most consistently rebellious of these cities, revolting in 761, 784–6, 788, 797, 872, 873 and 887, as well as successfully maintaining its freedom, despite attempts at suppression throughout the years 829 to 837, and 853 to 857 or later. Mérida was another centre of revolt in the years 807–8, 810–812, 828 (twice) and 868. It too, after the second revolt of 828, enjoyed a period of independence from external control in the years 828 to 833. Only the destruction of its fortifications in 868, on the orders of the amir Moḥammed I, and the rise of Badajoz further down the Guadiana, finally undermined its resistance and sent the city into an irreversible decline.[6] The Ebro valley and Catalonia were also often centres of urban rebellions, as in Zaragoza in 781–2, 788–92, 797–800, 802, 843–4 and 881, Barcelona in 788 and Huesca in 800.

The aims and causes of these revolts were varied. Some resulted from internal tensions between mutually hostile sections of the local populace, as in some of the outbreaks in Mérida, where hostility between Arabs, Berbers, *muwallads* and Christians was a frequent cause of disturbance which could escalate into rebellion against central authority. Little as we know of the details, such popular revolts may be similar to that of Cordoba against the Visigothic monarchy in the mid sixth century.

Personal ambitions and even dynastic disputes could manipulate local susceptibilities in the search for a base from which rebellion could be launched. The displaced elder brothers of Hishām I gained enough support in Toledo in 788 to make it the centre of their revolt against the new amir.[7] Mérida, already the base for Yūsuf al-Fihri's abortive rising against ʿAbd al-Raḥmān I in 758–9, also joined them. These garrison cities in the marcher zone were especially volatile, as they were the centres of concentration of large numbers of Arab and Berber warriors, whose primary allegiance was not to any amir but rather to their tribal leaders. In fact a complicated web of personal and tribal loyalties must have existed, together with attendant feuds and antipathies, that created local authority and also developed a network of alliances that united towns and tribes over wide areas. The imposition of oaths of loyalty to the new ruler at the outset of each reign, to be taken by all office-holders and tribal leaders, attempted, as in the Carolingian Empire, to harness local power to the central authority by means of supernatural sanctions.[8]

The independence and ambitions of some governors with entrenched local support made them particularly difficult to control from Cordoba. The most striking case is that of the Banu Ḳasī, who dominated the Ebro valley throughout the ninth century. The activities of this family feature frequently in the *Muktabis* of Ibn Ḥayyān. Although their claim to descent from a Count Cassius of Visigothic date is most improbable, it is certain that they were *muwallads* and their careers show how deeply rooted their power in the upper Ebro actually was. Belief in a family history that extended back to the social élites of the Visigothic past was shared by them with the chronicler Ibn al-Kūtiyya and the kings of the Asturias amongst others, but in all of these cases this may have been more the accompaniment of contemporary social status than its cause.[9]

In the case of the Banu Kasī, this tradition of their high descent in terms of peninsula society was cunningly interwoven with other elements intended to magnify their pedigree as Muslims. Fortun, the son of their eponymous ancestor Cassius, was reported to have travelled to Damascus after the fall of the Visigothic kingdom, and there to have affirmed his loyalty in person to the caliph Walid I and embraced Islam as the client (*mawali*) of the Umayyads. These frankly apocryphal tales come from the work of the scholar and courtier Ibn Ḥazm (994–1064), chief minister of ʿAbd al-Raḥmān V, who claimed noble Persian descent but was generally suspected of being a Spanish *mawali*. Such pretensions were probably not

uncommon in the upper ranks of society in the later Umayyad
period.[10]

The Banu Kasī first come into prominence at the very end of the
eighth century as allies of a *mawali* rebel in Zaragoza and Huesca
called Bahlūl ibn Marzuk (*c.* 796). One of the family was governor of
Pamplona and was murdered by the citizens in 799. This did not stop
the Banu Kasī from allying later with Iñigo Arista, the king of
Pamplona, whose dynasty was created in the ensuing chaos; these
links, bonded by marriage ties, continued throughout the ninth
century. The despatch of a *mawali* general Amrūs ibn Yūsuf by the
amir in 802 led to the suppression of Bahlūl, the chastising of the Banu
Kāsi and the sacking of Pamplona. Amrūs fortified Tudela prior to his
death in 812, and organised a march in the upper Ebro around it.
However, the beneficiaries of his activity were to be the Banu Ḳasī.
Mūsa ibn Mūsa, impossibly claimed as the grandson of that Fortun
who had gone to Damascus in 714, was governor of Tudela by 842, in
which year he was in revolt against his Umayyad master. In alliance
with the king of Pamplona, he defeated an army sent against him by
the amir, but they were routed when 'Abd al-Raḥmān II led an
expedition to the march in person the following year. Yet so essential
and irreplaceable did Mūsa seem to be that when he submitted in 844
he was restored to his governorship, only to revolt again with
impunity in 847. For the next fifteen years he acted in practice as an
independent ruler, and was even talked of as 'the third king in Spain'.
He died in 862.[11]

Later members of his family were equally ambitious and hard to
control, although after Mūsa's defeat by the Asturians in 862 none
were able to exercise such extensive power as he. His three sons made
themselves masters of Tudela and Zaragoza in 871 and 872, although
one of them fell into the hands of the amir Moḥammed I, and was
crucified at Cordoba. Zaragoza remained theirs, despite attempts to
retake it, until 890, when a grandson of Mūsa sold it back to the
Umayyads. This Moḥammed ibn Lope ibn Mūsa (*d.* 898) went on to
make himself master of Toledo in 897, and Mu'tarrīf, one of his sons
who succeeded him there, took the title of king, before being
murdered by the citizens in 906. His brother Lope, the last of the line,
held Lérida, and directed his ambitions against Catalonia before
being killed in battle in 907. Despite occasional destructive but
inconclusive expeditions from Cordoba, and, more successfully, the
building up of an alternative power in the region through the Arab

family of the Tudjibites, the Umayyads were unable to crush or to do without the Banu Kasī, who made many agreements and honoured few. Accidents of war and assassination finally eliminated them, but in their careers and the difficulties they posed for the amirs they were far from unique. Even Amrūs ibn Yūsuf, who had killed Bahlūl, and put down the first Banu Kasī revolt in the name of Al-Ḥakem I, was soon suspected of conspiring with the Franks and plotting rebellion.

The activities of successful bandits could also assume the dimensions of a military uprising and often required as much effort to suppress. The difficulties presented by the terrain of the peninsula provided excellent opportunities for rural rebels or bandits to wage what was effectively guerrilla warfare against the government and its representatives, largely in the interests of their own enrichment. One of the best examples may be found in the career of the Berber leader Chakya of the Miknassa tribe, who in 768 surprised and killed the governor of Santaver and looted Coria. For the next four years he successfully avoided armies sent against him, twice commanded by 'Abd al-Raḥmān I in person, by dodging into the mountains. In 771 he nearly captured one of the amir's generals and later tricked and killed the governor of Medellin. In 774 he was again able to ravage Coria, thanks to the collusion of its Berber garrison, and he eluded the avenging army of 'Abd al-Raḥmān to escape once more into the mountains. In 772 and 776 he was able successfully to resist sieges of his mountain stronghold. However, in the latter year he was murdered by his own men, who sent his head and their submission to the amir. Chakya was thus almost the prototype of the ferocious bandit – or heroic guerrilla – of more recent centuries in Spain and Latin America.[12]

The Berbers in the peninsula were particularly suited for such roles, as many of them were mountain-dwellers in North Africa, unlike the Arabs who found such terrain hostile. However, they were far from having a monopoly on such activities. A Méridan *mawali* called Moḥammed ibn 'Abd al-Djabba held out very successfully in southern Extremadura between 833 and 840 against the armies of 'Abd al-Raḥmān II, until, having established himself in Christian territory, he was killed by the forces of Alfonso II of the Asturias.[13] Similar problems in the control of large tracts of hostile and virtually inaccessible land, favouring banditry and the use of guerrilla tactics, had almost certainly faced the Visigothic kings in the sixth century and probably did in the seventh too. The experiences of the Muslim rulers suggest what might have been some of the problems of their predecessors: conciliar enactments and liturgy of the seventh century relating to warfare and royal military undertakings can take on a reality and be seen in a practical context when considered in the light of the more fully documented Islamic period.

However, the Visigoths may have been spared one of the additional troubles of the Umayyads – the bitter but localised civil wars between hostile elements of the population. Such conflicts often occurrred between the Berbers and indigenous *muwallads* and Christians, as in Tarragona in 794. There was particularly intense fighting between the Toledans and the Berbers of Calatrava in 834–6, 853–7 and 873, doubtless exacerbated by blood feud. The Yemenis and the Kais, antagonists in the civil wars of the 740s, conducted a protracted civil war in the region of Tudmir (around Almeria and Murcia) between 822 and 828, despite the intervention of 'Abd al-Raḥmān II and his taking of hostages. The conflicting parties had eventually to be forcefully suppressed by the amir.[14]

In such circumstances, rulers could not for long rely on the indigenous military resources of their subjects, whose rivalries and mutual alliances made them difficult to control and untrustworthy. In addition, the settling of the Arabs and some of the Berbers that probably took place in the early Umayyad period limited the military use that the amirs could make of them. By the end of the eighth century the rulers were drawing their troops, at least in terms of the standing forces that attended them in Cordoba, from new sources. The responsibility for innovation in this direction is attributed to Al-Ḥakem I: 'Al-Ḥakem was the first monarch of this family who surrounded his throne with a certain splendour and magnificence. He increased the number of mamelukes (slave soldiers) until they amounted to 5,000 horse and 1,000 foot. ... he increased the number of his slaves, eunuchs and servants; had a bodyguard of cavalry always stationed at the gate of his palace and surrounded his person with a guard of mamelukes. ... these mamelukes were called Al-Ḥaras (the Guard) owing to their all being Christians or foreigners. They occupied two large barracks, with stables for their horses.'[15] According to Ibn Khaldūn he was also the first ruler to issue regular pay to his troops. In addition he employed a body of secret agents to keep him informed of public opinion in the capital.

Such developments in the increasing magnificence of the ruler's court and its remoteness from the populace have parallels in the

'Abbāsid Caliphate of the same period. So too has the employment of standing armies of alien mercenaries or slaves. In the case of the 'Abbāsids, from the early ninth century onwards it was the Turks who provided the manpower. The racial composition of the slave armies of Al-Andalus is not so clear, though some were certainly Christians. By the second half of the ninth century it is revealed in many references that one major component of such forces was Slavonic.

Slave-trading in early Medieval Europe is still much under-studied, although it is clear that it did exist on a major scale and was a vital feature of the society and economy of the period.[16] The Vikings, who first come into prominence with their attacks on Anglo-Saxon and Irish monasteries at the very end of the eighth century, played a large part in it. Many of their raids, which grew in intensity and geographical range throughout the middle of the ninth century, had as an end the obtaining of slaves as well as silver and gold. Captives of wealth and status might be ransomed, but the many others who fell into their hands during their carefully co-ordinated raids were sold as slaves. A ready market, especially for men of fighting age, could be found in Umayyad Spain, with its need for supplies of new mamelukes. Other victims could be sold in Africa and some exported further east.[17] As well as those taken in raids on Britain, Ireland and Francia, cargoes of Slavs from the Baltic could have been brought by the Vikings to the slave markets. There was also a land route for the westward trade in slaves out of central Europe, one of the main *entrepôts* for which was Verdun, and it is quite conceivable that slaves reached Spain in this way too.

Once arrived, wherever from, the Umayyads' slaves came to add another element to the already very mixed racial and cultural composition of the peninsula. Some of them were culturally self-conscious: during the ascendancy of Al-Manṣūr one of them, called Fatin (*d.* 1029) was noted as an Arabic stylist and book collector, while another, called Habib, wrote a work entitled *Clear and Victorious Arguments against Those who Deny the Excellencies of the Sclavonians.*[18] The slave soldiers and eunuchs of the palace of the Umayyads never came to isolate the ruler and dominate the court in the way that their Turkish counterparts did in the 'Abbāsid Caliphate. This could largely be due to their never achieving an unchallenged ascendancy: alternative sources of strength could be found to match them. Under the dictatorship of Al-Manṣūr (*c.* 980–1002), a new wave of Berber mercenaries was introduced into Al-Andalus, though with ultimately fatal results for the Caliphate. For they took an active part in the civil wars between rival Umayyad candidates from 1009 onwards, and even supported the pretensions of a rival African dynasty, the Hammūdids, that tried briefly to seize power in Spain. In 1010 the Berber mercenaries looted Cordoba and destroyed the two great suburban palace complexes of Medina Azahara and Medina Azahira, erected by 'Abd al-Raḥmān III and Al-Manṣūr. After the dissolution of the Caliphate in 1031, some of the Berbers established small kingdoms for themselves in the ruins, notably at Granada, while some of the slave soldiers seized power in Valencia and Almeria.[19]

Whatever their value as purveyors of slaves, the Vikings, by their raids on Spanish towns and cities, added a new component to the disorders of ninth-century Al-Andalus. Recent attempts to portray them as 'traders not raiders' cannot obscure their violence and destructiveness. They were dangerous and potentially treacherous trading partners, and while their role in the slave trade in Spain remains largely hypothetical, their depredations are clearly recorded. Raids on Al-Andalus by Vikings are reported in the years 844, 859, 966 and 971, conforming to the general pattern of such activity concentrating in the mid ninth and late tenth centuries.[20] The attacks in 844 and 859 were also linked with descents made on the coasts of the kingdom of the Asturias recorded in the *Chronicle of Alfonso III*.[21] In the first of these, having received a drubbing at the hands of King Ramiro I of the Asturias, the Vikings sailed south and surprised Seville. They defeated forces sent against them from Cordoba, looted at will in the lower Guadalquivir valley, and, evading 'Abd al-Raḥmān II's fleet, raided Niebla, Beja and Lisbon before sailing home. In 859 Vikings, probably from Norway as previously, again descended on Seville, burning the mosque, and went on to make attacks on the coast of North Africa and the Spanish Levant. Also, although it is not clear where or how, they captured King García of Pamplona and extorted a large ransom of 60,000 gold pieces for him.[22]

In the aftermath considerable efforts were made to prevent a repetition of these disasters. Moḥammed I (852–886) is recorded as having built a new fleet, as did 'Abd al-Raḥmān III in 956, while 'Abd al-Raḥmān II constructed shipyards in Seville and a naval base was developed at Almeria. These moves proved efficacious, for the Viking raids of 966 and 971 were successfully resisted by the Umayyad fleet.[23]

As well as the activities of the Vikings with their large expeditions – fleets of fifty-four ships being recorded for 844 and sixty-two for 859 – smaller-scale piracy was probably on the increase in the western Mediterranean in this period. In 953 Otto I of Germany sent Abbot John of Gorze to Cordoba to try to persuade ʿAbd al-Raḥmān III to suppress piratical raiding, doubtless from North African and possibly from Spanish ports.[24] The account of this embassy in the Abbot's *Life* is one of the few contemporary Latin references to Umayyad Spain. It is unlikely that the envoys, who encountered severe diplomatic difficulties over religious differences, met with much success in their task, as such piracy may well have been a valuable source of much-needed slaves.

These then, in outline, are some of the internal problems faced by the Umayyad rulers, and it is against this background that their dealings with the Christian states of the north of the peninsula must be seen. The latter were often provided with opportunities to take advantage of the disunity of their southern neighbours, just as Charlemagne had been called into Spain in 778 by a rebel in Zaragoza. Thus, in 854, the aid of Ordoño I of the Asturias was sought by rebels in Toledo. The powerful Banu Kasī of the Ebro valley often involved the kings of Pamplona, to whom they were linked by marriage, in their revolts. Unsuccessful rebels or bandits could on occasion take refuge in Christian territory, whilst the Christian rulers themselves or their marcher lords in Leon and Castille conducted frequent raids for plunder, not territorial expansion, into the Muslim-dominated lands. Finally the counts of Catalonia, the former Frankish march, were drawn as mercenaries into the Umayyads' civil wars, and undertook a bloody and not very remunerative expedition to Cordoba in 1010 on behalf of one of the rival claimants.[25]

However, the initiative remained generally with the Umayyads. The Islamic annals record, from the time of ʿAbd al-Raḥmān I onwards, an almost unceasing despatch of military expeditions from Cordoba against the Asturias and Pamplona, and to a lesser extent the Frankish march. For instance in the reign of Hishām I (788–796), after an initial period of civil war against his brothers, we find in 791 the amir leading an army into Alava and Castille, while his general Yūsuf ibn Bokht campaigned further westward, defeating Vermudo I of the Asturias. In 792 the general Ibn Mugeyth raided Alava and Castille and in 793 the same commander expelled Frankish forces from Gerona and Narbonne. In 794 two expeditions are recorded, one into Alava and the other into the Asturias, sacking Oviedo, its new capital. In 795 Ibn Mugeyth led an army to Astorga, driving Alfonso II before him.[26]

Such prodigious activity, although not consistently maintained, was by no means unusual. One or often two expeditions a year are recorded, frequently over extended periods of time, throughout the Umayyad era, culminating in the remarkable campaigns of Al-Manṣūr. A similar pattern of annual or twice-yearly raids into Byzantine Asia Minor was conducted by the Syrian Umayyad caliphs in the first half of the eighth century. Now it may be wondered why, under such a barrage of attack, the Christian states were able to survive. However, there are a number of very important features to be noticed in the accounts of the fighting found in the chronicles of both sides. For one thing, pitched battles are very rare and never decisive: the nearest approach to battles of any significance are the defeat of Vermudo I (788–791) in 791, and the victory of Ramiro II of Leon over 'Abd al-Raḥmān III at Simancas in 939.[27] The first of these had internal effects upon the Asturian kingdom, in that it reversed the results of a disputed succession and led to the probably constrained abdication of Vermudo and the elevation of Alfonso II (791–842). The second provided a valuable boost to morale in the Leonese kingdom, and also determined 'Abd al-Raḥmān III never to lead his armies in person again. Neither engagement was in any sense decisive militarily. In general fighting seems to have been small scale and often with such unclear results that it is possible to find both sides claiming victory in their respective historiography. By and large the military response of the Christian realms took the form of guerrilla activity, to hinder and harass the raiding armies from the south, and on occasion, as at Simancas, this could offer the chance of a descent upon a negligent and over-confident enemy on the march.

A second distinctive feature of these conflicts is their geographical limitation. Although occasional raids into the Asturias are recorded, and Pamplona was sacked in 803 and 843, the Umayyad expeditions were directed in the greatest number of cases at Alava and Castille. On some occasions these regions, the western and eastern frontier zones of the kingdoms of Pamplona and the Asturias respectively, were subjected to annual incursions. These territories were not the heartlands of the realms to which they belonged, nor did they guard the sole routes of access to them. It is, however, probable that it was from the frontier lordships of these regions that most of the smaller-scale raiding on the Muslim lands to the south was conducted.

A look at the overall picture of the Umayyads' military operations against the Christian states gives the distinct impression that they made no attempt to conquer them. This they might have been able to achieve with only limited difficulty, especially after so many of the internal problems besetting Al-Andalus were resolved early in the reign of 'Abd al-Raḥmān III. However, not even the impressive and uniformly successful campaigns of Al-Manṣūr, who sacked Barcelona in 985, Leon in 988 and Santiago in 997, were aimed at such an end. In every case he withdrew with his troops to Cordoba at the end of the campaigning season.

The Muslim rulers might have been unable to hold down conquests in the difficult northern terrain, or the nature of their military organisation may have been such that they lacked the resources to garrison them. However, Al-Manṣūr's importation of Berbers provided plenty of manpower for new military settlement, but no attempt was ever made to take over the Christian states, who conversely never sought significantly to extend themselves into Muslim-occupied territory during the Umayyad period. Their expansion, such as it was, directed itself towards the previously evacuated and depopulated regions, notably in the Duero valley and Castille.

What then was the purpose of this incessant Umayyad military activity? In some specific cases, as with the sacking of Pamplona, exceptional measures were taken to bring to heel and punish a Christian state that had ignored the tacit agreement on the *modus vivendi* that seems to have existed between Al-Andalus and its neighbours. In this case it was the involvement of King Garcīa with the rebel Banu Kasī that led to the exemplary punishment. The general run of campaigning had much less specific and more limited objectives. They are best characterised by the description in the *Bayān al-Moghrib* of the purposes of an expedition sent out in 795, which destroyed settlements and strongholds and ravaged the countryside.[28]

The despatch of such expeditions from Cordoba, whose exact composition is unfortunately never specified, probably had a number of parallel aims. For one thing, loot obtained, of which a fixed proportion went to the ruler, enhanced state revenues, limited by Islamic conventions in respect of tax. Further, it could have had a deterrent or punitive effect upon the Christian marcher nobles, whose depredations might thereby be limited. It provided military

experience for the Arab, Berber and slave forces, amongst whom
individuals who performed acts of outstanding bravery were
rewarded by gifts of gold arm-rings. It may also, as the expeditions
had to pass through the turbulent frontier regions of Al-Andalus,
have served as a useful check on the ambitions of the governors and as
a reminder of their master's power. In view of the limitations of direct
government from Cordoba, the passing of the armies through the
marches, where possibly some of their manpower was recruited,
could have proved as valuable in terms of the internal politics and
cohesion of Al-Andalus as in respect of any effects upon the Christian
kingdoms.

The kingdoms of Asturias-Leon and of Pamplona-Navarre,
especially in the tenth century, were in many respects dependent
states of the Umayyad Caliphate. Religion was not a major
determining factor in political alliances or in the relations between the
realms. Thus Al-Manṣūr, on his expedition of 997 that culminated in
the sack of Santiago and the destruction of the cathedral that housed
the reputed body of St James, was accompanied by Christian lords,
who all received a share of the spoils at the end of the campaign.[29] This
is not to say that the Christian states became regularly tributary to
Cordoba. However, their freedom of action was related directly to the
conditions that prevailed in the south. Economic links, of which we
are now too ill-informed, may have reinforced the interdependence of
the parts of the peninsula that was stronger than is often recognised.[30]

The political ties of the Asturias to Cordoba became more explicit
in the period of instability following the death of Ramiro II in 955.
Factions developed, with the participation of the King of Pamplona-
Navarre and the Count of Castille in supporting the claims of
contesting candidates for the throne. One of these, Sancho I 'the Fat',
was expelled by his own subjects after a brief reign (955–957) for
being too obese even to mount a horse. On the advice of his uncle
King Sancho of Navarre, who was also related to the Umayyads by
marriage, he appealed to 'Abd al-Raḥmān III for help. In 964,
having been slimmed down by the caliph's doctor, he was restored by
the forces of Al-Ḥakem II to his throne. His ejected supplanter,
Ordoño IV 'the Bad', in turn took the road to Cordoba to supplicate
the aid of the Umayyad ruler.

Ibn Ḥayyān has left us a long description of Ordoño's reception by
the caliph, which illustrates something of the splendour of the
Umayyad court in its heyday in the tenth century. Prostrating himself

before Al-Ḥakem II, Ordoño addressed him: 'I am the slave of the Commander of the Faithful (one of the caliphal titles), my lord and master, and I am come to implore his favour, to witness his majesty and to place myself and my people under his protection. May he be pleased to grant me his powerful patronage and consent to receive me into the number of his slaves.' Having presented his petition, Ordoño 'rose to retire, walking backwards so as not to turn his face from the caliph ... he plainly exhibited on his countenance the reverential awe with which he had been struck, and his utter astonishment at the magnificence and splendour displayed before him as indicative of the power and strength of the Caliphate. In passing through the hall, the eyes of Ordoño fell on the vacant throne of the Commander of the Faithful; unable to repress his feelings, he advanced slowly towards it, and having prostrated himself before it, remained for some time in that humble position, as if the caliph was sitting on it.'[31] Even allowing for the rhetoric, the image of Ordoño IV before the empty throne of the caliph captures something of the awe that must have struck those northerners, when brought fully into contact with the sophistication of the civilisation that had developed in Al-Andalus and to whose orbit, as however reluctant satellites, they were attached.

The Land of Three Religions

THE Umayyad caliphs shared the delight of their contemporaries the Macedonian emperors of Constantinople in mechanical marvels, especially those which could be used to heighten regal mystique by the display of apparently wondrous powers. Thus in the great audience chamber of his palace at Medina Azahara, 'Abd al-Raḥmān III placed a large marble bowl filled with mercury, so contrived that a light touch could set it swaying in motion. Beams of light, aimed through the controlled access of windows placed high up in the chamber, were reflected off the rapidly moving mercury and sent flashing around the hall like thunderbolts. This device, like the throne of the Byzantine emperors that could be mechanically elevated into the air, was intended to impress and intimidate those received in audience, especially the envoys of less sophisticated peoples.[32]

The power of Umayyad Spain, which under 'Abd al-Raḥmān III and Al-Manṣūr also extended across the straits to encompass parts of North Africa, and its eminence as one of the great cultural centres of the Islamic world, led its rulers and those of the foremost states of Christendom, notably Byzantium, into relations of mutual respect and civility. The *parvenu* German empire of the Ottonians lacked the expertise and *savoir faire* of the Byzantines in such diplomatic exchanges, and in 956 John of Gorze had to be persuaded not to present Otto I's letter to the caliph, as it was couched in such offensively Christian terms as to prejudice the end to which it had been sent and to endanger the ambassadors and the Christian community of Cordoba.[33] On the other hand the Byzantines, with experience of the cultural aspirations of Arab rulers stretching back to the early days of the Syrian Umayyad Caliphate, knew the value of art and scholarship as aids to diplomacy. In the tenth century an Emperor sent marble columns to 'Abd al-Raḥmān III for use in the building of his palace at Medina Azahara, and in 949 Constantine VII Porphyrogenitos sent, amongst other gifts, a particularly splendid illuminated manuscript of the botanical work of Dioscorides, then much appreciated by Arab physicians in the East.[34]

Although several schools of translators of Greek texts had flourished in the lands of the 'Abbāsid Caliphate in the later ninth and tenth centuries, their Arabic version of Dioscorides may not yet have made its way to Spain and, more strikingly, there was no one in Cordoba with enough knowledge of Greek to be able to translate the newly received manuscript. In 951, at the request of 'Abd al-Raḥmān III, the Emperor sent a monk called Nicholas from Constantinople to help in making the gift comprehensible to its recipients. In this he collaborated with the caliph's physician, a Jewish scholar called Ḥasdai ibn Shaprut, the man who was later to cure the fatness of King Sancho I of Leon.[35]

With Ḥasdai the golden age of the Jews in Spain may be said to begin. Until his death in either 970 or 990 he was one of the most influential figures at the Umayyad court, although holding no office beyond that of physician to the caliph. He was on occasion used for diplomatic purposes, as on a mission to the Navarrese court (*c.* 960) and in the negotiations with John of Gorze and the German envoys. However his greatest significance lay in his patronage of the Jewish community in Cordoba, by whom he was accorded the honorific title *Nasi*, or Prince.[36] As well as in displays of liberality to the Jews of Al-Andalus, he was a noted benefactor of the great Jewish academies of the Talmud at Sura and Pumbedita in Mesopotamia. He also patronised individual Jewish scholars in other Islamic realms.

Dunash ibn Tamim, a pioneer in scientific study amongst the Arabic-speaking Jews, and physician to the Fatimid caliphs at Kairouān, dedicated an astronomical treatise to him.[37] A further indicator of the cosmopolitan character of Mediterranean Judaism at this time and of Ḥasdai's importance in it is his extant letter to the king of the Khazars. This nomadic people of the south Russian steppes had recently converted to Judaism in a remarkable achievement of proselytising, and Ibn Shaprut wrote to their ruler to tell him of the whereabouts of Al-Andalus and of its neighbours. The authenticity of this letter is now generally accepted, although that of the Khazar king's reply is not, and from an acrostic preface it seems clear that it was written for Ḥasdai by his secretary Menachem Ben Saruk.[38]

This man, one of Ibn Shaprut's most distinguished clients, was a noted philologist who produced a very influential Hebrew dictionary, the *Mahberet*. Having in this criticised one of the greatest Jewish teachers of the previous generation, Saadia, *gaon* or head of the academy at Sura, he was in turn attacked by one of the latter's pupils, Dunash Ben Labrat, who had been attracted over from Africa by the lure of Ḥasdai's patronage. The ensuing academic feud, in which Dunash ousted his opponent from Ibn Shaprut's favour, was pursued on into the next generation by pupils of the two antagonists. Arid as a fight over philology may now seem, it is testimony to the new found strength of Jewish learning in Al-Andalus.[39]

This was further developed by the arrival in Cordoba and supporting by Ḥasdai of the great religious teacher Rabbi Moses. Under him and his son Rabbi Ḥanok, who died in 1026 when his pulpit collapsed under him, an academy was created in Cordoba that even eclipsed the long-established ones in the East as a centre of Jewish study of the scriptures, the Mishnah and the rabbinical commentaries on them.[40] As well, the poetic innovations of Dunash Ben Labrat, who had adopted Arabic poetic metres for use in Hebrew verse, evoked responses in subsequent generations. With Samuel Ha-Nagid (993–1056), Solomon ibn Gabirol (1021/2–*c.*1058) and Judah Ha-Levi (*c.*1075–1141) a 'renaissance' took place in Hebrew poetry, matched in the same period by the production of such classics of Jewish religious and philosophical exposition as Moses Maimonides' *Guide for the Perplexed* and Ha-Levi's *Kuzari*, a fictitious dialogue with the king of the Khazars.[41]

Although from the mid eleventh century onwards Jewish communities were subjected increasingly to periodic violence and oppression, under the Umayyads they were untroubled. Under the direction of leaders with influence at court such as Ḥasdai, and his successor in the time of Al-Manṣūr, Jacob ibn Jau, communal life was preserved and religious toleration assured.[42] New synagogues were built, such as the one founded in Cordoba by Ḥasdai ibn Shaprut's father Isaac, while a ban existed on the erection of Christian churches. Like the Christians, the Jews were obliged, as non-Muslims, to wear distinctive dress, and both groups were forbidden, by a survival of principles from earlier Roman and Visigothic legislation, to own Muslim slaves. Their other slaves could in theory obtain liberty by embracing Islam, but it is tempting to wonder if the difficulties of applying these rulings in practice differed appreciably from those of earlier centuries.

Hebrew was their liturgical language but by the late tenth century the common speech of the Jewish communities in Al-Andalus was Arabic, as it was for the Christians, replacing the Latin or possibly Aramaic of the Visigothic period. Cultured Muslims, such as the caliph Al-Ḥakem II, displayed an interest in Jewish learning, and a pupil of Rabbi Moses, called Joseph ibn Shatnash, is said to have interpreted the whole of the Talmud in Arabic for the Umayyad ruler.[43] The same caliph sent a Jewish doctor Ibrāhīm ibn Jacob to bring back for him an account of the lands of central Europe. In the course of these travels Ibn Jacob had an audience with the Emperor Otto I.[44] The network of their communities that stretched from Al-Andalus to Persia made Jews invaluable as diplomats and obtainers of information, with contacts that extended over both the Islamic and Christian worlds.

Relations between Jews and Christians in Spain under Umayyad rule, so dramatically transformed by the events of 711, are poorly documented and there is little evidence for the attitudes that existed on both sides. However one strange episode from a slightly earlier period does suddenly light up an underworld of intellectual tension between the two religions. This comes from our knowledge, limited as it is, of the remarkable career of Bodo-Eleazar.[45] Of eastern Frankish origin, Bodo was a Christian deacon at the court of the emperor Louis the Pious (814–840), by whom he was well esteemed. However he became convinced of the error of his religious adherence thanks to arguments put to him by certain unnamed Jews, who were enjoying considerable tolerance at the hands of the Frankish monarchs at this time, and he secretly prepared to accept their faith. Despite the favour then extended to the Jews, an open conversion would have been illegal in Francia, and so Bodo persuaded the emperor to let him undertake a pilgrimage to Rome, in the course of which he made public his change of religion, obtained the conversion of his nephew who accompanied him, and, according to embittered Frankish accounts, sold his attendants into slavery. He escaped Christian wrath by flight to Al-Andalus, where he established himself in Zaragoza, completing his conversion by circumcision, marriage and the growth of a beard. He also changed his name to Eleazar.

With the enthusiasm of a neophyte, he threw himself into conflict with his former co-religionists. He attempted to persuade the amir 'Abd al-Raḥmān II to force his Christian subjects to abjure their faith, expecting that they would thereby be driven into the folds of Islam or Judaism. Christians, for whom the Frankish ruler was the only possible protector if such enforced conversion should be attempted, sought to persuade King Charles the Bald (840–878) to seek Bodo-Eleazar's extradition, although to no avail. He himself had meanwhile been engaged in a polemical literary debate with Paul Alvar of Cordoba, a leading Christian layman of possible Jewish descent. Their exchange of letters survives in only one manuscript and unfortunately at some subsequent point an offended Christian cut out Eleazar's contribution. However it has been possible for this to be reconstructed with a fair degree of probability from Alvar's citations of his opponent's arguments.[46]

Eleazar attacked Christianity at one of its most vulnerable points, its claim to be heir to the promises made by God to Israel in the Old Testament. The continued survival of the Jews was a particular stumbling block here, and Eleazar pointed out very pertinently that their present low material condition was no guarantee of the validity of Christian claims. Had not the temples of the pagans once been magnificent? He also criticised some Christian arguments based upon key Biblical texts, but which depended upon mistranslation of the central Hebrew words. He also accused the Christians of worshipping three gods not one, of making a mortal man divine and of believing in the impossible in their doctrine of virgin birth.

Eleazar's attempt to persuade the amir to act against the Christians went unheeded and nothing is known of his eventual fate. Paradoxically his aim of destroying Christianity in Al-Andalus by means of the action of the state was probably the product of ways of thought that survived from his own discarded past, for, as in the case

of the Visigothic kingdom, secular compulsion towards religious
uniformity and orthodoxy was very much a product of the late Roman
Christian tradition. Normally Jewish proselytising was eirenic and,
as with Bodo-Eleazar's own conversion, aimed at individuals using
the kind of rationalist and exegetical arguments that he had advanced
against Alvar. The Christians of Al-Andalus had far more to fear from
the challenge of Islam than from that of Judaism, although, as in the
Visigothic period, there is evidence from the eighth century of Jewish
ideas and practices influencing local Christian communities. In about
730 Evantius, Archdeacon of Toledo, wrote condemning Christians
of Zaragoza who were claiming that anyone eating the blood of
animals would thereby become unclean, and from 764 comes the
fragment of a letter rebuking Cordoban Christians who wished to fast
jointly with the Jews on the Day of Atonement.[47] It seems clear that
the two communities coexisted in sufficient physical proximity in the
towns for their religious ideas to be mutually influential. It is possible
too that Jews, driven or persuaded into conversion during the
Visigothic period, still maintained links with their former co-
religionists.

The overthrow of the Visigothic kingdom altered the position of the
Christians in the peninsula, in that their religion was no longer that of
the rulers of the state. They thus lost their identification with the
secular power that had been characteristic of the previous period, and
could no longer turn to it for aid in the suppression of heterodoxy.
However, a complete divorce of church and state does not seem to
have occurred, in that the Umayyad amirs appear to have had a
controlling interest in the appointment of bishops and were required
to give their approval for the holding of councils. Thus the chancery
official Reccimund obtained the bishopric of Elvira (Granada) from
'Abd al-Raḥmān III as his reward for undertaking a diplomatic
mission to Otto I of Germany. This also gave him status in the eyes of
the Christians to whom he was being sent. A number of councils were
held in the ninth century at irregular intervals, although the acts of
only one of them have survived.[48] As well as requiring the prior
sanction of the Muslim ruler for their calling, they were possibly also
attended by Christian officials of the court, as in Visigothic days.

Most of the local Christian communities seem to have been initially
little affected by the conquest. This was largely as a result of the
agreements made by the conquerors with members of the Visigothic
aristocracy then holding regional authority. The name of one of these,

Theodemir, is recorded in a contemporary Latin chronicle, and the text of a treaty that he made with 'Abd al-'Aziz ibn Mūsa dated 5 April 713 has been preserved in a thirteenth-century Arabic biographical dictionary.[49] By it the Christian inhabitants of seven towns in south-east Spain – Orihuela, Valencia, Alicante, Mula, Bigastro, Eyyo (Elche?) and Lorca – were guaranteed their freedom, under the lordship of Theodemir, and liberty of their religion, in return for an annual tribute of one dinar and a specified quantity of cereals, vinegar, honey and oil per person, with a half rate to be paid for each slave. In addition they were required not to receive deserters or enemies of 'Abd al-'Aziz, or attack those under his protection. Theodemir is reported to have visited Damascus to receive confirmation of this treaty from the caliph in person, and it was still in force in 754 by which time he had been succeeded by his son Athana(g)ild. A reference in the Toledan Chronicle of that year to the Goths having elected counts to negotiate with the Muslims may also suggest that Theodemir had not been alone in what he did, in creating what was effectively a principality under Arab suzerainty, or as the treaty put it 'under the clientage of God and of his Prophet'.

Such enclaves of immune Visigothic and Christian rule probably did not long survive the creation of the Umayyad Amirate in Al-Andalus. They are never heard of after 754. Even so it seems very probable, as the report of Ibn Ḥaukal, an Arab geographer who travelled in Spain in 948, suggests, that large numbers of indigenous Christians, especially in the lower ranks of society, survived in rural areas and in many provincial towns throughout the Umayyad period.[50] They may well have still constituted the majority of the population, despite a rise in the number of conversions to Islam and the settling of the conquerors, and in the countryside at least may have proved as resistant to Arab culture as to religion. The urban and rural lower classes tend to escape from the net of available historical evidence as easily in the Umayyad as in the Visigothic period.

For Christians in Cordoba, Seville and other centres of Arab settlement and administration conditions were inevitably very different. Problems of coexistence had to be faced from the start. The initial small size of the Muslim community in Cordoba is perhaps indicated by their sharing of the Church of St Vincent with the Christians.[51] This, the basilica of the principal martyr-patron of the city, was divided, with the Muslims taking one half for their mosque. Such a choice by the conquerors, in occupying part of the Christians' main place of worship and focus of urban religious loyalty, can hardly have been accidental. In the time of 'Abd al-Raḥmān I it was determined that a proper mosque should be built on the site, and the Christians were persuaded to vacate their portion of the church by allowing them to erect a new one, which was, however, to be established outside the city, across the Guadalquivir. Over St Vincent's church the first stage of the great Umayyad mosque came into being.

Apart from such, perhaps symbolic, episodes, the urban Christian communities were reasonably well treated by the Muslim rulers. They were forbidden to build new churches or to advertise their worship by the ringing of bells, but beyond these limits and a prohibition on Christians attempting to convert Muslims or openly controverting Islam, persecution did not exist, nor was there any overt pressure put on the Christians to change their religion. They could be employed in government service and several individuals rose to hold high office in the Umayyad court, but they were vulnerable by reason of their religion in times of Muslim orthodox reaction. Thus the accession of Moḥammed I in 852 was marked by a purge of Christian officials from the court. This admittedly was probably not unconnected with the failed attempt by the influential Christian eunuch Nasr to prevent the amir's succession and secure that of one of his half brothers instead.[52]

In consequence the temptation for Christians who sought or had obtained high office to change their faith was considerable. A case in point is that of Gomez ibn Antonian ibn Julian, a court functionary who converted to Islam early in the reign of Moḥammed I in order to obtain appointment to the office of secretary to the amir, a post that contemporary Muslim opinion felt that a Christian should not hold.[53] The society of the ruling élite could best be entered through conversion, and thus the ranks of the *muwallads* were swelled as the Umayyad period advanced. The attractions of the material and intellectual culture of the upper-class Arabic society must also have contributed to the attractiveness of conversion, at least in centres such as Cordoba, receiving added impetus from the internal openness of the Islamic world, and the new departures in literature, learning and sophisticated living to be found in the capital of Al-Andalus in the ninth century.

Although Cordoba dominates not only our records, but also in all probability the lives of the leading Christians of Al-Andalus, it should not be assumed that it was the principal urban stronghold of the religion. Christianity was probably little touched in many rural areas. Also, although giving only a shadowy impression of itself in the few extant sources, an urban episcopate and ecclesiastical hierarchy still stretched over much of southern and central Spain. In terms of prestige, Toledo, although now an embattled marcher fortress, still remained the primatial see. Cordoba itself, as in Visigothic days, was subject to the metropolitan authority of the bishops of Seville. Of the other former metropolitan sees, only Mérida remained, for both Tarragona and Braga were deserted, and Narbonne fell into the hands of the Franks in the course of the eighth century. The Council of Cordoba held in 839 and presided over by Bishop Wistremir of Toledo was attended by bishops from Seville, Mérida, Guadix, Ecija, Cabra, Malaga and Granada. References to another council held in 862 in the *Apologeticus* of Abbot Samson, who was there accused of heresy, indicate that in addition the sees of Baeza, Baza, Urci, Elche and Sidonia were still in existence.[54]

It was not Muslim rule alone that broke many of the ties that had once linked the Church in Spain to that in Rome and in other parts of western Europe and which were not negligible during the Visigothic period. While the Umayyads clearly sought to monitor the contacts of their Christian subjects with fellow religionists across the frontiers, the marked isolation of the Church in Al-Andalus from the ninth century on, that kept it immune from the influence of virtually all of the developments in ecclesiastical thought and organisation elsewhere in Europe, may have been a product of the divisions created by the Adoptionist controversy.

This episode, which briefly brought the Spanish Church to the notice of its peers in western Europe, began as the accidental consequence of another obscurer dispute. About 780 a certain Egila, probably by his name of Gothic origin, either arrived in or returned to Al-Andalus as an itinerant bishop without a fixed see, having a special commission from his consecrator Archbishop Wilcharius of Sens and, apparently, papal backing. Such peripatetic bishops had been employed with much success earlier in the century in the spreading of Christianity to the Frisians, Saxons and other peoples to the east of the Rhine. These missionaries, linked to the papacy, had also fulfilled useful functions in encouraging reform within already established churches. The papacy, through the agency of Wilcharius, a noted Frankish reformer, may have been experimenting in the despatch of Egila with an extension of similar practices into Spain.

However their instrument was to prove a disappointment. Egila either was or became the follower of a certain Migetius, whom the Spanish episcopate under the direction of Bishop Elipandus of Toledo condemned for his unorthodox theological views in 785. His teachings are said to have included a belief that the divinity comprised three corporeal persons, manifested as King David, Jesus and St Paul. Once Pope Hadrian was made aware of his representative's involvement with Migetius, he was forced to disown him and warn the Spanish episcopate to have no further dealings with him.

This murky episode is important for a number of reasons. We only have Migetius's opponents' account of his ideas, preserved in a letter addressed to him by Bishop Elipandus.[55] It is quite conceivable that Elipandus distorted Migetius's views in the interests of controversy. However some of the features of this letter are very revealing when put in conjunction with the two letters sent by Pope Hadrian I to his agent Egila in 782. It seems that Migetius and his followers felt that the Spanish Church was falling into deviations from orthodoxy under the influence of its new Muslim masters, and that there was too much dangerous fraternisation taking place between individual Christians on the one hand, and Jews and Muslims on the other. Mixed marriages were explicitly condemned by the Pope at Egila's urging. Migetius and his disciples openly looked to Rome as the source of orthodoxy, and of the authority necessary to correct what they saw as the imperfections of the Spanish Church and Christians.

The chance survival, although in mutilated form, of the acts of the council of 839 provide a final glimpse of the fortunes of this sect, for the similarities in thought and practice between those condemned by the council under the name of 'Cassianists' and the followers of Migetius make their identity virtually certain. They were then entrenched in the region of Cabra, where they had at least one rural church, and they maintained a separate clergy. They had detached themselves from contact with the rest of the Spanish Church and other Christians, and the only ordinations that they held to be valid were those conferred by 'Agila of Ementia' (Mérida?).[56] This Agila is probably to be identified with Egila, whose consecration in Gaul and papal authority gave his sacraments a legitimacy that these sectarians felt to have been lost to the rest of the Spanish episcopate.

Times of persecution or subordination for the Church often produced such groups of uncompromising rigorists, such as the

Novatianists and the Donatists had been in the fourth century, who regarded their more flexible co-religionists as tainted. For the ultra-orthodox the sacraments administered by such clergy as those who compromised with non-Christianity would have no validity. The ordinations performed by their bishops were thus held to be ineffective. That such a sect, holding itself aloof from contamination by contact with Muslims and Jews and with those Christians held to have been tainted by it, should have come into existence in Spain after the Arab conquest is not surprising. Unfortunately we know little about it. However its existence does indicate, as do the complaints that its members made, that other Christians in Al-Andalus and the hierarchy of the Church found much less difficulty in associating with the new Muslim element in the population and with the Jews.

In attempting to resolve the problems created by the Migetians and the interference of Rome through Egila, the Spanish Church became embroiled in a new and more wide-ranging conflict. In his letter condemning Migetius Elipandus of Toledo had written of Christ *adopting* his human nature. This terminology was criticised by an Asturian monk called Beatus, the author of a commentary on the Apocalypse, and by his friend Etherius, subsequently Bishop of Osma. In October 785 Elipandus wrote to their superior, Abbot Fidelis of the monastery of San Torribio at Liebana, urging him to suppress their criticism, but this instead led to their composing a treatise denouncing the Bishop of Toledo's errors.[57]

The controversy rapidly spread. It quickly became known at Rome, for when Hadrian I wrote to the Spanish bishops in approval of their condemnation of Migetius he also upbraided Elipandus for his Christological ideas, but without effect. Here the matter might have rested but for the approval given in 792 to the controversial teaching by Felix, Bishop of Urgell in the Pyrenees, a town then in Frankish hands. In view of the prior papal condemnation, Felix was summoned to Charlemagne's court at Ratisbon to be lectured on the error of his beliefs by Bishop Paulinus of Aquileia. Having then recanted, he was sent to Rome, where being kept a virtual prisoner, he was made to sign a confession of faith. Not surprisingly, once permitted to return to his see, Felix took refuge in Muslim Spain and revoked his previous recantation. In 794 Charlemagne summoned a great ecclesiastical council to Frankfurt, which bishops from Italy and the Anglo-Saxon kingdoms also attended. This gathering produced two lengthy and detailed condemnations of the

Christological teachings of Elipandus and his friend Felix. Charlemagne, who had previously been admonished by the Bishop of Toledo to beware the example of Constantine the Great, who had fallen into heresy in his final years, sent the two treatises together with a covering letter into Spain.[58] A further, though less intellectually impressive, condemnation was produced by a synod held by Pope Leo III in St Peter's in Rome in 798, but neither these councils nor an exchange of letters between Elipandus and Charlemagne's adviser Alcuin had any effect upon the Spanish Church. Felix of Urgell's fate was different. Having returned to his see, he was removed to Aachen and forced once again to denounce his own views after a theological debate with Alcuin. However he was not this time allowed to return to Spain and ended his life in 818 confined in a monastery in Lyon. After his death Agobard, the Archbishop of Lyon, claimed to have found amongst his papers a treatise by the incorrigible Felix once more setting out his support for Adoptionism.

Inside Spain, Elipandus's Adoptionist terminology seems, apart from the reactions of Beatus and Etherius, to have generated remarkably little controversy. The ninth-century writer Paul Alvar of Cordoba asserted that a Bishop Teudula of Seville opposed the Toledan bishop's doctrine, but his treatise is now lost and a Bishop Ascaric, author of an acrostic epitaph, was singled out by Pope Hadrian I for condemnation as an Adoptionist.[59] The debate, at least on the part of its Spanish protagonists, was frequently abusive, with Elipandus denoucing Etherius as an ass and Beatus as the disciple of Antichrist and stinking with the vices of the flesh.[60]

It is possible that Elipandus received the general backing of the Spanish episcopate, as manifested in their corporate letter to Charlemagne, because of the peculiar pre-eminence of the see of Toledo that had existed since Visigothic times. Thus similarly in 684 the Christological views expounded by Julian of Toledo had been accepted by his colleagues as being those of the whole Spanish Church in the face of criticism from Rome.

The arguments used by Elipandus and his supporters drew heavily on their native intellectual tradition, employing citations from Isidore and Ildefonsus and also going back to such established mentors of the Spanish Church as Augustine and Fulgentius. Some of this drew abusive retorts from their opponents in 794 who claimed not to know of Isidore, Fructuosus and Ildefonsus, and who depended instead upon a battery of more widely accepted authorities.[61] This does not seem to have impressed the Spanish bishops other than Felix of Urgell, and even he later changed his mind.

In fact the arguments of Elipandus involved a distortion of the sense of the original passages on which he relied, and earlier use of Adoptionist terminology in the peninsula, as for example in passages in the liturgy, had different and unimpeachably orthodox intent. The Spanish bishops of the late eighth century were not in reality defending the ancient theological traditions of their Church, but what matters is that they thought they were. The barrage of criticism from across the Pyrenees, linked to that from Rome, already compromised by its involvement with Migetius, Egila and their followers, cannot but have contributed to the self-isolation of the Church in Al-Andalus, which left it uninfluenced by developments elsewhere and in its liturgy and learning largely a fossil of the Visigothic past.

Within the peninsula Beatus' and Etherius's sharp but inexact criticisms of Elipandus in 785 have been seen as marking an attempt by the independent and self-confident Asturian kingdom to overthrow the old pattern of ecclesiastical allegiances and to break free of the primatial authority of Toledo.[62] Such a view has little foundation. Toledo remained the primatial see, although it was not to fall into the hands of the heirs of the Asturian kings until 1085. No attempt was ever made to elevate Oviedo or Leon into a metropolitan see – the terms 'archbishop' and 'archbishopric' were not used formally in the Spanish Church before the late eleventh century – and the transfer of that of Mérida to Santiago in the early twelfth century was the product of quite different causes.[63] Nor can we assume that Beatus and Etherius spoke for the whole of the Church in the Asturias, the silence of whose bishops is marked.

The increasing detachment of the Church in Al-Andalus from the influence of its peers in western Christendom and the general freedom of movement and exchange of ideas that characterised the Muslim world perhaps made it more receptive to communication with other Christian communities living under Muslim domination. This is a subject as yet little studied, but a number of interesting pointers to such a conclusion may be found. A visitor to Cordoba in the 850s, who allowed himself to be swept up into the martyr movement that occurred in the city in that decade with fatal consequences to himself, was a monk called George, an eastern Christian who had spent twenty-seven years in the famous monastery of St Saba, near Jerusalem, before making his way via Africa to Spain.[64] In addition some of the liturgical manuscripts found in the monastery of St Catherine in Sinai display surprising Visigothic palaeographical features, and even if their full significance cannot yet be understood, they may prove indicative of some level of contact and exchange, as might the existence of the veneration of martyrs, whose cults are of Spanish origin, testified to in the same manuscripts.[65]

Although the language of the Christian liturgy in Al-Andalus remained Latin, the hold of Arabic in most other areas of daily life clearly grew as the Umayyad period proceeded, and not only the Bible but also the acts of the church councils of the Visigothic period were translated into Arabic, probably in the tenth century. However a spoken form of Latin, that increasingly deviated from the classic grammatical rules of the language, continued to exist and developed into early Spanish Romance.[66] If an ascription to the eleventh century be correct, the first appearance of the latter in extant written form was in an Arabic context, encapsulated in lines of verses called *kharjas*.[67] The Arabic of Al-Andalus, at least in spoken form, may well have been influenced by the linguistic company that it had to keep. One commentator, Ibn Sa'īd, wrote of it: 'The Moslem inhabitants of Andalus being either Arabs or Mustarabs, their language as well may be inferred was no other than Arabic. However it cannot but be said that the common speech both among the higher and the lower classes, has considerably deviated from the rules of Arabic grammar.'[68]

The growing attraction of Arab culture and language, and with it the danger of the lure of the religion of Islam that was inextricably associated with it, became a matter of deep concern to a small group of Christians in mid ninth-century Cordoba. This band, many of whom were closely linked together by ties of family and friendship, deliberately sought martyrdom at the hands of the Muslim authorities by public denunciations of Mohammed and of Islam, offences known to be punishable by death. The whole episode is described in the *Memoriale Sanctorum*, written by the Cordoban priest and later Bishop elect of Toledo, Eulogius, who acted as spiritual adviser to some of them, and who himself was to die by decapitation in 859, when found harbouring an Arab girl who had converted to Christianity. With his execution our principal source of information is lost but it seems likely that this act also marked the ending of the movement that he had defended and glorified.

The beginnings of the Cordoban martyr movement were largely accidental, although indications in the works of Eulogius and of his friend Paul Alvar suggest that the decline of traditiohal Christian Latin culture and the growth of Arabising were already a matter of deep concern to them and their friends. In 850 a monk called Perfectus from one of a number of small monasteries in the surrounding countryside was goaded into a theological discussion in the market place in Cordoba with a group of Muslims, in the course of which he denounced Moḥammed as a false prophet. Although this had no immediate effect, on a subsequent visit to the city he was recognised and seized by an angry crowd which carried him before the *qadi*. After being held in prison he again publicly abused the Prophet of Islam and was executed at the end of the month of Ramadan, the Muslim fast. His fate was not initially of his own choosing in that it was the result of Muslims deliberately pressing him to give his views on their prophet, but once driven to speak he was inevitably committed.[69]

By contrast the successors of this protomartyr actively sought their own deaths. For example Isaac, the subject of the second of the Passions in Eulogius's *Memoriale*, came from one of the noble families of Cordoba, but gave up his career as an administrator in Umayyad service to become a monk. Three years later, in 851, he went down to the city and persuaded the *qadi* publicly to expound the tenets of Islam to him on the pretext that he was considering conversion. In the middle of the exposition Isaac rounded on his informant and began to abuse him and his religion. Although the *qadi* at first assumed that he was drunk or mad, he was driven into having Isaac imprisoned and he was subsequently executed on the orders of the amir.[70] This precipitated a series of self-sought martyrdoms that took place throughout the summer of 851, mostly on the part of monks and clerics, but also involving a Basque soldier in the amir's guard called Sancho, who was one of Eulogius's pupils.

Not surprisingly such deliberate conflict provoked Muslim anger, and the amir Moḥammed I is reported to have considered imposing forcible conversion, but it also produced much disquiet in more moderate Christian circles. The validity of self-sought martyrdom became a matter of urgent debate, and the Church hierarchy led by Bishop Reccafred of Seville condemned the movement, possibly through a council held in Cordoba in 852. Eulogius was briefly imprisoned by the bishop. In response both Eulogius and Alvar wrote works in justification and defence of the martyrs and their actions. The former produced his *Memoriale* in three parts, in the years 851

and 853, which was largely an account of the passions of the individual confessors, to which in 857 he added a sequel in the form of his
Apologeticus Martyrum, whilst Alvar's *Indiculus Luminosus* of 852 and
854 was cast more as a general apologetic of the principles upon which
the movement was based.

Although they could not claim that the Muslims persecuted the
Church with violence in the way that the pagans had in the third and
early fourth centuries, they did regard the destruction of churches, in
implementation by Moḥammed I of the ban on new Christian
buildings, the discriminatory taxes, to which as non-Muslims they
were subjected, and the low social role accorded to their priests by the
constitution of society, as sufficient 'molestation' to justify the
martyrs' deeds, and they also cited the examples of earlier voluntary
martyrs even going back to John the Baptist. Interestingly Eulogius
in his attack on Moḥammed as a false prophet made use of a *Life* of
the founder of Islam that he had brought back from his visit to
Pamplona in 848.[71]

This journey, which Eulogius initially undertook in search of his
brothers then delayed at Mainz in the east of the Frankish kingdom,
had important consequences for the Christian community in
Cordoba. Being unable to leave the peninsula as a result of the
disturbed conditions then prevailing across the Pyrenees and around
Barcelona, he was persuaded to remain at Pamplona in the hope that
safe passage across the passes might eventually become possible.
Under the guidance of Bishop Wiliesind of Pamplona, Eulogius
whiled away some of the time in visiting monasteries in that region,
and in one of them he discovered a store of texts that were not
available at that time in the south, and which, when he decided to
abandon his plan and to return to Cordoba, he took back with
him. These manuscripts included Augustine's *City of God*, Virgil's
Aeneid, the *Satires* of Horace and various other poetic works by
Juvenal, Aldhelm, Optatianus Porphyrius and Avienus. On the basis
of these Eulogius began to instruct his friends in Cordoba in the rules
of Latin metre, thus initiating a small poetic revival, now best
represented in a small collection of verses by Alvar, which in form and
content very much followed the lines of similar works composed in the
Visigothic period by Eugenius of Toledo and others.[72] These and the
prose writings generated by the controversy over the martyr
movement mark the first flourishing of Latin literature in the south of
the peninsula since the end of the Visigothic kingdom.

The works of Eulogius and his friends were often intended to be deliberately evocative of a lost past, that of the departed realm of the Goths, that had been 'foremost in the blessed practice of the Christian faith, flourishing in the worthiness of most venerable bishops and radiant in the most beautiful building of churches'.[73] They looked to the literary heritage of that idealised past to illuminate their own writings and to provide the materials for a renaissance of Spanish-Christian Latin culture in a society in which they felt beleaguered. Their Latin style was as a result highly mannered, and they drew an almost absurdly archaic vocabulary from the writings of Isidore, notably the *Etymologiae*, that allowed them for instance to refer to the regnal years of the amirs as 'consulships' and to call young men 'ephebes'.

The numbers of those who took the road to voluntary martyrdom were relatively small. Eulogius chronicles the deaths of thirteen of them in the year 851, in which the movement effectively came into being. About the same number followed suit in the next year and between June of 853 and July 856 some seventeen martyrdoms are recorded. Apart from two girls called Alodia and Nunila, who met their deaths in Huesca, all of the executions took place in Cordoba, though not all of the victims were native to the city.[74] Several of them came from other towns in the upper Guadalquivir valley, such as Ecija and Carmona, and some, such as the priest Gumesind, from as far off as Toledo. However in all such cases they had come to Cordoba for other reasons, in some instances for the purposes of study, and once there had been drawn into the martyr movement. Several of the individuals are characterised as being of noble birth, some such as Aurea, executed in 856, being of Arab descent, but others such as Argemir clearly of Romano-Gothic origin. A common denominator for many of them was association with a small group of monasteries in the hinterland of Cordoba, of which that of Tabanos features most prominently in the sources. This appears to have been, as were some of the others, a double monastery, housing both monks and nuns under the separate rule of an abbot and an abbess. It was a family foundation, being the creation of a certain Jeremias and his wife Elizabeth. Here the martyr Isaac, a relative by marriage of the founding family, and the first voluntarily to seek his own death, spent three years as a monk. A number of others associated with the monastery, including the Palestinian monk George and also the founder of the house, Jeremias, who, having installed his wife and her brother Martin as first abbot and abbess, had withdrawn to lead the life of a lay hermit, were martyred in the early stages of the movement. However after the voluntary immolation of the nun Digna in 853 the monastery was destroyed by order of the amir Moḥammed I on the grounds that its creation had infringed the prohibition on the erection of new churches.[75]

In addition several of those who came forward to seek death by martyrdom were secret Christians, in that they were either converts from Islam or Christians who had lapsed into Islam only to reconvert to their original faith. The existence of both such classes of Christian who, for their ties to Islam however short-lived, were then liable to execution as apostates in Muslim law, is indicative of the religious fluidity that existed at least in certain sectors of society in mid ninth-century Cordoba. The tide of conversion did not run in just one direction. However most cases involving members of Muslim families who converted to Christianity concern the products of mixed marriages, in which the existence of a Christian mother or other female relatives led to the conversion of the children, often after the death of their Muslim father. In some such instances the children themselves became divided, with the boys retaining the paternal faith while the daughters secretly adopted their mother's Christianity. This was the case of Flora and an unnamed sister, whose brother denounced them to the *qadi* as lapsed Muslims in 845, for which he had them flogged. They then ran away from home to live secretly with Christian friends at Martos.[76]

While Muslim men could take Christian wives, the reverse was not possible. Thus an unusual case was that of the parents of Maria and Walabonsus, children of a humble Christian father from Elche and an Arab mother, who was persuaded by her husband into accepting his religion. As a result the family had to keep permanently on the move and in hiding until the wife died. Then their father put Maria into the convent of Cuteclara, under the direction of its abbess Artemia, herself the mother of two children, Adulphius and John, who had been martyred in obscure circumstances in 822, and Walabonsus was entrusted to the monastery of St Felix. Walabonsus became a deacon and one of the spiritual directors of Cuteclara, before volunteering himself for martyrdom in June of 851, amongst the first wave of those taking up the example of Isaac. Maria, who had a vision of her brother in which he told her that she too would soon be a martyr, met Flora, the fugitive convert from Islam, praying in the basilica of St

Acisclus and the two women thereupon decided to go to the the *qadi* and publicly denounce Moḥammed. Having done this and resisting the attempt of the *qadi* to convert them, they were executed in November of 851.[77]

In several of the cases, notably that of Eulogius himself, as recorded in the *Life* by Alvar, it seems that the Muslim judges were reluctant to press matters to their final conclusions, even when conversion to Islam was the only admissible alternative to execution. Eulogius was apparently offered the chance of a purely nominal conversion: 'Say only a word in this hour of need, and afterwards practice your faith where you will. We promise not to search for you.'[78] But in all such cases attempts at compromise were resisted and if necessary further insults were directed against Islam and its Prophet in order to ensure that the *qadi* pronounced sentence of death.

Difficulties exist in the evaluation of these accounts, not least in that they bear close resemblance to the early Christian passions of the martyrs, and it is not possible to be sure how far purely literary parallels are being made or to what degree the Cordoban martyrs deliberately emulated the conduct of their third- and early fourth-century predecessors. Likewise the blandishments and apparent worldly wisdom of the Muslim *qadis* and officials are identical in tone to many of the arguments put into the mouths of pagan Roman judges and governors in the earlier passions.

It is apparent in a number of the individual cases, so fully described by Eulogius in his various works, that the secrecy forced upon them by the strict rules against conversion and the problems created by mixed marriages drove a number of the martyrs into making their public declarations of faith and repudiation of Islam. But not all of the instances fall into such a pattern: it looks as if an attempt was being made by a small group of Christians in Cordoba to turn their community in the city into a martyr Church, following the pattern set in the great Diocletianic persecution of 303–312. Their aim was to halt the slide into Arabicising and into Islam by setting their Church into violent opposition to the Muslim establishment. The result should have been a smaller but more assured and self-defined Christian community, dwelling in but detached from Muslim Al-Andalus.

Limited geographically and in time as the Cordoban martyr movement was, it is probably indicative of major changes taking place initially in the heart, but soon to spread to most other parts, of

Umayyad Spain. Another symptom of these was the northward migration into the lands of the Christian states of communities of Mozarabic monks. The term 'Mozarab' is not unambiguous in its meaning. It was used for instance by Ibn Sa'īd to refer to indigenous Arabicised Muslims in Spain. However its general and current significance is to designate those Christians of Al-Andalus who, while retaining their religion, had adopted a large measure of Arab culture.

References in the extant Latin writings of the mid ninth century indicate the existence of several Christian monasteries in the countryside in the vicinity of Cordoba. Some of these may have survived from Visigothic times, but others, such as Tabanos, were recent foundations, and indeed the religious tensions developing in the city may have driven many Christians, who, if not willing to seek martyrdom, at least sought to commit themselves more fully to their religion, into adopting the monastic life. However from the second half of the ninth century on, something of a flight of members of religious houses into Leon and Catalonia can be seen getting under way, which increased in intensity in the tenth century. From the evidence of foundation inscriptions of churches in these regions and from their charters, the period from *c.* 910 to *c.* 940 saw the greatest such activity.[79] Not surprisingly, where the place of origin of these fugitive monks is known it generally turns out to be Cordoba.

There are few historical records of the actual migrations but the Mozarabs are so culturally distinctive that the traces of their presence in the north are not hard to find. They were given lands on which to settle and found new monasteries by the Christian rulers, particularly in the recently colonised frontier regions of the kingdom of Leon. The architecture that they employed, although used in a Christian context, was strongly affected by the styles of Al-Andalus. Particularly striking in their many extant churches are the narrow columns topped by 'horseshoe' arches, which are identical in design to the types of arch and arcading to be found in Umayyad Cordoba, as for example in the Great Mosque, and which are also demonstrably different to the features of the churches of the Asturias, which derive from Visigothic tradition.

The Mozarabic monks also brought with them a distinctive style of manuscript illumination, that is best exemplified in the magnificent decorated copies of Beatus of Liebana's *Commentary on the Apocalypse.* The earliest of these dates from 930 and the series stretches on into the early twelfth century, with the Silos manuscript, currently in the

British Museum. Other important manuscripts may be found in the cathedrals of Seo de Urgel and Burgo de Osma, and in the Pierpont Morgan Library in New York. The places of origin of some of the manuscripts are known: the Escorial Beatus (*c.* 950) is from the scriptorium of San Millan de la Cogolla, while the Pierpont Morgan of 962 is from Escolada. They, like the architecture, seem quite distinct from the contemporary and parallel products of the Christian states, although attempts have been made recently to argue that what is at issue is the creation of a new Leonese style of manuscript painting, rather than the importing of an already established Mozarabic one.[80] However, it is highly unlikely that this frontier zone was as Arabicised, or as culturally sophisticated, as such arguments would require us to believe.

Unfortunately, the origins of the Mozarabic style of manuscript decoration are obscure. No certain examples of Visigothic illuminated manuscripts are available for comparison; the attribution of the only possible contender, the Ashburnham or Tours Pentateuch, is still a matter of dispute. The highly schematic, stylised architectural designs to be found in some of the Beatus manuscripts clearly reflect the actual styles of Mozarabic churches, and of Al-Andalus. Although from the early eighth century onwards a general prohibition on the depiction of figures in art seems to have existed throughout the Islamic world, this was not observed in Spain, in respect of the minor arts at least, and its general application has probably been exaggerated. Thus, it is theoretically possible for figurative styles of art in Al-Andalus to have directly affected those of the Mozarabs. However, the almost total absence of contemporary manuscripts and the diminutive rate of survival of any artefacts of Umayyad Al-Andalus inhibit judgement.

The Mozarabic refugees made their distinctive mark on the north, and in the abbey of San Miguel de Cuxa, even across the Pyrenees.[81] Their churches and manuscripts may, in many cases, still be seen, although they had little apparent influence on the subsequent traditions of the regions in which their creators came to settle. Less palpable but possibly of greater significance was the effect of their bringing of books from the south with them. From these stem some of the collections of monastic libraries and cathedrals of later centuries. They may also have been instrumental in spreading interest in the cult of the Cordoban martyrs in the Christian states, so that by 883 Alfonso III was concerned enough to acquire the relics of Eulogius from the amir Moḥammed I in the course of diplomatic negotiations. He may also have obtained some of Eulogius's collection of books at the same time.[82]

What were the reasons for the exodus of Mozarabs from the south during the course of the ninth and tenth centuries? It may have been the result of deliberate persecution by the amir Moḥammed I. Alvar of Cordoba, writing soon after 859, spoke of 'the time when the savage rule of the Arabs miserably laid waste all the lands of Spain with deceit and imposture, when King Mohammed with unbelievable rage and unbridled fury determined to root out the race of Christians . . .'.[83] However, this was in respect of the fates of the martyrs of Cordoba, who had in most cases deliberately provoked Muslim hostility. No Arab source records any change from normal practices in relation to the Christians. The idea of a systematic and sustained persecution that would have been required to engineer the continuous migration of Mozarabic monks cannot be established.

A more probable explanation might lie in the effects of the violent and almost uncontrollable conflicts that affected most regions of Al-Andalus throughout the reigns of Al-Mundhir, 'Abd-Allāh and the opening years of 'Abd al-Raḥmān III (880s to c. 920). With the effective disintegration of the authority of the central government and the local civil wars in which Arabs, muwallads and Christians all became involved, the monasteries, however poorly endowed, must have been natural targets for aggression. In such circumstances, flight into the currently better-ordered Christian realms would be an attractive proposition.

However, the removal of these, the most militantly Christian elements in the society of Al-Andalus, may be closely related to the emergence from the period of conflict of a more stable and powerful Muslim state. As in other parts of the Islamic world, the cumulative effects of conversions to Islam would have been making themselves felt by the late ninth century, even though Muslims might still have constituted a minority of the population. For one thing, the growth of substantial numbers of muwullads challenged the survival of the traditional tribal organisation of the Arabs in Al-Andalus. The latter had also ceased to be of direct value to the state with the reliance on large slave armies. Tensions between Arabs and muwallads clearly grew in the course of the ninth century, as did those between both of these groups and the remaining Berbers. Conflicts are frequently recorded in all of the extant Arabic sources. Likewise, the divergencies between Cordoba, with a large population of *muwallads* and of slaves, and the rest of the Umayyad realm, were strongly marked. Distributions of largesse to the soldiers and remissions of taxes, together with the advantages of the rulers' architectural and artistic patronage, benefited the citizens of the capital. It is notable that the collapse of the Cordoban Caliphate was followed by a brilliant flowering of culture in many provincial centres in the succeeding *Taifa* period.

These and other problems came to a head in the reign of 'Abd-Allāh, although the last years of Moḥammed I and the brief rule of Al-Mundhir were also very troubled. Ibn Ḥayyān provides the fullest account of the revolts and disturbances under 'Abd-Allāh, who is strangely neglected by Al-Makkarī and Ibn al-Athīr.[84] The Banu Kasī, threatened by the rise of the Tojibids, were active once more in the upper Ebro valley, and also captured Toledo in 896. However, this powerful family was brought to an abrupt end when its head Moḥammed was killed besieging Zaragoza in 898, and his son Lope fell in battle in 907. With their demise, relative order and stability returned to the Ebro valley and the central march for the rest of the century.

More serious for the regime in Cordoba were the many *muwallad* revolts occurring in the west in Badajoz, Mérida, Beja and Faro, and in the east over a wide area in the regions of Jaen, Granada and Malaga. Also, various local potentates established themselves as effectively independent over long stretches of time, as in the case of Abū Farānik, who ruled a region of north-western Andalus untouched by the central government for twenty years. After his death he was succeeded by his nephew, who held out for another five years before having to submit to 'Abd al-Raḥmān III in 930.

Of all the rebels of this period, 'Umar ibn Ḥafṣūn is the most remarkable. He successfully defied the authority of four successive amirs, and as leader of most of the *muwallads* of south-eastern Andalus dominated the region until his death in 917/8. His power rested in the holding of a large number of small fortresses, with Bobastro as his main base. Successive expeditions from Cordoba failed to make headway against his strongholds, each in turn holding out against siege, delaying the advance of the Umayyad forces. On occasion, as when Bobastro itself was threatened, Ibn Ḥafṣūn took to the mountains to carry on successful guerrilla campaigning, or when it suited him, he would make token submission to the amir, who was powerless to replace him. In 890 he tricked the rebel governor of Jaen, murdered him and sent his head to the amir, while in the same year his own followers were even raiding in the vicinity of Cordoba.

The roots of Ibn Ḥafṣūn's power, probably like that of *muwallad* leaders such as 'the Galician', lay in the inability of the Umayyads to suppress local conflict. What was virtually a civil war raged around Granada between Arabs and *muwallads* in the 890s. As successive Arab leaders were murdered, so the violence and obligations of blood feud intensified. Neither side had much use for the Cordoban regime, except when it suited them. The *muwallads*, hard pressed by the Arabs, called for the aid of the governor of Jaen, promising to restore their allegiance to the amir, but when he was defeated trying to assist them, no more was heard of that. Instead, help was sought from Ibn Ḥafṣūn. From a series of local conflicts and rebellions, together with the assassination of rival *muwallad* leaders, the regional strength of Ibn Ḥafṣūn was created. It did not survive his death, as his several sons fell to quarrelling and murder, and a series of campaigns by 'Abd al-Raḥmān III finally broke the power of the last of them in 927.[85]

It is possible that this period of disturbances marks a time of some religious ambivalence. The family of Ibn Ḥafṣūn converted to Islam around 840, but according to the *Anonymous Chronicle of 'Abd al-Raḥmān III*, an Arabic source probably of the eleventh century, when the amir finally took Bobastro in 927 he had the body of Ibn Ḥafṣūn exhumed, and found that he had been given Christian burial. Ibn Ḥafṣūn is also reported to have built a church in Bobastro, as had his father before him. These may be no more than rumours put out to discredit a dead but dangerous man in the eyes of his followers and later generations of *muwallads*, but it is possible, although we cannot really see it in our sources, none of which are contemporary, that these revolts represent not a Christian revival but a reaction to the prospect of a more fundamental Islamisation of Al-Andalus.

What is clear is that 'Abd al-Raḥmān III, unlike his grandfather 'Abd-Allāh, was able to make substantial and fairly speedy headway against the rebellions and disorders that had virtually torn apart the state in previous reigns. By about 930 they were all at an end. It is hardly insignificant that this was the point, in 929, that he took the titles of Caliph and Commander of the Faithful. A new Umayyad Caliphate came into being. It was the name of 'Abd al-Raḥmān, and no longer that of the ephemeral 'Abbāsid in distant Baghdad, that was publicly mentioned in prayers as that of the leader of the community of Muslims. This marks not only a new self-confidence in terms of the secular power of the state, but more strikingly, a greater sense of religious assurance. Islamic Al-Andalus was there to stay, or so men might have thought.

7. The Christian Realms

The Asturias and Leon

THE century that follows the Arab invasion of the peninsula in 711 is probably the darkest in its history as far as the survival of evidence is concerned. There are very few contemporary records, but for the first half of the century there is a reasonably substantial chronicle, known from the date of its final entry as the *Chronicle of 754.* It was very probably compiled in Toledo, which briefly retained its position as the centre of learning in the peninsula, and its author, although anonymous, was clearly a Christian. He knew something of the history of the Visigothic kingdom and cast his work as a continuation of Isidore's *History of the Goths* rather than a series of annals. His main sources of information on seventh-century Spain were the secular laws and a collection of conciliar acts, but he was better informed about the history of the Arabs and of the Byzantine Empire. For these he was able to use another continuation of Isidore compiled in all likelihood in Cordoba soon after the date of its final entry in 741. This work, the *Chronicle of 741*, although written in Spain, concerns itself solely with the history of the Arab Caliphate and the Byzantine Empire. It is conceivable that its author, who wrote in Latin, came from Africa. It is striking how concerned both chronicles are with the deeds of the new conquerors and the author of the *Chronicle of 754* in particular was interested in putting their history into the context of that of the recent past of the peninsula, adding it on to the Isidoran tradition. Indeed he was doing for the Arabs something of what Isidore had done for the Visigoths in respect of the historically minded intelligentsia of the conquered population. From a reference in his *Chronicle* it appears that he also composed a history of the civil wars that had just taken place in Spain in the middle of the century between the rival groups of Arabs.[1] This work, now lost, may have followed the model of Julian's *History of Wamba*. It is perhaps typical of the perspective from Toledo, and of the centralising traditions of the Visigothic church, that he either never knew of or was not interested in the revolt in the Asturias, and the creation of its tiny Christian kingdom.

Extant Arabic sources for the history of eighth-century Spain are all later in date than the events described, and in view of the growing importance of the Asturian kingdom and other Christian states in the north of the peninsula in the subsequent centuries, might have been expected to display some interest in their origins. In fact they have very little to say on the history and society of these realms, or on the Visigothic past. It is noticeable that more interest is displayed in these subjects by Arab authors writing in the East than by those of Al-Andalus. Thus for example Ibn al-Athīr, working in Mesopotamia, seems to have been better informed on the chronology of the Visigothic kings than were the Christians in Spain, who claimed to be their heirs. On the other hand the caliph and historian Al-Ḥakem II is reported to have commissioned the writing of a *History of the Franks* by a Bishop of Gerona and an Arabic translation of Orosius, but seems to have displayed no such interest in the past of the Christians of northern Spain.[2] The attitude of the Andalusis may seem strange, but then Isidore would never have considered writing a history of the Basques or of the Cantabrians, and no one in Visigothic Spain would have wished for one.

For the history of the formative period of the Christian states of northern Spain, we have to turn to their own sparse records in the form of some short chronicles, some genealogies and regnal lists, and various collections of charters. In the case of the Asturias, the earliest of these realms to come into being, the first charter is a deed issued by King Silo (774–783) granting some lands for the foundation and support of a monastery and is dated 23 August 775.[3] There is a handful of other genuine eighth-century charters, some interpolated, and a larger number of later forgeries. However, for the ninth, and particularly the tenth, centuries, this source of evidence becomes more plentiful and informative, although the problems of ascertaining authenticity remain formidable. Such documents are invaluable for the history of settlement and landholding in the kingdom, but it is the chronicles, supplemented by the regnal lists that provide the outline of events.

These chronicles of the Asturian realm are all products of its final stage in the late ninth and early tenth centuries, and present many problems of transmission and interpretation. In their present form the earliest of them is probably the so-called *Prophetic Chronicle* written in April 883, which, on the basis of a spurious and pseudo-Biblical prophecy that the author attributes to Ezechiel, predicts the imminent expulsion of the Arabs from Spain, an event due to occur one year and seven months from this time of writing. That the Arabs did not leave Al-Andalus on 11 November 884 as predicted may have robbed the prophecy of its value, but the work, which is not a true chronicle in form, was preserved, probably thanks to the historical and chronological information that its author included as the basis for his calculations. Amongst other materials was a regnal list of the Asturian royal dynasty, which was subsequently continued up to 928, in the reign of Alfonso IV.

Of chronicles proper that 'of Alfonso III' was so called because it was long believed to have been written by that king, who ruled from 866 to 910. It covers the period from the accession of Wamba in 672 up to the death of Ordoño I in 866. Although it is possible that the work was first compiled in the reign of Alfonso III, it now survives in two versions, dated in their prologues to the reigns of his sons Garcia (910–914) and Ordoño II (914–924). The first of these, from the Navarrese see of Roda, is the fuller of the two and seems to display a Galician and ecclesiastical bias, whilst the other, the Oviedo text, is Asturian and regal in outlook. Argument exists as to which is the earlier: it used to be thought that priority should be given to the Roda text, but, although in its present state later in date, it is likely that the Oviedo version is the original and may represent the royal annals of the dynasty.[4]

The last of these chronicles, that 'of Albelda' was possibly the first to be written. It takes its name from the Navarrese monastery of Albelda, where the text was continued up to the year 976, but the first section covering the years 672 to 881 was probably written in the Asturias, as was its first continuation, from 881 to November 883. In form this work, like the two versions of the *Chronicle of Alfonso III*, follows Isidore's *History of the Goths* in providing brief notices of each individual reign, rather than a year by year account. Common to all these chronicles appears to be a belief that Isidore's *History* finished with the reign of Reccesuinth. This suggests that there may once have existed a continuation of Isidore's work from the reign of Suinthila up to that of Reccesuinth. The real authors of these chronicles are unknown, but their writings testify to the interest in history in the Christian courts of northern Spain in the late ninth and early tenth centuries. Alfonso III may well have commissioned both the *Albelda Chronicle* and the Oviedan version of the one that bears his name, whilst the Roda text was included in an early tenth-century manuscript compiled for the Navarrese court at Nájera.

Inevitably the perspective of these works on the early period of the history of the Asturian kingdom was coloured by developments which had taken place closer to the time of their being written. The significance of Pelagius' initial victory over the Arabs at Covadonga has been exaggerated and the event itself misdated; also the conscious presentation of the Asturian kingdom as the heir and successor to that of Toledo was a product of the reign of Alfonso II and not inherent from the start. Although there is much force to these and other criticisms and some of these distortions of perspective can be detected and compensated for, the lack of surviving evidence from the earlier centuries leaves no alternative to the looking back over the history of this small kingdom through the eyes of the court historians of the reigns of Alfonso III and his sons.

Taking either the traditional date of 718, or, as has been recently argued as being more probable, that of 722, it was only a few years after the Arab victory over the Visigoths before the Asturias was in revolt against its new masters. A defeat of the Arab or Berber garrison and the death in battle of the governor of Gijon cleared the province of them once and for all. In retrospect the battle at Covadonga, which may in reality have been a very small-scale affair, represents the first stage of the gradual Christian recovery of the peninsula, the *Reconquista*; however in the context of the early eighth century it may perhaps typify the advantage that this, and other related northern mountain areas, were quick to take over central authority should the latter seem weak. There is more continuity here with the kind of resistance that the Asturians, Cantabrians and Basques presented to the Romans and the Visigoths than later interpretations of the victory might have us believe. Before the late ninth century the battle of Covadonga had taken on quite legendary proportions. The wooden cross borne before Pelagius in the fray became a sacred treasure for his descendants, one of whom, Alfonso III, had it encased in gold and precious stones. An elaborate oral epic, full of robust dialogue and improbable personal confrontations between the participants, was composed; some of it survives in the two versions of the *Chronicle of Alfonso III*, and in due course the battle came to be associated with a miraculous appearance of the Virgin Mary.[5]

The truth is more prosaic. In the first place this was obviously a purely Asturian rising, and the chroniclers say as much. Its leader Pelagius is a shadowy figure. The *Chronicle of Albelda* had him being expelled from Toledo by King Wittiza, but, as this monarch and his descendants are objects of the particular opprobrium of this and other chroniclers writing after 711, conflict between him and the founder of the line of the Asturian kings may well be a personalising and legendary accretion. Pelagius could certainly have been an Asturian noble.[6] No substantial movement of refugees from the heartland of the former Visigothic kingdom into the northern mountains could have taken place before the battle, and in view of the realities before 711 it was hardly an obvious area for them to think of fleeing to. Besides, the Asturias, overrun by Mūsa in 714, was as much under Arab military domination as other regions of the peninsula.

Pelagius, who, according to the chroniclers, had been elected king by the Asturians prior to the battle, made his capital at Cangas de Onis, probably little more than the site of a royal residence and church, and ruled his small realm until his death in 737, facing no serious attempt by the Arabs to restore their authority. The exact extent of the Asturian kingdom in his day is hard to determine; it probably included little if any of Galicia, and Cantabria, its neighbour to the east, had its own *dux* or duke. What kind of formal relationship Duke Peter had with the Asturian monarch is unclear, but it was to be his son Alfonso who ultimately reaped the benefits of Pelagius' achievements, for he married the latter's daughter Ermosinda. When Pelagius's son Fafila was killed by a bear in 739 it was his brother-in-law who was chosen to succeed him. With the rule of this king, Alfonso I 'the Catholic' (739–757), the small realm starts to take on a clearer shape.

He and his father, unlike Pelagius, are linked genealogically with the former Visigothic monarchs in the chronicle, being described as descendants of Leovigild and Reccared. This is probably a false claim, but the parallel between Leovigild and Reccared, the creators of the Toledan kingdom and the Catholic monarchy respectively, and Peter and Alfonso 'the Catholic' was deliberate. In the reign of Alfonso I, taking advantage of the internecine wars of the Arabs in the south of the peninsula in the 740s and 750s, several of the main towns of Galicia and the Meseta were raided by the Asturians, including Lugo, Tuy, Oporto, Braga, Salamanca, Astorga, Leon and Zamora. Lacking the military strength and perhaps the desire to hold this large and exposed area against eventual Arab counter-attack, the urban populations were carried off back into the Asturias, and the whole Duero valley and western Galicia was devastated and depopulated, leaving a no-man's land between the Christian kingdom and the newly created Umayyad Amirate of Cordoba. Although such a depopulation can hardly have been total, the demolition of fortifications and the destruction of settlements would have left any remaining inhabitants little defence or basis for organisation. With the creation of the Umayyad marches across the centre of the peninsula it is likely that this empty frontier zone became a practical reality.

With the establishment of the Amirate and the stilling of the internal conflicts in the south, the Asturian kingdom became the target for almost annual raids by the Umayyads' expeditions, but this never presented a real threat to its continued existence, and occasionally could give rise to morale-boosting victories in skirmishes. One such is recorded in the reign of Alfonso's son Fruela 'the Cruel' (757–768), in the course of which a son of 'Abd al-Raḥman I is reported to have been captured and executed.[7] No reference to this is found in the Islamic sources. Of greater significance for the future of the kingdom were the campaigns of harassment and massacre directed against the surviving Berber garrisons in Galicia that finally led to their withdrawal from the region and return to Africa, after which Fruela was able to reverse some of his father's work and repopulate Galicia as far as the river Minio. Also from this reign comes the first record of conflict between the Asturians and the Basques, the latter rebelling unsuccessfully against the king in Cantabria. The extent of Basque lands under Asturian rule is uncertain, but, together with the Galicians, they added a third culturally distinctive and self-conscious element to the composition of the kingdom, the future politics of which was to be seriously affected by the rivalries and conflicts between the components. King Fruela himself married a Basque called Munia before meeting a violent death at the hands of his own followers. None of the chroniclers gives a clear reason for this, but their account of his death is put in juxtaposition with that of his murder of his own brother Vimara.

Although the families of Pelagius and Alfonso I managed to maintain a monopoly on the kingship, this was not due to a new acceptance of hereditary succession, for, as in the Visigothic kingdom, royal inheritance depended more upon military capacity than upon primogeniture. Thus in 768 the infant son of Fruela and Munia was passed over in favour of the late king's cousin Aurelius, son of Alfonso I's brother (see Table I). That the dynastic line was maintained despite such vicissitudes may represent continuity with traditions from the tribal past in the northern regions, and may also reflect the more limited bases of power of the nobility in the Asturian kingdom as opposed to the Visigothic. From the scant references of the chronicles it looks as if king-making, in the form of choosing between the various possible candidates from the royal dynasty, was the prerogative of an Asturian Palatine nobility. Their choice could be challenged by a claimant with sufficient backing in Galicia or amongst the Basques, ever willing to confront the central authority of the kingdom. Royal marriages and landholding gave rival branches of the dynasty particular ties to and claims on the leaders of these ready sources of manpower.

Aurelius ruled for six years (768–774), and during his reign and those of his two successors the kingdom and the Amirate of Cordoba appear to have been at peace, perhaps helped by some of the internal disorders in the latter. During this reign a servile revolt is reported, the causes and consequences of which are not reported beyond the fact that it was suppressed.[8] As in the Visigothic past there probably existed a substantial population of rural slaves tied to the land and sold with it on most estates including even quite small ones.

Aurelius was succeeded by an Asturian noble called Silo, who had married Adosinda, the daughter of Alfonso I, and who ruled for nine years (774–783). At some point in his reign he successfully faced a revolt in Galicia, and he moved the court from Cangas, where it had been based since the time of Pelagius, to Pravia, where he built a church dedicated to Santa Inés (Agnes). A charter of this king survives, which is notable for its primitive character. The more sophisticated formal documents of subsequent decades suggest that many of the governmental traditions of the Visigothic kingdom were not inherited directly by the Asturian, but may even have come from borrowings from Frankish practices in the time of Alfonso II in the early ninth century.

On the death of Silo his widow and the officers of the court proclaimed Alfonso, the son of Fruela I, but power was successfully seized instead by Mauregatus, an illegitimate son of Alfonso I, and the young Alfonso was forced to flee for refuge to his mother's Basque relatives in Alava (see Table I). Whether it was these Basque connections or his military inexperience that led to Alfonso's unpopularity is unknown, but he was passed over again when Mauregatus died after a brief reign (783–788), and Vermudo I (788–791), brother of Aurelius, was elected to succeed. This monarch is known popularly as 'the Deacon', for he abdicated to become a cleric. As has been previously suggested, this may not have been an entirely voluntary act, coming as it did after a humiliating military defeat.

Now at last Alfonso II (791–842) obtained the throne, which, but for the brevity of his predecessors' reigns, he might have lost all chance of. He ruled for fifty-two years, but his hold on the throne was not always secure. In his eleventh year as king (801/2) he was deposed by a revolt and relegated to a monastery, only to be restored in a counter-coup by a noble faction. Early in the reign he moved the site of the court once again, to its final resting place in the newly founded town of Oviedo. Here the king and his architect Tiodo deliberately set out to revive the traditions of Visigothic Toledo. As the Albelda chronicle puts it: '. . . he established the order of the Goths as it had been in Toledo in church and palace alike.'[9] The reign of Alfonso II probably marked a reaction against the indigenous traditions of the Asturias and an attempt to revive those of the lost Visigothic kingdom. Certainly the surviving buildings in Oviedo from this period, and the remarkable wall-paintings in one of them, the Church of St Julian, are clearly the products of metropolitan rather than provincial artistic styles.[10] The probable influx of fugitives from the Umayyad realm and particularly its frontier regions, which now included Toledo, will have brought more of the art, law and learning of the Visigothic past into the small Asturian kingdom, an area little touched by them in the seventh century.

Alfonso II did not just look to the south and to the departed kingdom of the Goths for help in moulding his state. He also turned to a new power that was starting to interest itself in the peninsula: the Carolingian kingdom of the Franks, which by the reign of Charlemagne (768–814) had extended itself southwards to the Pyrenees. Although that monarch's attempt to intervene in the Ebro valley in 778 proved a fiasco, relations were subsequently opened between Oviedo and the Frankish court. Spanish chronicles are uniformly silent on this, but Einhard's *Life of Charlemagne*, written in the early 830s, refers to diplomatic exchanges between the two courts and to Alfonso's referring to himself as being the Frankish Emperor's man.[11] A suspect and probably twelfth-century Spanish source purporting to give the acts of an ecclesiastical council held in Oviedo during this reign suggests that information on the church reforms being implemented in Francia was sent to the Asturias by the medium of Bishop Theodulf of Orleans, himself of Gothic descent.[12]

Alfonso, who seemingly deserved his nickname 'the Chaste', died without heirs, and was buried in Oviedo in the church of Santa Maria, his own foundation, leaving an uncertain succession. Power was taken, perhaps by election, by Nepotian, probably a nephew of the late king and Count of the Palace, the chief officer of the royal court (see Table I). However, he was immediately opposed by Ramiro, son of the former king Vermudo I, who was absent from court getting married at the time of Alfonso II's death. His support came from Galicia – and it is interesting to note that his name is Suevic – whilst that of his rival was Asturian and Basque. However, the latter appears to have been half-hearted, and Nepotian's followers deserted him when he marched against Ramiro. He was captured in flight by Counts Scipio and Sonna, and blinded on the victor's orders. Interestingly two tenth- or eleventh-century regnal lists include Nepotian as a legitimate king.[13] The appearance of names like Scipio, drawn from a very distant Roman past, may indicate something of a classicising tendency in the court circles of Alfonso II.

The short reign of Ramiro I (842–850), probably already elderly at his accession, continued to be plagued by disaffection and conspiracy. Two subsequent Counts of the Palace, Aldoratus and Piniolus, were executed for treason, the latter together with his seven sons. No other Asturian king is known to have had so much trouble with his court nobility, and this may reflect the hostility of the Palatine aristocracy towards a ruler whose strength lay in Galicia. Ramiro, perhaps deliberately avoiding the constructions of Alfonso II, built a new palace complex, comprising throne-room, chapel and baths, much of which still survives, on Monte Naranco to the north of Oviedo. Interestingly the decorative styles displayed on the extant hall (now a church) and chapel are notably different from those to be seen in Alfonsine Oviedo and may perhaps be Galician. Ramiro I died peacefully on 1 February 850 and was succeeded by his son Ordoño I (850–866).

Over a century after the depopulation of the Duero valley by Alfonso I, the Asturian kingdom was at last able to expand itself south of the Cantabrian mountains into the Meseta, and under Ordoño I a number of towns in the north of the region, including Leon and Astorga, were reoccupied. At the same time a gradual eastward expansion of the realm into Alava in the upper Ebro valley brought it into conflict with the neighbouring kingdom of Pamplona and the power of the Banu Kasī, who from their strongholds in Tudela,

Huesca and Zaragoza were seeking to dominate the region. However, the defeat of their leader Mūza and his son-in-law King García of Pamplona by Ordoño I at Albelda in 862 established Asturian hegemony in Alava for the next half century.

During the middle of the ninth century the region of Castille, between the Asturian kingdom and the towns of the north-western Meseta on the one hand and the upper Ebro valley on the other, began to be developed. It was an area lacking in major urban settlements, and its principal town of Burgos was not founded until 884, but, as its name implies, it was a region of castles, small fortresses and strongholds. Its early history is obscure despite its subsequent prominence as the greatest Christian Spanish kingdom of the later Middle Ages. In the ninth and tenth centuries it was just a vulnerable frontier zone of the Asturian kingdom, but one whose nobility and their followers enjoyed greater privileges and freedom from royal control than other parts of the state in the interests of promoting settlement and the resources for self-defence. Authority in Castille was exercised by a count appointed by the king but enjoying a large measure of practical independence. Even some of the earliest charters from the region juxtapose the names of the king 'ruling in Oviedo' and the count 'ruling in Castille'. In the time of Ordoño I this was a Count Didacus (Diego).[14]

It was in Castille that the new king Alfonso III 'the Great' (866–910) had to take refuge soon after succeeding his father, expelled from his throne by Froila, Count of Galicia, possibly a rival member of the dynasty. However, the usurper was promptly murdered by some of Alfonso's supporters and a remarkable reign was begun. The principal success of Alfonso's rule lay in the carrying to completion of the occupation and extensive repopulation of the Duero valley and Castille commenced by his father, aided by the political disintegration of the Umayyad frontier marches, which now made possible a southward extension of the Asturian kingdom. Settlements were either founded or restored in such naturally defensible sites as Zamora and Toro, which together with Leon became the centres of the colonisation of the north-western Meseta. These strongholds became the targets for attack by expeditions from the south, which continued sporadically despite the growing internal chaos of the Amirate, and after the first settlement had been destroyed by an Arab army Zamora had to be refounded by Alfonso III in 893. Such attacks were not always the work of organised expeditions from

Cordoba. In 901 a self-proclaimed *Mahdi*, or Islamic Messiah, tried to seize Zamora with the support of Berber tribesmen, but was defeated, executed and his head displayed on the walls.[15] The collapse of order in the centre of the peninsula could thus present as many problems to the Asturian monarchs as to the amirs.

It did however also provide opportunities of a predatory kind for Alfonso and his nobility. Much of the Amirate's western march, around Mérida and Badajoz, was subjected to raids and devastation by the Asturians in the early 880s, and again in the first quarter of the tenth century, until a truce had to be negotiated by Moḥammed I in 883. This same period of weakness gave Alfonso the chance of expelling the garrison of Conimbria (Coimbra – in the centre of modern Portugal) and resettling it with Christians. New settlements were also made further north in Braga, Oporto, and Viseu and also in southern Galicia. This period also saw the foundation of Burgos in 884 and of other fortified sites in Castille. In these latter the work was carried out by the count Roderic. It is this era of confidence and expansion that saw the production of the '*Prophetic Chronicle*', and helps to explain its air of facile optimism in forecasting the imminent collapse of Islam in the peninsula and the restoration of the kingdom of the Goths by Alfonso.

Such hopes were ill-founded and the period of expansion in the early part of the reign was followed by a quieter time of consolidation and defence. Internal divisions also materialised within the kingdom. Alfonso's brother Vermudo, previously blinded for his involvement in a conspiracy, successfully rebelled in Astorga and maintained an independent kingdom there for seven years with Arab support. Nor were the Asturian ruler's problems confined to his southern frontier as he was twice faced by revolts by his Basque subjects in Alava that required forcible suppression.

Despite such difficulties, the growth of the kingdom under Alfonso III marked its most substantial expansion since its foundation and before the late eleventh century. This was a time of self-confidence for its monarchy that is reflected in a programme of royal building that included a new palace in Oviedo and the commissioning of such masterpieces of the jeweller's art as the 'Cross of Victory', now housed in Oviedo Cathedral, and the agate casket in Astorga.[16] Alfonso, as ruler over the Asturians, Galicians, Basques and the newly arrived Mozarabs, had the necessary qualifications for *imperium* or imperial rule, and the ideology of 'the Spanish Emperor' that was developed during the reigns of his successors Alfonso VI and Alfonso VII is thought to make its first appearance in his time. Any such conception of the *imperium* of the Asturian king was probably most influenced by Frankish ideas and the example of the Carolingians. It has no real roots in the Visigothic past or in Roman tradition as applied to Spain. An interesting though somewhat interpolated letter survives from Alfonso III sent in 906 to the monks of the Abbey of St Martin at Tours in which he expressed interest in purchasing a Carolingian imperial crown that he believed them to possess; he also offers to send them what from its description can only be a copy of the *Lives of the Fathers of Mérida*.[17] No reply is known.

The most striking visual survival from the times of Alfonso III is the monastic church of San Salvador de Valdedios in the eastern Asturias, founded by the king in 893, and where he spent his last days. It retains traces of its original wall paintings which are stylistically akin to those of Alfonso II's church of St Julian in Oviedo. In cultural and artistic terms and in the encouragement of the Visigothic ideology of the Asturian kingdom, the reigns of Kings Alfonso II and III show striking continuity across something of a period of reaction in the time of Ramiro I. Alfonso III also continued the work of his namesake in respect of the cult of St James. He built the second church at Santiago de Compostela (*c*. 879–896) to replace the smaller one erected by Alfonso II a century earlier. This, however, was to be destroyed by Al Manṣūr in 997 and eventually succeeded by the present magnificent Romanesque cathedral.

The question of the cult of St James, the brother of St John, and its significance in the period of the Asturian kingdom is a very vexed one.[18] The principal source for the early history of the cult and the reverence it received is the twelfth-century *Historia Compostelana* (Compostelan History), which is a prejudiced witness. The belief that St James preached in Spain and that after his death in Jerusalem his body was brought back to the peninsula for burial near Iria Flavia in Galicia has left no trace in the Roman and Visigothic periods, although from outside of Spain there is a reference in a poem of the English monk Aldhelm, Bishop of Sherbourne (*d*. 708) to St James having preached in the peninsula.

In the ninth century, traditionally in 813, but it may have been two or three decades later, Bishop Theodemir of Iria Flavia (now called Padrón) claimed to have discovered the body of the saint buried in a rural site a few miles from his see. Successive churches, as has been mentioned, were erected on the spot to honour and house the relics, and the settlement of Compostela, the etymology of which name is disputed, came into being. In 1095 the episcopal see was transferred from Iria to Compostela and in 1120 it was elevated into an archbishopric by means of the abolition of that of Mérida. By that time pilgrimage to the shrine of St James was attracting Christians from all over western Europe and its popularity scarcely waned throughout the rest of the Middle Ages.

St James became the patron of the whole of Spain, and as the result of reports of his miraculous appearance in a number of crucial battles he received the epithet of 'Matamoros' or 'Moor-slayer', and is frequently thus represented in Spanish art. The first of these manifestations occurred supposedly at a battle of Clavijo in 834, in consequence of which King Ramiro I granted the proceeds of a special and perpetual tax to the bishopric. However, Ramiro I was not ruling in 834, no battle of Clavijo took place and the whole episode, especially the financial arrangement, resulted from the concoction of a spurious charter, forged in Compostela in the early twelfth century, the practical consequences of which it took over half a millenium to undo. The history of the cult of Santiago is peculiarly rich in such frauds.

It was given its distinctive character and impetus in the early twelfth century largely thanks to the work of a group of Compostelan clergy headed by Diego Gelmirez, the first archbishop. Its earlier history, behind the veil of the falsifications, is not so easy to detect. Archaeologically the foundations of the two churches on the site give grounds for belief in the existence of reverence for important relics there during the Asturian period. Below the level of the earlier of these, providing a possible explanation for the origin of the relics, a cemetery of late Roman or Suevic date has been found.

In the Early Middle Ages, the discovery and subsequent honouring of the remains of saints, especially martyrs, was a common feature of religious practice with a very definite role to play in expressing or fostering the self-consciousness and unity of communities. It was usually associated with the rise to eminence of a particular group, which could range in size from the inhabitants of a section of a town or of a village up to a whole race. It could give a local church its roots and provide a patron. The emergence of the cult of St James at this time is probably indicative of the self-assertion of the Galicians, not least towards the Asturian kings to whom they were subject. Why it was

James in particular who came to play this role for them remains
mysterious. It has been argued that this is the result of the translation
of relics of the saint from Mérida, as certainly occurred in the case of
Eulalia.[19] However, the Méridan evidence consists only of the
dedication inscription of a late sixth-century church, recording the
relics that were deposited under its altar, a normal part of
consecration.[20] Although the name of St James is found there it occurs
seventh out of twelve in the list. Nothing as important as the whole
body of an Apostle, which is what the Galicians claim to have, could
have been referred to in this way. The origin of the Galician relic thus
remains unknown.

It is certain, though, that before its development in the eleventh
and twelfth centuries, which was to lead to its pre-eminence in Spanish
Christianity, the cult of Santiago was an essentially Galician affair.
The Asturian kings, who often had difficulties in retaining the
loyalties of the Galicians, obviously found it prudent to associate
themselves with the cult by such acts of patronage as church-building
and doubtless the giving of votive offerings, such as the jewelled cross
presented by Alfonso III in 874. However, it was Oviedo that
remained the centre of their realm and there they began to build up a
powerful collection of relics of their own, some of which may still be
seen in the *camara sancta* in the Cathedral. In the capital it looks as if St
Eulalia, whose body had been carried off from Mérida, rather than St
James, was the preferred royal saint. Her relics are still preserved
there. More interest in Santiago was evinced in the succeeding
Leonese kingdom in the tenth century, in which settlers from Galicia
probably played a prominent part. However it remained only one of a
number of cults that attracted royal support, while in Castille at this
time veneration of the sixth-century hermit Aemilian came into
prominence.[21] This cult doubtless articulated the growing Castillian
sense of identity in the way that of Santiago did for the Galicians.

The transference of power from Alfonso III to his sons in 910 marks
the end of royal residence in the Asturias, and the final removal of the
centre of government from the former heartland of the kingdom into
the recently settled frontier regions to the south. Outgrown, the
Asturias were thenceforth left behind in the continuing development
of the Spanish Christian kingdoms, and it is customary to refer to the
state ruled by the sons and heirs of Alfonso III as the Kingdom of
Leon, its new centre of administration and the court. The details of
the movements of population from the old settlements to the new and

migration from the increasingly Islamicised south are poorly recorded beyond the brief details of foundations recorded in charters, but the transportation of the royal government from behind the shelter of the Asturian and Cantabrian mountains into the relative openness of the Meseta is symptomatic both of the sense of the solidity of the new settlements and of the self-confidence of their rulers.

Even when compared with their Asturian predecessors the kings of Leon in the tenth century seem obscure. The quantity of charters surviving from the Leonese kingdom greatly exceeds that produced previously in the Asturias but this type of evidence is very limited in its application, and the Leonese and Asturian charters are less varied and more restricted in their style and contents than those of the contemporary counties of Catalonia. However, it is in historical writing that this kingdom is deficient. For most of the tenth century, from the last stages of the reign of Alfonso III to that of Ramiro III (967–982) the chronological outline has to be taken from the *Chronicle of Sampiro*, written by a court notary early in the succeeding century, who may have become Bishop of Astorga (*c.* 1040). This survives in two versions: one, probably faithful to the original, transmitted in the twelfth century through the Castillian monastery of Silos, and the other, heavily interpolated and expanded and with a continuation compiled (*c.* 1119) by Bishop Pelagius of Oviedo, a notorious forger of texts. This latter becomes the only source for the last two decades of the tenth century and for the final stage of the Leonese kingdom, which went down in military defeat at the hands of Ferdinand I, the Navarrese king of Castille, in 1037. The only supplement to the Sampiro tradition, apart from the brief references in Arab historians, comes from the continuation of the Albelda chronicle up to 976 written by Abbot Vigila.

From these sources some account of the history of the kingdom can be drawn. The events preceding the deposition of Alfonso III by his sons in 910 are not clear, and it is possible that Sampiro was as baffled by their chronology as we are. It seems that at the end of a period of some military successes against Umayyad expeditions, and the expansion achieved by the repopulation of the Duero valley and the frontier regions of Castille, Alfonso discovered a plot in which his eldest son García was implicated, and he had him arrested at Zamora. This action precipitated a revolt in Galicia led by its count, who was García's father-in-law, and a further conspiracy by Alfonso's other sons which resulted in the king's forcible deposition in 910. The initial causes of discontent, other than the old monarch's inconvenient longevity, are unknown, but one immediate consequence appears to have been the transfer of the capital from Oviedo, perhaps at first to Zamora, but within a decade to Leon. The new king, García (910–914) had previously been identified with this frontier region, having been associated with his father in the repopulation of the Duero, and governing it from Zamora and Toro in Alfonso's later years. Little is known of his short reign beyond the success of a great raid that he led into Extremadura, and on his death the succession passed to his brother Ordoño II (914–924), previously governor or subordinate king in Galicia. This reign saw a further expansion of the kingdom, principally eastwards from Castille into the Rioja in alliance with King García Sánchez of Pamplona (905–925), until checked by the defeat of the two kings by 'Abd al-Raḥmān III in 920. Ordoño was the effective founder of the medieval city of Leon, and was the first of the kings to be buried there, in the Church of St Mary, formerly a Roman bath-house and later royal palace which he had had transformed into the episcopal seat.[22]

Both Ordoño II and his short-lived brother and successor Fruela II (924–925) encountered problems in their dealings with their marcher aristocracies, particularly in Castille. With the growth of the power of the kings of Pamplona in the Rioja from the 920s onwards, the counts in Castille, notably Fernan Gonzalez (931–970), were able to play off the ambitions of that rising realm against the authority of their own nominal overlords in Leon. In this they were assisted by the existence of a series of disputed successions in the later kingdom, some of which, through a network of marriage alliances, also led to the involvement of the rulers of Pamplona.

The succession in turn of three sons of Alfonso III created serious problems of royal inheritance, for both Ordoño II and Fruela II, who died of leprosy, left male heirs. The eldest son of the former succeeded in Leon as Alfonso IV (925–931) but another Alfonso, probably the son of Fruela II, seems to have established an independant kingdom in Galicia that lasted for nearly a decade. According to Sampiro, Alfonso IV would much rather have been a monk than a king and he eventually resigned his throne to his brother Ramiro II (931–950).[23] This story may conceal the reality of a bloodless coup, for no sooner had the new king left Leon for Zamora to take command of a raiding expedition, than Alfonso returned to his former capital and resumed his throne. Ramiro, however, speedily retook the city and had his brother blinded, together with three sons of Fruela II, in order to render them incapable of ruling. Forceful if ruthless, Ramiro II was probably the most outstanding, at least in military terms, of the Leonese kings. He conducted a series of highly successful raids on Arab strongholds along the frontier, and won the notable victory at Simancas in 939 over 'Abd al-Raḥmān III's counter-offensive. He dominated the Rioja, eclipsing the kings of Pamplona, and the Muslim ruler of Zaragoza submitted himself and his city, albeit only temporarily, to Leonese authority. In consequence repopulation could proceed apace: Salamanca was occupied, as was Ledesma, while Osma, Oca, Clunia and other strongholds in the frontier zone were either founded or restored by local counts on royal orders.

Ramiro's predecessors had had difficulties with the counts in Castille and Alava and a number of these had been executed by Ordoño II. Opposition to the new king by two of his counts in particular, Fernan Gonzalez and Diego Muniz, had led to their capture and imprisonment, but it is symptomatic of the local power that such men and their families were attaining in the vulnerable frontier regions, that Ramiro found it expedient to release them and restore their offices, while seeking to gain loyalty by marrying Fernan Gonzalez's daughter Urraca to his own son and heir Ordoño. This alliance was to have significant consequences, for it involved the ambitious count in the turbulent dynastic politics of the Leonese rulers in the succeeding decades.

When Ramiro II died, soon after a final victory over an Umayyad army at Talavera, his eldest son succeeded as Ordoño III (950–955). Fernan Gonzalez, although father-in-law of the new king, joined in a conspiracy with King García Sánchez of Pamplona to replace him by his younger brother Sancho. An attempt to expel Ordoño from Leon failed and the count was forced to take refuge in Castille and submit, while his daughter was then repudiated by the king. However, Ordoño III, who led a very lucrative raid on Lisbon and showed promise of continuing his father's successes, died prematurely, to be followed to the throne by his brother Sancho 'the Fat' (955–957, 960–967), whose obesity led to his expulsion in favour of Alfonso 'the Bad' (957–960), probably a son of Alfonso IV. This dispute provided opportunities not only for the Umayyads to make a decisive intervention in 960, but also for the Count of Castille to further his own independence by playing off the rival parties. Although formerly the ally of Sancho, he took a prominent part in his expulsion and arranged the marriage of his daughter Urraca to the new king. When Ordoño 'the Bad' was in turn driven out, Fernan Gonzalez found it expedient to make his peace with the restored Sancho and ordered Urraca to abandon her husband, who went into fruitless exile in Cordoba.

Sancho I, restored by the caliph, was in no position to undertake the raids on Umayyad territory that had marked the reigns of several of his predecessors, but instead he concentrated on an attempt to impose royal authority effectively on Galicia. This, however, was to prove a fatal venture, for in the course of negotiations in 967 he was poisoned by Gonzalo, Duke of Galicia in the newly created western frontier zone of the kingdom, an area roughly equivalent to the centre of modern Portugal and he left the throne to a son aged five, who succeeded as Ramiro III (967–984). A regency was exercised for him by his aunt Geloira (Elvira), daughter of Ramiro II and abbess of the convent of St Saviour in Leon. This long regency and another which marked the early years of the reign of Alfonso V (999–1027) are indicative of a significant change in attitude to royal government on the part of the dominant elements in society. To some extent it is suggestive of the hold now exercised by dynastic loyalty and the principle of primogeniture that the succession of a legitimate but infant monarch should be preferred to the selection of a maturer candidate from a minor branch of the royal line. However, more significant may be the fact that the powerful marcher aristocracies now had a vested interest in keeping royal authority weak, something easily achieved during a minority. This same period saw the first establishment, at least as far as the available evidence is concerned, of an entrenched hereditary nobility, able to pass office as well as family wealth and social standing from generation to generation. The emergence of such aristocratic dynasties, as occurred from the later ninth century on in the Frankish Carolingian Empire, reduced the practical importance of the monarchy and produced smaller but stronger units of local self-government in the form of virtually independent counties.[24] The scale of such a development in the Leonese kingdom was reduced by its much more limited size, and the marriage links of the family of Fernan Gonzalez of Castille with the royal dynasty of Pamplona (or Navarre) led in 1035 to the transformation of that almost autonomous county into a small kingdom.

Even in the centre of government the great lords of the frontier marches could play a preponderant role, eclipsing the Palatine nobles who had been so important in earlier decades. This resulted from their military strength, based on the growing population of the frontier counties, and their need to be self-sufficient in defence. Thus, during the minority of Alfonso V, the chief prop of the régime of his mother Queen Elvira, the regent, was the Galician count Menendo Gonzalez. Conflicts between active Leonese kings exercising their own rule and the great marcher counts, who were in theory only their appointed representatives, was scarcely avoidable. Sancho I had perished as a consequence and his son was no more successful in curbing his overmighty subjects. Unspecified difficulties with the counts in Castille and Galicia led to a revolt in the latter region and the crowning of a rival king at Compostela in the person of Vermudo II. Whether a purely Galician kingdom, a revival of that which had existed briefly earlier in the tenth century, was envisaged by the supporters of this monarch, the son of Ordoño III by a second marriage, is unknown, for the legitimate king Ramiro III failed in an attempt to dislodge his rival and died almost immediately, supposedly of natural causes. (See Table II.)

The standing of Vermudo II (982–999) may have been further weakened by doubts as to his legitimacy as well as by the nature of his succession. His mother Elvira had been the second wife of Ordoño III, but the legality of that king's dismissal of his first spouse, Urraca, daughter of Fernan Gonzalez, was questionable. Whether as a result of this initial fragility in his position or not, Vermudo II is recorded, uniquely amongst the Asturian and Leonese kings, as having formally confirmed the continued application in his realm of the Visigothic lawcode and the acts of the Church councils.[25] No new version of either seems to have been issued, and no extant manuscript can be associated with the king's decree, but the importance attached to them at this period may be illustrated by the existence of two great manuscripts containing full collections of ecclesiastical and secular laws that were produced in the Navarrese monastery of Albelda in 976 and 992.[26] These lavish products of both the calligrapher and the illuminator's art, the *Codex Vigilanus* (named after the abbot who commissioned it) and the *Codex Aemilianensis* (named after the monastery of San Millan, its later home) have been associated with King Ramiro III of Leon by reason of a full-page illumination that is common to both, and which depicts in three rows the Visigothic kings Chindasuinth, Reccesuinth and Egica, to whom the manuscripts ascribe responsibility for the *Forum Iudicum*, then below them a Queen Urraca, a King Sancho and a King Ramiro, and in the bottom row three scribes, these latter differing in the two codices. Dating alone might cast doubt on the ascription of the central figure to Sancho I of Leon and the one to the right of him to his son Ramiro III. It is perhaps more likely that the ruler represented in the dominant central position is King Sancho Garcés II of Pamplona (970–994), who is known to have had a wife, Queen Urraca, and whose brother Ramiro (d. 991) bore the title King of Viguera. (See Table II.) This makes the manuscripts and their royal patron Navarrese, not Leonese as is usually believed, a conclusion of some importance not least for the history of the monastery of Albelda. But their evidence for renewed royal interest in the legal heritage of the Visigoths in both the civil and ecclesiastical spheres, as also attested to by the act of confirmation by Vermudo II, is unequivocal.

The reign of the latter monarch in Leon was principally marked by the destructive raids directed against the kingdom by Al-Manṣūr which resulted in the sacking of the city of Leon in 988 and of Santiago in 997. The cathedral erected by Alfonso III was destroyed but the relics of the Apostle were left undisturbed, a surprising decision on the part of Al-Manṣūr if, as is usually believed, he was motivated by religious fanaticism and sought the complete obliteration of the Christian states. Vermudo II began the work of restoration and a new church was consecrated in 1003, but by that time the king was dead, leaving a three-year-old child as his successor.

The resulting minority, together with a growing threat from Navarre now under the rule of its most forceful monarch, Sancho Garcés III 'the Great' (1000–1035), limited the ability of the Leonese to take advantage of the sudden decline and eventual collapse of the Umayyad Caliphate that followed the ending of the ascendancy of the sons of Al-Manṣūr in 1008. Alfonso V (999–1027) showed considerable political and military skill, but was killed beseiging Viseu in an attempt to resume his kingdom's expansion in central Portugal. Ten years later his son Vermudo III (1027–1037), the last of the direct line of the heirs of Alfonso I, fell in battle with his brother-in-law Fernando I, the creator of a new kingdom of Castille and Leon. (See Table II.)

Stark as the narrative history of the kingdom must be as a result of its limited sources, some additional information can be gleaned from the corpus of extant charters. In particular several of the kings emerge as patrons of monasticism. Sahagún, which was to become the centre of Cluniac observance in Spain from the late eleventh century on, makes its first appearance in a charter of donation of Alfonso III in 904, and many of his successors, notably Ramiro II, followed with further benefactions. Another royal foundation was Carracedo, established by Vermudo II in 990. Some monasteries, as for example Celanova and Samos in Galicia, attracted considerable royal interest both in the form of gifts and also in confirmations by charter of the donations of lesser benefactors.[27] Other houses, as far as their surviving records go, only attracted less distinguished concern. But whoever the patrons and however small many of the individual gifts that monasteries received, the surviving charter evidence, which only represents a fraction of what once existed, demonstrates a widespread interest in monastic foundation and endowment in tenth- and eleventh-century Leon and Galicia.

The Rule of St Benedict, that had become the principal guide to the organisation of monastic life in many other parts of western Europe during the ninth and tenth centuries, had at this time made virtually no impact on Spain outside of Catalonia, where it was imposed by Carolingian patronage and example, and it was not to do so much before the reign of Alfonso VI (1072–1109) in Castille. Some of the monasteries of the Leonese kingdom, such as Samos in the diocese of Orense in Galicia, had originated in the Visigothic period, and it is likely that the Rule of St Fructuosus, their founder, was still employed. Monastic pacts made between monks and their abbots, that first appear in the Visigothic kingdom, continued to be employed in Galicia, Castille and the Rioja into the tenth century. No examples of these have come from Leon and it has been suggested that such agreements were not employed there and represent a Galician peculiarity that was later deliberately introduced into the newly colonised frontier regions of Castille and the upper Ebro.[28] However, this may reflect no more than the random survival of our evidence.

Monasteries were the educational centres of the kingdom. The few extant manuscripts tell us a little about this but more informative are a small number of lists of books, principally to be found in wills, which give some impression of the lost literary resources of these houses.[29] Neither the Asturian nor the Leonese realms can be regarded as having made any major or original contribution to intellectual culture. The only new works to have been composed within their frontiers were the monk Beatus of Liebana's voluminous *Commentary on the Apocalypse* of 786 and the brief contribution that he and his friend Etherius made to the Adoptionist controversy in the form of their letter to Elipandus of 785. The *Commentary*, that appeared in three versions, probably in 776, 784 and 786, although of vital importance in having preserved otherwise lost fragments of earlier patristic exegesis of the Apocalypse, was purely a labour of compilation. However, Beatus's citations show that he did have works by Ambrose, Jerome, Augustine, Tyconius and Fulgentius to hand to aid him in his task, as well as texts of Spanish authors such as Apringius of Beja and Isidore. He had enjoyed royal patronage, notably from Queen Adosinda the daughter of Alfonso I and wife of King Silo, until both he and his benefactress were forced into monastic retirement by the death of that monarch in 783. The fairly substantial literary resources that Beatus had at his disposal were possibly those of a royal library.

Not until the later ninth century, when Leon became the beneficiary of the movement of books from the south of the peninsula that accompanied the migration of the Mozarabs, does more evidence as to the intellectual culture of the kingdom emerge. The main influx of texts to supplement those that had survived from the Visigothic period probably took place at this time. A list of books appended to a manuscript dated 882 probably records one such import of works from Cordoba, which may have been part of the collection once formed by Eulogius, whose relics were transported to the Asturias in the same year. The list includes poetic texts as well as grammatical and exegetical ones. Adding to this the books whose existence is recorded in wills, notably that made in 927 by Bishop Cixila of Leon in favour of his monastery of Abeliare, a substantial number of works can be seen to have been available in the tenth-century Leonese kingdom, including the poetry of Virgil, Juvenal, Avitus, Dracontius, Corippus and Aldhelm.[30] Some of the manuscripts in question may have started their wanderings in the Carolingian Empire.

However, the greatest quantity of books referred to in these sources were liturgical. One manuscript of Virgil hardly makes a 'Renaissance', and most of the texts in Leonese and Galician monasteries were of strictly practical use, being either service books or aids to the study of scripture. A few monasteries, such as Abeliare, can be seen to have possessed a large and varied selection of books, but the majority are likely to have had only a handful and those being of strictly utilitarian value. However, all of these houses may have provided some level of education, not only for boys placed within their walls as future monks but also for the children of the aristocracy, amongst whose ranks literacy does not seem totally unknown. Clerics and royal clerks, such as the notary and historian Sampiro, must have received their training in monasteries or in episcopal households, which might be, as in the case of Bishop Cixila and Abeliare, indistinguishable. In very few cases is it likely that such education extended beyond the ability to write and some acquaintance with liturgy and parts of the scriptures.

Monasteries, together with a small number of noble families, the roots of whose status is impossible to trace, were the principal landowners in the frontier regions, although there was also a substantial number of smaller property-owners of free status encouraged to settle there in the periods of repopulation by special concessions.[31] For if the towns in the Duero valley and Castille, reoccupied or newly created by the Asturian and Leonese kings, were to be made into permanent and secure settlements, as was needed if the regions were to be retained successfully, a larger population was required. In the conditions that existed in these marcher zones tangible inducements were often necessary to bring in new settlers to occupy and defend the towns and related countryside. Considerable concessions were made by the kings and great lords in respect of autonomy and the privileges granted to the citizenry in these frontier towns. These generally varied from place to place and represent individual agreements made between the citizens and their overlord and these were generally in written form. Such charters of municipal rights, called *fueros*, could also include modifications of existing law and special legal regulations that then became part of the privileges of the citizenry. *Fueros* are known from later reissues to have been granted to Burgos and Castrojeriz in the tenth century, and the extant ones of Leon date from the early eleventh. Some of these early *fueros* became models for later ones. Similar practices were followed from the eleventh century in the kingdoms of Navarre and Aragon, and the confirmation of municipal *fueros* by successive kings became an important feature of Spanish political life. One consequence of the growth of *fueros* was the increasing limitation of the application of the law of the *Forum Iudicum* or *Fuero Juzgo* as it became in the vernacular. Castille in particular became a stronghold of localised law and custom, as opposed to Leon where the *Fuero Juzgo* remained generally in force until the thirteenth century. *Fueros* did not necessarily have to be royal concessions, as they could be granted by any landowner to his dependants. The tenth-century counts of Castille made the earliest such grants in that region. In addition, special classes of subjects might have their own *fueros*. Thus by the reign of Alfonso VI Jews in Leon had separate *fueros* from those of the Christians.[32]

The general *fueros* of Leon first appear in the ordinances of a council held in the city by Alfonso V in 1020.[33] It is conceivable that some of the regulations and concessions there written already existed and that the council was codifying current practice and committing it formally. The decrees relating to Leon and the rights of its citizens are not coherently collected together in the acts of the council but make up the greatest part of the business of the meeting.

The privileges granted were not just confined to the inhabitants of the city but were also extended to those living in certain specified areas outside of the walls. Those thus encompassed were required to come into the city to give and receive justice and could take refuge there in time of war. They were exempted from any tolls on goods that they sold there, but were required to assist in defence and in restoring the city walls. The government of Leon was entrusted to a council, the composition of which is not specified, but on the first day of Quadragesima each year all citizens, from both within and without the walls, were to gather in the square of St Maria de Regula to elect officers to oversee weights and measures employed in the city's markets. This assembly also fixed the wage to be paid for labour for the year. Further regulations in the council laid down penalties to be imposed on dealers in bread and meat who attempted to cheat their customers with false measures, and free access of all goods for sale in the city was also guaranteed.

The citizens were protected from harassment by royal officials: the *saio*, a judicial officer appointed by the king, and the *majorinus* (mayor) were forbidden to enter a citizen's home or break down its doors. Women might not be arrested or tried in the absence of their husbands. Members of various lower social orders, who might have legal ties elsewhere, could not be extradited from the city, and even slaves were similarly protected. However, in their case, if their servile status were proved in a legal process by the affirmation of 'truthful men', they might be returned to their lords, whether Christian or Muslim, a remarkable indication that distinctions of status were held to transcend religious divisions. All of these and other concessions were later confirmed by Queen Urraca in 1109 on her accession.[34]

A significant proportion of the inhabitants of the new towns of the frontier were Mozarabs and their descendants. The Christian states of northern Spain other than Catalonia had had little experience of urban life and organisation before the tenth century. Oviedo and Pamplona were their nearest approaches to such settlements and it is unlikely that the former was much more than a fortified palace complex. As a result the period of urban development that began under the Leonese kings owed much to the town life of Islamic Spain in terms of borrowings of institutions and of terminology. These were most probably mediated through the Mozarabs.

The Kingdom of Pamplona and the County of Aragon

THE history of the smallest of the Christian states of the Umayyad period, the kingdom of Pamplona, is both obscure and highly controversial. It has left us no contemporary chronicles and very few charters but for the tenth century at least is rich in genealogies. How Basque the realm of Pamplona, which formed the nucleus of the later kingdom of Navarre, a term first appearing in 1087, was is hard to determine, because what slender evidence there is relates almost exclusively to a limited geographical region, that of Alava and the Rioja Alta. Virtually nothing is known of the mountainous areas to the north of Pamplona beyond the fact that there were officials bearing the title *Comes Vizcayae* (Count of Biscay), and an administrative region with the archaic name of Gallia Comata in those parts subject to the authority of the kings.[35] The valley of Aragon to the east of Pamplona, which emerges from obscurity for the first time in the ninth century, was, like the northern regions, Basque in character as can be shown from the evidence of place and personal names in the charters. The racial and cultural composition of Alava in the upper Ebro, long open to penetration from the south during the Roman and Visigothic periods, is much harder to determine. However, Pamplona apart, the principal towns of the whole region remained in Arab or *muwallad* hands until the eleventh century.

Only three events can be chronicled with any degree of confidence in respect of this area in the eighth century. About 740 the inhabitants of Pamplona expelled their Arab governor and his garrison and in 778 Charlemagne occupied the city during his march on Zaragoza, whether taking it from its own citizens or from renewed Muslim rule not being known.[36] During his subsequent retreat he had the walls, once the subject of the praises of a fifth-century treatise *De Laude Pampilone* (sic), or 'In praise of Pamplona', demolished.[37] Possibly in consequence the city had an Umayyad governor again by 799. This was Mutarrīf ibn Mūsa of the Banu Kasī, and in that year it is recorded that he and his troops were massacred by the citizens. However, by 803 The Banu Kasī, in revolt at Tudela against their Umayyad overlords, had allied themselves with the Pamplonans, then probably under the authority of a certain Velasco.[38] Some of them may have taken refuge in the city after the suppression of the rebellion. Perhaps as a consequence of the Umayyad military activity in the upper Ebro valley, Pamplona submitted to the Franks in 806, only to be in revolt by 813 when an army had to be sent against it under King Louis of Aquitaine.[39] Whether Pamplona and its region was placed under the administrative authority of a Basque called Sancho Lopiz, the *dux* of Frankish Vasconia (Gascony), or was formed into a separate unit in its own right is unknown. However, a Frankish marcher county was established in the valley of the river Aragon, where another Basque, Asnar Galindez, was appointed the first count.[40]

The newly created march, that paralleled the one created at the same period in Catalonia at the eastern end of the Pyrenees, proved to be short-lived. By 824 Pamplona was again in rebellion, and an expedition under the Frankish counts Eblo and Asnar, the latter conceivably the Count of Aragon, having taken the city, was destroyed in the pass of Roncesvalles. This second battle of Roncesvalles is perhaps of greater importance than that of 778, for it seems to have put an end to Frankish intervention across the western Pyrenees, and led to the establishment of an independent kingdom in Pamplona, whose first ruler was probably Enneco Aritza. Of the Frankish counts taken in the battle, Asnar, as a fellow Basque, was released but Eblo was sent as a present to the Umayyad amir, an indication perhaps that the new kingdom saw the Franks as a greater threat than Cordoba.

The small county of Aragon seems soon to have come under the suzerainty of Pamplona, to which it was linked geographically. This resulted from a family drama recorded in one of the tenth-century genealogies preserved in the Roda codex.[41] The elder son of Count Asnar, called Centolle, having made fun of his brother-in-law, was murdered by him. This man, known as García 'the Bad', with the assistance of Enneco Aritza of Pamplona and some unidentified

Mauros, that is to say Arabs or Berbers, then evicted Asnar from his county. This may be related to the latter's involvement in the disastrous campaign of 824. García, divorcing Asnar's daughter Matrona, married an unnamed daughter of Enneco Aritza, whose suzerainty he accepted, while the unfortunate Asnar was compensated with appointment to the newly created office of Count of Cerdanya and Urgell in Catalonia by the emperor Louis 'the Pious'.

If this story is to be believed, Asnar was succeeded in his offices by his second son Galindo, who was, however, dispossessed by the emperor in 834, probably for having supported the usurpation of Louis's sons in the previous year. The exiled Galindo returned to Aragon where he succeeded in expelling García 'the Bad', but having then married Enneco Aritza's granddaughter Onneca he continued the association of the county with the kingdom of Pamplona. Thenceforth Aragon, under the descendants of Galindo, remained, if in practice largely independent, a division of that realm, until elevated into a kingdom in its own right for Ramiro I (1035–1063), the youngest son of Sancho 'the Great' of Navarre.

As for the kingdom of Pamplona, after this reasonably well-documented period of the first quarter of the ninth century, an almost impenetrable darkness descends upon its history until the appearance of a new dynasty on its throne in 905. Little is known of the doings of Enneco Aritza and his descendants beyond their almost consistent alliance with the Banu Kasī, of which family the leading figure, Mūsa ibn Mūsa, married another granddaughter of the Pamplonan ruler, called Assona.[42] These ties were not always beneficial for the small kingdom. In 843 King Enneco was defeated together with his Banu Kasī allies, by the Amir 'Abd al-Raḥmān II: his brother Fortun was killed and Pamplona sacked.[43] Later his grandson, also called Fortun, was captured by the Umayyads and spent some two decades as a hostage in Cordoba.[44] Fortun's daughter Onneca subsequently married the Amir 'Abd-Allah. It is likely that the unusual closeness of the links between the Aritza dynasty in Pamplona with the Muslim powers in the Ebro valley and Cordoba was prompted by fear firstly of the Franks, and then of the Asturians who were seeking throughout the century to extend their control eastwards into Alava.

It may have been the lengthy captivity of Fortun that opened the way for a new dynasty, that of the Jimeno family, to challenge the rights of the heirs of Enneco to the throne. The origins of this line are much disputed and the view that the original Jimeno was a count in

Frankish *Vasconia*, forced to take refuge in Pamplona after unsuccessful rebellion in 815, is now strongly challenged.[45] At any rate a King García Jiménez is recorded as having ruled at some point in the later ninth century by the genealogies, but as the use of patronymics was only introduced in the tenth century, the ninth-century charters cannot reveal whether their references to a King García are to this man or to the son of Enneco Aritza. If García Jiménez did rule during the captivity of Fortun, the latter does seem to have eventually gained his throne, possibly around 882, but in 905 the Jimenos obtained power definitively in the person of King Sancho Garcés I (905–925). Later medieval chronicles, admittedly of uncertain worth, refer to the voluntary abdication of Fortun to the monastery of Leyre after the premature deaths of all of his heirs.

Leyre is the only monastery whose foundation can be ascribed to the Aritza dynasty with any degree of certainty. If a probably ninth-century account of the translation of the relics of the martyr saints Nunila and Alodia be believed, it became their royal pantheon.[46] Enneco Aritza, Fortun Garcés and probably other members of their line were buried there. The subsequent Jimeno dynasty naturally enough looked elsewhere, and devoted itself instead to the house of San Juan de la Peña. As the account of his time spent in the kingdom in the letter to Bishop Wiliesind and in his *Life* show, Eulogius's visit indicates the existence of other monasteries in the region of Pamplona in the mid ninth century and also the relative wealth of literary texts to be found in some of them.

The only significant expansion of the kingdom during this period occurred in the early part of the tenth century. In 918 Sancho Garcés I extended his frontiers southwards into the vicinity of Nájera and Tudela, only to be driven back by an Umayyad army under 'Abd al-Raḥmān III in 920. Sancho and his ally Ordoño II of Leon were then defeated in battle at Valdejunquera. Typical of the frontier conflicts of this age, this had little effect, and in 921 Sancho Garcés took Viguera and Ordoño II captured Nájera in 923. They were deprived of their new conquests by the amir in the following year, and he went on to sack Pamplona. However, in 925 Sancho Garcés, without Leonese aid, regained all of the lost territory, including Nájera, and made himself master of the Rioja Alta. This adjustment of the frontier seems to have been accepted by the Umayyads, and no further campaigning ensued to attempt to dislodge the Pamplonan rulers from their new acquisition. During the regency of Queen Toda, that followed the death of her husband Sancho Garcés I, close ties seem to have been forged again between Pamplona and Cordoba, with the queen putting her realm under the protection of the caliph.

No further expansion of the still diminutive realm down the Ebro valley was attempted until the middle of the eleventh century. In 1045 Calahorra was taken and the Rioja Baja added to the kingdom. Similarly in Aragon, Huesca was not captured until 1096. On their western frontiers the kings of Pamplona had been subjected to the pressure of Leonese expansion. The foundation of Burgos in 884 brought the centre of the county of Castille close to areas of interest to the Pamplonans and, as has been seen, the Leonese kings were campaigning in Alava in the early tenth century. These developments may explain the shift after 925 of the centre of the kingdom from Pamplona to Nájera, and the kings thenceforth styled themselves by reference to both places. However, the danger of Leonese hegemony declined with the death of Ramiro II in 955, and the counts of Castille, who developed a virtually proprietary interest in the monastery of San Millan de la Cogolla near Nájera, were increasingly drawn into the Navarrese orbit and became linked with its royal dynasty when Sancho Garcés II married Urraca, the much-wedded daughter of Fernan Gonzalez. It was their great grandson Fernando I, the first King of Castille, who was to subjugate Leon (see Table II).

The Frankish March in Catalonia

BECAUSE of the geography of the peninsula, the old Romano-Visigothic provinces of Tarraconensis, comprising the Ebro valley and the Catalan seaboard, and of Narbonnensis, to the north of the Pyrenees, were less susceptible to direct control or military attack from the Cordoban Amirate than the Asturias, Galicia and Leon. These north-eastern regions had frequently resisted the authority of the Visigothic kings, and in so doing had on occasion looked northward to their Frankish neighbours for assistance. Such links were made concrete by the annexation of some of this territory by the Carolingian monarchy in the early ninth century. The period that precedes that, from 711 to the end of the eighth century is, however, peculiarly dark. It is certain that an independent kingdom existed briefly in the two provinces after the defeat of Roderic. A King Achila struck coins at Narbonne, Gerona and Tarragona.[47] He also features in ninth- and tenth-century regnal lists of the Visigothic kings, where he is given a successor called Ardo, of whom no coins are known.[48]

This realm survived for a short period as the new conquerors were busy imposing their rule on the rest of the peninsula, but in 720 an Arab expedition reached and captured Narbonne, probably ending the life of this kingdom. The three-year reign of Achila II, who was in all likelihood initially in rebellion against Roderic, of whom no coins are known from this region, would thus fall into the years 710 to 713, and the seven years of Ardo into the period 713 to 720. Although garrisons were established in the principal towns, no Arab or Berber settlement is recorded as having been made north of the Pyrenees, whereas the Ebro valley was so heavily colonised that no significant inroads could be made upon it by the Christian powers before the eleventh century.

Military expeditions under successive governors of Al-Andalus did expand Arab conquests along the Mediterranean coast of southern France, reaching as far as Avignon in 730, but the main thrust of such undertakings was into Aquitaine via Pamplona. The effect of these, from the vantage of hindsight, was to be seriously counter-productive, for so threatening did the successive Arab incursions into Aquitaine become that eventually its duke, Eudes, who like his predecessors had long resisted the claims of Frankish royal authority, had to call on Charles 'Martel', the Carolingian Mayor of the Palace, for aid, resulting in the defeat and death of the Arab governor 'Abd al-Raḥmān at the battle of Poitiers in 732. Although this in itself did not put an end to the incursions, it did bring revived Frankish royal authority firmly into Aquitaine and Provence. This was not achieved instantly, for Charles's son Pepin III and grandson Charlemagne had to face continued military opposition from the Aquitainian dukes and eventually had to suppress their line, but the process was begun by the Poitiers campaign.[49] Once involved, the Frankish rulers were also able to fulfil one of the ambitions of their sixth-century Merovingian predecessors by bringing all of southern France under their control. The Arabs were dislodged from recent gains in Provence by Charles 'Martel' in the late 730s, and Pepin, the first Carolingian king, went on to take Narbonne in 759, and thus finally added all the old Visigothic Septimania to the Frankish crown.

The revitalised Frankish monarchy soon became involved in the affairs of the peninsula itself, and, as in the Visigothic past, appeals for aid could be directed to it against the authority of the central power in Spain, now the Umayyad Amirate. In 778 Charlemagne, fresh from the conquest of Italy and successful campaigns against the Saxons, was invited to come to the assistance of the governor of Zaragoza, then planning revolt against his overlord in Cordoba. This proved a disaster as the city of Zaragoza was held against the Frankish king and in retreat the rearguard of his army was annihilated by the Basques in the pass of Roncesvalles.

No further Frankish involvement occurred until the beginning of the next century, but in the meantime Charlemagne increased his hold on Aquitaine, having his son Louis crowned as its king in 781. It was from this new kingdom of Aquitaine, under the direction of Louis with the supervision of his father, that Frankish penetration across the eastern end of the Pyrenees was successfully carried out. In 801 a Frankish army under Louis seized Barcelona. Its governor Zatun had previously offered to accept Frankish suzerainty in 797 as part of his own political machinations, but the expedition of 801, which is glorified in epic verse by the Aquitainian poet Ermoldus Nigellus, made this a reality, and from then on the city and the territory between it and the Pyrenees remained in Christian hands.[50] Attempts to expand this new march of the Carolingian Empire yet further proved fruitless; in 808 Tarragona was captured but then had to be abandoned and in 809 Louis failed in a bid to take Tortosa, and the frontier created in 801 remained little changed until the eleventh century.[51]

A system of administration was established by the new rulers in the aftermath of their conquest, dividing up the region into counties ruled by royal officials responsible for their defence, the conduct of justice, and accounting to the fisc of royal revenues. All deserted lands were held to be royal property and former Arab holdings were probably also appropriated. Because of the lack of information on earlier centuries, it is impossible to know if the counties that came into existence in the Frankish march in the first quarter of the ninth century, that is to say Barcelona, Ausona (Vich), Gerona, Cerdanya, Pallars and Ribagorça, had any continuity with the administrative divisions of the previous Visigothic realm, but it is clear enough from many explicit citations in the multitude of surviving charters that the law that was employed in the region was that of the *Forum Iudicum*, the Visigothic lawbook.[52]

The counts themselves were, for much of the ninth century, drawn from the ranks of the Frankish aristocracy, and many of them also held similar offices in other parts of the Carolingian Empire. Their own political interests generally lay closer to the royal court and few of them seem to have had significant landholdings in the new frontier territories. Not surprisingly they were often absent and their routine administrative duties could be fulfilled by their deputies the Viscounts, though any major military operation usually required the personal involvement of the counts themselves. Quite frequently one individual would be entrusted with responsibility for a plurality of counties in the frontier regions and he might in addition be invested with the title *Marchio* (Marquess or March Warden). At the eastern end of the Pyrenees there were two such marches, divided by the mountains: to the north that of *Gothia*, the old Visigothic Septimania, and to the south that of *Hispania*, the newly conquered territories. The Count of Toulouse, overseeing the central Pyrenees, usually also held the title *Marchio*, while further west lay the kingdom of Aquitaine with its own frontier counties. The administrative system was, however, extremely fluid. The counties that might be assigned to an individual *marchio* frequently varied and never fitted into a constant pattern. It was apparently often royal policy to build up the power of rival *marchios* in order to prevent the absolute dominance of any one of them on the frontier. When such a consideration was ignored it could lead to serious consequences, for most of the leading Frankish officials entrusted with responsibilities on the Pyrenean marches in the ninth century turned to rebellion and had to be violently dispossessed.[53]

One family in particular had a dramatic career in the region during this period. This was the dynasty of St William of Toulouse, a cousin of Charlemagne who took a prominent part in the campaign of 801. He is particularly notable as a monastic patron, founding Gellone in 804, whither he retired. His immediate descendants are better known or notorious for their secular political involvements, although one of his great grandsons was later to be the founder of the great reforming monastery of Cluny. William was Count of Toulouse from *c.* 790 to 804, and one of his sons called Gaucelm was entrusted with command of the Gothic march in 812. Another son, Bernard of Septimania, came into prominence in 827, when, as Count of Barcelona, he successfully resisted the revolt of a deposed former count called Aizo, who had obtained assistance from the amir Al-Ḥakem I of Cordoba. Bernard was subsequently summoned to the Carolingian court in 829 as royal chamberlain, and his rise to influence there was a major contributory factor in the rebellion of the Emperor Louis' elder sons against their father, in the course of which Bernard had to flee for refuge to the march and his brother Gaucelm was executed. With the restoration of Louis' authority in 834, Bernard was reinstated as Count of Barcelona and of most of the other counties of the Hispanic march. These he continued to hold, together with the title of *marchio*, until, suspected of treason, he was seized and executed by the West Frankish king Charles 'the Bald' in 844.

Not surprisingly Bernard's elder son William threw in his lot with Charles's enemy Pippin II, King of Aquitaine, who made him Count of Bordeaux. But in 848, after the final overthrow of Pippin, when Sunifred the next Count of Barcelona died, William took advantage of the ensuing disorder to descend on the march and take the city of Barcelona. He was defeated by royal forces the following year and after being captured in Barcelona was executed. William's younger brother Bernard 'Plantevelue', despite the fate of his relatives, subsequently rose to favour in the West Frankish court late in the reign of Charles 'the Bald', and was entrusted with the counties of Toulouse in 872 and Narbonne in 874. He took a leading part in the aristocratic revolt against the king in 877, and subsequently continued to conspire against the latter's heirs in the interest of the East Frankish ruler Charles 'the Fat' until killed in battle in 886.

Three generations of this family were thus associated with the Pyrenean marches and, with the exception of the first William, all of them proved disloyal to their royal overlords. In this they were not unusual. Other great Frankish office-holders whose power had been deliberately built up by the Carolingian rulers proved equally untrustworthy. Thus the *marchio* Humfrid had to be expelled for rebellion in 864 or 865, as was Bernard 'of Gothia' in 878. In remarkable contrast to this was the career of an indigenous family which, like that of William of Toulouse, held office on the march during successive generations but proved consistently loyal to the Carolingian dynasty. The precise origins and ancestry of this family are disputed, but it is accepted that it was of local extraction from either *Gothia* or *Hispania*. Its probable first major representative was Sunifred, Count of Urgell and Cerdanya in the Pyrenees, who was appointed Count of Barcelona and *Marchio* on the execution of Bernard 'of Septimania'. On his death in 848, his offices were redistributed, but in 870 his son Wifred was given the county of Urgell. In 878 Wifred and and his brother Miro, Count of Conflent, attacked the supporters of the rebel Bernard 'of Gothia' and were rewarded by the grant of his counties: Wifred acquiring Barcelona,

Gerona and Ausona, together with the title of *Marchio*, while Miro and another brother called Radulf were entrusted with Rossello and Besalú under his authority.[54]

From 878 onwards, until the merging of this family with the royal dynasty of Aragon in 1137, Wifred's heirs continued to rule all of the Frankish counties south of the Pyrenees, with the exception of the two central Pyrenean ones of Pallars and Ribagorça, without interruption. This has led to the rise of Wifred 'the Hairy' in the 870s being regarded as marking the birth of an independent Catalonia. However, it is important to note that Wifred and his heirs were content to retain their comital title, which was of Frankish creation, and continued, as did the other landowners in the march, to date their documents by the regnal years of the Frankish kings. Although in practice the ties between the county of Barcelona and the increasingly debilitated French monarchy declined after the middle of the ninth century, they were never formally broken and certainly until the extinction of the Carolingian dynasty in the late tenth century most of the leading lay and clerical magnates thought it worthwhile to have their charters confirmed by their nominal royal overlords.[55] The long survival of political loyalty to the Frankish monarchy on the Spanish march is in striking contrast to the behaviour of other parts of the former Carolingian Empire, as for example in Italy, Burgundy and Provence, where independent royal dynasties had come to power by the end of the ninth century. Even in the western Pyrenees the tiny kingdom of Pamplona had been created out of a Frankish march, and it was not for lack of precedent that the family of Wifred did not transform itself into a royal line. Nor had this anything to do with fear of retaliation or a dependence on Carolingian military aid, for, from early in the reign of Charles 'the Bald' on, it seems clear that the march was left to find its own protection and could not, as in 827, look for royal assistance.

The reasons for this remarkable survival of loyalty to the French crown are not easy to establish. It was more than a matter of sentiment on the part of the comital family, for the charters alone indicate that their attitude was common to all major sectors of society on the march. The notion of the Franks as the protectors of the region, to whom its inhabitants could turn when in conflict with other powers in the peninsula was an old one with its roots in the Visigothic period. Cultural and economic ties with Aquitaine and Provence were also long-standing, if liable to fluctuation. But little of this had much practical significance in the tenth and eleventh centuries. The charters do suggest from their survival in surprising quantity despite the vicissitudes of centuries, that written title to land was held to be of the greatest importance and from the late eighth century onwards this was guaranteed by numerous acts of royal confirmation. The Frankish kings did have a role to play, however impotent they were in their ability to enforce their authority, in providing the grounding in which land tenure in the march was rooted. Although Catalonia was in practice independent from the time of Wifred 'the Hairy' onwards in terms of the power and authority of its rulers, the comital dynasty, too much stress on this can obscure and conceal the interesting relationship that did exist between the inhabitants of the Hispanic march and the French crown, and can also give an anachronistic impression of the character of Catalonia in these centuries.

The geographical term was not employed at this period, although it is being used here for convenience, nor were the early limits of the Frankish county of Barcelona equivalent to the later boundaries of the medieval state. After the initial Frankish conquest of 801, no further territorial expansion was achieved before the eleventh century; the old ecclesiastical centre of the region, Tarragona, the seat of a Visigothic metropolitanate, did not revert permanently to Christian control until 1089, and most of the southern parts of modern Catalonia remained in Islamic hands until the thirteenth century. At the same time, as in the Visigothic period, there were strong links between the Christian lands south of the Pyrenees with the Frankish counties north of the mountains in the former Septimania. In due course both of these areas were to be united under the rule of the kings of Aragon, and 'French' Catalonia was only lost to the Spanish monarchy in the seventeenth century. In terms of political frontiers Catalonia is hard to define, precisely because of the many fluctuations that occurred in them over the centuries, but at the same time the concept is expressive of the cultural and economic cohesion of the coastal regions to the north and south of the eastern end of the Pyrenees irrespective of artificial administrative and political divisions.

The narrative history of tenth-century Catalonia is virtually non-existent. The handful of brief chronicles that constitute the only historiography in the region before the twelfth century generally start their accounts with the sack of Barcelona by Al-Manṣūr in 985.[56] Thus all too little is known of the pattern of events between the death of Wifred I in 897 or 898, only recorded in the *Muktabis* of Ibn Hayyān, and the rule of his descendant Count Ramon Borrel I (992–1017). However, the region compensates in the survival of its charters: literally thousands of originals, let alone the wealth of copies in later diocesan and monastic cartularies, are to be found in the Catalan archives, many of them still unedited. Whereas, such an important monastery as Albelda in the Rioja has only left us twenty-nine charters of pre-eleventh-century date, some of the Catalan monastic houses such as San Cugat de Valles, or San Benet de Bages, can offer several hundred. The collections in such cases are complex in their ramifications, as in many instances earlier documents have been preserved relating to property that only subsequently came into the possession of the monastery. Also the charter holdings of small monastic houses that later became dependancies of greater ones were often merged with the general collections of the mother house.

From these rich and varied materials much information can be gleaned. It is possible to see how, in the period of expanding settlement in the later ninth and tenth centuries, a mass of churches and tiny monasteries were founded by small landowners, who could sometimes only endow them with a handful of fields and vineyards. After a time this explosive growth slowed and the small foundations, some of which can have been barely economically self-supporting, were granted by their owners, for they generally remained propriet-ary churches and monasteries, to larger and more flourishing institu-tions. Some of these were in turn put under the authority of others, cathedral churches or a handful of greater monasteries. The effect was a gradual reduction in the numbers of independent and privately owned churches and monasteries and a greater regulating of church organisation in the course of the later tenth and eleventh centuries.

It is possible to see, if only from the rather formal viewpoint of changes in ownership and authority, how much secular interest there was in the founding of these churches and small monasteries in the earlier period. There were private institutions, often with slaves attached to them who could be given away at will. In some cases the founders and their heirs reserved certain rights, such as the selection of abbots. This could lead to abuses, which by the end of the tenth century, with the growth of reforming idealism throughout the church in most of western Europe, became less tolerable. In 1005 the monks of San Benet de Bages sent a memorial to the papacy in a successful bid to free the election of their abbots from control by their founder's descendants. This family had recently foisted one of their own number on to the monastery as abbot, who had proved less than satisfactory in that he had sold some of its books and had then made off with a silver chalice and paten. Pope Benedict VIII took the house under direct papal patronage.[57]

Documents like this memorial and a range of other judicial and quasi-legal texts form a small but significant proportion of the surviving corpus of charters, most of which comprise deeds of sale or of gift. Fortunately local practice involved the inclusion of substantial accounts of proceedings into these records of trials and hearings, in some cases reporting the statements of participants in direct speech. Generally disputes were resolved by recourse to groups of witnesses, the side having 'more or better' of them being in theory the winner, but in practice, as far as the documents reveal, only the successful party in the dispute seems to have produced any witnesses at all. This may have been thanks to the procedure whereby they were first required to swear on the altar, on relics and on the four Gospels before giving their testimony. Trials appear to have been held in churches and were presided over by the count assisted by a panel of about half a dozen judges and in the presence of a similar number of 'good men'. In many instances the parties to a dispute were represented by advocates of their own choosing called *mandatarii*. In some cases, and particularly in criminal trials, the ordeal was employed. In this, and in the resolution of civil disputes, the procedures laid down in the Visigothic law were followed, and in some of the documents the specific texts of the *Forum Iudicum* relevant to the issue are cited.

In general, the importance placed upon written records in these cases is striking, and concern for documentation distinguishes the legal procedures of this region not only from those of other parts of Christian Spain but also from the rest of the Carolingian Empire other than northern Italy. A case that illustrates both this attention to documents and written title to land, and also the use of witnesses for the resolution of disputes, comes from the archives of the monastery of Cuxa (now lost). In 878, when the monastery of St Andrew at Eixalada was destroyed by flood, one of its former patrons, realising that his deed of gift had thus been lost, attempted to repossess some land he had previously granted to the house. Witnesses who could testify that to their knowledge the disputed estate had been in the hands of the monks prior to the flood secured judgement in favour of the monastery. This case ended with the defendant signing an 'evacuation', a formal renunciation of the false claim by its author, which bound him and his heirs not to resurrect it at any future point.[58]

The administrative division of Carolingian Catalonia into a series of counties, some of very small size, was maintained in the tenth century, though some new units were also created. The counties were ruled in a number of combinations by various branches of the family of Wifred I, the senior line of which retained Barcelona and the title of *Marchio*, which seems to have implied a supervisory power over other counties not ruled directly. The count-marquesses of Barcelona enjoyed not only a pre-eminence of prestige but also some measure of control over the affairs of the other counts, and on occasion conducted trials and hearings in their territories, as well as signing or confirming charters from areas outside their immediate jurisdiction.

The comital dynasty had strong ties to the Church, and on occasion members of the family held ecclesiastical office, as for example did Miro Bonfil (d. 4), who was simultaneously Count of Besalú and Bishop of Gerona. His nephew Oliba inherited the tiny county of Bergueda in 990, which he surrendered to his brothers in 1003 to enter the monastery of Ripoll, founded by his ancestor Wifred I in 888. In 1005 he was elected its abbot, and also that of the monastery of Cuxa, across the Pyrenees, and in 1018 he was in addition consecrated Bishop of Vich.

Such close involvement with the secular rulers of the region brought enormous benefit to the Church in Catalonia, contrary to the tenor of the arguments of the eleventh-century ecclesiastical reformers. The comital house, from the time of Wifred I onwards, was the foremost patron of monasticism in the area. As well as for actual foundations of such important monasteries as Ripoll, San Juan de las Abadesses and San Pedro de Roda, the counts were responsible for an almost unbroken series of donations to most of the major houses. They were also active patrons and defenders of learning and reform. The monk Gerbert of Aurillac, later Pope Sylvester II (999–1003), came to Catalonia to study under Bishops Atto of Vich and Miro Bonfil of Gerona. Under Oliba, Ripoll and Cuxa became major centres of learning, all the more remarkable when contrasted with other such institutions in most parts of Christian Spain and western Europe. Manuscripts, especially of mathematical and scientific interest, were available there, probably obtained from Cordoba, and a number of poems have survived that were composed by monks under Oliba's rule as well as some by himself. At the same time the library at Ripoll, in which small beginnings had been made in earlier decades, underwent a substantial expansion, and its collection continued to grow in subsequent centuries.[59] Much of it was still in existence when the monastery was sacked by the local populace in 1835 when the Spanish religious houses were secularised.

Although Cordoba was probably the source of much of the learning that flourished in Catalonia in the late tenth and early eleventh centuries, and this is further testimony of the interdependence of the different regions of the peninsula in many varying ways, some borrowings were also made from France. The monasteries of the region that began their lives or were restored in the eighth and ninth centuries did so under the guidance of the *Rule of St Benedict*, which was promoted as the norm for monastic observance by the Carolingian rulers.[60] This distinguished Catalonia from the rest of the peninsula where older traditions survived unchallenged. Similarly the old Visigothic liturgy was eclipsed in the region by the introduction of new service books that followed the rites of Rome, though these were adapted to suit local needs and the cults of indigenous saints.

This tide did not just run in one direction. Distinctive contributions were made to the Carolingian Church and to the government of the state by a number of individuals who came from the former Visigothic lands on both sides of the Pyrenees. Amongst the most distinguished of these were the poet Theodulf, Bishop of Orleans (d. 821), the chronicler Prudentius, Bishop of Troyes (d. 867) and Benedict of Aniane (d. 821), the great monastic reformer and adviser of the Emperor Louis 'the Pious', whose original name had been Wittiza. In addition, some of the products of the learning of Visigothic Spain, notably many of the writings of Isidore of Seville and the great *Hispana* canonical collection, were influential in the ninth-century intellectual revival of the Frankish Church.

Although, as has been mentioned, the physical limits of the part of Catalonia under Christian rule hardly expanded after 801, the surviving documents show that an intensive repopulation of that area took place in the course of the next century and a half. The process began in the areas north of the Pyrenees during the reign of Charlemagne and was extended to the south and then further westward in the course of the ninth and tenth centuries. A significant though unquantifiable proportion of those who were settled on the formerly abandoned lands were immigrants from Umayyad-

controlled Spain, and are referred to in the sources, principally
Carolingian royal charters, as *Hispani*. Where they originated is not
certain, though it might as easily have been the Ebro valley as
Cordoba. Some of the new monasteries, notably Cuxa, also show
clear evidence of Mozarabic architectural and artistic influence.

These new settlers are first recorded in the time of Charlemagne,
and they received special treatment from the Carolingian regime,
anxious to maintain by repopulation its initially precarious hold on
the region, which as a result of decades of conflict was seriously
under-occupied. It is clear from the charters that significant amounts
of land in the area, both to the north and the south of the
Mediterranean end of the Pyrenees, were deserted and had thereby
become the property of the royal fisc. From these, estates were
granted to the new settlers, who also received privileges denied to the
indigenous population. They were freed from the supervision of the
counts and were taken directly under royal protection. They received
their estates free of any tax obligations and were permitted to sell or
otherwise exchange them amongst themselves.

The initial recipients of these benefits were clearly men of some
substance, as the setting up of the estate of one *Hispanus* called John,
which is unusually well recorded in surviving documents, indicates,
for he further subdivided his newly-acquired lands amongst his own
followers, whe were also subject to his jurisdiction for all but the most
serious of offences.[61] Names such as Christianus and Tamunnus
amongst John's men are indicative of a Mozarab or possibly even
Christianised Arab origin. The case of this John, who received his
property in the county of Narbonne after signal service fighting for
the Frankish king on the Spanish march, also suggests that some of
the grants were intended as rewards for military activity. In other
instances, from the records of later disputes over ownership, it looks
as if groups of immigrants or displaced persons just occupied deserted
lands, and by bringing them into cultivation they were able to acquire
a title, which the Frankish crown was prepared to recognise and on
occasion confirm by charter.

It is not certain how long the process of the immigration of the
Hispani continued, but in the last years of the reign of the West
Frankish king Charles 'the Bald' (840–878), control over deserted
lands and the property of the royal fisc was transferred absolutely to
the local counts.[62] This coincides with the effective transformation of
the status of the latter from being appointed royal officials to being a

hereditary nobility, as can be seen in the case of Catalonia in the careers of Wifred I and his descendants. Thenceforth the process of the distribution of vacant lands and of their resettlement became the prerogative of the counts, and the *Hispani* cease to feature in the records as a separate class of landowner. New settlers from Muslim-controlled Spain doubtless continued to arrive in the march, but they no longer constituted a group requiring special attention or privileges. It is probable that many of the inhabitants of the settlements created by Wifred I and his heirs came from within the Catalan counties, and were attracted to the expanding frontier by land-hunger or the special concessions granted by the counts.

From the later tenth century on, paralleled by the appearance of the *fueros* in Leon and Castille, charters were issued by the counts of Barcelona and other lesser landowners such as the bishops, which gave exceptional rights to their recipients, the inhabitants of the newly-created frontier towns and smaller fortified settlements and their related rural territories. The earliest of those now extant is the charter issued by Count Borrel II (954–992) to the inhabitants of Cardona, though references in deeds of confirmation make it seem likely that even earlier examples once existed.[63] Cardona, founded by Wifred I, is probably a case in point as Borrel II makes an unspecific reference to a document issued by his ancestor. In the extant text of 986 the count-marquess guarantees the inhabitants security of tenure for their properties and freedom from some taxes and tolls. They were required to continue payment of a tithe to the Church of St Vincent in Cardona and to maintain the walls and towers of the settlement for defence against both 'pagans and Christians'. The Viscount Ermemir and his heirs were established by the charter to act as patrons to the citizens and with their 'ministers' to provide local government. No one else was to be allowed to try to make themselves senior amongst them. The inhabitants were required to take part in comital 'hostings', that is turn out to fight offensively or defensively at the ruler's command, and anyone failing to assist in the defence of the town was to be excommunicated and deprived of his goods by his fellows.

Although similar in principle to the near contemporary *fueros* of Leon, the Cardona charter shows that important differences existed between the Leonese kingdom and the county of Barcelona in such matters as the measure of self-government allowed to the citizens. In the Leonese case authority was principally vested in a council, and important functionaries such as the market officials were elected by the community, whereas in Cardona all governmental power lay with the Viscount, appointed by the Count of Barcelona whose family was henceforth to enjoy hereditary tenure. In the Catalan case lordship was being created, whilst in Leon the emphasis was on autonomy, at least for the upper ranks of the citizenry in a society that was highly stratified. On the other hand, in Cardona the inhabitants were envisaged as being equal under the lord, and were expressly required to pull down any of their number who sought to claim superior status to his fellows. Varied and complex as was the history of these societies in the course of the centuries to follow, it is clear that the roots of the differences in social structure and political life between the kingdoms of Aragon and Castille in the later Middle Ages can be traced to this earliest period of their existence.

Catalonia, once subjected to Frankish influence and with its distinctive cultural, legal and administrative traditions, was patently distinguishable from the rest of the peninsula and had a long future of political independence ahead of it. However, this should not obscure the fact that it was one amongst several parts of a greater whole. The richness of Spain in the diversity of its regional cultures and their histories is one of its greatest glories, though perhaps for those who seek to rule all of it, one of the greatest difficulties that they have to face. Problems that troubled the Romans, the Visigoths and the Umayyads still survive to confront their successors.

At the end of the first millennium AD, what may have looked like a stable pattern of political relationships had been created in the peninsula. The Caliphate of Cordoba, a formidable Mediterranean power that ruled not only most of Spain but also, from Fez, parts of North Africa, had risen in prestige, military strength and physical magnificence throughout the course of the tenth century. The Christian states to the north, under their own rulers, lived in its shadow. Toda, Queen-Regent of Pamplona-Navarre, had put her state under the protection of 'Abd al-Raḥmān III, and one of her successors, Sancho Garcés II sent a daughter to marry the great Al-Manṣūr. 'Abd al-Raḥmān III, himself the grandson of a Pamplonan princess, received suppliant kings from Leon, and even distant Catalonia had been shown its vulnerability by the sacking of Barcelona in 985. Despite the vicissitudes of the two previous centuries, the Umayyads had come as near as their Roman and

Visigothic predecessors to achieving the unification of the peninsula under a single dominant authority. They were to be the last so to do for over five hundred years.

Yet within the first forty years of the eleventh century the whole political complexion of Spain had radically altered. The Umayyad dynasty destroyed itself in civil wars between rival candidates, a process in which the dependants of Cordoba, Christian and Muslim alike, and its own military servants, the Berbers and the slave armies, took an active part, and the caliphate was extinguished. The weakening of the role of the Umayyad caliph during the minority of Hishām II and the achievement of dictatorial power by Al-Manṣūr played an important part in subverting the established basis of authority in Al-Andalus, but the career of the great vizier, whose palace of Az-Zahira rivalled that of ʿAbd al-Raḥmān III at Az-Zahara, shows that the effective imposition of a single will could still maintain the rule of Cordoba. His elder son ʿAbd al-Mālik, to whom in 1007 the puppet caliph gave the title of Al-Muẓaffar, 'the Victor', and who had served as his father's deputy in Fez, was able to keep the system created by Al-Manṣūr in being for a few years more, but his death in 1008, possibly poisoned by his half brother 'Sanchuelo', son of the Pamplonan princess, finally exposed the fragility of the central authority, almost as effectively as had the defeat of Roderic on the Guadelete in 711. Over twenty years of strife ensued that left Cordoba irreparably damaged physically, and its caliphate an irrelevancy. The history of Spain has demonstrated consistently that once the hand in the centre is weakened its hold over the diverse and restive peripheral parts of the peninsula is lost.[64]

In the north the career of Sancho 'the Great' of Pamplona (1000–1035), who achieved a brief pre-eminence over neighbours weakened by the campaigns of Al-Manṣūr and Al-Muẓaffar, led, paradoxically, not to the permanent aggrandisement of his tiny kingdom, but to the creation, through the division of his territories amongst his sons in 1035, of the new kingdoms of Aragon and Castille, the second of which speedily absorbed the older Asturian-Leonese monarchy (see Table II). With the demise of the latter in 1037 and the destruction of the Umayyad Caliphate the two poles of the political order of the peninsula during the previous three centuries disappeared.

Within a hundred years Spain was to be exposed to more new forces and influences than perhaps in the whole of its history since the coming of the Romans. From the north came ideas, individuals and institutions that further undermined the vestiges of the old order. The Visigothic-Mozarabic liturgy was suppressed in the interests of a Rome-inspired uniformity of Christian practice, Cluniac monasticism and the Rule of St Benedict obtained firm holds, especially in the kingdom of Castille, whose monarchs Fernando I and Alfonso VI made themselves the most munificent patrons of the mother house of Cluny. French knights and others too were drawn into the peninsula by the influence of new ideas of crusade, and by the increasingly attractive prospects of the acquisition of wealth by the sword. In art and in the Church foreigners found patronage and opportunities for advancement in the increasingly flourishing Christian kingdoms, soon to include the new realm of Portugal amongst their number. In the south, older ways were submerged by a new wave of Berber influence and a more rigid and fundamentalist Islam that accompanied the rule of the Almoravid and Almohad dynasties. Like the fifth and eighth, and the sixteenth to follow, the eleventh century and early twelfth marked a period of profound change in the peninsula, in which the ideology of the *Reconquista* was first born. But there remains in Spanish history an essential continuity that transcends such times of cataclysm and upheaval, born perhaps out of the shared experience of the aspirations towards unity, and the resistance to them, both deeply rooted in the past and in the geography of the land, that remain as strong today as in the time of the Romans, Visigoths and Umayyads.

Bibliographies

Introductory Note

THESE have been divided into two sections: A listing works in English and B listing those in other languages. Each is in turn subdivided roughly by the character of subject matter:
1. GENERAL
2. POLITICAL AND LEGAL HISTORY
3. SOCIAL AND ECONOMIC
4. CULTURE AND THE CHURCH

Sources, both in translation and the original texts, are listed in the appropriate sections. Obviously limitations of space prevent these bibliographies from being anything other than selective, although the attempt has been made to make that in English reasonably comprehensive. In making the choice of material for inclusion greater weight has been given to primary rather than secondary sources, for obvious reasons. Each section is further subdivided chronologically, or as between Umayyad Al-Andalus and the Christian states. Some additional bibliography on detailed points will be found in the references.

Abbreviations

L.V.   *Leges Visigothorum*, the Codes of Reccesuinth and Ervig, in K. Zeumer (ed.) *M.G.H., Leges* I (Hanover and Leipzig, 1902)

M.G.H.   *Monumenta Germaniae Historica*, divided by series:
         A.A.   *Auctores Antiquissimi*
         Leges
         S.R.G.   *Scriptores Rerum Germanicarum*
         S.S.   *Scriptores*

P.L.   *Patrologia Latina*, ed. J.P. Migne

V.S.   *Visigothic Spain: New Approaches*, E. James (ed.) (Oxford, 1980)

A. WORKS IN ENGLISH

1. GENERAL

For general treatments of the history of Spain in the Middle Ages see J.F. O'Callaghan, *A History of Medieval Spain*, (Ithaca, 1975) and G. Jackson, *The Making of Medieval Spain*, (London, 1972). D.W. Lomax, *The Reconquest of Spain*, (London, 1978) concentrates on the later medieval centuries, but gives a short outline of the earlier ones too. H. Livermore, *The Origins of Spain and Portugal*, (London, 1971) covers the period from the fourth to the ninth centuries, and is the only book in English to attempt to bridge the supposed divide caused by the Arab conquest, but it contains occasional errors of fact. There are short accounts of the Visigothic and Umayyad periods in the *Cambridge Medieval History* vols II and III, but these are now too old-fashioned to be other than a hindrance.

2. POLITICAL AND LEGAL

(a) The Later Roman Empire and the Fifth Century

For the end of Roman rule in most of Spain, and the entry of the Alans, Vandals and Sueves, two of the major sources available are Orosius, *Seven Books of History against the Pagans*, translated by R.J. Deferrari, *Fathers of the Church*, vol. 50, (Washington, 1964) and Zosimus, *Historia Nova*, translated by J.J. Buchanan and H.T. Davis, (San Antonio, Texas, 1967). The fragments of the work of Olympiodorus, preserved in the *Bibliotheca* of the Patriarch Photius, are translated in C.D. Gordon, *The Age of Attila*, (Michigan, 1966). Late Roman law, and its adaptation and abridgement by the Visigoths in the *Breviary* of Alaric, is found in C. Pharr, *The Theodosian Code*, (New York, 1969).

F.J. Wiseman, *Roman Spain*, (London, 1956) provides a general history, and a useful account of extant remains. For the early history of Mérida, see I.A. Richmond, 'The first years of Emerita Augusta', *Archaeological Journal*, 87 (1930) pp. 98–116, and for the North-East, his 'Five Town-Walls in Hispania Citerior', *Journal of Roman Studies*, 21 (1931) pp. 86–100. The collapse of Roman rule and the ensuing Suevic kingdom in the peninsula are studied, somewhat controversially, in E.A. Thompson, 'The End of Roman Spain', *Nottingham Medieval Studies*, 20–23, and 'The Conversion of the Spanish Suevi to Catholicism', *V.S.*, pp. 77–92. On the establishment of the Visigoths in south-western Gaul and their kingdom there, see *idem*, 'The settlement of the Barbarians in Southern Gaul', *Journal of Roman Studies*, 46 (1956) pp. 65–75, and 'The Visigoths from Fritigern to Euric', *Historia*, 12 (1963) pp. 105–26. Some of their earlier history before entering the Roman Empire, and their conversion to Arianism, are discussed in *The Visigoths in the Age of Ulfila* (Oxford, 1966) by the same author.

(b) The Visigothic Period

E.A. Thompson, *The Goths in Spain* (Oxford, 1969) provides a detailed general coverage of social and economic as well as political aspects of the Visigothic kingdom, though some of its interpretations require challenging. There is a useful brief treatment in J.M. Wallace-Hadrill, *The Barbarian West*, 3rd edn. (London, 1967) ch. 6, that is particularly good on law and on the major intellectual figures of the time. The reign of Leovigild has attracted most scholarly attention, not least for its relative abundance of source material, of which Isidore of Seville, *History of the Goths, Vandals, and Suevi*, translated by G. Donini and G.B. Ford (Leiden, 1970) is available in English, and gives brief accounts of the reigns of the rulers of these three peoples in the fifth and sixth centuries. For interpretations of events in Spain towards the end of the latter, and notably the rebellion of Hermenigild, see J.N. Hillgarth, 'Coins and Chronicles: Propaganda in Sixth Century Spain', *Historia*, 16 (1966), pp. 482–508, and R.J.H. Collins, 'Mérida and Toledo: 550–585', *V.S.*, pp. 189–219. An approach to the writing of history in late sixth and early seventh-century Spain, which sees it as being largely controlled by the royal court, a view that may not achieve universal acceptance, may be found in J.N. Hillgarth, 'Historiography in Visigothic Spain', *Settimane di Studio*, 17, (Spoleto, 1970) pp. 261–313. The major legal compilation of the Visigothic kingdom, the *Forum Iudicum* of Reccesuinth and Ervig, has been translated in S.P. Scott, *The Visigothic Code*, (Boston, 1910). P.D. King, 'King Chindasvind and the First Territorial Law-Code of the Visigothic Kingdom', *V.S.*, pp. 131–57 argues in favour of Chindasuinth having been the progenitor of *Forum Iudicum*. *Law and Society in the Visigothic Kingdom*, (Cambridge, 1972) by the same author contains much of interest on many aspects of government and society in this period, and a particularly good chapter on the family, but approaches these subjects through the law-code in an overly abstract way, often confusing reality with the normative aspirations of the legislators. On Visigothic law see also, F.S. Lear, 'The Public Law of the Visigothic Code', *Speculum*, 26 (1951) pp. 1–24, and *Treason in Roman and Germanic Law* (Austin, Texas, 1965) chs 4–6. There is depressingly little on the later stages of the Visigothic kingdom, but see F.X. Murphy, 'Julian of Toledo and the Fall of the Visigothic Kingdom in Spain', *Speculum*, 27 (1952) pp. 1–21, and R.J.H. Collins, 'Julian of Toledo and the Royal Succession in Late Seventh-Century Spain' in P.H. Sawyer and I.N. Wood (eds) *Early Medieval Kingship* (Leeds, 1977) pp. 30–49. R.D. Shaw, 'The Fall of the Visigothic Power in Spain', *English Historical Review*, 21 (1906) pp. 209–28, would be a mildly amusing historical curiosity, if its absurd arguments did not have modern devotees.

(c) The Umayyad State

There are a number of general histories of Islamic Spain, covering its whole span from 711 to 1492, which are therefore relevant to the Umayyad period; the best of these, although very brief, is W. Montgomery Watt and P. Cachia, *A History of Islamic Spain*, (Edinburgh, 1965). A. Chejne, *Muslim Spain, its History and Culture*, (Minneapolis, 1974) is full of information, but suffers from its author's over-literal approach to the sources. Unfortunately, books on the Islamic period, in dealing with the Arab conquest and its immediate effects, display remarkable ignorance or prejudice in respect of the preceding Visigothic period, though largely as a result of being misled by the often dismal secondary literature, which has all too often treated the fall of the Gothic kingdom in terms of 'decadence and decline'. T.F. Glick, *Islamic and Christian Spain in the Early Middle Ages*, (Princeton, 1979) has suffered particularly in this respect, but offers very important insights on the mutual interrelationship of the Muslim and Christian states from the eighth to thirteenth centuries. His arguments on conversion should, however, be checked against those of his very thought-provoking source, R.W. Bulliet, *Conversion to Islam in the Medieval Period*, (Harvard, 1979).

Few of the sources for Al-Andalus in the Umayyad period are currently available in English, but there is Ibn 'Abd al-Ḥakem, *History of the Conquest of Spain*, translated by J.H. Jones, (Göttingen, 1858), a version of the *Futūh Misr*. A substantial part of the historical work of Al-Makkarī is made available in P. de Gayangos, *The History of the Mohammedan Dynasties in Spain*, 2 vols (London, 1840–3). On these and other Arab historians and writers of the Umayyad period, see brief accounts in R.A. Nicholson, *A Literary History of the Arabs*, 2nd edn, (Cambridge, 1930) ch. 9, and D.M. Dunlop, *Arab Civilisation to AD1500*, (London and Beirut, 1971) especially chs 3 and 5. Entries on individuals, as well as on subjects, for example history (*Tarikh*) will be found in the extremely valuable *Encyclopedia of Islam*, 1st edn, 4 vols (Leiden, 1913–42); 2nd edn (not yet completed), vols I–IV (Kha), (Leiden, 1960–78), which can be consulted with profit on virtually all of the topics relating to Islamic Spain.

The fullest account of the career of Mohammed can be found in W. Montgomery Watt, *Muhammad at Mecca*, (Oxford 1953) and *Muhammad at Medina*, (Oxford, 1956), and in briefer form in M. Robinson, *Mohammed*, (Harmondsworth, 1971). The best translation of the Koran is that of A.J. Arberry, *The Koran Interpreted*, 2 vols (London and New York, 1955). The traditional interpretations of early Islam have recently been severely challenged by P. Crone and M. Cook, *Hagarism, the Making of the Islamic World*, (Cambridge, 1977), now supplemented by P. Crone, *Slaves on Horses*, (Cambridge, 1980) and M. Cook, *Early Muslim Dogma*, (Cambridge, 1981).

A useful political history of Islamic Spain in the periods of the governors and of the Umayyad amirs and caliphs can be found in P.K. Hitti, *History of the Arabs*, 10th edn (London, 1971), chs 24–28, and a considerably shorter handling by A. Huici in *The Cambridge History of Islam*, vol. II (Cambridge, 1970), ch. 7, part 7. A helpful introduction to Islamic law is available in N.J. Coulson, *A History of Islamic Law*, (Edinburgh, 1964), and see also J. Schacht, *The Origins of Muhammadan Jurisprudence*, (Oxford, 1950).

(d) The Christian Realms
There is nothing of note in English on the history of the Asturian and Leonese
monarchy in this period; for the kingdom of Pamplona, there is a brief treatment in
R.J.H. Collins, 'The Basques in Aquitaine and Navarre' in J.C. Holt (ed.) *War,
Government and Society in the Middle Ages*, (Ipswich, 1964). For Catalonia, particularly in
respect of the ninth century, there is R.J.H. Collins, 'Charles the Bald and Wifred the
Hairy' in M. Gibson and J. Nelson, *Charles the Bald: Court and Kingdom*, (Oxford, 1981)
pp. 169–89.

3. SOCIAL AND ECONOMIC

(a) Later Roman Empire and the Fifth Century
J. Percival, *The Roman Villa*, (London, 1976) pp. 59–61, and R. Chevalier, *Roman
Roads*, (London 1976) pp. 155–8, give short accounts of the Spanish dimension of their
subjects. For the fifth century see E.A. Thompson, 'End of Roman Spain' (A2–*a*).

(b) The Visigothic Period
For aspects of town life, as illustrated particularly in the case of Mérida, a most
valuable source is made available in the text and translation of J.N. Garvin (ed.), *The
'Vitas Patrum Emeretensium'*, (Washington, 1946). For some of the uses that can be made
of it see R.J.H. Collins, *Mérida and Toledo, 550–585, V.S.*, pp. 189–219. Some
indications concerning rural society can be gleaned from Braulio of Zaragoza's *Life of
St Aemilian*, translated by C.W. Barlow in *Fathers of the Church*, vol. 63, (Washington,
1969) pp. 113–39. For a hitherto neglected social group see D. Claude, 'Freedmen in
the Visigothic Kingdom', *V.S.*, pp. 159–88, and on an important region, E. James,
'Septimania and its Frontier: An Archaeological Approach', *V.S.*, pp. 223–42. The
Visigothic coinage is catalogued and studied in G.C. Miles, *The Coinage of the Visigoths
of Spain, Leovigild to Achila II*, (New York, 1952), and one important aspect of it is
analysed, with perhaps overly pessimistic conclusions, in P. Grierson, 'Visigothic
Metrology', *Numismatic Chronicle*, 6th series, 13 (1953) pp. 74–87.

(c) The Umayyad State
T.F. Glick, *Islamic and Christian Spain*, (A2–*c*) makes many valuable contributions,
especially on the Eastern Mediterranean origin of some of the distinctive features of the
economy and social organisation of Umayyad Spain. See also A.M. Watson, 'The Arab
Agricultural Revolution and its Diffusion, 711–1100', *Journal of Economic History*, 34
(1974) pp. 8–35. S.M. Imamuddin, *Some aspects of the Socio-Economic and Cultural History
of Muslim Spain*, (Leiden, 1965) is less relevant than it sounds. A brief general analysis
will be found in J. Vicens Vives, *An Economic History of Spain*, (Princeton, 1969). For
coins see G.C. Miles, *The Coinage of the Umayyads of Spain*, 2 vols (New York, 1950).

(d) The Christian Realms
See A.R. Lewis, *The Development of Southern French and Catalan Society, 718–1050*, (Austin,
1965).

4. CULTURE AND THE CHURCH

(a) Later Roman Empire and the Fifth Century
M.C. Diaz y Diaz, 'Early Christianity in Lugo', *Classical Folia*, 32 (1978) pp. 243–59,
raises some important questions about the early diffusion of Christianity in northern
Spain. E.A. Thompson, 'The Conversion of the Spanish Suevi to Catholicism', *V.S.*,
pp. 77–92, looks into the dating of that event. Translations of the works of Prudentius
(*fl. c.* 400) will be found, with the texts, in H.J. Thompson (ed.), *Loeb Classical Library*

Series. The dating of the substantial corpus of Spanish liturgical passions is studied in M.C. Diaz y Diaz, 'Notes for a Chronology of the Passionario Hispanico', *Classical Folia*, 24 (1970) pp. 28–45.

(b) The Visigothic Period

S. McKenna, *Paganism and Pagan Survivals in Spain up to the Fall of the Visigothic Kingdom*, (Washington, 1938), and J.N. Hillgarth, 'Popular Religion in Visigothic Spain', *V.S.*, pp. 3–60 (with full bibliography) deal with important areas of religious behaviour and belief. A.K. Ziegler, *Church and State in Visigothic Spain*, (Washington, 1930) is still useful, although its main concern with the question of whether the Church dominated the State or vice versa is now somewhat anachronistic. There are valuable considerations of the dissemination of the influence of the Visigothic Church in J.N. Hillgarth, 'The East, Visigothic Spain and the Irish', *Studia Patristica*, 4 (Berlin, 1961) pp. 442–56, and *idem*, 'Visigothic Spain and Early Christian Ireland', *Proceedings of the Royal Irish Academy*, 62 (1963) pp. 167–95, and also M. Herren, 'On the Earliest Irish Acquaintance with Isidore of Seville', *V.S.*, pp. 243–50. *Individuals*: Leander's sermon to III Toledo is translated by C.W. Barlow in *Fathers of the Church*, vol. LXII (Washington, 1969) pp. 229–35, as is his *Rule for Nuns*, *ibid*. pp. 183–228. Sections of Isidore's *Etymologiae* are translated in E. Bréhaut, *An Encyclopaedist of the Dark Ages, Isidorus of Seville*, (New York, 1912). Other convenient translations are *Isidore of Seville's History of the Goths, Vandals and Sueves*, translated by G. Donini and G.B. Ford (Leiden, 1970), and *The Letters of St Isidore of Seville*, edited and translated by G.B. Ford (Amsterdam, 1970). See also J.N. Hillgarth, 'The Position of Isidoran Studies: A Critical Review of the Literature since 1935' in *Isidoriana* (Leon, 1961) pp. 11–74, also R.E. McNally, 'Isidoriana', *Theological Studies*, 20 (1959), P.J. Mullins, *The Spiritual Life according to Saint Isidore of Seville*, (Washington, 1940), and R.E. Reynolds, 'The Isidoran Epistula ad Leudefredum', *V.S.*, pp. 251–72, which disproves its authenticity. On Sisebut see J. Fontaine, 'King Sisebut's Vita Desiderii and the Political Function of Visigothic Hagiography', *V.S.*, pp. 93–130. The works of Braulio are translated in *Fathers of the Church*, vol. 63 (Washington, 1969), and there is a comprehensive study in C.H. Lynch, *Saint Braulio of Saragossa* (Washington, 1938). For Eugenius, C. Codoñer Merino, 'The poetry of Eugenius of Toledo', *Papers of the Liverpool Latin Seminar*, 3 (1981), and for Ildefonsus, A. Braegelmann, *The Life and Writings of Ildefonsus of Toledo*, (Washington, 1942). On Julian see the articles by Collins Murphy (A2–*b*) and also F.X. Murphy, 'Julian of Toledo and the Condemnation of Monotheletism in Spain', *Mélanges J. de Ghellinck*, (Gembloux, 1951) pp. 361–73; C.H. Beeson, 'The Ars Grammatica of Julian of Toledo', *Studi e Testi*, 37 (1924) pp. 50–70; J.N. Hillgarth, 'Towards a critical edition of the works of St Julian of Toledo', *Studia Patristica*, 1 (Berlin, 1957) pp. 37–43 and *idem*, 'St Julian of Toledo in the Middle Ages', *Journal of the Warburg and Courtauld Institutes*, 21 (1958) pp. 7–26, for his subsequent influence.

Visigothic monastic texts are translated by C.W. Barlow in *Fathers of the Church*, vols 62 and 63 (Washington, 1969); there is a translation, although the text has now been superseded by that of Diaz y Diaz, in F.C. Nock, *The 'Vita Sancti Fructuosi'*, (Washington, 1946), and the 'autobiographical' works of Valerius, together with an overall study, are presented in C.M. Aherne, *Valerio of Bierzo*, (Washington, 1949). On supposed 'pactual monasticism' see C.J. Bishko, 'The date and nature of the Spanish Consensoria Monachorum', *American Journal of Philology*, 69 (1948), pp. 377–95.

On the liturgy of the Visigothic Church (inextricably linked with that of the Mozarabs) see M.C. Diaz y Diaz, 'Literary aspects of the Visigothic Liturgy', *V.S.*, pp. 61–76, W.C. Bishop, *The Mozarabic and Ambrosian Rites*, (Alcuin Club Tracts XV, 1924), T.C. Akeley, *Christian Initiation in Spain c. 300–1100*, (London, 1967), and for its influence on the Frankish liturgy, E. Bishop, 'Spanish Symptoms' in his *Liturgica*

Historica, (Oxford, 1918) pp. 165–210. Small sections of some of the councils of the Visigothic Church have been translated in recent issues of *Classical Folia*, and there is a plan to publish a full English version in the near future.

For the Jews in Visigothic Spain see the general treatment of S. Katz, *The Jews in the Visigothic and Frankish Kingdoms of Spain and Gaul*, (Cambridge, Massachusetts, 1937). Somewhat ideosyncratic attempts to go beyond the laws to analyse the causes of the ill treatment of the Jews in the Kingdom can be found in J.duQ. Adams, 'Ideology and the Requirements of "Citizenship" in Visigothic Spain: The Case of the Judaei', *Societas*, 2 (1972), pp. 317–32, and B. Bachrach, 'A reassessment of Visigothic Jewish Policy', *American Historical Review*, 78 (1973) pp. 11–34.

(c) The Umayyad State and the Mozarabs

For outline treatments of the culture of Islamic Spain see the general books listed above (A2-c). For the Mozarabs there is a very useful and comprehensive introduction to the sources, both Latin and Arabic, in E.P. Colbert, *The Martyrs of Cordoba*, (Washington, 1962). There is a less than sympathetic assessment of the martyr movement in N. Daniel, *The Arabs and Medieval Europe*, (London and Beirut, 1975), ch. 2. For a study of one of its leading apologists, together with a translation of his *Life of Eulogius*, see C.M. Sage, *Paul Albar of Cordoba*, (Washington, 1943). For another aspect of their literary activity there is R.J.H. Collins, 'Latin Poetry in Ninth Century Spain', *Papers of the Liverpool Latin Seminar*, 4 (1983).

(d) The Christian Realms

See the introduction to H.A. Saunders (ed.), *Beati in Apocalipsin Libri Duodecim*, (Rome, 1930) for Beatus of Liebana. R.J.H. Collins, 'Latin Poetry', (A4-c) deals with all that is known of the literary culture of the ninth century kingdom of Pamplona, and is also relevent for the Asturian realm.

For the art and architecture of Spain after the fall of the Visigothic kingdom, see C.R. Dodwell, *Painting in Europe, 800–1200*, (Harmondsworth, 1971) chs. 6 and 11, A. Grabar and C. Nordenfalk, *Early Medieval Painting*, (New York, 1957) pp. 62–8, 161–75, and K.J. Conant, *Carolingian and Romanesque Architecture*, (Harmondsworth, 1966) pp. 87–99, 111–18. There is a lavishly-illustrated short treatment in J. Williams, *Early Spanish Manuscript Illumination*, (London, 1977), and a distinctive artistic product of late tenth-century Umayyad Cordoban court art is studied in J. Beckwith, *Caskets from Cordoba*, (London, 1960). The best general account, which is full of excellent illustrations, is P. de Palol and M. Hirmer, *Early Medieval Art in Spain*, (London, 1969).

B. WORKS IN OTHER LANGUAGES

1. GENERAL

Several volumes of the massive *Historia de España*, initiated and edited by R. Menendez Pidal, are relevant to this period. A completely new edition of vol. II on Roman Spain is due to appear shortly. Vol. III is *España Visigoda*, various authors (Madrid, 1940), now a little old-fashioned in some respects. Vols IV and V, *España Musulmana, 711–1031* (Madrid, 1950) are Spanish translations of the three volumes of E. Lévi-Provençale's *Histoire de l'Espagne Musulmane* (see below B2-c, B3-c). Vol. VI is J. Perez de Urbel and R. del Arco y Garay, *España Cristiana, 711–1038: Comienzos de la Reconquista*, (Madrid, 1956). This has now been supplemented by vol. VII, part 1, C. Sanchez-Albornoz, *El Reino Astur-Leones, 722–1037*, (Madrid, 1980); part 2, on the Christian realms in the Pyrenees, is in preparation. In a smaller compass there is L.G. de Valdeavellano,

Historia de España, part I, 2 vols (Madrid, 1968). There are two useful historical encyclopedias: G. Bleiberg (ed.), *Diccionario de Historia de España*, 2nd ed., 3 vols (Madrid, 1968) and Q. Aldea *et al.* (eds), *Diccionario de Historia Eclesiástica de España*, 4 vols (Madrid, 1972–5). For ecclesiastical history, Z. Garcia Villada, *Historia Eclesiástica de España*, 2 vols (Madrid, 1929–33), is still very valuable, and can now be supplemented by R. Garcia Villoslada (ed.), *Historia de la Iglesia de España*, of which vol. I, *La Iglesia en la España Romana y Visigoda*, (Madrid, 1979) has appeared.

2. POLITICAL AND LEGAL

(a) Later Roman Empire and the Fifth Century
For the history of the early fifth century, there is Orosius, *Historiarum Adversum Paganos Libri VII*, ed. C. Zangemeister, (Hildesheim, 1967) and Zosimus, *Historia Nova* (in Greek) ed. L. Mendelssohn, (Leipzig, 1887). Hydace, *Chronique*, ed. A. Tranoy, (*Sources Chrétiennes*, vols CCXVIII–CCXIX) (Paris, 1974)), is the best edition of Hydatius, and has useful commentary and a French translation. The fragmentary 'Chronicle of Zaragoza' is edited by T. Mommsen, *M.G.H., A.A.* XI (Berlin, 1894) pp. 222–3. The Roman inscriptions of Spain will be found in A. Hübner (ed.), *Corpus Inscriptionum Latinorum*, vol. II and Supplement (Berlin, 1869 and 1892), and for some recent discoveries see S. Mariner Bigorra, *Inscripciones Romanas de Barcelona*, (Barcelona, 1973). On the Suevic kingdom, see W. Reinhart, *Historia General del Reino Hispánico de los Suevos*, (Madrid, 1952), and on their coinage, *idem*, 'Die Münzen des Swebenreiches', *Mitteilungen der Bayerischen Numismatischen Gesellschaft*, 55 (1937) pp. 151–90. On the beginings of Visigothic settlement, there is *idem*, 'Sobre el Asentamiento de los Visigodos en la Península, *Archivo Español de Arqueologia*, 17 (1945) pp. 124–39; and for the most powerful Visigothic king of the period, K.F. Stroheker, *Eurich, König der Westgoten*, (Stuttgart, 1937).

(b) The Visigothic Period
There are a number of general histories of the Visigothic kingdom, of which J. Orlandis, *Historia de España: La España Visigótica*, (Madrid, 1977), M. Sanz Agüero, *Historia de España: Los Visigodos*, (Madrid, 1978) and D. Claude, *Adel, Kirche und Königtum im Westgotenreich*, (Sigmaringen, 1971) are particularly notable. Of the principal historical texts, Isidore of Seville's *Historia Gothorum, Wandalorum, Sueborum*, and his *Chronica*, are edited by T. Mommsen in *M.G.H., A.A.* XI (Berlin, 1894) pp. 267–303, 424–81. So is the *Chronicle of John of Biclar*, ibid. pp. 211–20, of which there is another edition and study in J. Campos, *Juan de Biclaro, Obispo de Gerona*, (Madrid, 1960). There is yet another, together with Spanish translation, in P. Alvarez Rubiano, 'La Crónica de Juan Biclarense', *Analecta Sacra Tarraconensia*, 16 (1942) pp. 7–44.

    For the archaeology of Visigothic settlement, limited and controversial as it is at present, see H. Zeiss, *Die Grabfunde aus dem Spanischen Westgotenreich*, (Berlin, 1934), and also W. Hübener, 'Zur Chronologie der Westgotenzeitlichen Grabfunde in Spanien', *Madrider Mitteilungen*, 11 (1970) pp. 187–212. There are few treatments of individual reigns, but K.F. Stroheker, 'Leowigild' in his *Germanentum und Spätantike*, (Zurich/Stuttgart, 1965) pp. 134–91, H.J. Diesner, 'König Wamba und der Westgotische Frühfeudalismus', *Jahrbuch der Österreichen Byzantinischen Gesellschaft*, 18 (1969) pp. 7–36, and *idem*, 'Politik und Ideologie im Westgotenreich von Toledo: Chindasvind', *Sitzungsberichte der Sächsischen Akademie der Wissenschaften zu Leipzig*, 121 (Berlin, 1979), offer some interesting if debatable perspectives. Other studies of features of the political life and organisation of the Visigothic kingdom include J. Orlandis, 'El Poder Real y la Succession al Trono en la Monarquía Visigoda', *Cuadernos del Instituto Jurídico Español*, 16 (1962) pp. 1-136, C. Sanchez-Albornoz, 'La Ordinatio Principis en la España Goda y Postvisigoda', in his *Estudios sobre las*

Instituciones Medievales Españolas, (Mexico, 1965), and *idem*, 'El Aula Regia y las Asambleas Politicas de los Godos', *Cuadernos de Historia de España*, 5 (1946) pp. 5–110. The notion of the essential isolation of Spain in the Gothic period is developed most fully in R. Gibert, 'El Reino Visigodo y el Particularismo Español', *Settimane di . . . Spoleto*, vol. III: *I Goti in Occidente* (Spoleto, 1956) pp. 537–83. Against this might be contrasted J. Orlandis, 'Communications et Échanges entre l'Espagne Wisigothique et la France Mérovingienne', *Annales de la Faculté de Droit et des Sciences Economiques de Toulouse*, 13 (1970) pp. 253–62, and for dealings with the Byzantine Empire, K.F. Stroheker, 'Das Spanische Westgotenreich und Byzanz', *Bonner Jahrbücher*, 163 (1963) pp. 252–74. For Byzantine Spain see also P. Goubert, 'Byzance et l'Espagne Wisigothique', *Revue des Études Byzantines*, 2 (1944) pp. 5–78, and *idem*, 'L'Administration de l'Espagne Byzantine', *ibid.* 3 (1945) pp. 127–42, and 4 (1946) pp. 70–134. The law codes of Euric and Reccesuinth-Ervig are edited by K. Zeumer in *M.G.H., Leges* I (Hanover and Leipzig, 1902).

(c) The Umayyad State

As well as Ibn 'Abd al-Ḥakem (A2-*c*), there are two other sources of great value for the history of the Arab conquest of Spain and its immediate aftermath: the eleventh century *Fath al-Andalus*, translated by J. de Gonzalez, *Fatho-l-Andaluçi: Historia de la Conquista de España*, (Argel, 1889), which continues with short notices on the Umayyad amirs, and the *Bayān al-Moghrib*, translated by E. Fagnan, *Al-Bayano'l-Mogrib* 2 vols (Algiers, 1901, 1904), which is a much more substantial work, and is particularly valuable as a source for North African history. The extremely useful annalistic account of Ibn al-Athīr, which together with the Bayān constitute the principal narrative sources for the political and military history of Umayyad Al-Andalus, is also translated by E. Fagnan, *Ibn al-Athīr: Annales du Maghreb et de l'Espagne*, (Algiers, 1901). The work of the late tenth-century grammarian and historian Ibn al-Kūtiyya has not survived in its original form, and although it is believed that, as it now stands, it represents a version made by his students from their notes, its textual history is conceivably more complicated still. It contains some interesting if idiosyncratic material on the conquest, but is most valuable for its account of the mid ninth century. There is a Spanish translation: J. Ribera (ed. and tr.) *Historia de la Conquista de España de Abenalcotía el Cordobés*, (Madrid, 1926). Another initially eleventh-century source with a complicated and suspicious subsequent textual history is translated in E. Lafuente y Alcántara, *El 'Ajbar Machmua'*, (Madrid, 1867). There is an extremely interesting short chronicle of the opening years of the reign of 'Abd al-Raḥmān III, translated into Spanish in E. Lévi-Provençale and E. García Gomez (ed. and tr.), *Crónica anónyma de Abderrahman III*, (Granada, 1950). The sections of the geographical work of Ibn Ḥaukal pertinent to Spain are translated by M.J. Romani Suay in *Ibn Hawkal: Configuración del Mundo*, (Valencia, 1971), and there is a full French translation by J.H. Kramers and G. Wiet in *Configuration de la Terre*, (Paris, 1964). The very valuable but fragmentary *Muktabis* of Ibn Hayyān, of especial interest in its account of the tenth century and of events in the marches, has not yet even been edited in full, but various sections are available in translations in successive volumes of the periodical *Cuadernos de Historia de España* vols XIII, XXI, XXII, and so on. That part of his text dealing with the reign of the caliph Al-Ḥakem II has been edited by A.A. al-Ḥajjī, *Al-Muqtabis fī Akhbār Balad al-Andalus*, (Beirut, 1965).

There are two Latin chronicles, both of the mid eighth century, that 'of 741', or the *Chronica Byzantina-Arabica*, probably written in Cordoba, and that 'of 754', or the *Chronica Mozarabica*, a product of Toledo. They are edited in J. Gil, *Corpus Scriptorum Muzarabicorum*, 2 vols (Madrid, 1973) pp. 7–54. On the former see C.E. Dubler, 'Sobre la Crónica Arabigo-Bizantina de 741 y la Influencia Bizantina en la Península Ibérica', *Al-Andalus*, 11 (1946) pp. 283–349.

The standard political history of Islamic Spain in the Umayyad period is E. Lévi-Provençale, *Histoire de l'Espagne Musulmane*, vols I and II (Leiden, 1950), which supersedes all earlier surveys. See also C. Sanchez-Albornoz, *La España Musulmana*, 2 vols (Buenos Aires, 1946). On Cordoba in the immediate aftermath of the abolition of the caliphate there is K. Soufi, *Los Banū Ŷahwar en Cordoba 1031–70, 422–462 AH*, (Cordoba, 1968).

(d) The Christian Realms

The principal historical sources for the kingdom of the Asturias are the three late ninth-century chronicles. Of these the *'prophetic'*, the *Albelda Chronicle* and the Roda version of that of Alfonso III are found in M. Gomez Moreno (ed.), 'Las Primeras Crónicas de la Reconquista', *Boletín de la Real Academia de la Historia*, 100 (1932) pp. 600–23. The Roda and Oviedo texts of the Alfonso III Chronicle are published together in A. Ubieto Arteta, *Crónica de Alfonso III*, (Valencia, 1971), and it is to this edition that reference is made in the notes below. For the kingdom of Leon, the two versions of the text of the *Chronicle of Sampiro* are available, together with a study of the author and some of the charters he may have drafted as a royal notary, in J. Perez de Urbel, *Sampiro, su Crónica y la Monarquía Leonesa en el Siglo X*, (Madrid, 1952), and for its continuation in the Silos version, see J. Perez de Urbel and A. Gonzalez Ruiz-Zorrilla, *Historia Silense*, (Madrid, 1959).

The fullest study of the Asturian kingdom will be found in the massive volumes of C. Sanchez-Albornoz, *Orígenes de la Nacion Española: El Reino de Asturias* 3 vols (Oviedo: 1972–5), which contain reprints of some of his older articles and much new material, and provide an exhaustive political and military account. There are some interesting pieces to be found in the collection, *Estudios sobre la Monarquía Asturiana*, (Oviedo, 1971), which concentrate principally upon Alfonso II and his period. The only full-length study devoted to an individual Asturian king is A. Cotarelo, *Historia Crítica de la Vida de Alfonso III el Magno*, (Madrid, 1933).

The Leonese monarchy has not yet been treated in such detail, but there is a valuable study of its greatest king in J. Rodriguez, *Ramiro II, Rey de León*, (Madrid, 1972). Articles relating to this period will be found in the occasional publication *León y su Historia* (Leon, vol. I, 1969; vol. II, 1973 etc.). For Galicia see P. David, *Études Historiques sur la Galice et le Portugal du VI–XIe Siècles*, (Lisbon, 1947).

For the history of the kingdom of Pamplona the sources are very sparse. The principal indigenous records are a set of genealogical lists probably composed in the tenth century at the court at Nájera. They are edited in J.M. Laccara, 'Textos Navarros del Códice de Roda', *Estudios de Edad Media de la Corona de Aragon* I, (Zaragoza, 1945) pp. 193–275. For the events of the ninth century a very limited framework can be created with the aid of Frankish chronicles (see references to ch. 7, part ii) and the works of the Arab historians. Text and translation into Spanish of the relevant sections of Ibn Hayyān are provided in E. Lévi-Provençale and E. Garcia Gomez, 'Textos Inéditos del Muktabis de Ibn Hayyān sobre los Orígenes del Reino de Pamplona', *Al-Andalus*, 19 (1954) pp. 295–315. The general lack of evidence gives the greatest opportunity for controversy. For some of the rival interpretations of the early history of the kingdom see J. Perez de Urbel, 'Lo Viejo y lo Nuevo sobre el Origen del Reino de Pamplona', *Al-Andalus*, 19 (1954) pp. 1–42, and a whole series of studies by C. Sanchez-Albornoz, which are conveniently collected in his *Vascos y Navarros en su Primera Historia*, (Madrid, 1976). Another volume of collected articles, this time dealing principally with the tenth century, will be found in A. Ubieto Arteta, *Trabajos de Investigacion I*, (Valencia, 1972). There is an overall, though no less controversial, perspective on the medieval history of Navarre in J.M. Lacarra, *Historia Politica del Reino de Navarra desde sus Origenes hasta su Incorporacion a Castilla* 3 vols (Pamplona, 1972–3), of which vol. I treats of the period covered in this book.

There are no contemporary historical writings produced in Catalonia at this time, and thus the chronological framework of its political history is extremely obscure, particularly in the tenth century. The best guide is R. d'Abadal i de Vinyals, *Els Primers Comtes Catalans*, 3rd ed. (Barcelona, 1980). Sections of the Arab historians concerning the region are published in J.M. Millas Vallicrosa, 'Els Textos d'Historiadors Musulmans Referents a la Catalunya Carolíngia', *Quaderns d'Estudi*, 14 (1922) pp. 125–61. Some of the most important studies of R. d'Abadal are conveniently collected, together with a full bibliography of his writings, in his *Dels Visigots als Catalans* 2 vols 2nd ed. (Barcelona, 1974). See also F. Mateu y Llopis, 'De la Hispania Tarraconense Visigoda a la Marca Hispánica Carolina', *Analecta Sacra Tarraconensia*, (1947) pp. 1–122.

For the rise of Castille see J. Perez de Urbel, *Historia del Condado de Castilla* 3 vols (Madrid, 1945), and for the greatest of the early counts there is a lavishly illustrated treatment in V. De la Cruz, *Fernan Gonzalez*, (Burgos, 1972). See also T. Lopez Mata, *Geografia del Condado de Castilla a la Muerte de Fernan Gonzalez*, (Madrid, 1957).

3. SOCIAL AND ECONOMIC

(a) Later Roman Empire and the Fifth Century

There is a short general survey, J.M. Blazquez, *Historia Social y Económica: La España Romana, Siglos III–V*, (Madrid, 1975), and a series of regional studies on a large scale are being produced, of which the first to appear is A. Tranoy, *La Galice Romaine*, (Paris, 1981). There are two useful articles on the Late Roman senatorial aristocracy of Spain in A. Balil, 'Aspectos Sociales del Bajo Imperio (IV–VIs) – Los Senadores Hispánicos', *Latomus*, 24 (1965) pp. 886–904, and K.F. Stroheker, 'Spanische Senatoren der Spätrömischen und Westgotischen Zeit', *Madrider Mitteilungen*, 4 (1963), pp. 107–32. For a substantial archaeological survey see P. de Palol, *Arqueologia Cristiana de la España Romana*, (Madrid and Valladolid, 1967).

(b) The Visigothic Period

An overall perspective can be gained from J. Orlandis, *Historia Social y Económica: La España Visigoda*, (Madrid, 1975). On towns there is an overly pessimistic survey in J.M. Lacarra, 'Panorama de la Historia Urbana en la Península Ibérica desde el Siglo V al X', *Settimane di … Spoleto*, 6 (Spoleto, 1959) pp. 314–59, paralleled by a study of their administration in C. Sanchez-Albornoz, 'El Gobierno de las Ciudades en España del Siglo V al X', *ibid.*, pp. 359–92. The question of the survival or otherwise of the institutions of Roman town-life into the Visigothic period is considered in C. Sanchez-Albornoz, *Ruina y Extinción del Municipio Romano en España e Instituciones que le Reemplazan*, (Mendoza, 1944). The same author has devoted much attention to 'feudal' relationships in the Visigothic kingdom, and to studies of vassalage and the *beneficium*: see his *En Torno a los Orígenes del Feudalismo*, vol. I (Buenos Aires, 1974) which reprints his 'Fideles y Gardingos en la Monarquía Visigoda' and 'Raices del Vasallaje y del Beneficio Hispanos'; see also his *El 'Stipendium' Hispano-Godo y los Orígenes del Beneficio Prefeudal*, (Buenos Aires, 1947). On these subjects there is also L.G. de Valdeavallano, *El Feudalismo Hispanico y Otros Estudios de Historia Medieval*, (Barcelona, 1981). On slavery in Spain there is an important section in the pioneering study, C. Verlinden, *L'Esclavage dans l'Europe Médiévale*, vol. I: *Péninsule Ibérique – France*, (Bruges, 1955). A revealing small text that has value for the understanding of a rather neglected area of social formation, that of education, is considered in P. Riché, 'L'Education a l'Époque Wisigothique: les Institutionum Disciplinae', *Anales Toledanos*, 3 (1971) pp. 171–80; see also by the same author *Éducation et Culture dans l'Occident Barbare*, (Paris, 1962).

(c) The Umayyad State

E. Lévi-Provençale, *Histoire de l'Espagne Musulmane*, vol. III (B2-*c*) is devoted to a study
of social and intellectual life in Al-Andalus, from a largely Cordoban perspective. The
most fundamental reappraisal of the nature of the Arab settlement and the society
created in the peninsula by the conquest is to be found in P. Guichard, *Tribus Arabes et
Berbères en Al-Andalus*, (Paris, 1973), Spanish translation: *Al-Andalus*, (Barcelona,
1976), which challenges the long-held beliefs of traditional historiography in the speedy
disappearance of tribal structures in Al-Andalus. J. Vernet, *Los Musulmanes Españoles*,
(Barcelona, 1961) is useful introductory survey. On urban life see the studies of L.
Torres Balbás, 'Plazas, Zocos y Tiendas de las Ciudades Hispano-Musulmanas',
Al-Andalus, 12 (1947) pp. 437–76, 'Los Contornos de las Ciudades Hispano-
Musulmanas', *Al-Andalus*, 15 (1950) pp. 437–86, and 'Estructura de las Ciudades
Hispano-Musulmanas', *Al-Andalus*, 18 (1953) pp. 149–77. For the palace of 'Abd
al-Raḥmān III, see R. Castejon, *Medina Azahara*, (Leon, 1976).

(d) The Christian Realms

The charters of the Asturian kingdom are edited in A.C. Floriano, *Diplomática Española
del Periodo Astur*, 2 vols (Oviedo, 1949–51). Those of the Leonese monarchy have not yet
received such comprehensive treatment, but can be found partially in various editions
of the charter collections of individual monasteries, as for instance in M. Yanez
Cifuentes, *El Monasterio de Santiago de León*, (Leon and Barcelona, 1972), and P.
Floriano Llorente, *Colección Diplomática del Monasterio de San Vicente de Oviedo*, (Oviedo,
1968). The substantial studies of C. Sanchez-Albornoz on the social organisation and
economy of the Asturian and Leonese monarchies are conveniently collected in his
Viejos y Nuevos Estudios sobre las Instituciones Medievales Españolas, vols I and II (Madrid,
1976) vol. III (Madrid, 1976). For the city of Leon there is the same author's *Una Ciudad
de la España Cristiana hace Mil Años* 6th ed. (Madrid, 1976).

Few charters have survived from the kingdom of Pamplona, but there are some later
monastic cartularies containing some early documents, a large percentage of which,
however, look to have been falsified or interpolated. Some of these have been published,
notably by A. Ubieto Arteta: *Cartulario de Siresa*, (Valencia, 1960), *Cartulario de San Juan
de la Peña* (Valencia, 1962), and *Cartulario de Albelda*, (reprinted Zaragoza, 1981). The
documents of the cartulary of San Millan de la Cogolla, a Pamplonan foundation that
became the principal monastery in early Castille, were transcribed by L. Serrano,
Cartulario de San Millan, (Madrid, 1930), and have been re-edited with additions by A.
Ubieto, *Cartulario de San Millan de la Cogolla, 759–1076*, (Valencia, 1976). The estates of
the monastery have been studied in J.A. García de Cortazar, *El Dominio del Monasterio de
San Millan*, (Salamanca, 1969). The few extant original documents from the Rioja are
now edited in I. Rodriguez de Lama, *Colección Diplomática Medieval de la Rioja*, vol. II
(Logroño, 1976) docs. 923–1168. For Aragon see A. Ubieto Arteta, *Historia de Aragón*,
vol. I (Zaragoza, 1981).

The enormous wealth of Catalonia in charter evidence has hardly yet been tapped.
Some of the texts were published in the seventeenth and nineteenth centuries, notably
in the appendices to P. de Marca, *Marca Hispanica*, (Paris, 1688), ed. S. Baluze, and J.
de Villanueva, *Viage Literario a las Iglesias de España* 16 vols (Valencia, 1803–51). Since
then some of the documents have been lost, and a few more published. Frankish royal
diplomas granted to churches and individuals in the march have been edited in R.
d'Abadal, *Catalunya Carolíngia* II 2 vols (Barcelona, 1926 and 1950), and the
indigenous documentation of the mid-Pyrenean counties of Pallars and Ribagorça in
ibid. III, (Barcelona, 1955). The important, though relatively small, documental
holdings of the bishopric of the Seu d'Urgell up to the year 1010 have been published by
C. Baraut in vols I–III of the new periodical *Urgellia*, (Seu, 1979–81). The enormous

collections in the Archivo de la Corona de Aragón and the Monastery of Santa Maria de Montserrat are still largely unedited.

The fullest study of the society and economy of Catalonia in the tenth and eleventh centuries (with substantial bibliography) is P. Bonnassie, *La Catalogne du Milieu de X^e à la Fin du XIe Siècle*, 2 vols (Toulouse, 1975–6) – Catalan translation: *Catalunya Mil Anys Enrera*, (Barcelona, 1979). See also G. Feliu Montfort, 'Las Ventas con Pago en Moneda en el Condado de Barcelona hasta el Año 1010', *Cuadernos de Historia Económica de Cataluña*, 5 (1971) pp. 9–43, and *idem*, 'El Condado de Barcelona en los Siglos IX y X: Organización Territorial y Económico-Social', *ibid.* 7 (1972) pp. 9–32. For the history of the city of Barcelona see F. Udina Martorell and J.M. Garrut, *Barcelona, Dos Mil Años de Historia*, (Barcelona, 1963).

4. CULTURE AND THE CHURCH

(a) The Later Roman Empire and the Fifth Century

C. García Rodriguez, *El Culto de los Santos en la España Romana y Visigoda*, (Madrid, 1966) very usefully categorises, with extensive references, the cults of the saints venerated in the peninsula. The only substantial study of the Church in the Suevic kingdom will be found in K. Schäferdiek, *Die Kirche in den Reichen der Westgoten und Suewen bis zur Errichtung der Westgotischen Katholischen Staatskirche*, (Berlin, 1967). For art see the sections on 'Arte Romano' and on 'Arte Paleocristiano' by T. Aguirre and B. Huguet in *Ars Hispaniae* II, (Madrid, 1947), and also H. Schlunk and T. Hauschild, *Hispania Antiqua*, (Mainz, 1978), which is also relevant to the Visigothic period.

(b) The Visigothic Period

For two short attempts at synthesis see M.C. Diaz y Diaz, 'La Cultura de la España Visigótica del Siglo VII', *Settimane di . . . Spoleto*, 5 (Spoleto, 1958) pp. 813–44, and J. Fontaine, 'Conversion et Culture chez les Wisigoths d'Espagne', *ibid.* 14 (1967) pp. 87–147. The texts of the acts of the ecclesiastical councils are found in J. Vives (ed.), *Concilios Visigóticos e Hispano-Romanos* (Barcelona and Madrid, 1963). For the *Hispana* canonical collection see G. Martínez Díez, *La Colección Canónica Hispana* I, (Madrid, 1966). Two of the most important of the texts of the Visigothic-Mozarabic liturgy are published in M. Férotin (ed.), *Liber Ordinum*, (Paris, 1904), and *Liber Mozarabicus Sacramentorum*, (Paris, 1912). Some of the liturgical pieces contained in these books are compositions of the Visigothic Church, but it is not easy to separate them from later sections. Other liturgical manuscripts are published in the *Monumenta Hispaniae Sacra, Series Liturgica*, vols I–IX (Madrid and Barcelona, 1946–72), including the early eighth century *Liber Orationum*, (vol. I) and the *Leon Antiphonal* of 976 (vol. V), which copies a lost original of the reign of Wamba. Further liturgical editions are now appearing from the Instituto de Estudios Visigoticos-Mozarabes in Toledo. On the liturgy see the studies in J.F. Rivera Recio (ed.), *Estudios sobre la Liturgia Mozárabe*, (Toledo, 1965), and *Liturgia y Musica Mozárabes*, (Toledo, 1978).

The leading figures of the Spanish Church in the Visigothic kingdom are in most cases the subjects of a considerable number of studies and only a small number can be listed here. On Leander of Seville there is U. Dominguez del Val, *Leandro de Sevilla y la Lucha Contra el Arianismo*, (Madrid, 1981). Not surprisingly the bibliography on Isidore is enormous, but the outstanding study of his thought is J. Fontaine, *Isidore de Séville et la Culture Classique dans l'Espagne Wisigothique*, 2 vols (Paris, 1959). Surprisingly, many of Isidore's works have not been re-edited since the eighteenth century, when the edition of F. Arevalo was published. This is reprinted in *P.L.* vols LXXXI–LXXXIV. It can be augmented by newer versions of individual works, such as W.M. Lindsay (ed.), *Isidori*

Etymologiae sive Origenes, 2 vols (Oxford, 1911), although a new monster edition of the *Etymologiae* in twenty volumes is currently in preparation. The *De Natura Rerum*, accompanied by the verse epistle of King Sisebut appears in J. Fontaine, *Isidore de Séville: Traité de la Nature*, (Bordeaux, 1960). The *Regula* and an edition of the *Sententiae* will be found in J. Campos and I. Roca, *Santos Padres Españoles* II, (Madrid, 1971).

For a biography of Isidore there is J. Perez de Urbel, *San Isidoro de Sevilla*, 2nd ed. (Barcelona, 1945). On the political dimension of his thought there are two very interesting articles by M. Reydellet, 'La Conception du Souverain chez Isidore de Séville', *Isidoriana* (Leon, 1961) pp. 457–66, and 'Les Intentions Ideologiques et Politiques dans La Chronique d'Isidore de Séville', *Mélanges d'Archeologie et d'Histoire de l'École Française de Rome*, 82 (1970) pp. 363–400; see also now his *La Royauté dans la Littérature Latine de Sidoine Apollinaire à Isidore de Séville*, (Rome, 1981) ch. 10. For the *De Viris Illustribus* there is the edition of C. Codoñer Merino, *El 'De Viris Illustribus' de Isidoro de Sevilla*, (Salamanca, 1964). On Isidore's literary style see J. Fontaine, 'Théorie et Pratique du Style chez Isidore de Séville', *Vigiliae Christianae*, 14 (1960) pp. 65–101, and for the subsequent dissemination of his writings, B. Bischoff, 'Die Europäische Verbreitung der Werke Isidors von Sevilla', *Isidoriana*, (Leon, 1961) pp. 317–45.

On Sisebut's verse epistle see V. Recchia, 'La Poesi a Cristiana: Introduzione alla Lettura del Carmen de Luna di Sisebuto di Toledo', *Vetera Christianorum*, 7 (1970) pp. 21–58; W. Stach, 'König Sisebut ein Mäzen des Isidorianischen Zeitalters', *Die Antike*, 19 (Berlin, 1943), and L.J. Van der Lof, 'Der Mäzen Konig Sisebuts und sein "De Eclipsi Lunae"', *Revue des Études Augustiniennes*, 18 (1972) pp. 145–51. The letters of Sisebut, together with those of Count Bulgar and a few others of early seventh-century date, are edited, along with the king's *Vita Desiderii*, in J. Gil (ed.), *Miscellanea Wisigothica*, (Seville, 1972). The letters of Braulio are edited in L. Riesco Terrero, *Epistolario de San Braulio*, (Seville, 1975) and for the life of St Aemilian there is L. Vazquez de Parga, *Sancti Braulionis ... Vita S. Aemiliani*, (Madrid, 1943). The Spanish translation of the book by C.H. Lynch (A4-*b*) contains useful additional sections: C.H. Lynch and P. Galindo, *San Braulio, Obispo de Zaragoza (631–651), Su Vida y Sus Obras*, (Madrid, 1950).

On the Toledan bishops see J.F. Rivera Recio, 'Encumbramiento de la Sede Toledano durante la Dominación Visigótica', *Hispania Sacra*, 8 (1955) pp. 3–34. The poetic works of Eugenius II are edited by F. Vollmer in *M.G.H., A.A.* XIV (Berlin, 1905). The texts of Ildefonsus will be found in C. Codoñer Merino, *El 'De Viris Illustribus' de Ildefonso de Toledo*, (Salamanca, 1972), and for his theological writings see V. Blanco and J. Campos (eds), *Santos Padres Españoles I: San Ildefonso de Toledo*, (Madrid, 1971). On the former see J. Fontaine 'El De Viris Illustribus de San Ildefonso de Toledo: Tradición y Originalidad', *Anales Toledanos* 3 (1971) pp. 59–96, and for the latter, J.M. Cascante, *Doctrina Mariana de S. Ildefonso de Toledo*, (Barcelona, 1958).

The works of Julian are conveniently collected in *Corpus Christianorum Series Latina*, vol. CXV (Turnholt, 1876), which contains reprints of T. Mommsen's edition of the *Historia Wambae*, B. Bischoff's edition of the *Epistola ad Modoenum* (*Hermes* 87 (1959), pp. 247–56), together with new versions by J.N. Hillgarth of all the other writings, apart from the *Antikeimenon*, which is promised for a further volume. See also J.N. Hillgarth, 'Las Fuentes de S. Julián de Toledo', *Anales Toledanos*, 3 (1971) pp. 97–118, and two articles by J. Madoz: 'San Julián de Toledo', *Estudios Eclesiasticos*, 26 (1952) pp. 39–69, and 'Fuentes Teológico-Literarias de San Julián de Toledo', *Gregorianum*, 33 (1952) pp. 399–417.

For an introduction to monasticism in the Visigothic period see A. Mundó, 'Il Monachesimo nella Peninsola Iberica fino al Secolo VII', *Settimane di ... Spoleto*, 4 (Spoleto, 1957). The most substantial treatment, which extends into subsequent centuries, will be found in A. Linage Conde, *Los orígenes del Monacato Benedictino en la*

Península Ibérica, 3 vols (Leon, 1973). Texts of the monastic regulations of Fructuosus are edited in J. Campos and I. Roca (eds), *Sanctos Padres Españoles* II, (Madrid, 1971). The *Life of Fructuosus,* with recently discovered additional sections, is edited in M.C. Diaz y Diaz, *La Vida de San Fructuoso de Braga,* (Braga, 1974), and for the writings of Valerius of Bierzo see R. Fernandez Pousa, *San Valerio: Obras,* (Madrid, 1942), apart from a series of acrostic verses by him, which may be found in M.C. Diaz y Diaz, *Anecdota Wisigothica* I, (Salamanca, 1958).

The inscriptions, mostly sepulchral, dating from Late Roman and Visigothic times are collected in J. Vives, *Inscripciones Cristianas de la España Romana y Visigoda* 2nd ed. (Barcelona, 1969). For the Jews in Visigothic Spain see the important general treatment of B. Blumenkranz, *Juifs et Chrétiens dans le Monde Occidental, 430–1096,* (Paris, 1960). Art is conveniently surveyed in H. Schlunk, 'Art Visigodo', *Ars Hispaniae* II, (Madrid, 1947), and receives more extended coverage in J. Fontaine, *L'Art Préroman Hispanique,* (La Pierre-Qui-Vire, 1973).

(c) *The Umayyad State and the Mozarabs*

The best account of the intellectual culture of Al-Andalus is J. Vernet, *La Cultura Hispanoárabe en Oriente y Occidente,* (Barcelona, 1978), and for its role in the wider Islamic world, see M.A. Makki, *Ensayo sobre les Aportaciones Orientales en la España Musulmana y su Influencia en la Formacion de la Cultura Hispano-Árabe,* (Madrid, 1968). The texts of all the Mozarabic writers—Elipandus, Eulogius, Alvar, Samson and the rest—will be found in J. Gil (ed.), *Corpus Scriptorum Muzarabicorum,* 2 vols (Madrid, 1973), to which should be added C. Pellat (ed.), *Le Calendrier de Cordue,* (Leiden, 1961), a mixed Latin and Arabic work containing a combination of liturgical and astronomical information, dating from the tenth century. The principal studies of the Mozarabs are F.J. Simonet, *Historia de los Mozárabes de España,* (Madrid, 1903), and I. de las Cagigas, *Los Mozárabes,* 2 vols (Madrid, 1948). For their establishment in the north see M. Gomez-Moreno, *Las Iglesias Mozárabes,* (Madrid, 1919), and on the art of the illuminated *Beatus* manuscript H. Stierlin, *Die Visionen der Apokalypse,* (Zurich, 1978). For a detailed survey of Mozarabic art there is J. Fontaine, *L'Art Mozarabe,* (La Pierre-Qui-Vire, 1977). See also the studies in *Arte y Cultura Mozárabe* (Toledo, 1979).

(d) *The Christian Realms*

The great commentary on the *Apocalypse of Beatus of Liébana* is edited by H. Saunders, *Beati in Apocalipsin Libri Duodecim,* (Rome, 1950). See also L. Vazquez de Parga, 'La Biblia en el Reino Astur-Leones', *Settimane di . . . Spoleto,* 10 (Spoleto, 1963) pp. 258–80. On the art of the Asturian kingdom there is H. Schlunk, 'Arte Asturiano' *Ars Hispaniae* II, (Madrid, 1947). For learning and the copying of manuscripts in the kingdom of Pamplona see M.C. Diaz y Diaz, *Libros y Librerías en la Rioja Altomedieval,* (Logroño, 1979). There are three important studies of Oliba, the leading figure in the intellectual life of early Catalonia: R. d'Abadal i de Vinyals, *L'Abat Oliba i la Seva Època* (Barcelona, 1948), E. Junyent, *Commemoració Millenària del Naixment de l'Abat-Bisbe Oliba: Esbós Biogràfic,* (Montserrat, 1971), and the substantial biography, A.M. Albareda, *L'Abat Oliba: Assaig Biogràfic,* (Montserrat, 1972). For his monastery of Ripoll see E. Junyent, *El Monastir Romanic de Santa Maria de Ripoll,* (Barcelona, 1975). For its scientific learning see J.M. Millas Vallicrosa, *Assaig d'Historia de les Ciències Físiques i Matemàtiques a la Catalunya Mig.eval,* (Barcelona, 1931), and for its school of poetry of the time of Oliba, N. d'Olwer, 'L'Escola Poètica de Ripoll en els Segles X–XIII', *Anuari de l'Institut d'Estudis Catalans,* 6 (1915–20). For the distinctive art of the region there is W. Neuss, *Die Katalanische Bibelillustration um die Wende des ersten Jahrtausends und die altspanische Buchmalerei,* (Bonn-Leipzig, 1922).

ADDENDA TO THE BIBLIOGRAPHIES

On questions of language there is now R.P. Wright, *Late Latin and Early Romance in Spain and Carolingian France* (Liverpool, 1982). The results of a major excavation of a Visigothic church and monastic site, with briefer treatment of two comparable structures, have been published in L. Caballero Zoreda and J.I. Latorre Macarrón, *La iglesia y el monasterio visigodo de Santa Maria de Melque (Toledo), San Pedro de la Mata (Toledo) y Santa Comba de Bande (Orense)* (Madrid, 1980). For Muslim Spain the augmented later editions of C. Sanchez-Albornoz, *La España Musulmana*, which collects in systematic chronological order Spanish translations of the principal Arabic sources, should be consulted in preference to the first edition of 1946 (6th edn Madrid, 1982). Sources in Spanish translation relating to the history and topography of Cordoba in the Umayyad period are now conveniently collected together in A. Arjona Castro, *Anales de Córdoba Musulmana* (Cordoba, 1982). There is a useful social and administrative analysis, covering the whole period from 711 to 1492, in R. Arié, *España Musulmana* (Barcelona, 1982), part of a new history of Spain in ten volumes. The second of these, J.J. Sayas Abengochea and L.A. Garcia Moreno, *Romanismo y germanismo. El despertar de los pueblos hispánicos* (Barcelona, 1982) is also relevant to the period of this book. Welcome publication of archival materials continues, and for Leon there is now G. del Ser Quijano, *Documentación de la Catedral de Leon (Siglos IX-X)* (Salamanca, 1981), and, based on a previous edition of texts, there is an important economic study of a Leonese monastery, later to be the foremost Cluniac house in Spain, in J.L. Minguez Martin, *El dominio del monasterio de Sahagún en el siglo X* (Salamanca, 1980). There are further controversial studies of the development of society in the north of the peninsula from the Visigothic to the Leonese periods in A. Barbero and M. Vigil, *La formacción del feudalismo en la península ibérica* (Barcelona, 1978). For the creation of the kingdom of Aragon and its first monarch see A. Duran Gudiol, *Ramiro I de Aragon* (Zaragoza, 1978).

References

INTRODUCTION

1. Ammianus Marcellinus, *Res Gestae* XXXI, vol. III ed. J.C. Rolfe (Loeb Library, 1939) pp. 376–505 (Latin with English translation), for the relations between the Romans and the Visigoths, the battle of Adrianople, and the rise of the Huns.

2. Cf. O. Lattimore, *The Inner Asian Frontiers of China*, (New York, 1951), ch. 4 and pp. 542–9.

3. E.A. Thompson, *The Goths in the time of Ulfila*, (Oxford, 1966), chs 4 and 5.

4. For example A. Barbero and M. Vigil, *Sobre los Orígenes Sociales de la Reconquista* (Barcelona, 1974), also N. Santos Yanguas, *El Ejército y la Romanizacion de los Astures*, (Oviedo, 1981).

5. See the collected studies in *Les Empereurs Romains d'Espagne*, (Paris, 1965).

6. J.F. Matthews, 'A Pious Supporter of Theodosius I: Maternus Cynegius and his Family', *Journal of Theological Studies*, n.s. XVIII (1967) pp. 438–46.

7. A. Balil, *Historia Social y Económica: La España Romana (Siglos I–III)*, (Madrid, 1975).

8. R. Thouvenot, *Essai sur la Province Romaine de Bétique*, (Paris, 1940), for the south; for Galicia, see Tranoy (*n.* 12 below). Studies of the other provinces of Roman Spain are currently being undertaken.

9. *Epistle to the Romans* XV. 24, 28.

10. J.M. Blazquez, 'The Possible African Origin of Iberian Christianity', *Classical Folia* XXIII, (1969) pp. 3–31. Cf. contra: *Historia de la Iglesia de España* I (B1) part I, ch. 4.

11. H. Chadwick, *Priscillian of Avila*, (Oxford, 1976), also A. d'Alès, *Priscillien et l'Espagne Chrétienne à la fin du IVe Siècle*, (Paris, 1936).

12. See most recently, A. Tranoy, *La Galice Romaine*, (Paris, 1981).

13. J. Caro Baroja, *Sobre la Lengua Vasca*, (San Sebastian, 1979). The origins of the Basque language still remain a subject for dispute.

14. Strabo, *Géographie* III, ed. F. Lasserre (Paris: Ed. Budé, 1966), vol. II.

1. THE EMERGENCE OF A NEW ORDER

1. Augustine, *De Civitate Dei* I passim, ed. C. Tauchnitz, (Leipzig, 1877) pp. 3–38.

2. A.H.M. Jones, *The Later Roman Empire*, 3 vols (Oxford, 1964) pp. 756–7, 774–5, 777–8; R. Thouvenot, 'Salvian and the Ruin of the Roman Empire', *Antiquity*, VIII (1934) pp. 315–27.

3. S. Mazzarino, *The End of the Ancient World* (Eng. tr. London, 1966) chs 1 and 4.

4. Sidonius Apollinaris, *Poems and Letters*, 2 vols, ed. and tr. W.B. Anderson (Loeb Library, 1936); see especially his description of the court of the Visigothic king Theoderic II, ep. I.2, vol. I, pp. 334–45.

5. Orosius (Bibliog. A2-*a*) prologue, pp. 3–5.

6. J.F. Matthews, 'Olympiodorus of Thebes and the History of the West (AD407–425)', *Journal of Roman Studies*, LX (1970), pp. 79–97.

7. Orosius (Bibliog. A2-*a*) VII. 40, pp. 356–7; Zosimus (A2-*a*) V.27, p. 222; Olympiodorus (A2-*a*), pp. 30–1.

8. Orosius (A2-*a*) VII. 40, p. 356; Zosimus V. 43, VI.1 and 5.

9. Orosius (A2-*a*) VII. 40, p. 357; Hydatius (B2-*a*) 42, p. 114.

10. Orosius (A2-*a*) VII. 42, p. 359; Olympiodorus (A2-*a*), pp. 36–7; Gregory of

Tours, *Historiarum Libri Decem* II.9, ed. B. Krusch and W. Levison, *M.G.H., S.R.G.* I (new edition, Hanover, 1951), tr. Q.M. Dalton (Oxford, 1927) vol. II p. 52.

11. Olympiodorus (A2–*a*), p. 36; Hydatius (B2–*a*) 48, p. 116.

12. Orosius (A2–*a*) VII. 40, p. 357; E.A. Thompson, 'The End of Roman Spain' (A2–*a*), pt. I, pp. 18–28.

13. Orosius VII. 42, p. 359.

14. Olympiodorus (A2–*a*), pp. 40–2.

15. Hydatius (B2–*a*) 77, p. 124; *Chronica Gallica* 107, ed. T. Mommsen, *M.G.H., A.A.* IX, p. 658.

16. Hydatius (B2–*a*) 91, p. 130.

17. Hydatius (B2–*a*) 111–75, pp. 134–56.

18. Hydatius (B2–*a*) 96, p. 130.

19. Hydatius (B2–*a*) 91, 96, 100 (Galicia); 137, 142 (the North East); 119, 123 (Lusitania and Baetica), pp. 130, 132, 136, 138, 142.

20. Hydatius (B2–*a*) 137, p. 142.

21. Hydatius (B2–*a*) 134, p. 140.

22. Hydatius (B2–*a*) 168, p. 152.

23. Hydatius (B2–*a*) 175, p. 156.

24. Hydatius (B2–*a*) 181, 188, 190, 193, 195, 198 (Maldras); 139, 180, 187 (Agiulf); 188, 189 (Framtane); 193, 202–3, 219 (Rechimund); 201, 203, 223 (Frumarius); 220, 223, 226, 233, 237, 238, 251 (Remismund).

25. Hydatius (B2–*a*) 186, 192, pp. 158, 160.

26. *Chronica Gallica A DXI* 651–2, ed. T. Mommsen, *M.G.H., A.A.* IX (Berlin, 1892), pp. 664–5.

27. See the discussion in W. Goffart, *Barbarians and Romans AD418–584: The Techniques of Accommodation*, (Princeton, 1980).

28. J. Vives, *Inscripciones Christianas de la España Romana y Visigoda* (B4–*b*) no. 363, pp. 126–7.

29. E.A. Lowe, *Codices Latini Antiquiores*, no. 626 (Paris B.N. lat. 12161), editions by K. Zeumer and A. d'Ors (B2–*b*).

30. *L.V.* II.i.5;

31. A. d'Ors, *El. Código de Eurico* (Rome and Madrid, 1960) pp. 47–281; see also R.J.H. Collins, 'Theodebert I, Rex Magnus Francorum' in P. Wormald (ed.), *Ideal and Reality in the Early Middle Ages*, (Oxford, 1983).

32. Isidore, *H.G.* 51 (A2–*b*), p. 24; (B2–*b*), p. 288.

33. Due to appear as *Estudios Visigoticos IV: El Código de Leovigildo*, ed. R. Gibert, in *Cuadernos del Instituto Juridico Español en Roma*.

34. *Codex Euricanus* (B2–*b*) 277 and 305, ed. Zeumer pp. 5 and 16.

35. Cf. C.P. Wormald, *'Lex Scripta* and *Verbum Regis'* in P.H. Sawyer and I.N. Wood (eds), *Early Medieval Kingship*, (Leeds, 1977) p. 129. The reference in Sidonius's Epistle VIII.iii is surely a *topos*.

36. Isidore, *H.G.* 35 (A2–*b*), p. 17; (B2–*b*), p. 281.

37. Cf. J.M. Wallace-Hadrill, *The Long-Haired Kings*, (London, 1962) pp. 179–81.

38. *Lex Gundobada* constitutio I.3, ed. L.R. de Salis, *M.G.H.*, Leges II.i (Hanover, 1892).

39. A. d'Ors, *El Código de Eurico* (B2–*b*), pp. 2–12.

40. W. Ashburner, 'The Farmer's Law', *Journals of Hellenic Studies*, XXXII (1912) pp. 87–95; Greek Text *ibid.* XXX (1910) pp. 97–108.

41. *Codex Euricanus* (B2–*b*) 335, ed. Zeumer, p. 27.

42. Edictum Theodorici Regis, ed. J. Baviera in *Fontes Iuris Romani Anteiustiniani* II (Florence, 1968) pp. 684–710. A controversial attempt to attribute it to the Visigothic king Theoderic II is found in G. Vismara, 'El Edictum Theodorici', *Estudios Visigóticos I*, (Rome and Madrid, 1956) pp. 49–89.

43. A.H.M. Jones, *The Later Roman Empire* 3 vols (Oxford, 1964) p. 473.

44. M.J. Hunter, 'The Gothic Bible' in *Cambridge History of the Bible*, II (Cambridge, 1969) pp. 338–62, 525–6.

45. *Acta* edited by C. de Clercq in *Corpus Christianorum Series Latina*, CXLVIII (Turnholt, 1963) pp. 189–228.

2. THE IMPOSITION OF UNITY

1. Gregory of Tours, *Historiarum Libri Decem*, II.37, tr. O.M. Dalton, (Oxford, 1927), vol. II pp. 77–8; see also Cassiodorus, *Variae* III. 1–4, ed. T. Mommsen, *M.G.H., A.A.* XII, pp. 78–81 for Ostrogothic attempts at mediation.

2. Jordanes, *Getica*, ed. T. Mommsen, *M.G.H., A.A.* v.i (Berlin, 1882), tr. C.C. Mierow, *The Gothic History of Jordanes*, 2nd edn (Princeton, 1915): Isidore, *H.G.* 36 (A2–*b*), p. 18.

3. Isidore, *H.G.* 37–8 (A2–*b*), pp. 18–9.

4. Jordanes LVIII (*n*. 2 above), tr. Mierow, p. 137.

5. Isidore, *H.G.* 39 (A2–*b*), p. 19; Arcipreste de Talavera, *Vida de San Isidoro*, ed. J. Madoz, (Madrid, 1962) ch. 1, p. 70.

6. Gregory of Tours (*n*. 1 above) III.10, tr. Dalton, pp. 92–3; Isidore, *H.G.* 40 (A2–*b*), p. 19.

7. *Chronicorum Caesaraugustanorum Reliquiae*, ed. T. Mommsen, *M.G.H., A.A.* XI (Berlin, 1894) pp. 222–3. I hope to demonstrate these conclusions in a future paper.

8. *Ibid.* p. 222.

9. Ammianus Marcellinus, *Res Gestae* XXVII. v.6, ed. J.C. Rolfe, (Loeb Library: 1939) vol. III, p. 32; H. Wolfram, 'Athanaric the Visigoth: Monarchy or Judgeship. A study in Comparative History', *Journal of Medieval History*, I (1975) pp. 259–278.

10. Sidonius Apollinaris, *Panegyric on Avitus* (Carmen VII), line 505, ed. W.B. Anderson, (Loeb Library, 1936) vol. I, p. 160. Is *avus* here exact?

11. Procopius, *History of the Wars*, v. xii. 50–4, ed. H.B. Dewing (Loeb Library, 1919), vol. III, pp. 130–3.

12. Isidore, *H.G.* 42 (A2–*b*), p. 20.

13. Isidore, *H.G.* 43 (A2–*b*), pp. 20–1; *Lex Theudi Regis, L.V.*, pp. 467–9. (B2–*b*).

14. Isidore, *H.G.* 44 (A2–1*b*), p. 21: Jordanes LVIII (*n*. 2 above), tr. p. 138.

15. Isidore, *H.G.* 45 (A2–*b*), pp. 21–22.

16. E.A. Thompson, *The Goths in Spain*, (A2–*b*), pp. 320–3, gives the arguments.

17. P. Grierson, 'Una Ceca Bizantina en España', *Numario Hispanico*, IV (1955) pp. 305–14.

18. Jordanes LVIII (*n*. 2 above), tr. p. 138.

19. Fredegar, *Chronicle* IV. 42, ed. J.M. Wallace-Hadrill, (London, 1960), p. 35; J. Nelson, 'Queens as Jezebels: the Careers of Brunhild and Balthild in Merovingian History' in D. Baker (ed.), *Medieval Women*, (Oxford, 1978) pp. 31–77.

20. Isidore, *H.G.* 48 (A2–*b*), pp. 22–3; John of Biclar, *Chronicle* (B2–*b*), p. 213.

21. *V.P.E.* (A3–*b*), v. v. 2-vi. 2, pp. 200–9.

22. J. Vives, *Concilios* (B4–*b*), pp. 53–64.

23. Isidore, *D.V.I.* XXXI (B2–*b*), pp. 151–2.

24. *Victoris Tonnennensis Episcopi Chronica*, ed. T. Mommsen, *M.G.H., A.A.* XI, pp. 184–206.

25. J. Vives, *Concilios* (B4–*b*), pp. 155, 157, 161, 162.

26. *V.P.E.* (A3–*b*), pp. 208–10.

27. Gregory of Tours, *Histories* (see *n*. 1 above) V.37, tr. pp. 208–9, and *De Miraculis Sancti Martini* I.11, *P.L.* LXXI, cc. 923–5.

28. John of Biclar, *Chronicle* (B2–*b*), pp. 212–5.

29. *Ibid.* p. 215; K. Raddatz, 'Studien zu Recopolis I: Die Archaolögischen Befunde', *Madrider Mitteilungen*, V (1964), pp. 213–33.

30. John of Biclar, *Chronicle* (B2–*b*), p. 215.

31. Gregory of Tours, *Histories* (see *n.* 1 above), V. 38, tr. p. 209.

32. John of Biclar, *Chronicle* (B2–*b*), p. 216.

33. See the arguments of R.J.H. Collins, 'Mérida and Toledo, 550–585', *V.S.*, pp. 215–8. (A2–*b*).

34. He is treated as a martyr in the *De Vana Saeculi Sapientia* of Valerius of Bierzo, ed. R.F. Pousa, *San Valerio: Obras*, (Madrid, 1942) pp. 145–57.

35. G.C. Miles, *Coinage of the Visigoths* (A3–*b*), pp. 182–98.

36. Gregory of Tours, *Histories* (see *n.* 1 above), VI.43, tr. p. 275; John of Biclar, *Chronicle* (B2–*b*), p. 216, also Isidore *H.G.* 91 (A2–*b*), p. 42.

37. *Epistulae Austrasicae* 27, 28, 43–5, ed. W. Gundlach, *Corpus Christianorum Series Latina*, CXVII (Turnholt, 1957), pp. 450–7, 465–7.

38. Gregory the Great, *Dialogues* III. xxxi, ed. A de Vogüé, *Sources Chrétiennes*, 260 (Paris, 1979) pp. 384–91.

39. John of Biclar, *Chronicle* (B2–*b*), pp. 216–7.

40. J.N. Hillgarth, 'Coins and Chronicles' (A2–*b*).

41. *V.P.E.* (A3–*b*) V. iv. 1–8, pp. 198–201.

42. Isidore, *D.V.I.* XXX (B4–*b*), p. 151.

43. John of Biclar, *Chronicle* (B2–*b*), p. 216.

44. Isidore, *D.V.I.* XXVIII and XXX (B4–*b*), pp. 149–51.

45. R.J.H. Collins, 'Mérida and Toledo, 550–585', *V.S.* (A2–*b*).

46. Gregory the Great, *Registrum Epistolarum*, I. 41, ed. P. Ewald and L.M. Hartmann, *M.G.H., Epp.* I (Berlin, 1957) pp. 56–8.

47. J. Vives, *Concilios* (B4–*b*), p. 160.

48. *V.P.E.* V. xi. 15 (A3–*b*), pp. 242–3.

49. Ibid. V. xii. 2–5, pp. 244–7.

50. J. Vives, *Concilios* (B4–*b*), pp. 154–5.

51. John of Biclar, *Chronicle* (B2–*b*), pp. 219–20.

3. A CHURCH TRIUMPHANT

1. Nanctus: *V.P.E.* III (A3–*b*), pp. 154–61; Donatus: Ildefonsus, *D.V.I.* (B4–*b*), pp. 121–2.

2. R.J.H. Collins, 'Fulgentius von Ruspe', *Theologische Realenzyklopädie* XI.

3. Isidore, *D.V.I.* XIV (B4–*b*), p. 142; J. Fontaine, *Isidore de Séville* (B4–*b*), pp. 857–9.

4. Isidore, *D.V.I.* VIII, XIX, XXV, (B4–*b*), pp. 138–9, 144, 147; Fontaine, *op. cit.* pp. 857–9.

5. e.g. the *Contra Varimadum*, ed. B. Schwank, *Corpus Christianorum Series Latina*, XC (Turnholt, 1961) pp. 1–134, and vii–x.

6. As indicated by the numerous citations throughout the whole corpus of extant Visigothic Latin texts.

7. R. Grégoire, *Les Homéliaires du Moyen Âge*, (Rome, 1966) pp. 161–85 and Appendix 2.

8. L.A. Garcia Moreno, *Prosopografia del reino visigodo de Toledo* (Salamanca, 1974) nos. 178 and 192.

9. *Ibid.* no. 179.

10. *Ibid.* no. 245; Ildefonsus, *D.V.I.* VI (B4–*b*), pp. 125–6.

11. J. Vives, *Concilios* (B4–*b*), p. 222.

12. C.H. Lynch and P. Galindo, *San Braulio* (B4–*b*), pp. 356–61 (text).

13. *Etymologiae*, ed. Lindsay (B4–*b*), III. 29 (no page refs).

14. *Differentiae* I. 6, *P.L.* LXXXIII, c. 10.

15. A. Reise (ed.), *Anthologia Latina*, (Leipzig, 1906), no. 483; J. Fontaine, *Isidore de Séville: Traité de la Nature*, (Bordeaux, 1960).

16. Isidore, *Ep.* XI (A4–b), pp. 56–7.

17. Redemptus, *Liber de Transitu S. Isidori*, *P.L.* LXXXI, cc. 30–2.

18. J.M. Wallace-Hadrill, *The Barbarian West* (A2–b), p. 124.

19. Isidore *H.G.* 61 (A2–b), p. 28; 62, pp. 28–9.

20. *Vita et Passio Sancti Desiderii*, ed. J. Gil, *Miscellanea Wisigothica*, (Seville, 1972), pp. 53–68.

21. Ep. VIII, ed. J. Gil, *ibid.*, pp. 19–27.

22. Fredegar, *Chronicle* IV. 33, ed. J.M. Wallace-Hadrill, (London, 1960), pp. 21–2.

23. Isidore, *H.G.* 61 (A2–b), p. 28.

24. Isidore, *D.V.I.* XXXIII (B4–b), p. 153.

25. L. Vazquez de Parga (ed.), *Vita S. Aemiliani*, (Madrid, 1943), p. 3.

26. Ildefonsus, *D.V.I.* (B4–b); Julian, *Elogium Ildefonsi*, *P.L.* XCVI, cc. 43–4; Felix, *Encomium Juliani*, *ibid.* cc. 445–52.

27. J. Vives, *Concilios* (B4–b), pp. 403–9.

28. R.J.H. Collins, 'Julian of Toledo and the Royal Succession' (A2–b).

29. Férotin (ed.), *Liber Ordinum*, cc. 149–56 (B4–b), some of which is translated by J.N. Hillgarth, *The Conversion of Western Europe* (Englewood Cliffs N.J., 1969), pp. 90–2.

30. R.J.H. Collins, 'Mérida and Toledo, 550–585' *V.S.* (A2–b), pp. 213–14; C. García Rodriguez, *El Culto de los Santos* (B4–b), pp. 246–53.

31. Braulio, Epp. 31–2 (A4–b), pp. 71–4; (B4–b), pp. 132–5.

32. Taio, *Epistle* and *Sententiae*, *P.L.* LXXX, cc. 723–990.

33. Ildefonsus, *D.V.I.* XIII (B4–b), pp. 132–5.

34. J. Madoz, *Le Symbole du XIeme Concile de Tolède*, (Louvain, 1938).

35. Ildefonsus, *D.V.I.* XIII (B4–b), p. 134; the Hymn: C. Blume, *Analecta Hymnica*, XXVII (Leipzig, 1897) pp. 125–7. C.H. Lynch, *Saint Braulio* (A4–b), pp. 236–40.

36. Ildefonsus, *ibid.*

37. C. Codoñer Merino, *El 'De Viris Illustribus' de Ildefonso de Toledo* (B4–b), pp. 46–58.

38. L.A. Garcia Moreno, *Prosopografia*, nos 250 and 584.

39. Ildefonsus, *De Virginitate Perpetua Sanctae Mariae* I, ed. V. Blanco Garcia (B4–b), p. 49.

40. For example the *Missa de Nativitate* (Alia) in the *Liber Sacramentorum* (B4–b), c. 54.

41. Ed. cit. (*n.* 39 above), pp. 12–23.

42. *Prognosticum*, ed. J.N. Hillgarth (B4–b), pp. XXV–XXXVI.

43. See the 'rehabilitation' by F.X. Murphy, 'Julian of Toledo and the Fall of the Visigothic Kingdom' (A2–b).

44. F.X. Murphy, 'Julian of Toledo and the condemnation of Monotheletism' (A4–b).

45. For a poem attributed to Bishop Sisbert, *Lamentum Poenitentiae*, ed. K. Strecker, *M.G.H., Poetae* IV (Berlin, 1923), pp. 770–83.

46. G.C. Miles, *Coinage of the Visigoths* (A3–b), p. 405. Vives, *Concilios* (B4–b), pp. 507–15.

47. *Chronica Muzarabica* 44, ed. J. Gil (B2–c), p. 32.

48. Ildefonsus, *D.V.I.* III (B4–b), pp. 120–2. For Eutropius at III Toledo, John of Biclar, *Chronicle* (B2–b), p. 219.

49. *Vita Caesarii* I. v. 42, *P.L.* LXVII, c. 1021; R.J.H. Collins, 'Caesarius von Arles' in *Theologische Realenzyklopädie*, VII, pp. 531–6.

50. J. Gonzalez Echegaray, *Los Cántabros*, (Madrid, 1966) pp. 236–8.

51. *Acta Sanctorum* Ianuarii I (Antwerp, 1643) pp. 738–43.

52. Venantius Fortunatus, *Opera Poetica*, IV. xi, ed. F. Leo, *M.G.H. A.A.* IV. i (Berlin, 1881) p. 87. For Asan as a source of bishops, see J.M. Wallace-Hadrill, *The Barbarian West* (n. 18 above), p. 127.

53. M.C. Diaz y Diaz, 'Early Christianity in Lugo', *Classical Folia*, XXXII (1978) pp. 243–59.

54. C.J. Bishko, 'The Date and Nature of the Spanish Consensoria Monachorum', *American Journal of Philology*, LXIX (1948) pp. 377–95.

55. Fructuosus, *Rule for the Monastery of Compludo*, tr. C.W. Barlow (A4–*b*), pp. 157–8, 168.

56. *Ibid.* p. 169.

57. Valerius of Bierzo, *Ordo Querimoniae*, VI, ed. and tr. C.M. Aherne (A4–*b*), p. 87.

58. R.F. Pousa, *San Valerio: Obras*, (Madrid, 1942), pp. 1–18.

4. THE SEVENTH-CENTURY KINGDOM

1. *V.P.E.* (A3–*b*), pp. 1–6.

2. M. Almagro *Guia de Mérida*, 6th ed. (Valencia, 1974).

3. I. Richmond, 'The First Years of *Emerita Augusta*' (A2–*a*).

4. M.-H. Quet, *La Mosaique Cosmologique de Mérida*, (Paris, 1981), which, however, argues for a second-century date.

5. For the inscription see note 28 to ch. I; the mosaic is illustrated in R. Bianchi Bandinelli, *Rome, the Late Empire*, (Eng. tr. London, 1971) plate 186, p. 195.

6. *España Sagrada*, XIII (Madrid, 1756), ch. 8.

7. *V.P.E.* IV. ii. 1–18 (A3–*b*), pp. 162–9.

8. P. Fabre, *Saint Paulin de Nole et l'Amitié Chrétienne*, (Paris, 1949) p. 36; Augustine, Epistle 125, *Corpus Scriptorum Ecclesiasticorum Latinorum*, XLIV (Vienna, 1904) pp. 3–7.

9. *V.P.E.* IV. vi. 7–8 (A3–*b*), pp. 178–9.

10. R.J.H. Collins, 'Mérida and Toledo, 550–585', *V.S.* (A2–*b*).

11. Laurence was in origin a Spaniard from Huesca, but his cult began in Rome, of which Church he was traditionally a deacon.

12. *V.P.E.* IV. x. 3–7 (A3–*b*), pp. 186–9.

13. *V.P.E.* v. iii. 11–12, p. 197.

14. *V.P.E.* v. ii. 3–4, pp. 191, 192.

15. J. de C. Serra Ráfols, *La Villa Romana de la Dehesa de La Cocosa*, (Badajoz, 1952).

16. M.C. Diaz y Diaz (ed.), *Vita Fructuosi*, 2, (B4–*b*), p. 82.

17. I.N. Wood, 'The Ecclesiastical Politics of Merovingian Clermont', in P. Wormald (ed.), *Ideal and Reality in the Early Middle Ages*, (Oxford, 1983).

18. H.J. Thomson (ed. and tr.), *Peristephanon*, III, (Loeb Library, 1953) pp. 142–57.

19. A. Fábrega Grau (ed.), *Passionario Hispanico*, (2 vols, Madrid and Barcelona, 1955) vol. I, pp. 255–60.

20. C. García Rodriguez, *El Culto de los Santos*, (B4–*b*), pp. 284–303.

21. P. Jaffé, *Regesta Pontificum Romanorum*, (Leipzig, 1885), no. 891.

22. Gregory of Tours, *Histories*, II. 23 (see note 1 of ch. 2 above), tr. p. 61.

23. *V.P.E.* v. xiv. 1–3 (A3–*b*), pp. 254–5.

24. R.J.H. Collins, 'Mérida and Toledo, 550–585' *V.S.* (A2–*b*), pp. 199–200.

25. *V.P.E.* III. 9 (A3–*b*), pp. 158–9.

26. For fragmentary extant diplomatics of the Visigothic period see M. Mundo Marcet, *Los Diplomas Visigodos Originales en Pergamino*, (Barcelona, 1974).

27. *V.P.E.* III. 11–15 (A3–*b*), pp. 158–61.

28. *Ars Hispaniae*, II (Madrid, 1947), pp. 249–59.

29. Hydatius, *Chronicle* (B2–*a*), 213, 222, pp. 166, 170.

30. C. Sanchez-Albornoz, *Ruina y Extincion del Municipio Romana en España*, (Buenos Aires, 1943).

31. L. Vazquez de Parga (ed.), *Vita Aemiliani*, 26, (Madrid, 1943) p. 34.

32. A. Barbero and M. Vigil, *Sobre los Orígenes Sociales de la Reconquista*, (Barcelona, 1974), pp. 188–90.

33. X Toledo Canon 2, XVI Toledo Canon 10: Vives, *Concilios* (B4–*b*), pp. 310, 509–12.

34. R.J.H. Collins, 'The Basques in Aquitaine and Navarre', in J.C. Holt (ed.), *War, Government and Society in the Middle Ages,* (Ipswich, 1984).

35. Fredegar, *Chronicle* IV. 73, ed. J.M. Wallace-Hadrill, (London, 1960) pp. 61–2.

36. Julian, *Historia Wambae*, 27–9, ed. Levison (B4–*b*), pp. 241–4.

37. *Epistulae Bulgaranis Comitis*, ed. J. Gil, *Miscellanea Wisigothica* (Seville, 1972) pp. 30–44.

38. *Desiderii Episcopi Cadurcensis, Epistolae*, II. 8, ed. W. Arndt, *Corpus Christianorum Series Latina*, CXVII (Turnholt, 1957) pp. 331–2.

39. *L.V.* II. i. 8 (B2–*b*), pp. 53–7; VI Toledo c. xii, Vives, *Concilios* (B4–*b*), p. 241.

40. C. Wickham, *Early Medieval Italy*, (London, 1981) pp. 31–2.

41. *Historia Wambae*, 3 (B2–*b*), pp. 219–20.

42. Taio of Zaragoza, *Epistola ad Quiricum*, *P.L.* LXXX, c. 727.

43. Fredegar, *Chronicle*, IV. 82, ed. Wallace-Hadrill, (London, 1960) pp. 69–70.

44. J. Vives, *Concilios* (B4–*b*), pp. 226–48, esp. V Tol. c. vi, p. 229 and VI Toledo Canon xiv, p. 242.

45. *L.V.* II. i. 6 (B2–*b*), pp. 48–52; Vives, *Concilios* (B4–*b*), p. 290.

46. Braulio, *Ep.* 37 (A4–*b*), pp. 83–5, (B4–*b*) p. 148.

47. V Toledo Canons ii, iv, v, VI Toledo Canons xii, xvii, xviii, cf. XII Toledo Canon iii, all in Vives, *Concilios* (B4–*b*); see also *L.V.* II. i. 6 (B2–*b*), p. 52.

48. E.A. Thompson, *The Goths in Spain*, (A2–*b*), p. 205.

49. G. Martínez Díez, *La Colección Canónica Hispana*, (Madrid, 1966) pp. 306–25.

50. Isidore *Ep.* 10 (A4–*b*), section 4, pp. 52–5.

51. G.C. Miles, *Coinage of the Visigoths*, (A3–*b*), p. 321.

52. XII Toledo Canon i, Vives, *Concilios* (B4–*b*), pp. 385–7.

53. J. Vives, *Concilios*, pp. 465–71.

54. Isidore, *Etymologiae* (B4–*b*) IX. iii. 1–5; *Sententiae*, III. xlix–li; IV Toledo Canon lxxv, Vives, *Concilios* (B4–*b*), pp. 217–21.

55. *Historia Wambae* 2 (B2–*b*), p. 218.

56. C.P. Wormald, 'Lex Scripta and Verbum Regis' in P.H. Sawyer and I.N. Wood (eds), *Early Medieval Kingship*, (Leeds, 1977) p. 130.

57. P.D. King, 'King Chindasvind and the First Territorial Law Code' *V.S.* (A2–*b*), pp. 131–57.

58. *L.V.* (B2–*b*), p. XIX = Manuscript R1, see *Codices Latini Antiquiores*, 111. (seventh century).

59. *C.L.A.* nos. 556, 617, 703a, 793, 950, 1059, 1064, 1199, 1324, 1362, 1395, 1576, 1637, 1752.

60. Leon Cathedral manuscript 15 (*C.L.A.* 1637), see Z. García Villada, *Catálogo de los Codices y Documentos de la Catedral de León*, (Madrid, 1919) pp. 43–50.

61. P.D. King, *op. cit.* p. 136.

62. T. Mommsen (ed.), *Codex Theodosianus*, V. viii with *Interpretatio*, (1904) pp. 224–5.

63. VIII Toledo Decretum, Vives, *Concilios* (B4–*b*), p. 294.

64. *Ibid.* p. 295.

65. *L.V.* II. i. 8 (B2–*b*), p. 54; on the breaking of the oath (VII Toledo Canon 1, Vives, *Concilios*, pp. 249–53) see VIII Toledo Canon ii, *ibid.* pp. 268–77.

66. Eugenius, *Carmen* XXV (B4–*b*), pp. 250–1.

67. *Edict of Rothari*, 2, tr. K. Fischer Drew, *The Lombard Laws* (Philadelphia, 1973), p. 53.

68. XII Toledo Canon vii, Vives, *Concilios* (B4–*b*), pp. 394–5, and Ervig's *Tome, ibid.* p. 383.

69. *Chronicle of Sampiro*: – Silos version (B2–*d*), p. 344.

70. F. Cantera and J.M. Millas Vallicrosa, *Las Inscripciones Hebraicas de España*, (Madrid, 1956).

71. L. García Iglesias, *Los Judios en la España Antigua*, (Madrid, 1978), pp. 95–9.

72. Isidore, *H.G.* 60 (A2–*b*), pp. 27–8; IV Toledo Canon lvii, Vives, *Concilios* (B4–*b*), pp. 210–11.

73. *Ibid.* pp. 210–14,

74. VI Toledo Canon iii, VIII Toledo Canon xii, *ibid.* pp. 236–7, 285.

75. Cf. B. Albert, 'Un Nouvel Examen de la Politique Anti-Juive Wisigothique', *Revue des Études Juives*, CXXXV (1976), pp. 4–29.

76. *L.V.* XII. ii. 12–14 (B2–*b*), pp. 417–23.

77. *L.V.* XII. ii. 1–11, *ibid.* pp. 411–17.

78. IX Toledo Canon xvii, Vives, *Concilios* (B4–*b*), pp. 305–6.

79. *L.V.* XII. iii. (B2–*b*), pp. 429–56.

80. E.A. Thompson, *The Goths in Spain* (A2–*b*), pp. 232–3.

81. XVI Toledo Canon 1, Vives, *Concilios* (B4–*b*), pp. 497–8.

82. *Ibid.* pp. 523–7, 534–6.

83. J. Gil (ed.), *Miscellanea Wisigothica*, (Seville, 1972) pp. 48–9.

84. F. Dahn (ed.), *Die Könige der Germanen*, VII (1885), pp. 650–3.

85. *L.V.* XII. ii. 17 (B2–*b*), pp. 425–6.

86. *P.L.* LXXXIII, cc. 449–538.

87. Epistle 3, J. Madoz (ed.), *Liciniano de Cartagena y Sus Cartas*, (Madrid, 1948) pp. 125–9.

88. *L.V.* XII. ii. 16 (B2–*b*), p. 424.

89. V Toledo Canon 1, VI Toledo Canon ii, XVII Toledo Canon vi. Vives, *Concilios* (B4–*b*), pp. 226–7, 235–6, 532, rising from annual to monthly observance.

90. A. Sharf, *Byzantine Jewry*, (London, 1971) pp. 42–60; Fredegar, *Chronicle* IV. 65, ed. Wallace-Hadrill (London, 1960) p. 54.

91. Cf. N. Bonwetsch (ed.), *Doctrina Iacobi Nuper Baptizati*, (Berlin, 1910).

92. As in Jerusalem after its fall to the Persians in 614: Antiochus Strategos, *Account of the Sack of Jerusalem*, trs. F.C. Conybeare, *English Historical Review*, XXV (1910) pp. 502–17.

93. *L.V.* XII. ii. 18 (B2–*b*), pp. 426–7.

94. J. Vallvé, 'España en el Siglo VIII: Ejército y Sociedad', *Al-Andalus*, XLIII (1978) pp. 51–112.

95. E.A. Thompson, *The Goths in Spain* (A2–*b*), pp. 271–4.

96. *L.V.* IX. i. 9, 16–18 (B2–*b*), pp. 356–8, 361–3.

97. *L.V.* VI. i. 3 (B2–*b*), pp. 250–1; E.A. Thompson, *The Goths in Spain* (A2–*b*), p. 259.

5. THE ARAB CONQUEST: THE NEW MASTERS

1. I. Goldziher, 'On the development of the Hadīth', in his *Muslim Studies*, II, ed. and tr. S.M. Stern (London, 1971) pp. 17–251.

2. In general, H.A.R. Gibb, 'Ta'rikh', in *Encyclopedia of Islam* (A2–*c*), Supplementary vol. (1938) pp. 233–45.

3. J. Ribera (tr., Spanish), *Historia de los Jueces de Córdoba*, (Madrid, 1914).

4.   J. Gil (ed.), *Chronica Muzarabica* (B2–*c*), pp. 16–32.

5.   A. Ubieto Arteta, *Crónica de Alfonso III* (B2–*d*), pp. 12–15.

6.   D. Catalan and M. Soledad de Andres (eds), *Crónica del Moro Rasis*, (Madrid, 1975).

7.   Ibn 'Abd al-Ḥakem (A2–*c*), pp. 18–21; also Ibn al-Athīr (B2–*c*) pp. 41–2; *Fatḥ al-Andalus* (B2–*c*) pp. 3–6, 20–1; see also R. Basset, 'Légendes Arabes d'Espagne: La Maison Fermée de Tolède, *Bulletin de la Société Géographique d'Oran*, (1898) pp. 42–58.

8.   For example W. Montgomery Watt, *History of Islamic Spain* (A2–*c*), pp. 13–14; and even E. Lévi-Provençale, *Histoire de l'Espagne Musulmane* (B2–*c*), pp. 12–16.

9.   J. Vallvé, 'Sobre Algunos Problemas de la Invasion Musulmana', *Anuario de Estudios Medievales*, IV (1967) esp. pp. 365–7.

10.   Ibn 'Abd al-Ḥakem (A2–*c*), p. 18; Al-Makkarī (A2–*c*), p. 273.

11.   *Ibid.* p. 268; Ibn 'Abd al-Ḥakem does not refer to them; the most extended treatment is to be found in Ibn al-Kūtiyya (B2–*c*), who claimed descent from them.

12.   (B2–*c*), pp. 28–9.

13.   G.C. Miles, *Coinage of the Visigoths* (A3–*b*), pp. 39–42.

14.   Al-Makkarī (B2–*c*), p. 268; *Fatḥ al-Andalus* (B2–*c*), p. 7.

15.   For example the arguments of L.A. García Moreno, *El Fin del Reino Visigodo de Toledo, Decadencia y Catastrofé*, (Madrid, 1975).

16.   Ibn 'Abd al-Ḥakem (A2–*c*), pp. 24–5; *Al-Bayān* (B2–*c*), pp. 23–4; *Fatḥ* (B2–*c*) pp. 11–12.

17.   *Ibid.* pp. 19–22; Ibn 'Abd al-Ḥakem, p. 28; *Al-Bayān*, pp. 25–9.

18.   *Ibid.* pp. 30–3; Al-Makkarī (A2–*c*), vol. II, pp. 30–1; *Fatḥ*, pp. 23–5.

19.   P. Crone and M. Cook, *Hagarism* (A2–*c*), pp. 3–34.

20.   R.H. Charles (tr.), *Chronicle of John (c. 690 AD) Coptic Bishop of Nikiu*, (London, 1916).

21.   F. Macler (tr.), *Histoire d'Heraclius per l'Évêque Sebéos*, (Paris, 1904).

22.   The principal Arabic source for the life of Moḥammed, the *Sīrat Rasūl Allāh* of Ibn Isḥāk, is translated in A. Guillaume, *The Life of Muhammad* (Lahore etc., 1955).

23.   For a reconstruction of the chronology of the Suras of the Koran, see W. Montgomery Watt, *Companion to the Qur'an*, (London, 1967).

24.   Cf. P. Crone and M. Cook, *Hagarism*, p. 5, for possible interpretations.

25.   On the debts to the past and their transmission, see D. O'Leary, *How Greek Science Passed to the Arabs*, (London, 1949), and P. Hitti, *History of the Arabs* (A2–*c*), ch. 27.

26.   R.W. Southern, *Western Views of Islam in the Middle Ages*, (Cambridge, Massachusetts, 1962) pp. 1–33.

27.   O. Grabar, *The Formation of Islamic Art*, (New Haven and London, 1973) esp. pp. 48–67, 109–38; L. Golvin, *Essai sur l'Architecture Religieuse Musulmane*, vol. II (Paris, 1971).

28.   D. Dennett, *Conversion and the Poll Tax in Early Islam* (Cambridge, Massachusetts, 1950).

29.   M.A. Shaban, *The 'Abbāsid Revolution*, (Cambridge, 1970) pp. 138–68.

30.   Al-Makkarī (A2–*c*), Bk. v. ch. iii, vol. II, pp. 19–29.

31.   *Ibid.* pp. 15–7.

32.   Ibn Khallikān, *Biographical Dictionary*, III. 375, tr. W. Macguckin de Slane, (Paris, 1868).

33.   See H.T. Norris, *The Berbers in Arabic Literature*, (London and Beirut, 1982).

34.   Al-Makkarī (A2–*c*), vol. I, p. 153.

35.   On Berber settlement there are three regional studies: J. Bosch Vilá, 'El Elemento Humano Norteafricano en la Historia de la España Musulmana', *Cuadernos de la Biblioteca Espanola de Tetuan*, II (1964) pp. 17–37. P. Guichard, 'Le Peuplement de la Région de Valencia aux Deux Premiers Siècles de la Domination Musulmane'

Mélanges de la Casa de Velazquez V (1969) pp.103–56; J. Oliver Asin, 'En Torno a los Orígenes de Castilla', *Al-Andalus*, XXXVIII (1973) pp.319–91.

36. *Fath al-Andalus* (B2–*c*), p.39 (Mérida), Ibn al-Athīr (B2–*c*), pp.178, 181 (Tarragona, Talavera).

37. C.-E. Dufourcq, 'La Coexistence des Chrétiens et des Musulmans dans Al-Andalus et dans le Maghrib du Xe Siècle', *Occident et Orient au Xe Siècle*, (Paris, 1979), pp.209–20.

38. R.W. Bulliet, *Conversion to Islam in the Medieval Period*, (Harvard, 1979) pp.114–27.

39. Al-Makkarī (A2–*c*) V. v, vol. II, p.45, and n.17.

40. E. Lévi-Provençale, *Histoire de l'Espagne Musulmane* (B2–*c*), vol. 1, p.39.

41. Al-Makkarī (A2–*c*) V. v, vol. II, pp.41–2; *Al-Bayān* (B2–*c*), pp.44–7, *Fath al-Andalus* (B2–*c*), pp.34–9; Ibn al-Kūtiyya (B2–*c*), p.15.

42. Good examples of the working of Arab feuds can be found in the books of W. Thesiger: *Arabian Sands* and *The Marsh Arabs*; for Germanic feud: J.M. Wallace-Hadrill, 'The Bloodfeud of the Franks' in his *The Long-Haired Kings*, (London, 1962) pp.121–47.

43. Al-Makkarī (A2–*c*) V. v, pp.43–4.

44. *Ibid.* p.49; NB no such story is to be found in *Al-Bayān*

45. Taken from the *Muktabis* of Ibn Hayyān, in Al-Makkarī (A2–*c*), vol. II, pp.58–61.

46. P. Guichard, *Al-Andalus* (B3–*c*), pp.517–57.

47. Al-Makkarī (A2–*c*) V. iii, vol. II, p.24.

48. *Ibid.* I. viii, vol. I, pp.102–11.

49. Ibn Sa'īd in Al-Makkarī (A2–*c*) III. i, vol. I, p.201.

50. Al-Makkarī (A2–*c*) III. iii and iv, vol. I, pp.232–49 (including Medina Azahira).

51. *Ibid.* III. ii, vol. I, pp.213–31; O. Grabar, 'Formation of Islamic Art' (A4–*c*), ch.5.

52. Al-Makkarī (A2–*c*) VI. ii, vol. II, p.81.

53. *Ibid.* II. iii, vol. I, p.152.

54. *Ibid.* vol. II, pp.102–3; Ibn al-Athīr (B2–*c*), pp.177–9.

55. Al-Makkarī (A2–*c*), II. i, vol. I, p.112.

56. *Ibid.* VI. iii, vol. II, p.95.

57. *Ibid.* VI. iv, vol. II, 117–21.

58. *Ibid.* VI. vi, vol. II, p.168, and Appendix C, pp.XXXIX–XLII.

59. Ibn Hayyān, via Ibn Sa'īd, in Al-Makkarī (A2–*c*) I. viii, vol. I, p.98.

60. Al-Makkarī (A2–*c*), vol. I, pp.102–3, and *n.*25, p.397.

61. *Ibid.* VI. vi, vol. II, p.175.

62. *Anonymous Chronicle of 'Abd al-Rahmān III* (B2–*c*) 2, pp.41–5.

63. Al-Makkarī (A2–*c*), I. viii, vol. I, p.111.

64. G.C. Miles, *The Coinage of the Umayyads of Spain.* (A3–*c*), pp.20–2.

65. J.D. Breckenridge, *The Numismatic Iconography of Justinian II*, (New York: 1959) pp.69–77.

66. Al-Makkarī (A2–*c*) II. ii, vol. I, pp.113–15.

67. *Ibid.* VI. iii, vol. II, pp.107–12.

68. J. Vallvé, 'Espana en el Siglo VIII. . .' (B2–*c*).

69. Al-Makkarī (A2–*c*) I. viii, vol. I, p.110.

70. Ibn Sa'īd in al-Makkarī II. i, vol. I, p.116.

71. Ibn Haukal (B2–*c*), p.61.

72. Al-Makkarī (A2–*c*) II. iii, vol. I, p.148.

73. *Ibid.* p.149.

74. *Ibid.* VII. i, vol. II, p.202.

75. Ibn al-Kūtiyya (B2–c), p. 78 for Moḥammed ibn Walīd, Governor of Cordoba, a post that his father had held before him; pp. 49, 59, 70, 88, for three generations of administrators: Isa, Hadjib under 'Abd al-Raḥmān II, his son Umayya, a vizier under Moḥammed I, and his grandson 'Abd al-Raḥmān, Hadjib to the Amir Al-Mundhir.

6. THE UMAYYAD REGIME

1. Aimoin, *De Translatione SS MM Georgii, Aurelii et Nathaliae, P.L.* 115, cc. 942–60, in which Frankish monks used the evacuation to facilitate their departure from Cordoba.

2. C. Sanchez-Albornoz, 'Data del la Batalla de Covadonga' in his *Orígenes de la Nacion Española* (B2–d), pp. 97–135.

3. Ibn Ḥayyān, tr. P. de Gayangos, in his edition of Al-Makkarī (A2–c), vol. II, pp. 448–50.

4. Ibn al-Athīr (B2–c), p. 151; *Al-Bayān* (B2–c), p. 102.

5. Ibn Ḥazm in Al-Makkarī (A2–c) VI. iii, p. 107; Ibn al-Athīr (B2–c), pp. 168–70, 177–9.

6. M. Almagro, *Guia de Mérida*, 6th ed. (Madrid, 1965), pp. 29–33, on the Alcazaba erected by 'Abd al-Raḥmān II: see also pp. 18–21.

7. Ibn al-Athīr (B2–c), pp. 139–40.

8. *Anonymous chronicle of 'Abd al-Raḥmān III* (B2–c) 2, pp. 91–5.

9. For the Banu Ḳasī, see E. Lévi-Provençale, *Histoire de l'Espagne Musulmane* (B2–c), vol. I, pp. 154–6, 213–18, 323–9, 387–94, vol. II, pp. 30–2.

10. W. Montgomery Watt, *History of Islamic Spain* (A2–c), pp. 128–31; see also D.M. Dunlop, *Arab Civilisation to AD 1500* (London and Beirut, 1971), pp. 65–6 and note 195, p. 283.

11. C. Sanchez-Albornoz, 'El Tercer Rey de España', *Cuadernos de Historia de España*, 49–50 (1969) pp. 5–49.

12. Ibn al-Athīr (B2–c), pp. 118–25; *Al-Bayān* (B2–c), pp. 85–8.

13. Ibn al-Athīr, pp. 206–7; *Crónica de Alfonso III* (B2–d), pp. 44–5.

14. Ibn al-Athīr, p. 197.

15. Al-Makkarī (A2–c) VI. iii, vol. II, pp. 106–7.

16. C. Verlinden, 'Traite et Esclavage dans la Vallée de la Meuse', in *Mélanges Felix Rousseau*, (Bruxelles, 1958), pp. 673–86.

17. Ibn Ḥaukal (B3–c), p. 62.

18. Al-Makkarī (A2–c) VII. i, vol. II, p. 200, and *n.* 1, p. 482.

19. C.E. Bosworth, *The Islamic Dynasties*, (Edinburgh, 1967), pp. 14–17.

20. A.A. El-Hajji, 'The Andalusian Diplomatic Relations with the Vikings during the Umayyad Period' *Hespéris Tamuda*, 8 (1967) pp. 67–110.

21. *Crónica de Alfonso III* (B2–d), pp. 46–7, 50–1.

22. Al-Makkarī (A2–c) VI. iv, vol. II, p. 127, Ibn al-Athīr (B2–c), p. 235.

23. A.A. El-Hajji, *art. cit.* p. 75.

24. P. Guichard, 'Animation Maritime et Développement Urbain des Còtes de l'Europe Orientale et du Languedoc au Xᵉ Siècle', *Occident et Orient au Xe Siècle*, (Paris, 1979) p. 196.

25. S. Sobrequés, *Els Grans Comtes de Barcelona*, 3rd edn. (Barcelona, 1980) pp. 7–10.

26. Ibn al-Athīr (B2–c), pp. 143–4, 150, 151–2.

27. Al-Makkarī (A2–c) VI. iii and v, vol. II, pp. 98, 136–7.

28. *Al-Bayān* (B2–c), p. 102.

29. Ibn Ḥayyān in Al-Makkarī (A2–c) VII. i, vol. II, pp. 194–5.

30. See the arguments of T.F. Glick, *Islamic and Christian Spain in the Early Middle Ages*, (A3–c).

31. Ibn Ḥayyān in Al-Makkarī (A2–c) VI. vi, vol. II, pp. 163–4.

32. Al-Makkarī (A2−c) III. iii, vol. I, p. 237.

33. *Vita* of John of Gorze, ed. W. Pertz, *MGH, Scriptores*, IV, c. cxxi, p. 371f.

34. J. Vernet, *La Cultura Hispanoárabe en Oriente y Occidente*, (Barcelona, 1978), pp. 69−71 (with Spanish translation of the texts).

35. *Ibid.* pp. 36−7; *The Jewish Encyclopedia* 12 vols. (New York, 1901−6), vol. VI, pp. 248−50.

36. *Sefer ha-Qabbalah* of Abraham ibn Daud, ed. G.D. Cohen, (London, 1969) VII, 73.

37. *The Jewish Encyclopedia*, V, pp. 13−14.

38. *Sefer ha-Qabbalah* Epilogue, 28−30; D.M. Dunlop, *The History of the Jewish Khazars*, (New York, 1967) pp. 125−55.

39. E.I.J. Rosenthal, *Judaism and Islam*, (London and New York, 1961) pp. 73−6; *The Jewish Encyclopedia*, V, pp. 11−13, and VIII, pp. 470−1.

40. *Sefer ha-Qabbalah*, VII, 1−60, 68−79.

41. *Ibid.* Epilogue, 150−63.

42. *Ibid.* VII, 99−130, 139−67, showing that conditions were not always easy.

43. *Ibid.* VII, 70−1.

44. A. Miquel, 'L'Europe Occidentale dans la Relation Arabe d'Ibrāhîm b. Ya'qūb', *Annales*, 21 (1966) pp. 1048−64, with French translation.

45. B. Blumenkranz, 'Du Nouveau sur Bodo-Eleazar?', *Revue des Études Juives*, 112 (1953) pp. 35−42.

46. B. Blumenkranz, 'Un Pamphlet Juif Médio-Latin de Polémique Antichrétienne', *Revue d'Histoire et de Philosophie Religieuses*, 34 (1954) pp. 401−13.

47. J. Gil (ed.), (B4−c) *Corpus Scriptorum Muzarabicorum*, pp. 2−5, 58.

48. *Ibid.* pp. 135−41.

49. *Chronica Mozarabica, ibid.* 47, p. 34; for the text of the treaty, F.J. Simonet, *Historia de los Mozarabes de España*, (Madrid, 1903), pp. 797 ff.

50. Ibn Ḥaukal (B3−c), p. 63.

51. Al-Makkarī (A2−c) III. ii, vol. II, pp. 217−8.

52. Ibn al-Kūtiyya (B2−c), p. 61.

53. *Ibid.* pp. 67−70.

54. J. Gil (ed.), (B4−c), *Apologetius* II, praef. 8, p. 553.

55. J. Gil (ed.), (B4−c), Elipandus *Ep.* I, pp. 68−78; Letter of Pope Hadrian in P. Jaffé and W. Wattenbach, *Regesta Pontificum Romanorum* (Leipzig, 1885), no. 2479.

56. J. Gil (ed.) (B4−c), Council of Cordoba, p. 139.

57. J. Gil (ed.), (B4−c), Elipandus *Ep.* III, pp. 80−1.

58. J. Gil (ed.), (B4−c), Elipandus *Ep.* V, pp. 94−5.

59. J. Gil (ed.), (B4−c), Alvar *Ep.* IV, p. 181; Jaffé-Wattenbach no. 2479.

60. J. Gil (ed.), (B4−c), Elipandus *Eps.* IV and VI, pp. 92, 96.

61. For example the citations made by Alcuin in his *Contra Haeresim Felicis*, ed. G.B. Blumenshine, (Vatican, 1980), pp. 55−99.

62. R. d'Abadal i de Vinyals, *La Batalla del Adopcionismo en la Desintegracion de la Iglesia Visigoda*, (Barcelona, 1949).

63. A.G. Biggs, *Diego Gelmirez, First Archbishop of Compostela*, (Washington, 1949) pp. 153−6.

64. J. Gil (ed.), (B4−c), Eulogius, *Memoriale Sanctorum*, II. x. 25, pp. 426−7.

65. E.A. Lowe, 'An Unknown Latin Psalter on Mount Sinai', *Scriptorium*, 9 (1955) pp. 177−99; and 'Two Other Unknown Latin Liturgical Fragments on Mount Sinai', *ibid.* 19 (1965) pp. 3−29.

66. R. Menendez Pidal, *Orígenes del Español* 3rd edn. (Madrid, 1950) pp. 415−20; but compare with R.P. Wright, 'Speaking, Reading and Writing Late Latin and Early Romance', *Neophilologus*, 60 (1976) pp. 178−89.

67. S.M. Stern, *Les Chansons Mozarabs*, (Palermo, 1953).

68. Al-Makkarī (A2–c) II. iii, vol. I, p. 142.

69. J. Gil (ed.), (B4–c) *Memoriale Sanctorum*, II. i, pp. 397–401.

70. *Ibid.* II. ii, p. 402.

71. *Ibid.* I praef. 2, p. 367; J. Gil (ed.), (B4–c), Alvar, *Ep.* VI. 8–10, pp. 200–1.

72. J. Gil (ed.), (B4–c), pp. 344–61, 665, 685–93; See R.J.H. Collins, 'Latin Poetry in Ninth Century Spain', *Papers of the Liverpool Latin Seminar*, 4 (1983).

73. J. Gil (ed.), (B4–c), *Memoriale Sanctorum* I. xxx, p. 392.

74. *Ibid.* II. vii, pp. 406–8.

75. Many refs, see Gil *(ed.), cit.* (B4–c) index p. 722.

76. *Memoriale* II. viii. 1–8, 12–16, pp. 408–12, 413–15.

77. *Ibid.* II. viii. 9–16, pp. 412–5.

78. Alvar, *Vita Eulogii* 15 (A4–c), p. 340.

79. M. Gomez Moreno, *Iglesias Mozarabes*, (Madrid, 1919) p. 141 no. 3.

80. J. Williams, *Early Spanish Manuscript Illumination,* (London, 1977) pp. 16–21; compare with J. Fontaine, *L'Art Mozarabe* (B4–c), pp. 49–60.

81. M. Durliat, *Roussillon Roman*, (La Pierre-Qui-Vire, 1975) pp. 31–51.

82. R.J.H. Collins, 'Latin Poetry in Ninth Century Spain' (A4–c).

83. Alvar, *Vita Eulogii*, 12 (A4–c), p. 337; compare with *Memoriale* III. i (B4–c), pp. 439–40; Moḥammed's reputation amongst the Arab historians is very high: *Fatḥ al-Andalus* (B2–c) p. 81, and *Al-Bayān* (B2–c), p. 175.

84. Much of Ibn Ḥayyān's account of the reign of 'Abd-Allāh is translated by P. de Gayangos in his version of Al-Makkarī, vol. II, pp. 438–60 (n. 47 to VI. iv.).

85. *Anonymous Chronicle of 'Abd al-Rahmān III* (B2–c), pp. 118–47; *Al-Bayān* (B2–c), pp. 192–6, 217–21, 228–32, 237, 287–334.

7. THE CHRISTIAN REALMS

1. J. Gil (ed.), (B4–c), *Cronica Mozarabica* 70, p. 47.

2. J. Vernet, *La Cultura Hispanoarabe en Oriente y Occidente*, (Barcelona, 1978) p. 74.

3. A.C. Floriano, *Diplomatica Española del Periodo Astur* (B3–d) no. 9; also L.G. de Valdeavellano, 'La Época del Rey Astur Silo y el Documento del Año 775', in his *El Feudalismo Hispánico*, (Barcelona, 1981) pp. 163–96.

4. *Crónica de Alfonso III* (B2–d), pp. 8–12.

5. *Ibid.* pp. 32–5; R. Menendez Pidal (ed.), *Primera Crónica General de España*, 568, vol. II (Madrid, 1955), pp. 322–4.

6. *Crónica de Alfonso III* (B2–d), p. 36 (Oviedo version only).

7. *Ibid.* p. 38.

8. *Ibid.* pp. 40–1; *Albelda Chronicle* (B2–d), p. 602.

9. *Ibid.* p. 602.

10. *Ars Hispaniae* II (B5–d), pp. 398–405.

11. L. Halphen (ed.), *Vita Caroli Magni*, 16, (Paris, 1967) pp. 44–5.

12. C. Sanchez-Albornoz, *Orígenes de la Nacion Española*, II (B2–d), pp. 631–9, defends the authenticity of the council, but see also the critical treatment of F.J. Fernandez Conde, *El Libro de los Testamentos de la Catedral de Oviedo*, (Rome, 1971) pp. 130–7.

13. *España Sagrada*, 13 (Madrid, 1756), Appendix VI, p. 449; *Annales Castellani Antiquiores* s.a. 941, M. Gomez Moreno (ed.), *Discursos Leidos ante la Real Academia de la Historia*, (Madrid, 1917) pp. 23–4.

14. A. Ubieto Arteta (ed.), *Cartulario de San Millan de la Cogolla*, nos 9 ff., (Valencia, 1976).

15. A. Cotarelo Valledor, *Historia Critica ... de Alfonso III* (B2–d), pp. 446–50.

16. J. Manzanares Rodriguez, *Las Joyas de la Camara Sancta*, (Oviedo, 1972) pp. 12–20.

17. A.C. Floriano, *Diplomatica... Astur* (B3–*d*), no. 185. I am sceptical about the significance of the term *imperium* in the documents of this period.

18. T.D. Kendrick, *St James in Spain*, (London, 1960) ch. I.

19. J. Perez de Urbel, 'Los Orígenes del Culto de Santiago en España', *Hispania Sacra*, 5 (1952) pp. 1–33.

20. J. Vives, *Inscripciones* (B4–*b*), no. 548, pp. 314–15.

21. B. Dutton, *La 'Vida de San Millan de la Cogolla' de Gonzalo de Berceo*, (London, 1967), p. xi. See the documents in *Cartulario de San Millan* (*n.* 14 above).

22. *Chronicle of Sampiro* (B2–*d*), p. 311 (Pelagian version only).

23. *Ibid.* pp. 320–1.

24. Compare R.J.H. Collins, 'Charles the Bald and Wifred the Hairy' (A2–*d*).

25. *Chronicle of Sampiro* (Silos continuation) (B2–*d*), p. 344.

26. G. Antolín, *Catalogo de los Códices Latinos de la Real Biblioteca del Escorial*, 5 vols, (Madrid, 1910–23) vol. I, pp. 320–412.

27. A. Linage Conde, *Los Orígenes del Monacato Benedictino en la Península Iberica*, vol. III (Leon, 1973); *Monasticon* nos. 1254 (Sahagún), 350 (Carracedo), 395 (Celanova), 1268 (Samos).

28. C.J. Bishko, 'Gallegan Pactual Monasticism in the Repopulation of Castille', *Estudios Dedicados a Don Ramon Menendez Pidal*, Vol. II (Madrid, 1951) pp. 513–31.

29. C. Sanchez-Albornoz, 'Notas Sobre los Libros Leidos en el Reino de Leon hace Mil Años', *Cuadernos de Historia de España*, 1–2 (1944) pp. 222–38.

30. R.J.H. Collins, 'Latin Poetry in Ninth Century Spain' (A4–*c*).

31. M. Yáñez Cifuentes, *El Monasterio de Santiago de León*, (Leon and Barcelona, 1972) pp. 73–85 and documents.

32. *España Sagrada*, 35, Appendix I, document of AD 1091, pp. 411–14.

33. *Ibid.* pp. 340–7.

34. *Ibid.* Appendix II, pp. 414–15.

35. J. Gil (ed.), (B4–*c*), Eulogius, *Ep.* III, pp. 497–8; J.M. Lacarra, 'Textos Navarros' (B2–*d*), p. 238 and *n.* 17.

36. F. Kurze (ed.), *Annales Q.D. Einhardi* s.a. 778, *M.G.H., S.R.G.* (Hanover, 1895) p. 51.

37. J.M. Lacarra, 'Textos Navarros' (B2–*d*), pp. 268–9.

38. Ibn al-Athīr, (B2–*c*), pp. 164–5.

39. F. Kurze (ed.), *Annales Regni Francorum* s.a. 806, *M.G.H., S.R.G.* (Hanover, 1895) p. 122; *Vita Lludovici Imperatoris*, 18, R. Rau (ed.), *Quellen zur Karolingischen Reichsgeschichte*, vol. I, (Darmstadt, 1974) pp. 282–4.

40. J.M. Lacarra, 'Textos Navarros' (B2–*d*), p. 240.

41 *Ibid.* pp. 241–2.

42. *Ibid.* p. 229.

43. Ibn Ḥayyān, ed. and tr. E. Lévi-Provençale and E. García Gomez, 'Textos Inéditos del Muqtabis' (B2–*d*), pp. 298–303.

44. Al-Makkarī (A2–*c*) VI. iv, vol. II, p. 127 (year 861–2 AD).

45. M. Ilarri Zabala, *La Tierra Natal de Iñigo Arista*, (Bilbao, 1980).

46. *Translatio SS. Nunilonis et Alodiae, Acta Sanctorum Octobris*, IX, pp. 645–6.

47. G.C. Miles, *Coinage of the Visigoths* (A3–*b*), pp. 444–6.

48. K. Zeumer (ed.), *Chronica Regum Visegothorum*, (in his edition of *L.V.*–B2–*b*), p. 461.

49. M. Rouche, *L'Aquitaine des Wisigoths aux Arabes*, (Lille, 1977) pp. 101–24.

50. E. Faral (ed.), *In Honorem Hludowici*, 11. 102–571, (Paris, 1964) pp. 12–46.

51. *Vita Lludovici* cc. 8–18, R. Rau (ed.), *Quellen zur Karolingischen Reichsgeschichte*, (Darmstadt, 1974); but compare E. Lévi-Provençale, *Histoire de l'Espagne Musulmane* (B2–*c*), vol. I, pp. 178–85, for the perspective of the Arab sources.

52. W. Kienast, 'La Pervivencia del Derecho Godo en el Sur de Francia y en

Cataluña', *Boletín de la Real Academia de Buenas Letras de Barcelona*, 35 (1973/4) pp. 265–95.

53. R.J.H. Collins, 'Charles the Bald and Wifred the Hairy' (A2–*d*).

54. R. d'Abadal, *Els Primers Comtes Catalans* (B2–*d*), pp. 55–72.

55. Collins *op. cit.*; texts in R d'Abadal, *Catalunya Carolíngia* (B3–*d*).

56. M. Zimmerman, 'La Prise de Barcelone par Al-Manṣūr et la Naissance de l'Historiographie Catalane', *Annales de Bretagne*, 87 (1980) pp. 191–218.

57. Documents of the S. Benet de Bages collection in the archive of the Monastery of S. Maria de Montserrat, dated 20 March, 1005 and 16 December, 1016.

58. *Marca Hispanica* (B3–*d*) Appendices 39–41.

59. R. Beer, *Los Manuscrits del Monastir de Santa Maria de Ripoll*, (Catalan translation by E. Barnils y Giol, Barcelona, 1910); A.M. Albareda, *L'Abbat Oliba* (B4–*d*), pp. 255–80.

60. C. Baraut, 'El Monastir de Sant Sadurní de Tavèrnoles i els Orígens del Monaquisme Benedictí al Comtat d'Urgell', *Studia Monastica*, 22 (1980) pp. 253–9.

61. R. d'Abadal, *Catalunya Carolíngia* (B3–*d*) vol. II, pt. ii, pp. 307–11.

62. R.J.H. Collins, 'Charles the Bald and Wifred the Hairy' (A2–*d*), pp. 176–7, 181.

63. *Carta de Població de Cardona*, (Manresa, 1935) – facsimile and transcription.

64. Texts relating the history of these years can be found translated in P. de Gayangos' version of Al-Makkarī (A2–*c*), vol. II, Appendices A–C; for a narrative outline see E. Lévi-Provençale, *Histoire de l'Espagne Musulmane* (B2–*c*), vol. II, pp. 291–341.

Lists of Rulers

A dotted line indicates a change in dynasty

KINGS OF THE SUEVES[1]

Hermeric	by 409–441 (Hydatius, s.a. 419, 430, 433, 438, 441; Isidore *H.S.* 85)
Rechila	438–448 (Hydatius s.a. 438, 441, 448; Isid. (Reccila) 86)
Rechiarius	448–456 (Hyd. *passim*; Isid. (Recciarius) 87)
Maldras	456–460 (Hyd. *passim*; Isid. (Masdra, 457–60) 88)
Framtane	457 (Hyd.; Isid. (Franta) 88)
Rechimund	by 459–461/4 (Hyd. s.a. 459, 460, 461; Isid. (Reccimund) 88–9)
Frumarius	*c.* 460–465 (Hyd. s.a. 460, 465; Isid. 89)
Remismund	465–post 469 (Hyd. *passim*; Isid. 90, also *H.G.* 33)
unknown	*c.* 470–*c.* 550
Charraric	550s? (Gregory of Tours, *De Miraculis S. Martini I. xi*)
Ariamir	558/9–post May 561 (1st Council of Braga)
Theodemir	?–569/70 (Isid. 90–1; John of Biclar)
Miro	570–583 (Isid. 91; John of Biclar)
Eboric	583–584 (Isid. 92; John of Biclar)
Audeca	584–585 (Isid. 92; John of Biclar)

KINGS OF THE VISIGOTHS[2]

Alaric I	395–410
Athaulf	410–416
Sigeric	416
Wallia	416–419
Theoderic I	419–451
Thorismund	451–453
Theoderic II	453–466
Euric	466–484
Alaric II	484–507
Gesalic	507–511
Amalric	511–531 (under the Ostrogothic king Theoderic 511–526)
Theoderic (Theudis)	531–548
Theodisclus	548–549
Agila I	549–554
Athanagild	551–568
Liuva I	568–573
Leovigild	569–586
Reccared I	586–601
Liuva II	601–603
Witteric	603–610

Gundemar	610–612
Sisebut	612–621
Reccared II	621
Suinthila	621–631
Sisenand	631–636
Chintila	636–639
Tulga	639–642
Chindasuinth	642–653
Reccesuinth	649–672
Wamba	672–680
Ervig	680–687
Egica	687–702
Wittiza	698–710
Roderic	710–711
– – – – – – –	
Agila II	710/1–713
Ardo	713–720

THE ARAB GOVERNORS[3]

Mūsa ibn Nusayr	711–713/4
'Abd al-'Azīz ibn Mūsa	713/4–715/6
Ayūb ibn Ḥabīb al Lakhmi	6 months, 716–early 717
Al-Horr ibn 'Abd al-Raḥmān ibn 'Uthman at-Thakīfi	Jul/Aug 717–April/May 718
As-Samh ibn Mālik al-Khaulāni	April/May 718–May 721
'Abd al-Raḥmān ibn 'Abd-Allah al-Ghāfeki	May–Aug 721
Anbasah ibn Soḥaym al-Kalbi	Aug 721–Dec 725/Jan 726
Odhrah ibn 'Abd-Allah al-Fihri	Jan–Aug (?) 726
Yahyā ibn Sallāmah al-Kalbi	late 726–Nov/Dec 727
'Uthman ibn Abi Nasah al-Khathami	Dec 727–June/July 728
Ḥodjefah ibn al-Ahwan al-Kaysi	June/July 728–April 729
Al-Ḥaythan ibn Ubeyd al-Kelābi	April 729–March 731
Muḥammed ibn 'Abd-Allah al-Ashjai	March–May 731
'Abd al-Raḥmān ibn 'Abd-Allah al-Ghāfeki	(again) May 731–Oct 732
'Abd al-Mālik ibn Kāttan al-Fihri	Oct 732–Oct/Nov 734
Ukbah ibn al-Hejāji as-Saluli	Oct/Nov 734–739
'Abd al-Mālik ibn Kāttan	(in revolt) 739–Sept/Oct 741
Balj ibn Bashir	Sept/Oct 741–Sept 742
Tha'labah bin Sallāmah al-Amali	Sept 742–May 743
Abū al-Khāttar Ḥusam ibn Dhirar al-Khalbi	May 743–April 745
Thuabah ibn Yezīd	April 745–746/7

Yūsuf ibn 'Abd al-Raḥmān
al-Fihri   Dec 746/7 – May 756

UMAYYAD AMIRS OF CORDOBA[4]

'Abd al-Raḥmān I	756–788
Hishām I	788–796
Al-Ḥakem I	796–822
'Abd al-Raḥmān II	822–852
Moḥammed I	852–886
Al-Mundhir	886–888
'Abd-Allah	888–912
'Abd al-Raḥmān III	912–929

UMAYYAD CALIPHS[4]

Abd al-Raḥmān III	929–961
Al-Ḥakem II	961–976
Hishām II	976–1009, 1010–1013
Moḥammed II	1009, 1010
Suleyman	1009–1010, 1013–1016
'Abd al-Raḥmān IV	1018
'Abd al-Raḥmān V	1023–1024
Moḥammed III	1024–1025
Hishām III	1027–1031

HAMMUDID CALIPHS[4]

'Ali an-Nāsir	1016–1018
Al-Qāsim al M'amūn	1018–1021, 1022–1023
Yahyā al-Mu'talī	1021–1022, 1025–1027

KINGS OF THE ASTURIAS[5]

Pelagius	718/722(?)–737
Favila	737–739
Alfonso I 'the Catholic'	739–757
Fruela I 'the Cruel'	757–768
Aurelius	768–774
Silo	774–783
Mauregatus	783–788
Vermudo I 'the Deacon'	788–791
Alfonso II 'the Chaste'	791–842
Nepotian	842
Ramiro I	842–850
Ordoño I	850–866
Alfonso III 'the Great'	866–910

KINGS OF LEON[6]

García	910–914
Ordoño II	914–924
Fruela II	924–925

Alfonso IV	925–930
Ramiro II	930–950
Ordoño III	950–955
Sancho I 'the Fat'	955–957, 960–967
Ordoño IV 'the Bad'	957–960
Ramiro III	967–984
Vermudo II	982–999
Alfonso V 'the Noble'	999–1027
Vermudo III	1027–1037

KINGS OF PAMPLONA[7]

Enneco (Iñigo) Arista	early ninth century–852(?) (Ibn Hayyān, Genealogies)
García Iniguez	850s/860s (Ibn Hayyān, Genealogies)
García Jiménez	(?) (Genealogies, Charters?)
Fortun Garcéz	c. 882–905 (Genealogies, Charters)

Sancho Garcés I	905–925
García Sánches I	925–971
Sancho Garcés II	970–994
García Sánches II 'the Tremulous'	994–1000
Sancho Garcés III 'the Great'	1000–1035

COUNTS OF BARCELONA[8]

Bera	801–820 (*Vita Lludovici* 13; *R.F.A.* s.a. 820)
Bernard 'of Septimania'	by 827–829, 835–844 (*R.F.A.* s.a. 827; Nithard; *A.B.* s.a. 844)
Berenguer	c. 830–835
Sunifred I	844–848
William, son of Bernard	by seizure, 848–849/50 (*A.B.* s.a. 848)
Aleran	848–852
Odalric	852–c. 858
Humfrid	c. 858–864
Bernard 'of Gothia'	865–878
Wifred I	878–897/8
Wifred II Borrell	897/8–911/2
Suñer	911/2–954
Borrell II	954–992
Ramón Borrell III	992–1019
Berenguer Ramón I	1019–1035

NOTES

1. References are given here as the chronology and history of the Suevic kingdom are both complicated and disputed. Hydatius = the Chronicle of Hydatius (B2–*a*), Isidore *H.S.* = the Suevic section of Isidore's *History of the Goths, Vandals and Sueves* (A2–*b*). John of Biclar's Chronicle, see (B2–*b*). For I Braga, see the edition by Vives (B4–*b*). Gregory, *Miraculae S. Martini* ed. W. Arndt and B. Krisch, *M.G.H., S.R.M.* I.

2. Following K. Zeumer, 'Die Chronologie der Westgothenkönige des Reiches von Toledo', *Neues Archiv*, 27 (1902) pp. 411–44. See also the regnal lists in Zeumer's edition of *Leges Visigothorum* (B2–*b*), pp. 456–61.

3. Following Al-Makkarī (A2–*c*), although alternative datings can be found in other sources.

4. Following C.E. Bosworth, *The Islamic Dynasties* (Edinburgh, 1967), p. 11.

5. Compiled on the basis of the Asturian Chronicles (B2–*d*) and regnal lists (see *n*. 6).

6. See the *Nomina Regum Catholicorum Legionensium*, a section of the *Chronicon Albeldense*, in E. Florez, *España Sagrada*, 13 (Madrid, 1756) pp. 449–50; also the text of the Chronicle itself, *ibid*. pp. 450–59 (also edition cited in B2–*d*); for the tenth century see the Chronicle of Sampiro (B2–*d*), which ends with the reign of Ramiro III; for Vermudo II to Vermudo III dating by charters is possible (B3–*d*), and see *E.S.* 13, pp. 459–62.

7. The chronology of the ninth-century monarchy is highly controversial, but, in view of the limitations of the evidence, can never be more than conjectural. Ibn Hayyān: see E. Lévi-Provençal and E. García Gomez, 'Textos Inéditos del Muqtabis de Ibn Hayyān sobre los Orígenes del Reino de Pamplona' (B2–*d*); the tenth-century rulers can be dated by charter (B3–*d*); see also the genealogies in J.M. Lacarra, 'Textos Navarros del Codice de Roda' (B2–*d*).

8. This follows R. d'Abadal, *Els Primers Comtes Catalans* (B2–*d*), though dates in the period 849–878 are approximate rather than secure. *R.F.A.* = *Annales Regni Francorum*; *A.B.* = *Annales Bertiniani*; for these and the *Vita Lludovici* see R. Rau, *Quellen zur Karolingischen Reichsgeschichte*, vols. I & II (Darmstadt: 1974, 1972).

304

Genealogical Table I: The Asturian Succession

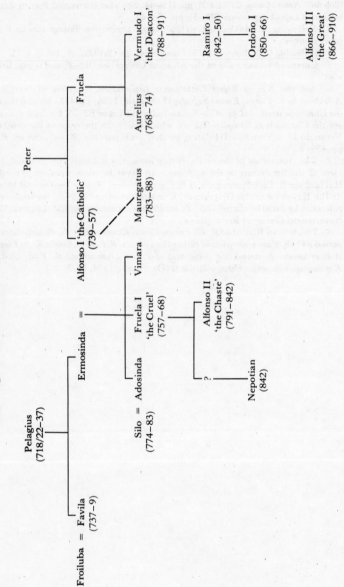

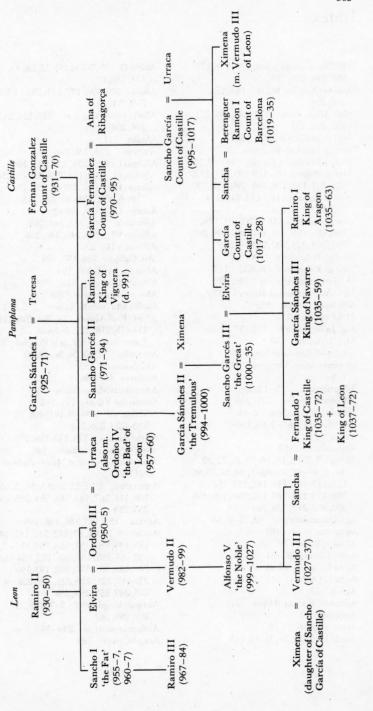

Genealogical Table II: The Leonese Succession, Castille and Pamplona

Index